PIETAS FROM
VERGIL TO DRYDEN

PIETAS FROM VERGIL TO DRYDEN

James D. Garrison

The Pennsylvania State University Press
University Park, Pennsylvania

Excerpts from *Jerusalem Delivered* by Torquato Tasso, An English Prose Version Translated and Edited by Ralph Nash, reprinted by permission of the Wayne State University Press. Copyright © 1987 by Wayne State University Press, Detroit, Michigan 48202.

Excerpts from *Orlando Furioso* by Ludovico Ariosto, An English Prose Translation by Guido Waldman, reprinted by permission of Oxford University Press, © Guido Waldman, 1974.

Library of Congress Cataloging-in-Publication Data

Garrison, James D.
    Pietas from Vergil to Dryden / James D. Garrison.

        p.   cm.
    Includes bibliographical references and index.
    ISBN 0-271-00787-7
    1. Dryden, John, 1631–1700—Knowledge—Literature. 2. Virgil—
Influence—Dryden. 3. Aeneas (Legendary character) in literature.
4. Turnus (Legendary character) in literature. 5. Literature,
Medieval—Roman influences. 6. Literature, Modern—Roman
influences. 7. Pietas (The Latin word) 8. Virtue in literature.
9. Piety in literature. 10. Duty in literature. I. Title.
PR3427.L5G37   1992
809'.93353—dc20   91–12139
                                                          CIP

It is the policy of The Pennsylvania State University Press to use acid-free paper for the first printing of all clothbound books. Publications on uncoated stock satisfy the minimum requirements of American National Standard for Information Sciences—Permanence of Paper for Printed Library Materials, ANSI Z39.48–1984.

For My Parents
Dale and Inez Garrison

Contents

Preface

This book brings together two topics of literary scholarship that have often been observed but never comprehensively studied. The first is the transformation of the Roman ideal of pietas as it is adapted to the cultural conditions of later times. The second is the appeal that Dryden's poetry makes to the example of Vergil. These two topics meet in the preface to Dryden's version of the *Aeneid,* where Dryden remarks upon the difficulty of translating the virtue celebrated in the character of Vergil's hero. Expanding this crux of translation, I have written a literary history of pietas that extends from classical Latin to neo-classical English literature and thus connects Vergil to Dryden. As Vergil provides the book with its organizing themes, so Dryden gives the book its point of view.

As it appears to Dryden at the end of the seventeenth century, and to many others both before and since, the Latin word *pietas* is impossible to translate accurately. I have therefore maintained the Latin form of the word without italics to refer to the general subject of the book. Italics are reserved to indicate the different forms of the word that occur in Latin and the derivative languages. All evidence is necessarily presented in the original languages, but footnoted translations are offered to assist with the originals. Unless otherwise specified, all translations from the Bible are taken from the King James Version. For classical authors I have used the translations in the Loeb Classical Library. For the Italian epics I have used Guido Waldman's version of *Orlando Furioso* with the permission of Oxford University Press, and Ralph Nash's version of *Gerusalemme Liberata* with the permission of Wayne State University Press. Other translations, from works less extensively cited, may be located in the Selected Bibliography. All unidentified translations are my own.

It is a pleasure to thank those who have given me guidance, criticism, and encouragement. I am especially grateful to my brother David Garrison, who read an earlier draft of this book, wrote insightful and consistently practical comments, and helped me through the process of revision. Wayne Lesser, Janice Rossen, and Wayne Rebhorn read the book in close to its final form and gave me valuable suggestions as I prepared the manuscript for publication. William J. Scheick recommended that I send it to The Pennsylvania State University Press. I am glad that I did, for it has been a pleasure to work with Philip Winsor in bringing the book out. Throughout the time that this study has been in process, I have been fortunate to have the friendship of three excellent department chairmen, Joseph J. Moldenhauer, William O. S. Sutherland, and Joseph Kruppa. For their support and encouragement I am very thankful. Finally I would like to thank my wife Susan and our children Emma and Paul, who have made sure that I have a life outside of the library.

Abbreviations

Introduction

For centuries the most revered name in the Western literary canon, Vergil has interpreted the culture and polity to which European civilization traces its origins. At the center of this interpretation is pietas, an idea that long sustains the highest claims of value even as it is accommodated to conditions and assumptions widely divergent from those articulated in the *Aeneid*.[1] This divergence is eventually reflected in the European vernaculars, creating a notoriously vexed problem for Vergil's translators. In the preface to his 1697 *Aeneis,* John Dryden calls attention to the difficulty of translation, adapting his remarks from Jean de Segrais, whose observations in French partially vouch for the assertion that "the word in *Latin* is more full than it can possibly be exprest in any Modern Language."[2] Dryden then defines the Latin word in English: "Piety alone comprehends the whole Duty of Man towards the Gods; towards his Country, and towards his Relations."[3]

Like most definitions of pietas, Dryden's acknowledges semantic change from within a framework of individual preoccupations. Taken on the example of Vergil to represent the religious, political, and ethical order of ancient civilization, the virtue of Aeneas is explained in Dryden's preface to reveal by contrast the relative disorder of the contemporary, as semantic history is here assimilated to a familiar fiction of loss: there once was a time and a language in which one word held together all that is now fragmented and scattered, expressible only by multiplying the words of "any Modern Language." To recover the fullness of the word is for Dryden to imagine epic in an age of satire, unifying metaphor in an age of irony. Yet the mode of his definition itself verges on satire, the discrepancy between *piety* and *pietas* exposing the present as an age less than congenial for the writing of an epic poem. Left to translate the poet he had once hoped to emulate, Dryden regards the descent of the English from the Latin word as a measure of cultural decline, as one aspect of the circumstances that limit his translation of Vergil.

Although others value pietas differently, attempting to escape rather than to reclaim the Vergilian aura, Dryden's perception that the history of pietas leads finally away from epic may be demonstrated by considering a preliminary outline of literary usage. (1) At what may be regarded as the climactic moment in the first half of the *Aeneid*, the hero's voyage to the underworld leads to reunion with his father, whose greeting is a celebration of his son's heroism: "venisti tandem, tuaque exspectata parenti / vicit iter durum pietas?"[1][4] This rhetorical question expresses the essential bond of the poem as a heroic virtue answerable to the demands of the voyage fiction: *pietas* conquers the journey. Although the terms of Anchises's praise are severely tested in the six books that follow, and *pietas victa* will be a recurrent countertheme of Latin literature after Vergil, the speech of Anchises introduces an unmistakably Roman ideal of principled conquest that confers the blessings of order exemplified by the devotion of sons to fathers. (2) In evident imitation of Vergil, Dante describes the journey of the *Inferno* as "la guerra / sì del cammino e sì de la pietate."[2][5] As Robert Ball has emphasized in an important article that speaks directly to the meaning of this line, Dante "does in fact draw on the Latin associations of *pietas* in such a way that *pietà* reinforces the typological comparison of the pilgrim's journey with those of Aeneas (*in bono*) and Ulysses (*in malo*)."[6] In elaborating this argument Ball shows how the poem is informed by the literary history of pietas, as the classical Latin sense of duty attends the evolved meaning of compassion that is the dominant sense of the derivative in medieval Italian. Untranslatable into modern English, this play of meaning in the *Inferno* is crucial to understanding the meaning of the journey itself. Aeneas grows into an understanding of his characteristic virtue on the way toward Rome; Dante's pilgrim engages a similar process of understanding on the way toward paradise. (3) As the spiritual journey reveals the risks of neglecting the Vergilian legacy of filial pietas, now directed toward God the Father, so two centuries later Erasmus will actually call the Christian pilgrimage "pietatis via." After praising Vergil's hero as a

[1] Art thou come at last, and hath the love thy father looked for vanquished the toilsome way?

[2] the strife, both of the journey and of the pity

model for the militant Christian, Erasmus distinguishes the way of the Christian from the way of the world: "Ad haec si maxime laboriosior esset pietatis via quam mundi, tamen hic laboris asperitas praemii spe lenitur nec deest unctio divina, quae facit, ut omne fel in mel vertatur."[3][7] Although this passage has but one word in common with the lines from *Aeneid* 6, the importance of the phrase that contains it is emphasized by the proximate and parallel phrase "Christi via."[8] The word so thoroughly expressive of *Romanitas* in Vergil assumes identity in Erasmus with the Messiah whose way is not the way of the world, much less the way of conquest. Erasmian *pietas* does not conquer the way, but is the way.

Once adopted by Christianity, however, the word that had proclaimed the epic heroism of Aeneas becomes increasingly vulnerable to irony, a word in twentieth-century translation more to the point of Richard Wilbur's *Tartuffe* than to Robert Fitzgerald's *Aeneid*. (4) That pietas finds its characteristic modern home in satire rather than epic is already indicated, for example, by a telling passage from book 4 of *Gulliver's Travels*. Here the adjectival form of the English derivative is given a specific historical setting with reference to the European colonial enterprise.

> Here commences a new Dominion acquired with a Title by *Divine Right*. Ships are sent with the first Opportunity: the Natives driven out or destroyed, their Princes tortured to discover their Gold; a free Licence given to all Acts of Inhumanity and Lust; the Earth reeking with the Blood of its Inhabitants: And this execrable Crew of Butchers employed in so pious an Expedition, is a *modern Colony* sent to convert and civilize an idolatrous and barbarous People.[9]

In Swift the inherited vocabulary is perceived as an instrument of power, as rhetorical cover for political exploitation. In modern dress, the civilizing mission of Rome and the evangelism of Christian Europe can be only ironically justified by the word *pious*. Its moral force here undermined by association with inhumanity and barbarism, the English *piety* eventually surrenders its claim on political discourse and retreats to the domain

---

[3] Even if the way of piety were infinitely more laborious than the way of the world, still the harshness of the struggle is alleviated by the hope of a reward, and the unction of divine grace is not lacking to change all gall into honey.

of private religious experience. In the process it descends the social scale to the level of those whom Swift calls enthusiasts and others, anglicizing the term derisively coined in German, call *pietists*. The negative associations of this name, first recorded in English in the year Dryden published his *Aeneis*, dominate the modern history of pietas, which manages to retain its positive connotation and ancient sanction only insofar as it opposes the public, the political, the heroic.

Nor is this development confined to English. (5) In *The Philosophy of Right*, for example, where Hegel would revive the Roman ideal to express the ability to recognize and act on obligations that are not the product of contract, the relevant institutional context for understanding pietas is the family: "in welcher die *Frau* ihre substantielle Bestimmung und in dieser *Pietät* ihre sittliche Gesinnung hat."[4][10] Contrasted to the male world of the state and the outer world generally, the domain of pietas is here restricted in a way that reverses the centrifugal force of the word in Vergil's epic. The classical exemplar is thus not Aeneas but Antigone: "Die Pietät wird daher in einer der erhabensten Darstellungen derselben, der Sophokleischen *Antigone*, vorzugsweise als das Gesetz des Weibes ausgesprochen."[5][11] Although Hegel appeals to an ancient text, what it exemplifies is a recognizably nineteenth-century ideal: "der *religiöse* Charakter der Ehe und Familie, die *Pietät*."[6][12]

As pietas thus turns inward, it becomes increasingly confined to the domain of religion. (6) Yet even in the field of religious discourse its already limited sanction may be called in doubt, as in Paul Tillich's *Systematic Theology*: "[I]n its distorted form, 'piety' becomes a tool with which to achieve a transformation within one's self. But anything which is imposed upon man's spiritual life by himself or by others remains artificial, producing anxiety, fanaticism, and the intensification of works of piety. It discloses the final failure of the pietistic way of self-salvation."[13] The semantic distortion, indicated by the quotation marks, designates a theological distortion that Tillich elsewhere characterizes as revivalist or fundamentalist. The word that had once pointed the way, has here come to designate religious deviation.

[4] Woman has her substantive destiny in the family, and to be imbued with family piety is her ethical frame of mind.

[5] Family piety is expounded in Sophocles' *Antigone*—one of the most sublime presentations of this virtue—as principally the law of woman.

[6] the religious character of marriage and the family, or *pietas*

In the larger view suggested by this series of citations, the broad curve of the word's literary history is from epic and toward satire, from an aristocratic to a middle- and finally lower-class social environment, from the public to the private domain. Although the decline of pietas both in influence and value is one of the most obvious features of its modern history,[14] its importance in earlier periods is confirmed by repeated attempts to claim it by definition. The different ways in which pietas has been defined by writers who would invoke its authority are therefore considered in chapter 1, as the first step toward recalling the cultural memory inscribed in this word.[15] The longer chapters that follow elaborate upon the significance of these changing conceptions of pietas in European literature from Vergil's epic to Dryden's translation.

The sources relevant to such an undertaking are many and diverse, but the natural starting point is the *Aeneid* and its numerous commentators.[16] Chapter 2 thus considers the accumulation of glosses on Vergilian *pietas* with particular emphasis on the allegorical tradition of commentary, in which the classical heroic is adapted to the ethics of Christianity. Among the passages from the poem that claim the most attention when the meaning of *pietas* is at stake include (1) the first epic simile, comparing Neptune to a political leader (1.148–56); (2) the proclamation of Rome's imperial mission by Anchises (6.851–53); (3) Aeneas's hesitation before abandoning Dido (4.388–96); (4) his parallel hesitation before killing Turnus (12.930–44). As later writers have often turned to these passages for essential definition of the poem's national themes of history and governance, and its heroic themes of love and war, they are here cited in advance as epigraphs for the four succeeding chapters of this book, which addresses these respective concerns as it follows the progress of the word chronologically.

Chapter 3 is devoted to pietas in the discourse of history from the age of Augustus to that of Augustine, and emphasizes the Roman concern for order expressed in the first simile of Vergil's epic. Here the character of the leader who calms the rebellious crowd is established by emphasis on the very quality that designates Aeneas.

> ac veluti magno in populo cum saepe coorta est
> seditio, saevitque animis ignobile volgus,
> iamque faces et saxa volant (furor arma ministrat),
> tum pietate gravem ac meritis si forte virum quem

conspexere, silent arrectisque auribus adstant;
ille regit dictis animos et pectora mulcet. (1.148–53)[7]

One of the most conspicuous versions of the poem's fundamental conflict between *furor* and *pietas,* this passage develops corollary distinctions between the many and the one, the vulgar and the venerable, the power of arms and the power of speech, sedition and rule. It is important to observe that this concept of order is not static: the simile illustrates the triumph of *pietas* over *furor* in time (hence "tum . . ."). But this vision of history coexists with the alternative of 7.586–600: in this revision of the first simile, comparing the Latian king to an ocean cliff battered by a tempestuous sea, later readers will discover the triumph of *furor* in Turnus, the submergence of *pietas* in the abdication of Latinus. Of these alternative visions of history, the first anticipates later panegyric, which locates *pietas* in the present as a guarantee of the future, while the second is confirmed in satire, which characteristically consigns *pietas* to the past. This double vision of Roman history thus anticipates the divergent tracks of the *civitas piorum* and the *civitas impiorum* in Augustine's historical synthesis.

Chapter 4 traces the uses of pietas in the political discourse of the Middle Ages, discourse that variously appropriates the implications of *Aeneid* 6.851–53, beginning with Augustine, who quotes the words of Anchises on the very first page of the *City of God:* "tu regere imperio populos, Romane, memento / (hae tibi erunt artes) pacique imponere morem, / parcere subiectis et debellare superbos" (6.851–53).[8] Whereas the initial simile of the poem and its later revision in book 7 both organize values hierarchically, the second denying the privilege of order granted in the first, the more famous proclamation of Roman power by Anchises connects its principal ideas with a coordinating conjunction. Though frequently cited in Western political writing, the last line of this passage rarely retains the balance it has in Vergil. Often enough the two phrases are recast in opposition to one another, the claims of one asserted at the expense of the other. This has specific bearing on the significance of

---

[7] And as, when oft-times in a great nation tumult has risen, the base rabble rage angrily, and now brands and stones fly, madness lending arms; then, if haply they set eyes on a man honoured for noble character and service, they are silent and stand by with attentive ears; he with speech sways their passion and soothes their breasts.

[8] Remember thou, O Roman, to rule the nations with thy sway—these shall be thine arts—to crown Peace with Law, to spare the humbled, and to tame in war the proud!

pietas, which gravitates historically toward the meaning of *parcere subiectis* and away from *debellare superbos,* and is thus understood not as a transcendent or comprehensive virtue but rather as one pole in argument over policy. Arguments limiting, even denigrating *pietas* in the political writing of the later Middle Ages leave it vulnerable to the competition of such alternative terms as *clementia,* which then supersede *pietas* in transit to political discourse in the modern languages.

The semantic evolution of the word toward *parcere subiectis* also bears heavily on interpretation of the hero's encounters with both Dido and Turnus, encounters widely imitated in Renaissance literature and the subject of chapters 5 and 6 respectively. In the case of Dido, the poem painfully expresses the alternatives at the moment of decision: "At pius Aeneas, quamquam lenire dolentem / solando cupit et dictis avertere curas, / multa gemens magnoque animum labefactus amore, / iussa tamen divum exsequitur classemque revisit" (4.393–96).[9] The diction of this passage registers the power of Dido's appeal, but the syntax places "pius Aeneas" on the side of the gods. Inner feeling for Dido is subordinated ("quamquam") to the outer action expressed by the sentence, as *amor* is sacrificed to *pietas.* However narrow this victory, it is one that Western writing about love, especially in modes other than the heroic, subjects to continuous revision. Later authors of Ovidian, pastoral, and Petrarchan poetry, for example, will find frequent occasions to reconsider the configuration of love and pietas as alternatives. Even in heroic poetry, moreover, imitations of Vergil's fourth book influence perception of the ideal represented by Aeneas, who will actually wind up in Ariosto's inferno for abandoning Dido.

Unlike Dido, Turnus does not invoke the word, but in his supplication of Aeneas he does appeal to the son-father relationship: "miseri te si qua parentis / tangere cura potest, oro (fuit et tibi talis / Anchises genitor), Dauni miserere senectae / et me, seu corpus spoliatum lumine mavis, redde meis" (12.932–36).[10] In hesitating, Aeneas is moved by Turnus's plea for mercy; in finally rejecting the plea, he is described as a figure of fury and wrath. How such a description might be reconciled with "sum

[9] But good Aeneas, though longing to soothe and assuage her grief and by his words turn aside her sorrow, with many a sigh, his soul shaken by his mighty love, yet fulfils Heaven's bidding and returns to the fleet.

[10] If any thought of a parent's grief can touch thee, I pray thee—in Anchises thou, too, hadst such a father—pity Daunus's old age, and give back me, or, if so thou please, my lifeless body, to my kin.

pius Aeneas" (1.378) is the subject of involved commentary from at least the time of Lactantius. Yet the difficulty of the ending is increased for later readers by the evolution of *pietas* toward *misericordia,* already acknowledged by Augustine in the fifth century.[17] As it changes, the language itself seems to tell against Aeneas, and nowhere more so than in the poem's last lines, which prompt imitations—even additions to the original poem—that would reconcile the hero's treatment of Turnus with latter-day understanding of pietas.

These passages from the *Aeneid* illustrate in different ways Vergil's characteristic vision, his extraordinary capacity to disclose the dimension of sacrifice that every choice entails.[18] As later writers adapt these several passages to their own conceptions of history, governance, love, and war, they too must often choose between Vergil's alternatives, emphasizing one dimension of the *Aeneid* at the expense of another. But if the history of response to the poem is a history of sacrificing Vergil's complex meaning, it is also a history of adding to that meaning conceptions of pietas that will support the cultural assumptions of later times. This is abundantly evident in the work of Dryden, the subject of chapter 7. Although Dryden retains the word in his *Aeneis,* he does so in the face of usage that increasingly renders pietas antithetical to the heroic. The pressures that weigh against pietas in Dryden's translation are, however, present much earlier, and are well indicated by the history of attempts to assert its true meaning.

1
Pietas

Durable agreement that pietas designates an ideal is affirmed by recurrent disagreement over how the word itself is to be understood, how it is related to other terms of value, and how contemporary usage is related to ancient meaning. This ongoing process of redefinition and challenge constitutes a dialogue about the ordering principles of Western culture, as the meaning of the word is reconciled to changing historical circumstances.[1] The tenor of this dialogue is expressed in overt attempts to say what pietas is, and this often means to say what it is not, as meaning is negotiated between the demands of the present and the different traditions of the past.

This is already evident in classical Latin literature, as writers before and after Vergil commonly anchor their own preferred definitions on the prior authority of Greek philosophy. Lucretius, for example, explains *pietas* in terms derived from the philosophy of Epicurus.

> nec pietas ullast velatum saepe videri
> vertier ad lapidem atque omnis accedere ad aras
> nec procumbere humi prostratum et pandere palmas
> ante deum delubra nec aras sanguine multo
> spargere quadrupedum nec votis nectere vota,
> sed mage pacata posse omnia mente tueri.[1][2]

[1] It is no piety to show oneself often with covered head, turning toward a stone and approaching every altar, none to fall prostrate upon the ground and to spread open the palms before shrines of the gods, none to sprinkle altars with the blood of beasts in showers and to link vow to vow; but rather to be able to survey all things with a mind at peace.

This definition emerges from a series of negatives, as the word is drawn into a specifically Epicurean system of value that has minimal use for the cultic. Although honoring the gods is not itself condemned, fearing them is perceived to be as pointless as performing sacrifices in order to win their favor. Such ignoble feelings are inconsistent with right thinking, which is the true essence of Lucretian *pietas*. Although this understanding of the word is not frequently invoked by later writers, the rhetorical pattern of this definition—"non . . . sed"—is to be very often repeated. Many after Lucretius will make a point of discrediting alternative definitions as mistaken or fraudulent, in order to proclaim instead *vera pietas*.

Although the Senecan aphorism—"nulla vis maior pietate vera est"[2][3]—expresses the heavy Roman investment in the word, the qualifying adjective acknowledges *pietas* as a focal point of philosophical disagreement, already evident in transit from Lucretius to Cicero. Foremost opponent of the Epicurean philosophy, Cicero defines *pietas* on several occasions, though never twice in exactly the same way. The most influential of his explanations occurs in the early rhetorical treatise on invention, where he admits the synonym *cultus* in conjunction with *officium,* for centuries afterward among the handiest terms for approximating the meaning of pietas: "pietas, per quam sanguine coniunctis patriaeque benivolum officium et diligens tribuitur cultus."[3][4] Almost as influential is the prescriptive definition of the word in the Platonic Dream of Scipio, where father advises son: "sed sic, Scipio, ut avus hic tuus, ut ego, qui te genui, iustitiam cole et pietatem, quae cum magna in parentibus et propinquis, tum in patria maxima est."[4][5] The importance of *iustitia* and *pietas,* endorsed by the testimony of the Scipios, is here validated from the perspective of eternity. But, whereas the meaning of *iustitia* is assumed to be self-evident, *pietas* requires explanation. As Cicero explains it here, *pietas* signifies the duty of the individual both to the family and to the state. Nor does the ordering of these relationships confront the possibility that these two might in some situations conflict; rather, this definition rests on the implied analogy between the family—or at least the noble family— and the state that it serves. The *pietas* of Cicero's *Republic* is more

[2] There is no power stronger than true love.
[3] Duty is the feeling which renders kind offices and loving service to one's kin and country.
[4] But, Scipio, imitate your grandfather here; imitate me, your father; love justice and duty, which are indeed strictly due to parents and kinsmen, but most of all to the fatherland.

than right thinking: it is a public virtue identified with the ethos of the ruling class.

Adapted from a republican to an imperial ideology of rule in Vergil's epic, *pietas* is attached not only to *iustitia* but also to *arma*. In the words of Ilioneus: "rex erat Aeneas nobis, quo iustior alter / nec pietate fuit, nec bello maior et armis" (1.544–45).[5] The essential and reiterated connection of *pietas* to *arma* in the character of Aeneas later becomes a cause for redefinition by Christian apologists. Although Lactantius, for example, readily acknowledges the moral power of the Roman poet in his *Divine Institutes,* he emphatically disputes Vergil's identification of *pietas* with the character of Aeneas: indeed, the apologist is intent on correcting Vergil's misconception and determined to deny the popular image of Aeneas as "maximum pietatis exemplum."[6] Reflecting particularly on the poem's conclusion, Lactantius wonders whatever happened to the *pietas* so often praised by the poet. The answer forthcoming is that Vergil never really understood the meaning of the word. Although Lactantius stops just short of actually replacing Aeneas's epithet with an antonym, he does replace Aeneas with a rather different exemplum. "Dicet hic aliquis: Quae ergo, aut ubi, aut qualis est pietas? Nimirum apud eos, qui bella nesciunt, qui concordiam cum omnibus servant, qui amici sunt etiam inimicis, qui omnes homines pro fratribus diligunt; qui cohibere iram sciunt, omnemque animi furorem tranquilla moderatione lenire."[6][7] The noun *concordia,* the adjective *tranquillus,* and the verb *lenire* locate important values in the Christian appropriation of the ideal that Lactantius would detach from the pervasive influence of Vergil's poem. The rhetorical force of Lactantius's attack on Aeneas thus measures the importance of *pietas* in the *Divine Institutes:* "pietas autem summa virtus est."[7][8] Although this phrase appears to be an adaptation of a passage from Cicero,[9] Lactantius's actual definition of the word in contradiction of Vergil is taken not from Cicero but translated from the Hermetic books: "ἡ γὰρ εὐσέβεια γνῶσίς ἐστι τοῦ θεοῦ" / "Pietas autem nihil aliud est quam Dei notio."[8][10]

[5] Our king was Aeneas: none more righteous than he in goodness, or greater in war and deeds of arms.

[6] Someone will say at this point: What, therefore, is piety, or where is it, or what sort of quality is it? Surely it rests with those who know not wars, who preserve harmony with all, who are friendly even to the unfriendly, who love all men as brothers, who know how to restrain wrath and to quell all fury of mind with tranquil moderation.

[7] Piety is the highest virtue.

[8] Piety is nothing other than a getting acquainted with God.

As Lactantius's translation indicates, *pietas* is the Latin word that commonly renders the Greek εὐσέβεια, a point emphasized by Augustine. For all his famous dislike of Greek, Augustine too depends on the language of the parent culture, but for him the relevant sponsor is not Epicurean, Platonic, nor Hermetic philosophy, but rather the revealed truth of the Greek Bible. In book 10 of the *City of God,* Augustine weighs the meaning of *pietas* against the language of the Septuagint: "Pietas quoque proprie Dei cultus intellegi solet, quam Graeci εὐσέββειαν vocant. Haec tamen et erga parentes officiose haberi dicitur. More autem vulgi hoc nomen etiam in operibus misericordiae frequentatur."[9][11] Searching for a single Latin word to express worship due to God, Augustine here considers the liabilities peculiar to *pietas.* In the process he offers three definitions. If usage could be restricted to the first of these, Augustine could end his search. But, unfortunately from this point of view, the word still expresses obligation to parents, and is now extended by popular association with *misericordia.* In his ensuing attempt to account for the popular meaning, Augustine observes a parallel vulgarization of εὐσέβεια, which he says explains the appearance of the more exact word θεοσέβεια in the Greek Scriptures. This conjectural exposition of the Septuagint serves to underline the parallel distinction between *pietas* and *vera pietas* in the *City of God* itself. The polemical adjective distinguishes the pure meaning Augustine would like the word to have from the inconvenient encumbrances of both classical ("erga parentes") and vulgar ("in operibus misericordiae") Latin. The added *vera* redirects attention away from actual usage, whether literary or popular, toward Augustine's own ideal definition offered six books earlier: "Pietas est enim verax veri Dei cultus."[10][12]

The influence of Augustine over subsequent definitions of *pietas* is equalled only by that of Cicero, and does not significantly begin to diminish until the thirteenth century, when the vocabulary derived from the Latin Aristotle places the word itself in a new light. The importance of Augustine's definition is well attested by Bernard of Clairvaux. In his treatise on consideration, where *pietas* is named as the quality to be preferred to all others, Bernard acknowledges the Augustinian definition

[9] Piety, again, or as the Greeks say, *eusebia,* is commonly understood as the proper designation of the worship of God. Yet this word also is used of dutifulness to parents. The common people, too, use it of works of charity.

[10] For piety is the true cult of the true God.

before proceeding to explain how *pietas* is consistent with *consideratio:* "Quid sit pietas quaeris? Vacare considerationi. Dicas forsitan me in hoc dissentire ab illo, qui pietatem diffinivit cultum Dei. Non est ita. Si bene consideras, illius sensum meis expressi verbis . . ."[11][13] As Bernard's understanding of the word is shown to be consistent with Augustine's, so his own theme of *consideratio* is shown to be an aspect of *pietas,* and its significance thus enhanced. Yet it may be observed that in a later work, Bernard offers a different definition in response to the question: "Quae sit vera pietas?" "Pietas," he now writes, "enim haec est iugis Dei memoria . . ."[12][14] He supports this definition from the text of 1 Timothy 4.8 ("pietas autem ad omnia utilis est"), which invites the semantic extension it receives in scholastic philosophy.[15]

Dispensing with overt claims to true meaning in his "quaestio de pietate," Thomas Aquinas circumvents Augustine by appealing to the classical example of Cicero, and by stressing the correct hierarchical relationship of man to his superiors, father, fatherland, God the Father. Like Cicero, and unlike Augustine, Aquinas approaches the problem of definition by analogy, distinguishing *pietas* from each of three related words: *caritas, religio, iustitia.* In the second instance, to illustrate, he argues that as the devotion due to God exceeds that due to parents and country, so *religio* surpasses *pietas.* But then invoking the principle that the greater subsumes the lesser, he concludes: "Unde per excellentiam pietas cultus Dei nominatur, sicut et Deus excellenter dicitur Pater noster."[13][16] After then asserting by appeal to Aristotle that it is impossible for *pietas* and *religio* to conflict, Aquinas turns in the next question ("de observantia") from the *pater/Pater* analogy to a version of Cicero's *pater/patria*. At issue in article 3 of this question is the word appropriate to the relationship between individual and ruler. The conclusion assigns *observantia* to the personal, *pietas* to the institutional aspect of this relationship. Where the common good is concerned: "non pertinet ad observantiam, sed ad pietatem, quae cultum exhibet non solum patri, sed etiam patriae."[14][17]

---

[11] What is piety, you ask? To take time for consideration. Perhaps you may say that I differ in my definition from the man who defined piety as worship of God. But that is not so. If you carefully consider, his meaning is expressed by my words . . .

[12] What is true piety? Piety is the memory of the yoke of God.

[13] Even as God, therefore, is called our father par excellence, in the same way homage to him is termed piety.

[14] It is not respect that is engaged but rather piety itself, the bearing of which is not solely towards parents but towards country as well.

Thus distinguished, *pietas* can serve Aquinas without the Augustinian *vera*.

In his dialogue with ancient authorities, Aquinas finds no occasion to comment on contemporary usage or to address the problem of vulgarization. This problem is addressed, however, by Dante in the second part of his vernacular *Convivio*. In his commentary on the Boethian Lady Philosophy, Dante finds definition of *pietà* necessary to distinguish it from *misericordia*. Not surprisingly, he summons Vergil to explain: "Per che Virgilio, d'Enea parlando, in sua maggior loda *pietoso* il chiama: e non è pietà quella che crede la volgare gente, cioè dolersi dell' altrui male; anzi è questo un suo speziale effetto, che si chiama misericordia, ed è passione. Ma pietade non è passione, anzi è una nobile disposizione d'animo, apparecchiata di ricevere amore, misericordia, e altre caritative passioni."[15][18] The admitted difference here is not between Latin and Italian, but rather between the literary and popular meanings of pietas common to both languages. Though echoing the parallel passage in the *City of God*, Dante bypasses Augustine's biblical evidence in favor of the Aristotelian distinction between disposition and passion: placed in their respective ethical categories, *misericordia* and *pietà* clearly cannot function as synonyms. In drawing this distinction Dante avoids the ongoing argument about the appropriate objects of pietas, limiting the context of definition so that *pietà* can characterize Aeneas without reference to Anchises, the Penates, or Troy. As the subjectivity of this definition thus illustrates the historical tendency of the word to turn inward, so too does the implicit comparison of Aeneas and Lady Philosophy in this passage detach the meaning of the word from the context of classical epic. Although the disposition Aeneas shares with her is described as "nobile," Lady Philosophy is herself "pietosa ed umile." As Dante defines it here, pietas depends less on the Vergilian heroic than it does on the paradoxical language of the New Testament. Although the references are classical, it is in a Christian sense that pietas irradiates every other mark of goodness ("fa risplendere ogni altra bontà col lume suo").

Dante's sometime teacher Brunetto Latini also defines the word in a medieval vernacular: "Pitiez est une vertus qui nos fait amer et servir

---

[15] Wherefore Virgil, in speaking of Aeneas, attributes to him piety as his greatest praise; and piety is not what the vulgar think, that is, it consists not in grieving over others' ills, but this is rather a particular effect of it which is called pity, and is a passion. But piety is not a passion; it is rather a noble disposition of mind prepared to feel love, pity, and other charitable emotions.

diligemment Deu et nos parens et nos amis, et nostre païs."[16][19] In Brunetto's French there are no exclusions, no explanatory analogies; the possible objects of pietas are impartially tallied. In this list "amis" stretches the lateral range of the word beyond the "propinquis" of Cicero, and affirms the affective force of "amer." In channeling the relationship between subject and multiple objects, the author complements "amer" with "servir," indeed underlining the latter with "diligemment" in the manner of Cicero's "diligens." Like the objects they govern, however, the verbs are joined by "et," thus allowing considerable room for equivocation between affection and obligation in "Pitiez." Given Brunetto's spelling, moreover, it is particularly remarkable that he takes no notice of the popular meaning observed by Augustine and Dante. Although the orthographic change that eventually serves to differentiate the literary (*piété*) from the popular (*pitié*) meaning is evident here, the definition itself indicates that this differentiation is far from complete in thirteenth-century French.

The Tudor translation of Erasmus's *Enchiridion* reveals that a similar uncertainty still prevails with English derivatives three centuries later. As Anne M. O'Donnell has carefully noted in her edition of the 1534 English version, Erasmian *pietas* enters English spelled in seven ways: *piete, pietie, pietye, pite, pitie, pyte, pytie.*[20] The translation itself, often with the aid of marginal glosses, offers various definitions in an attempt to mirror the full range of a word that occurs over one hundred times in the original. Consider, for example, Erasmus on the ways of the spirit and the ways of the flesh. First in the Latin original: "Ergo spiritus deos nos reddit, caro pecora. Anima constituit homines, spiritus pios, caro impios." Then in the English translation: "To conclude therfore / the spiryte maketh us goddes / the flesshe maketh us beestes: the soule maketh us men: the spiryte maketh us relygyous / obedyent to god / kynde and mercyfull. The flesshe maketh us dispysers of god / disobedyent to god / unkynde and cruell."[21] The series of four adjectives chosen to expound "spiritus pios" divides into pairs that recall Augustine's distinction between *cultus dei* and *misericordia,* and anticipates the later distinction in English between *piety* and *pity.* Yet it should be emphasized that in this passage the distinction suggests more immediately the dual obligation to God ("obedyent to god") and neighbor

[16] Piety is a virtue which causes us devotedly to love and serve God and our parents and our friends and our country.

("kynde and mercyfull") commanded by the New Testament. In contrast, the negation of a proper relationship with God and neighbor serves to render "caro impios." In both the negative and positive case, the very expansiveness of the translation implies that the English derivatives of *pius* and *impius* are in some ways inadequate to the importance of the argument. When derivatives are used in the translation, the reader is frequently assisted by a definition. In chapter 12, for example, there are two relevant glosses. The first of these is consistent with the translation cited above, although it omits the implied reference to one's neighbor in "kynde and mercyfull"; "Pietie signifyeth servyce/honour/reverence/obedyence due to god."[22] The second definition is quite different, and not merely in emphasis: "Piety is the reverent love and honour which the inferiors have towarde theyre superiors/whiche is chefly requyred/and therfore it is that perfytenes of a chrysten man."[23] Here there is no reference to God, and insofar as neighbors are present they have been organized into inferiors and superiors. Written on the eve of the English Reformation, this definition accommodates "Piety" to the demands of social order.

Similar ideas were still sufficiently alive at the end of the seventeenth century to elicit a refutation from John Locke. In his second treatise on government, Locke considers the word in specific relation to patriarchal theories of royal sovereignty. "And though that *Honour* and Respect, and all that which the *Latins* called *Piety,* which they indispensibly owe to their Parents all their Life times, and in all Estates, with all that Support and Defence [which] is due to them, gives the Father no Power of Governing."[24] Defining the word only to dismiss its political relevance, Locke implicitly distinguishes *piety* from *pietas,* and then denies the *pater/patria* analogy that had sustained the political significance even of the Latin word. What "the *Latins* called *Piety*" is not the same as what the English now mean by the word, and even if it were, appeal to this virtue would give "the Father no Power of Governing." Locke's manner here suggests that a political understanding of pietas is at best an anachronism that cannot be revived by Restoration nostalgia for the ideals of Roman civilization.

The subsequent naturalization of the word in English is evident in the sermon literature of the next century, when it is routinely defined as love of God and accommodated to the increasingly prevalent idea of innate human goodness. This is the case even in the sermons of the more orthodox divines such as Bishop Butler:

That which we more strictly call piety, or the love of God, and which is an essential part of a right temper, some may perhaps imagine no way connected with benevolence: yet surely they must be connected, if there be indeed in being an object infinitely good. . . . [T]he love of God as a being perfectly good, is the love of perfect goodness contemplated in a being or person. Thus morality and religion, virtue and piety, will at last necessarily coincide, run up into one and the same point . . .[25]

Although the word thus offers Butler some resistance, it is finally made to agree with the dominant vocabulary of the eighteenth-century moralists. But the moralists who would reconcile "virtue and piety" find their negative in the satirists of the period, who have little difficulty exposing the disengagement of virtue from piety in contemporary life. The passage from *Gulliver's Travels* cited above is not a lone instance, nor does the doubt thus raised by the contrast of moral theory to actual practice pass unnoticed. In 1749 David Hartley makes a point of observing that "Piety is not in general, and amongst the Bulk of Mankind, had in great Honour . . . and [the] Pretences to it are often made use of by Hypocrites to cover the worst Designs."[26] Writing in the same year, Henry Fielding applies the epithet of Aeneas not to his own epic hero Tom Jones but rather to Tom's hypocrite of a half-brother, last seen in the novel scheming to marry a Methodist widow.

From this point the decline of the word proves difficult to check, as the "sober, discreet, and pious"[27] Master Blifil must eventually share the epithet with (for example) the sadistic schoolmaster of *Nicholas Nickleby*. Dickens effectively defines the word in an early conversation between Squeers and Snawley, who negotiates with the pedagogue about teaching his stepchildren, expressing a desire that "their morals . . . be particularly attended to."[28] After receiving assurance that he has "come to the right shop for morals," Mr. Snawley turns the conversation to the schoolmaster's own character:

> "You are a moral man yourself," said Mr. Snawley.
> "I rather believe I am, sir," replied Squeers.
> "I have the satisfaction to know you are, sir," said Mr. Snawley. "I asked one of your references, and he said you were pious."
> "Well, sir, I hope I am a little in that line," replied Squeers.
> "I hope I am also," rejoined the other.[29]

The exchange alternates between assertion and acknowledgment, then concludes in agreement that represents a shared sense of "morals." Although Dickensian irony preserves in some degree the ancient dignity of the word, it is evident nonetheless that pietas has fallen into unsavory company. Even Squeers is cautious in claiming his reference, as if uncertain of the compliment intended. A far cry from "sum pius Aeneas," his "I hope I am a little in that line" attests the dubious status of the English adjective and begins to explain Wordsworth's poetic lament over the decay of "ancient Piety."[30]

Later in the nineteenth century the Latin word is thus reconsidered from a historical perspective by John Ruskin in his *Val D'Arno* lectures. Contemplating the odes of Horace, Ruskin devotes a substantial paragraph to the "piety" of the Roman poet.

> Note thirdly, then, his piety, and accept his assured speech of it: "Dis pietas mea, et Musa, cordi est." He is perfectly certain of that also; serenely tells you so; and you had better believe him. Well for you, if you *can* believe him; for to believe him, you must understand him first; and I can tell you, you won't arrive at that understanding by looking out the word "pietas" in your White-and-Riddle. If you do, you will find those tiresome contractions, Etym. Dub., stop your inquiry very briefly, as you go back; if you go forward, through the Italian pieta, you will arrive presently in another group of ideas, and end in misericordia, mercy, and pity. You must not depend on the form of the word; you must find out what it stands for in Horace's mind, and in Virgil's. More than race to the Roman; more than power to the statesman; yet helpless beside the grave, "Non, Torquate, genus, non te facundia, non te Restituet pietas."[31]

Here *pietas* clearly has a high status, but it is the status of a preserved artifact. Dismissing the accumulation of meanings attendant upon "the form of the word" (in effect, the subject of this chapter), Ruskin would have his audience open, not the dictionary, but the "mind" of the Latin poet. Ruskin's formulations of the meaning thus recovered disclose, however, the difficulty of the assigned task, a difficulty confirmed in the succeeding paragraph: "To know what love means, you must love; to know what piety means, you must be pious."[32] The shift from ancient poet to modern reader, from the Latin to the English form, leads Ruskin to a revealing admission: "Perhaps you dislike the word, now, from its vulgar use."[33] Although Ruskin does not specify "vulgar" here, the adjective might aptly describe the conversation of Squeers and Snawley. Ruskin's own sketch of the modern cleric in *Fors Clavigera* may serve as a second example, underlining the difference between ancient and modern usage. "And, in general, any man's becoming a clergyman in these days implies that, at best, his sentiment has overpowered his intellect; and that, whatever the feebleness of the latter, the victory of his impertinent piety has been probably owing to its alliance with his conceit, and its promise to him of the gratification of being regarded as an oracle, without the trouble of becoming wise, or the grief of being so."[34] Whereas *pietas* is a case of "more than" appears, *piety* is a case of less than appears, a word now associated with intellectual "feebleness," "conceit" and "gratification" of the self.

The decline of the word in modern discourse has been so decisive as to encourage deliberate attempts at resuscitation. As if addressing Ruskin's clergyman, George Santayana would elicit the historically submerged power of the word "in its nobler and Roman sense": "Piety, in spite of all its allegories, contains a much greater wisdom than a half-enlightened and pert intellect can attain."[35] To demonstrate the potential of pietas thus revived, Santayana reconsiders the problem of appropriate objects: "parents first, then family, ancestors, and country; finally, humanity at large and the whole natural cosmos." Up to the semicolon this expanding catalogue repeats Cicero's republican definition, while the extension of the ideal to "humanity" suggests late- and post-classical usage. Santayana's specific phrase, "Piety to mankind must be three-fourths pity," brings classical and medieval Latin meanings together in modern English. His "cosmic piety" completes the circle of definition back to the father, for (he maintains) the "universe is the true Adam." Radiating outward from the father and then returning to its source, Santayana's pietas—"man's reverent attachment to the sources of his being"—thus captures in modern idiom two of the broadest and most enduring senses of the word revealed by this series of passages: a sense of connectedness and a sense of reverence.

As this series also indicates, pietas repeatedly provokes definitions, indeed repeatedly calls for definition of society's highest values. The diverse meanings formulated by major writers from Lucretius to Santayana point to the truth of Kenneth Burke's remark in *Permanence and Change* that "One cannot long discuss the question of meaning, as applied to the field of art, without coming upon the problem of piety."[36] The converse is even more obviously true: one cannot long discuss the problem of piety without coming to the question of meaning. Burke confirms this by providing his own definition: "Piety is *the sense of what properly goes with what.*"[37] Burke's pietas, like Santayana's from which it derives, is an idea of range and power that necessarily operates in opposition to modern vulgarization of the word: "I would even go further in trying to establish this notion of piety as a response which extends through all the texture of our lives but has been concealed from us because we think we are so thoroughly without religion and think that the 'pious process' is confined to the sphere of churchliness."[38] In evident acknowledgment of this popular modern meaning— "churchliness"—*piety* is not included in Burke's "Dictionary of Pivotal Terms" that concludes his *Attitudes Toward History.* Nor does the word qualify for inclusion in Raymond Williams's book of *Keywords,* which calls attention to vocabulary whose uses bind together certain "ways of seeing" culture and society.[39]

No longer a "pivotal" or "key" term, as even efforts to revive it affirm, pietas nonetheless has a history unusually expressive of ways of seeing. Attempts such as those surveyed above to define, adapt, or otherwise appropriate the meaning of the word are commonly attempts to clarify or impose a certain vision. If these definitions thus suggest the advantage of approaching the topic historically, they also demonstrate that it cannot be approached as the history of an idea, for the idea represented by the word is precisely what is at issue.[40] This struggle over meaning typically signals conflict between different centers of intellectual as well as political power, between (for example) pagan and Christian, emperor and pope, Protestant and Catholic. Although this struggle may ultimately be for legitimation of power, the political sanction of pietas depends on the religious and ethical meanings that it derives not only from the *Aeneid* but also from the Bible.

2
Auctores Pietatis:
Classical and Christian Ideas of Pietas

In the *Fasti* Ovid describes Aeneas as "pietatis . . . auctor."[1] This phrase is repeated late in the fourth century by Chromatius Aquilensis, whose sermon on the raising of Lazarus proclaims Jesus Christ as the author of *pietas*.[2] Because the epic and the Gospels thus offer alternative, even contending models of *pietas*, this word becomes a site of the encounter between classical education and Christian faith. Contention over its meaning figures importantly in commentaries on both Vergil and the New Testament. These two lines of commentary eventually converge in the popular iconographies of the Renaissance, which gather classical and Christian exemplars of *pietas* under cross-referenced visual emblems. Predominant among these are the emblem of Aeneas with his father on his back, and that of the pelican with a cross in the background ("Pelecanus Christi Symbolum"). By the early seventeenth century, polarization of meaning evident in the commentaries and popularized in the emblem books is represented by two distinct but still complementary English words, as the Latin *pietas* divides into *piety* and *pity*. In the prose of George Herbert, for example: "God . . . out of his infinite pity hath set forth heaven for a reward to draw men to Piety."[3] Even as terms of Christian belief, however, *piety* and *pity* reflect an older semantic cleavage frequently remarked by Vergil's Latin commentators and well summarized in the sixteenth-century *Poetics* of Julius Caesar Scaliger: "Est autem pietas vox ambigua."[1][4]

[1] But pietas is an ambiguous word.

Vergilian Commentary

The ambiguity discerned by Scaliger is expressed in different ways in different periods, but from the fourth century to the seventeenth the glosses recurrently point to a fundamental distinction between *pietas in deum* and *pietas in homines*. The first meaning, consistent with the synonym *cultus* emphasized by Cicero, is discovered in passages of the epic that look upward through a patriarchal system of values to divine authority. The second meaning is attached to expressions of divine or parental compassion, thus offering evidence for the popular synonym *misericordia*. Acknowledging both ascending and descending perspectives of the word, the line-by-line commentaries of the fourth century are at pains to render the vocabulary of the poem consistent with its action. As practiced by Servius and Donatus, whose commentaries cling to the poem even into the Renaissance, this interpretive procedure has the eventual effect of withdrawing *pietas* from heroic *virtus*, thereby undermining the conjunction of *pietas* and *arma* in the characterization of Aeneas and setting a pattern of discussion consistent with the medieval neglect of *Aeneid* 7–12.

The two poles that attract *pietas* in the commentary of Servius are religion and justice, one defining the relationship between the hero and his gods, the other his relationship with mortals. One dimension of the word thus leads to a pure Aeneas whose virtue looks away from the world; the other yields a just Aeneas forced to act in the world. If this polarity suggests the union of the divine and human in Aeneas, or perhaps the difference between the hero of the first six books and the hero of the last six, Servius does not say so, but his remarks on specific passages do reveal the potentially conflicting responsibilities of the epithet *pius*. To define it, Servius appeals to etymology, asserting the connection between the adjective and the verb *piare:* "sane 'pius' potest esse et purus et innocens et omni carens scelere. piare enim antiqui purgare dicebant . . ."[2][5] The burdens that such synonyms as "purus" and "innocens" place on the epic hero are evident enough, but his situation is further complicated by the way in which Servius expounds Vergil's idea of justice. Describing Aeneas as "iustus" in his comment on *Aeneid* 1.10, Servius later defines *pietas* as a part of justice. But since the other part is

[2] To be sure, "pius" can mean both pure and innocent and entirely without wickedness. Indeed, ancient authors took "piare" to signify purification . . .

"severitas,"[6] *pietas* is driven toward a meaning that expresses compassion or mercy. The supreme test of this meaning is the final encounter with Turnus, where Servius strikingly credits Aeneas with *pietas* first for hesitating and then again for acting: "omnis intentio ad Aeneae pertinet gloriam: nam et ex eo quod hosti cogitat parcere, pius ostenditur, et ex eo quod eum interimit, pietatis gestat insigne . . ."[3][7] As *pietas* is thus called to designate mutually exclusive alternatives, the inherent polarities of meaning emerge under the pressure of decision as paradox. But in this context the paradox serves only to underline the basic assumption that everything in the poem is intended to reveal the glory of Aeneas.

This assumption is shared by Donatus, who understands the glory of Aeneas as central to the poem's imperial theme.[8] Although Donatus proclaims the hero to be without fault ("vacuum omni culpa"), preserving the blameless character of Aeneas over the course of the entire commentary necessitates involved explanations of *pietas*, beginning with the commentary on book 1. Here Donatus subdivides the qualities of the hero into those of mind and body: *pietas* and *iustitia* go with mind; *ultio* and *virtus* go with body.[9] The continuing consequence of this division becomes evident whenever the action of the poem tests the compatibility of *pietas* with violence. Whether referring to the animal sacrifice in book 8 or to the suicidal cry of Euryalus's mother in book 9, Donatus cannot conceal the difficulty he has in harmonizing *pietas* and slaughter, even within the framework of ritual. In the case of the sacrifice to Juno, for example, he first asserts that this act of "pius Aeneas" expresses cruelty rather than *pietas*.[10] To preserve the blameless hero he therefore distinguishes two meanings of *pius*: "non ita pium dixit quasi misericordem, sed pro loco supplicem numini et religiosum sacrificantem."[4][11] The second meaning makes good sense of the passage, but the very ordering of the comment—negation preceding affirmation—reveals the strain of reconciling Vergil's Aeneas to the evolving sense of the ideal he is taken to represent.

For Donatus, *pietas* is to *impietas* as *misericordia* is to *crudelitas*, but the terms thus defined are inconsistent with the action of the Iliadic books, as indicated especially by the commentary on books 9–12. Par-

[3] Everything tends toward the glory of Aeneas. For when he thinks of sparing his enemy, he is shown to be pious; and when he slays him, he bears the distinguishing mark of his piety . . .

[4] Thus he does not use pius in the sense of merciful, but in this case to refer to supplication of the gods and religious sacrifice.

ticularly revealing is the interrogative comment on the killing of Mezentius in book 10. The relevant words from the epic are: "tum pius Aeneas hastam iacit . . ." (10.783).[5] After first questioning the propriety of Vergil's adjective, Donatus counters with the argument that it is the duty of the pious (*officium piorum*) to abominate killing and to show mercy even when the logic of the times favors severity. Although he finally manages to save the passage and rationalize the hero's conduct by emphasizing the opposed sacrilegious character of Mezentius,[12] Donatus has to abandon his own understanding of the word in the process. The synonym *misericordia* simply will not match the conduct of the hero in this episode, and only by returning to his basic alternative synonym *cultus* can Donatus allow Aeneas to keep his epithet: "merito pii appellandi sunt qui integro ritu deorum cultus observant."[6][13] This semantic dissonance is still more evident in the account of book 12, where *ultio* as well as *virtus* is at issue. Again words must be harmonized with acts, the attributes of the mind with the deeds of the body, *pietas* with revenge. Like Servius, Donatus therefore separates the wish to spare Turnus from the act of killing him, but unlike Servius, Donatus does not use the same word for both the wish and the act, reserving *pietas* to mark the impulse to forgive, allowing *religio* to take credit for the actual deed.[14] From the commentator's point of view this interpretation has the advantage of dissociating the essential virtue of Aeneas from the last act of the poem, thereby preserving the hero's compassion. The problem thus reluctantly identified by Donatus is the same one that Lactantius had not so reluctantly pointed out in his *Divine Institutes:* certain heroic deeds performed by Aeneas in the poem, including especially the killing of Turnus, can be reconciled with *debellare superbos* but not with *parcere subiectis,* and it is the latter implication of the word that is rapidly gaining currency in the Latin of the later empire.

This alienation of *pietas* from *virtus* is inevitably encouraged by allegorical explanations of the poem. Derived from neo-Platonic interpretations of Homer, the allegorical approach to Vergil diminishes the philological attention devoted to Aeneas's distinctive virtue. When it is remarked, as in the influential commentary of Fulgentius, its meaning is usually disclosed indirectly. After stating his purpose in explicitly Christian terms, Fulgentius allegorizes the escape from Troy: "vir enim pius superbiae voces et

[5] Then good Aeneas casts a spear . . .
[6] Those who correctly observe divine worship are rightly called pious.

malorum poenas effugit ac pavescit."[7][15] Different in reference but similar in effect to the "omni carens scelere" of Servius and the "vacuum omni culpa" of Donatus, Fulgentius's conception of *pietas* is revealed by what is avoided rather than by what is achieved. As the starting point of a spiritual odyssey, the escape from Troy means flight from the world of heroic action. In the broadest sense the goal of the journey that begins in flight becomes the discovery of true faith. On the model of Fulgentius, then, medieval commentators invest the poem with theological understanding supported by biblical quotation; in the process, books 7–12 recede from view, and the inherited polarity of justice and religion is recast in hierarchical terms: the active life of justice ultimately yields to the contemplative life of religion.

Following the example of Fulgentius as elaborated by Bernardus Silvestris, whose twelfth-century commentary explains *pietas* as a step on the ascent to *religio*,[16] John of Salisbury shapes his interpretation to a refutation of Epicurean philosophy. Written later in the twelfth century as part of his *Polycraticus*, John's exposition of *Aeneid* 1–6 conventionally identifies the journey of Aeneas with the life of the human soul ("Aeneas, qui ibi fingitur animus").[17] Book 1 represents infancy, book 2 adolescence, book 3 the various errors of young manhood. Book 4 claims more detailed comment, for here is the turning point of the allegory as reason ("sub typo Mercurii") comes to persuade and teach the errant soul, taking as his text 1 Corinthians 13.11.[18] Sanctioned by reference to the biblical story of Joseph and illustrated from Horace, the wisdom of Mercury sets Aeneas on the right way toward the fifth age in which political maturity is achieved. The descent to the underworld in book 6 marks old age by providing an opportunity for the soul to recognize the errors of the whole life past and thus to reach the spiritual bliss signified by Italy.[19] Finally, the *pietas* of Aeneas represents the narrow way of the New Testament, in contrast to the broad way of the Epicureans ("Lata est ergo Epicureorum via . . .").[20] Though hardly original in outline, this interpretation is remarkable for its range of classical reference, including acknowledgment of a political dimension to *pietas* in the account of *Aeneid* 5. Whereas Bernardus had paraphrased Cicero on *pietas* without allowing this passage to disturb his Christian ideal of moral education, John of Salisbury, who elsewhere in the *Polycraticus* takes Aeneas as his exemplary magis-

---

[7] Certainly the pious man is alarmed by the voices of pride and the punishments of evil and flees from them.

trate, recognizes government as an expression of the hero's maturity, surpassed only by the achievement of spiritual beatitude.[21] The sequential ordering of *pietas* that serves the state (book 5) and *pietas* that serves God (book 6) establishes a hierarchy of significance, as spiritual meaning transcends without denying the political.

This hierarchical relationship between political and spiritual definitions of *pietas* is refined in the most interesting of the late medieval commentaries on the *Aeneid*. In the introduction to the fourth book of the *Camaldolese Disputations,* Cristoforo Landino observes to the Duke of Urbino that he will recognize his own customs and manners in the actions of Aeneas. This flattery is designed to educate the Duke in his office by revealing to him the philosophy of Vergil's poem, the subject of books 3 and 4 of the dialogue. "A philosophia enim habemus, ut pie vivamus, ut impietatem omnem abominemur et ab omni scelere abstineamus."[8][22] Thus borrowing Servius's description of Aeneas as "omni carens scelere," Landino characterizes the ideal ruler on the paraphrased authority of *Aeneid* 6.851–53: "iniuria oppressos sublevent, superbiam seditiosorum civium deiectam cupiant."[9][23] Rulers who meet this Vergilian standard of excellence are appropriately celebrated in Landino's tour of the Elysian fields; in contrast, the principal representations of *impietas* in the dialogue are tyrants and other false models of governance: Polyphemus, Mezentius, and above all the Titans and their offspring. Commenting on *Aeneid* 6.580–82, for example, Landino succinctly captures the character of the false ruler in the Titan figure responsible to neither God nor man: "impietatem in deos atque superbiam in homines."[10][24]

Having stressed the political importance of *pietas,* Landino then proceeds to subordinate this conception of the ideal to the higher calling of spiritual wisdom. Ciceronian *pietas* now becomes a temptation that Aeneas must overcome. Speaking largely through Leon Battista Alberti, Landino considers the active life of civic duty to be the principal subject of *Aeneid* 3 and 4 (not, as in the *Polycraticus,* of book 5). Both in Crete and in Carthage Landino's Aeneas is tempted by the will to rule ("cupiditas imperandi"); his later desertion of Dido at the urging of Mercury expresses abandonment of the active in favor of the contemplative life. The

[8] It is by philosophy that we live justly, detest all impiety, and abstain from all crime.
[9] They relieve the oppressed of injustice. They work to drive out the arrogance of subversive citizens.
[10] impiety toward the gods and pride toward men

pietas of civic duty is subordinated to a loftier understanding of its meaning that is underlined by significant distinctions of image and vocabulary: public life is associated with storm (*tempestas*), the contemplative with calm (*tranquillitas*), an image pattern that is carefully developed in the account of the storm raised at Juno's request in book 1 and again in a studied comparison of the landing in Italy with the landing in Africa.[25] Corresponding to this basic image pattern are important discriminations in vocabulary, as Landino distinguishes *prudentia*, which concerns such earthly affairs as government, from the loftier perspective afforded by *sapientia*.[26] His reading of *Aeneid* 4 is thus predicated on a further distinction by gender, female *prudentia* forsaken by male *sapientia*.

By bringing Aeneas to this idea of divine wisdom, Landino's interpretation brings the hero's epithet there too. As Thomas Stahel has written: "Landino's task is to bring to fruition the epithet 'pius Aeneas'; his version of the *Aeneid* depicts the progress of the singularly gifted man who truly *becomes* pious in the fully Platonic sense of wholeheartedly embracing contemplative virtues."[27] Landino's conception of *pietas* thus conforms closely to Lactantius's borrowed definition of this "summa virtus" as "notio Dei."[28] It corresponds even more exactly to the definition given in Augustine's *Enchiridion:* "Hominis autem sapientia pietas est."[11][29] Nor should this congruence with earlier Christian definitions surprise, since Landino's Vergil is himself a Christian in all but name: "O divinum ingenium! O virum inter rarissimos viros omnino excellentem et poetae nomine vere dignum! qui non Christianus omnia tamen Christianorum verissimae doctrinae simillima proferat."[12][30] The advice given to Federigo di Montefeltro on the authority of the *Aeneid*—"pie vivamus"—could have been given as well on the authority of 1 Timothy 2:2 ("quietam et tranquillam vitam agamus in omni pietate, et castitate"). The wisdom of Vergil is the wisdom of Paul.[31]

Landino's interpretive accommodation of the *Aeneid* to the Bible is directly attached to the poem in an elaborate edition of Vergil's works published in Florence in 1487. His commentary joins those of Servius and Donatus, which together substantially outweigh the poem itself. Although Landino here refers to the *Camaldolese Disputations*, the neces-

[11] But the wisdom of man is piety.

[12] O divine intellect! O man most excellent even among the choicest men, and most worthy of the name "poet!" Although not a Christian, everything he wrote is so similar to the very truths of Christianity!

sity of accounting for *Aeneid* 7–12 directs his attention from the idealization of Aeneas achieved in book 6 toward an *apologia* for his actions in
book 12. In the process the claims of *iustitia* as well as those of *religio* are
explicitly acknowledged: "Pietas iustitiae pars est qua diligens officium
tribuimus patriae et iis qui nobis propinquitate coniuncti sunt."[13][32]
Here, then, as in later editions of the poem, readmission of the last six
books to critical scrutiny points at least tentatively toward a more historically nuanced understanding of the Vergilian idea. To turn from the Florence edition of 1487 to the Venice edition of 1544, for example, is to
discover a style of commentary more philological than philosophical or
allegorical. In the most detailed comment on *pietas* in this edition, Augus-
tino Datho emphatically rejects Landino's neo-Platonism, charges that
even the grammarians have misunderstood Aeneas's virtue, and sets out
to establish its true meaning by reference to the writings of Cicero.

It is clear from the start, however, that Datho's interest in *pietas* is no
less dictated by religious concerns than Landino's, even though the nature of their concerns is not the same. Beginning with a rehearsal of
passages from Cicero, Datho patronizingly dismisses the early rhetorical
treatises as the primitive work of a preoccupied adolescent. The classic
Ciceronian definition of *pietas* from the early work on invention is thus
disregarded, as Datho proceeds to the time when Cicero began to think
more acutely ("acrius philosophari coepit"). It is specifically in the treatise on the nature of the gods that Datho finds the idea developed to his
satisfaction. He selects for quotation passages from this work that bring
out the religious dimension of the word, including one passage that
could hardly fail to impress a reader familiar with the religious polemic
of the sixteenth century: "In specie fictae simulationis, sicut reliquae
virtutes, ita pietas inesse non potest, cum qua simul sanctitatem et religionem tolli necesse est."[14][33] Stressing the connection with *religio,*
Datho does not extend his quotation to the end of Cicero's sentence,
where *pietas* is connected with *iustitia.* Instead he invokes another passage associating *pietas* with divine worship ("cultus deorum"),[34] and
from here it is but a short step to Augustine and the Septuagint: "Et qui
Job librum transtulere, ubi apud Graecos in eo volumine θεοσεβίαν

---

[13] Piety is the part of justice that obligates us to the fatherland and to those near to us
in kinship.

[14] Piety, however, like the rest of the virtues, cannot exist in mere outward show and
pretence; and, with piety, reverence and religion must likewise disappear.

repererunt, et σωφίαν converterunt pietatem et sapientiam."[15] Sustaining the correlation between Greek and Latin with quotation of passages from the Hermetic books already quoted by Lactantius, Datho then returns to Cicero in order to extract a religious meaning from the "iustitiam cole et pietatem" command in the *Republic*. Specifically concerned with the priority Cicero grants to *patria* in this passage, the commentator explains this emphasis by observing that civil societies are especially pleasing to God as ruler of the world. Thus corrected, or correctly understood, Cicero's meaning here must be *cultus divinus*. By reordering the objects of *pietas* to place God first, Datho mediates between Cicero and Augustine, and neglects Plato altogether.

Armed with this elaborately defended meaning, Datho raises the specific question: in what sense is Vergil's hero "pietate insignis"? The method is again corrective. Many think that Aeneas earns his epithet by the honor accorded to his father, and Datho agrees that Vergil's own words provide ample support for this view. After citing several relevant passages, however, he counters with another set of passages that display Aeneas as, above all, mindful of religion: "Et patria decedens Aeneas ante omnia pietatis ac religionis memor patrem hortatur. 'Tu genitor cape sacra manu patriosque penates.' "[16] The goal of Aeneas, in this reading, is not the contemplative life, nor is it religion in any neo-Platonic sense; the goal is, rather, the resettlement of the Trojan gods in Latium, religion in a ritual or institutional sense. It is the hero's attention to religious duty that accounts, then, for his epithet: "Aeneas . . . qui cerimonias semper ac sacros rituum unus omnium extitit diligentissimus, ut merito ab insigni poeta pius plerunque nuncupatus sit."[17] Datho's meaning is sufficiently classical to be recognized by Cicero and sufficiently medieval in its emphasis on religion to be understood by Landino, but the framework of understanding is contemporary.

The contemporary importance of the word is further indicated by Scaliger's *Poetics*, in which the meaning of the Vergilian ideal occupies an entire chapter.[35] Whereas Datho had approached ambiguity by empha-

[15] Those who have translated the book of Job have rendered the Greek theosebia and sophia as pietas and sapientia.

[16] On leaving Troy, Aeneas—above all mindful of piety and religion—urges his father: "Father, do thou take in thy hand the sacred things and our country's household gods."

[17] Because Aeneas was always exceptionally attentive in performing religious ceremonies and sacred rituals, the poet rightly distinguishes him by generally calling him pious.

sizing one meaning over all others, Scaliger aims at synthesis, and in this regard exerts a considerable influence over later Renaissance commentary. Scaliger characteristically proceeds from one balanced pair of familiar terms to another, as he weighs (for example) the ascendant *cultus* against the descendant *misericordia*. "Pietas interdum misericordiam quandam significat: interdum propensionem certi cultus."[18] Citing numerous passages from the *Aeneid* by way of illustration, Scaliger represents the full range of *pietas* in the idealized character of Aeneas. His emphasis is not on the ambiguity of any single passage, but rather on the diverse ways in which the hero's characteristic virtue is displayed over the course of the whole poem. As *cultor deorum* Aeneas shows *affectus* in 5.56 and 5.466, *officium* in 3.5; in 2.707 he is the perfect son, in 1.646 the perfect father. In his relationships with other mortals, Aeneas is shown, especially, to be capable of compassion. Calling attention to the hero's often tearful response to pathos, Scaliger notes that this feeling is not restricted by bonds of family or nation. "Quin etiam hostibus fuit, et placidus, et lenis, et clemens, et pius. nanque et Lausum miseratur interemptum."[19] Although reference to the death of Lausus makes an abrupt climax to this sequence of ideas, the association of *pietas* with mercy toward an enemy is striking nonetheless, especially in light of earlier interpretations of *Aeneid* 12. The encounter between Aeneas and Lausus proves to Scaliger that Vergil's hero is indeed *pius* even in the sense indicated by the parallel terms: *placidus, lenis, clemens*. Aeneas thus becomes for Scaliger not only the exemplar, but also the teacher of *pietas:* "non solum fecit Aeneas quae ad pietatem pertinebant, sed etiam et docuit, et professus est."[20] Such praise leads finally to a celebratory peroration, from which the hero emerges—without contradiction, complication, or inconsistency—as a walking ideal whose epithet expresses ethical as well as religious meaning, parental care as well as filial duty.

The influence of Scaliger's synthetic approach is evident at the turn of the seventeenth century in J. J. Spanmueller's exposition of Vergil, published under the name Jacobus Pontanus. Commenting on "insignem pietate virum" (1.10), Spanmueller refers the reader to the *Poetics:* "Eximiam, et multiplicem Aeneae pietatem in deos atque homines,

---

[18] Pietas sometimes means mercy, sometimes the inclination of true worship.

[19] Indeed even toward enemies, he was gentle, mild, merciful, and pious, for he pities even the slain Lausus.

[20] Not only did Aeneas do what piety required, but he also declared and taught it.

prolatis in medium e Virgilio locis, pulcherrime ostendit Scaliger."[21][36] This reference is both appreciative and accurate. Spanmueller's word *multiplex* is in fact truer to Scaliger's method than his own word *ambiguus*. Yet the comments of Spanmueller himself suggest that contention over the meaning of *pietas* has begun to subside, and that it is now possible to recover a more classical understanding of its implications. Working less by cross-reference within the *Aeneid* than by allusion to other classical sources, Spanmueller offers his most sustained discussion of *pietas* in response to *Aeneid* 2.707. To illuminate the image of Aeneas shouldering Anchises, he points to the non-Vergilian Aeneas of Ovid, Propertius, and Seneca, and to figures said to resemble Aeneas and Anchises in less prominent Roman writers. A consequence of this repetition of passages from ancient writers is to fix Vergil firmly in the pre-Christian past. The perspective thus acquired allows Spanmueller to view the events of the later books with a measure of dispassion. The problem posed by the death of Turnus, for example, is treated at length, the accumulated objections and reservations admitted; but the resolution to the difficulty of this passage is inherent in the initial assumption that Vergil cannot be held accountable to Christian ethical standards. Vergil's use of the word must instead be understood against the background of mistaken belief, its meaning admitted to be incongruent with Christian ethics. Accordingly, Spanmueller has no qualms about conceding that the *pietas* of Vergil sometimes does seem *impius* ("pietatem aliquando fuisse impiam"), as Lactantius had charged.[37] But whereas Lactantius had used this observation to challenge Vergil's understanding of the word, Spanmueller defends—even praises—Vergil for using it. Similarly, in contrast to Donatus's agonized explanation of "pius" at 10.783, he coolly observes: "Bene pius, qui deorum contemptorem interficit. Est enim pietatis tollere impios."[22][38] His point is not original—Donatus himself comes finally to a similar conclusion about the passage—but the ease with which he reaches it suggests the convenience of the historical approach.

The assimilation of Vergilian to Christian *pietas* evident in the allegorical commentaries of the Middle Ages has thus yielded by the close of the

[21] By passages adduced from Vergil, Scaliger very beautifully shows the distinctive and many-sided piety of Aeneas toward both gods and men.

[22] It was most proper for the pious hero to kill one who despised the gods. It is indeed an act of piety to destroy the impious.

sixteenth century to a more historically conscious acceptance of the *Aeneid*. Yet if the tendency to impose contemporary meaning on this ancient text is diminished and the emotional pitch of explanation lowered, the debate over meaning has nonetheless left an impression that is still quite evident in the later seventeenth-century Vergil of Charles de la Rue on which Dryden based his translation. Mining his glosses from various layers in the archaeology of the word, de la Rue explains *pietas* in his marginal paraphrase with synonyms dictated by his understanding of the immediate context. The range of possibilities extends from *virtus* to *caritas,* and comprehends the repeated distinctions of earlier commentators: *cultus* is admitted along with *misericordia,* and *religio* coexists with *iustitia.* But of these, the most often repeated is still *religio.* That de la Rue even admits *caritas* to his paraphrase,[39] moreover, is a sure sign that the gradual recovery of historical meaning occurs within a context of understanding shaped by the Bible.

Biblical Commentary

Reflecting on the first psalm, Martin Luther contrasts the eternal word of God to the variable customs and rites of men, contingent on time and place. In expanding this idea, he places the distinction between *pietas* and *impietas* on the side of eternity. "Nam etsi varient per tempora mores, personae, loca, ritus, eadem tamen vel pietas vel impietas transit per omnia saecula."[23][40] Although the Bible provides sanction for this view, interpretation of its different books is notoriously a function of "mores, personae, loca, ritus." Founded on the exegetical works of the church fathers, the tradition of biblical commentary early identifies *pietas* with Jesus Christ. As this identification is elaborated in scholastic exegesis, the pastoral epistles command special attention, most notably 1 Timothy, where the word appears more frequently than in any other book of the Vulgate New Testament: the specific passages recurrently cited from this epistle are 3.16 on the incarnation and 4.7–8 on spiritual exercise. In the commentary of humanism and reform, the pastorals are superseded by the major epistles in shaping comprehension of *pietas,*

[23] For although in the course of time customs, people, places, and usages may vary, godliness and ungodliness remain the same through all the ages.

and among the reformers especially, the emphasis is often on the negative. Romans thus becomes the crucial text, and in Protestant interpretation the "omnem impietatem" of 1.18 is asked to bear the weight of repeated comment.

This shift in textual focus is accompanied by a marked shift in usage. In patristic and medieval commentary *pietas* is a visceral quality, usually defined by the synonym *misericordia* or the antonym *crudelitas*. In the age of Erasmus and Luther, *pietas* is a mental or spiritual quality, closely associated with *eruditio* (and sometimes paradoxically with *stultitia*) or *spiritus*, depending on the commentator's attitude toward the nature of biblical authority and the scope of interpretation itself. The focus of debate over these issues is the value of classical erudition in expounding the Bible, a question long since evident in the writings of the church fathers and essential to understanding the evolution of *pietas*. From one perspective, exemplified by Ambrose, Christian *pietas* is continuous with the *pietas* of Cicero and Vergil; in the alternative view of Jerome, believing himself to have been reproved by divine vision for his pagan studies, Christian *pietas* denies its classical heritage.

For Ambrose, Christianity perfects the classical culture in which he was nurtured. His book on the duties of the clergy, for example, is modelled on Cicero, whose ideas are appropriately modified as they are applied to the needs of a Christian audience. After quoting Cicero's maxim that *pietas* is the foundation of all virtue, for example, Ambrose adds a religious explanation:

> Iustitiae autem pietas est prima in Deum, secunda in patriam, tertia in parentes, item in omnes: quae et ipsa secundum naturae est magisterium. Sequidem ab ineunte aetate ubi primum sensus infundi coeperit, vitam amamus tanquam Dei munus, patriam, parentesque diligimus, deinde aequales quibus sociari cupimus. Hinc charitas nascitur, quae alios sibi praefert, non quaerens quae sua sunt, in quibus est principatus iustitiae.[24][41]

[24] But the piety of justice is first directed towards God; secondly, towards one's country; next, towards parents; lastly, towards all. This, too, is in accordance with the guidance of nature. From the beginning of life, when understanding first begins to be infused into us, we love life as the gift of God, we love our country and our parents; lastly, our companions, with whom we like to associate. Hence arises true love, which prefers others to self, and seeks not its own, wherein lies the pre-eminence of justice.

Viewing *pietas* as the first part of justice, Ambrose places God before country in the line of duty, replaces Cicero's "propinquiis" with "omnes," and makes the principal objects of *pietas* dependent on the verb "diligimus." Finally modified to include relationships with equals based on love, classical *pietas* becomes the mother of Christian *caritas*.

Although Cicero is obviously important to Ambrose, equally important is Vergil, whose words and phrases repeatedly embellish the bishop's exegetical works. The extensive commentary on Luke suggests, in particular, the convergence of Vergilian and Christian *pietas*. Interpreting the parable of the banquet in Luke 14, for example, Ambrose develops the idea of discipleship by blending the easy yoke of Matthew 11.29–30 ("Tollite iugum meum super vos, et discite a me, quia mitis sum") with the emblematic *pietas* of *Aeneid* 2.707 ("ergo age, care pater, cervici imponere nostrae"): "Christum enim recepimus, qui cervicibus nostris pietatis suae iugum mite suspendit."[25][42] Christ is received by the Christian as the burden of Anchises is accepted by Aeneas. In the very act of receiving this burden, the Christian assumes the virtue of Aeneas, newly identified with the yoke of Christ: "pietatis . . . iugum." Even more pointed is the association of Jesus with Aeneas in the commentary on the resurrection of Lazarus. "Sed et ibi piae sororis lacrimis commovetur, quia mentem humana tangebant . . ."[26][43] The allusion here to perhaps the single most familiar line in the *Aeneid* ("sunt lacrimae rerum et mentem mortalia tangunt," 1.462) identifies the weeping Jesus of the Lazarus narrative with the weeping Aeneas of the murals episode. Yet this understanding is modified by the role of Lazarus's sister. Described as *pia soror,* she exemplifies not only compassion but also the bond of kinship, *officium* as well as *affectus*.

In light of this meaning, the several passages in Luke (8.19–21, 12.52–53, 14.26) that seem not only to weaken kinship ties but even to subvert the commandment to honor father and mother necessarily require careful exegesis. Ambrose's interpretive strategy is to argue that these passages do not deny the obligations of kinship, but that they do point toward a higher sense of duty: if we are obliged to show duty to parents, so much more are we bound to be dutiful to God.[44] To stress this priority, Ambrose elevates *religio* above *pietas,* concluding his comments on 12.52–53 with these words: "religio enim praestat pietatis offi-

[25] For we have received Christ, who places on our necks the mild yoke of his piety.
[26] But there he is moved by the tears of the pious sister, because human things touched his mind . . .

ciis."[27][45] Though repeated elsewhere in his writings,[46] this distinction is sometimes blurred, even by adding *vera* to *pietas:* "praeferenda est religio necessitudini, pietas propinquitati: ea est enim vera pietas, quae praeponit divina humanis, perpetua temporalibus."[28][47] Ambrose here characteristically turns potential alternatives into a hierarchy of preferences. The *pietas* of Aeneas still lives in Ambrose, but it is surpassed—perfected—by *vera pietas,* which places the divine and eternal above the human and temporal.

Jerome takes a much harder line. Commenting on Matthew 10.37 ("Qui amat patrem aut matrem plus quam me, non est me dignus"), for example, he envisions the possibility of disjunction between love of parents and love of God, in which case *pietas* is actually defined as hatred of parents ("odium in suos pietas in Deum est").[48] For friends of Jerome, moreover, this was not always a merely speculative possibility, as his letters urging them to pursue an ascetic life attest. In a letter of 374, he presses the argument with characteristic force: "Licet parvulus ex collo pendeat nepos, licet sparso crine et scissis vestibus ubera, quibus nutrierat, mater ostendat, licet in limine pater iaceat, per calcatum perge patrem, siccis oculis ad vexillum crucis vola! Pietatis genus est in hac re esse crudelem."[29][49] Jerome thus offers an image of *pietas* antithetical to *Aeneid* 2.707: the son trampling the father to reach the cross. The same two terms, *pietas* and *crudelitas,* are again joined in a later epistle urging a young woman to enter a monastery. To counter any possible worry that she might be blamed for abandoning her mother, Jerome argues: "Si quis te carpit, quod sis Christiana, quod virgo, ne cures, quod ideo dimiseris matrem, ut in monasterio inter virgines viveres; talis detractio laus tua est. Ubi non luxuria in puella Dei, sed duritia carpitur, crudelitas ista pietas est."[30][50] Here the paradoxical language announces two distinct communities of understanding.

[27] For religion is more important than the obligations of piety.

[28] Religion is to be shown toward friends, piety toward relatives: it is indeed true piety that places the divine above the human, the eternal above the temporal.

[29] Though your little nephew hang on your neck, though your mother with dishevelled hair and torn raiment show you the breasts that gave you suck, though your father fling himself upon the threshold, trample your father underfoot and go your way, fly with tearless eyes to the standard of the Cross. In these matters to be cruel is a son's duty.

[30] Heed it not if anyone criticizes you for being a Christian and a virgin, and for having left your mother to live in a monastery with other virgins. Such censure is your truest praise. When men blame one of God's maidens, not for self-indulgence, but for sternness, what they call cruelty is really devotion.

Although Jerome himself often reverts to more traditional usage,[51] he also uses the word to draw even finer distinctions than that between Christian and pagan. In various ways and contexts, *pietas*—or more often *impietas*—is used by Jerome to separate the truth as he sees it from the truth as others, including other Christians, see it. Such polemical use of the word occurs even in his less controversial writings, including the biblical commentaries: the prosperous evildoers ("facientes impietatem") of Malachi 3.15, for example, are personified in Jerome's commentary by Marcion and Valentinus.[52] Such polemics threaten to drain the words of any determinate meaning and reduce them to mere labels, interchangeable in accordance with one's point of view. That this does not happen more often is due in large part to the stabilizing force of the Bible itself. As biblical translator, Jerome exerts an incalculable influence on later understanding of *pietas*.

The meaning of the word in the Vulgate Old Testament emerges largely by negation: *impius* occurs over fifty times more often than *pius*.[53] Most frequent in the book of Proverbs, *impius* is generally predictive of a bad end, because the way of the impious is evil ("Abominatio est Domino via impii," 15.9). The divine order thus assumed by proverbial wisdom underlies the book of Job, where the word *impius* is also frequent, often in expressions of uncertainty, in questions and in subjunctive or conditional clauses. "Et si impius fuero, vae mihi est; / Et si iustus, non levabo caput" (10.15).[31] Here and elsewhere the word opposite *impius* is not *pius* but *iustus*. Thus Genesis 18.23: "Numquid perdes iustum cum impio?" and Ecclesiastes 3.17: "Iustum et impium iudicabit Deus."[32]

The closest the Old Testament comes to a more specific definition or image of *impietas* is in Zechariah 5.7–8, the obscure vision of the woman who personifies the evils afflicting Israel. In Jerome's version: "Et ecce talentum plumbi portabatur, et ecce mulier una sedens in medio amphorae. Et dixit: 'Haec est impietas.' "[33] In his commentary, Jerome remarks specifically on this word, explaining the variations from Hebrew to Greek to Latin, and implicitly justifying his change of the Old Latin *iniquitas* to *impietas* by offering a definition to suit the context:

[31] If I be wicked, woe unto me; and if I be righteous, yet will I not lift up my head.
[32] Wilt thou also destroy the righteous with the wicked? / God shall judge the righteous and the wicked.
[33] And, behold, there was lifted up a talent of lead: and this is a woman that sitteth in the midst of the ephah. And he said, This is wickedness.

"impietas, quam alio nomine idolatriam possumus appellare, et nega-
tionem Dei."[34][54] Commenting on the succeeding vision, in which two
women with wings appear to carry personified *impietas* off to Babylon,
Jerome adds that Babylon is its true home ("Vere enim in Babylone sedes
est impietatis").[55] Alluding to both the Tower of Babel and the Babylo-
nian captivity, Jerome views the "sedes . . . impietatis" as a place of
confusion and punishment, the seat of both idolatry and heresy. Since
impietas is also figured here as oppressive weight ("pondus impietatis
gravissimum"), Zechariah 5.7 is cited elsewhere by Jerome to illustrate
the burden of sin in contrast to the easy yoke of Matthew 11.30; and in
his commentary on this gospel passage, Jerome—although citing the
passage in the Old Latin—specifically refers to the lead weight of Zechariah 5.7.[56] The very same passage that is illuminated for Ambrose by the
emblematic *pietas* of the *Aeneid* recalls to Jerome the personified
iniquitas or *impietas* of the Old Testament. Where Ambrose proceeds to
definition by analogy, Jerome refines the word by division, contrast,
opposition, paradox. A word thus reflecting the continuity of classical
and Christian culture in Ambrose, *pietas* is often used by Jerome to
dramatize disjunction and to assert the authority of the Hebrew scriptures. The *pietas* of Ambrose tends toward universal *caritas,* whereas
that of Jerome serves to identify the orthodox or more often in the
negative to point a finger at heresy.

For all their differences, the two doctors share an understanding of
pietas as shaped by the morality of the Gospels. In later exegesis this is
affirmed by identification of *pietas* with the teacher of that morality. In
developing the correspondence between the spiritual gifts of Isaiah and
the beatitudes of Matthew, Augustine (for example) associates *pietas*
with the blessing of the meek, *pius* therefore with *mitis.*[57] This is an
association of no little significance, moreover; because *mitis* is the adjective used to describe the *pietatis iugum* in Ambrose, the adjective directly
linked in the Vulgate with Christ, who says in the same passage from
Matthew—not "sum pius"—but "mitis sum." In the commentaries of
Gregory, where the basic meaning of the word is *misericordia* and the
repeated phrase of note is *viscera pietatis,* Christ becomes the incarnate
image of divine mercy ("superna pietas"): "Quia enim omnipotens Deus
pietatis suae mysterio homo factus est."[35][58] The apparent scriptural

[34] Impiety, which we can call by its other name idolatry, is the denial of God.
[35] For indeed omnipotent God by the mystery of his piety became a man.

allusion here is to 1 Timothy 3.16. Gregory's "mysterio" transliterates the original: "καὶ ὁμολογουμένως μέγα ἐστὶν τὸ τῆς εὐσεβείας μυστήριον· ὃς ἐφανερώθη ἐν σαρκί . . ." His "pietatis" reflects Latin translation: "Et manifeste magnum est pietatis sacramentum, quod manifestatum est in carne . . ."[36] Whereas the Greek "ὃς" clearly marks a disjunction in the text, introducing lines understood as quotation, the Latin "quod" syntactically connects the hymnodic celebration of the incarnation to the preceding phrase "pietatis sacramentum."[59] The Latin translation thus provides the warrant for identification of *pietas* with Jesus Christ.

As interpreters explain this text, *pietas* is affirmed in its attachment to the doctrine of the incarnation. In the highly influential commentary of the anonymous Ambrosiaster, the word is pushed back to enhance the reference to the church in verse 15 and is defined in the process as "sacramentum veritatis."[60] To identify *pietas* with truth is further to bring this passage into agreement with Titus 1.1 ("agnitionem veritatis, quae secundum pietatem est in spem vitae aeternae") and to invest the word with ultimate doctrinal authority. The central truth sponsored by the church is then paraphrased by glossing the biblical "pietatis" with "mysterii Dei" and adding "Christus" to the relative clause: "Sacramentum mysterii Dei, quod est Christus in carne . . ."[37] This emphasis is affirmed in the ninth-century commentary of Hrabanus Maurus, who explains the passage as a response to heretical doctrines denying the full humanity of Jesus and defends the orthodox view in the phrase *doctrina pietatis*.[61] Attaching this doctrine to a fully developed conception of a merciful God, the twelfth-century Benedictine Herveus defines *pietas* as divine descent ("ex alto") into brotherhood ("ut sibi fratres acquireret") with mortal men. This literally descending conception of the word is expressed in the language of the fathers, as Herveus repeats the Gregorian correlation of *pietas* and *misericordia* to expound the doctrine of the incarnation.[62]

Additional synonyms for *pietas* are tested by medieval exegetes on chapter 4, verses 7 and 8 of the same epistle, where the doctrinal issue is superseded by a behavioral one: "exerce autem teipsum ad pietatem. Nam corporalis exercitatio, ad modicum utilis est: pietas autem ad omnia utilis est, promissionem habens vitae, quae nunc est, et

---

[36] And without controversy great is the mystery of godliness: God was manifest in the flesh . . .

[37] The sacrament of the mystery of God, which is Christ incarnate . . .

futurae."[38] The persistent focus of attention here is the phrase "pietas autem ad omnia utilis est," with "omnia" serving as the basis for extending the meaning and enhancing the importance of *pietas*. Commentators who naturally take the word as an expression of doctrine in 3.16 take the same word in 4.7–8 as a disciplinary rule— without any clear limits. If the phrase can validate the privilege of *misericordia,* as it does for those who follow Ambrosiaster ("omnis enim summa disciplinae nostrae in misericordia et pietate est"), it can also be extended by Hrabanus Maurus to mean *caritas* ("Pietas autem quae sine dubio charitas intelligitur, ad omnia utilis est") and by Peter Lombard to signify the commandment of brotherly love ("Pietas autem quae operatur bona fratribus").[63] By the time of Aquinas, then, 1 Timothy 4.7–8 can authorize the elevation of *pietas* among the spiritual gifts of Isaiah 11 and can be extolled as a universal good ("bonum universale").[64]

Renaissance usage is, in part, a reaction against this universality and specifically against the reiterated definitions that invoke the favored patristic synonym *misericordia.* Restriction on the meaning of the word is already evident in the first printed gloss on 1 Timothy 4.8, by Nicolaus of Lyra, who finds two senses of the word in this passage ("accipitur hic pietas dupliciter").[65] After acknowledging the Augustinian definition, "cultus divinus," Nicolaus adds: "pietas importat condescensionem ad proximum."[39] Reaching both up and down, *pietas* expresses the central moral idea of the New Testament: devotion to God and man. Although perfectly summarizing a view shared with prior commentators, Nicolaus's gloss is notably free of theological elaboration. The biblical "omnia" does not here become a license for gathering different applications of the word, nor does it produce any reference to patristic authority. Rather, it provides an opportunity for reestablishing a literal sense of the verse and for reasserting an idea of fundamental truth: *pietas* is beneficial in all things because it places men in right relationship with God and neighbor ("bene disponat hominem ad deum et ad proximum"). The relationship with God is here expressed by the phrase "cultus divinus," but Nicolaus avoids offering any equivalent phrase to

---

[38] Exercise thyself rather in godliness. For bodily exercise profiteth little: but godliness is profitable unto all things, having promise of the life that now is, and of that which is to come.

[39] Piety brings about graciousness toward one's neighbors.

explain *pietas* "ad proximum," pointedly neglecting the often-repeated *misericordia*.

Whereas Aquinas himself had already refined the distinction between these synonyms,[66] Lorenzo Valla (whose ironic encomium of Aquinas is today one of his best known works) refuses to admit *misericordia* as a synonym at all. In his annotations on the New Testament, Valla allows *pietas* to stand as the natural Latin translation of εὐσέβεια in the pastoral epistles; but in his invective against Bartolomeo Fazio, he ridicules his adversary's confusion of *pietas* with *misericordia*. Without deciding whether Fazio's misunderstanding is a function of his impudence or stupidity, Valla explains to him the correct sense of the word: "amor in deum, in parentes, in patriam, in pignora, sive (ut Cicero ait) iustitia adversus deum."[40][67] Valla clearly aims at a pure classical definition without the accretions of meaning gathered since the time of Cicero. To reject *misericordia* is to reject a tradition of glosses on the word dating back to the fourth century.

The relaxed grip of patristic and scholastic glosses evident in Valla's definition is diversely apparent in the exegetical discourse of humanism and reform. Although *pietas* has a range of important roles to play in this discourse, certain patterns of association are recurrently emphasized, often in combination with one another. The fundamental division in Christian usage between doctrine (1 Timothy 3.16) and discipline (1 Timothy 4.7–8) eventually overlaps the increasingly important distinction between *vera pietas* and *ficta pietas*. Metaphorically expressed as a contrast between what is inward and invisible and what is outward and visible, this distinction hardens as the Reformation progresses. A second repeated metaphor is the traditional one of the Christian pilgrimage, the "via Dei" of Luther's lectures on Romans, the "Christi via" of Erasmus's *Enchiridion*. But the place of *pietas* along the way—is it the goal? the path itself? the starting point?—depends on the writer's own way of interpreting the Bible as a guide to the journey. Crucial in this regard is the place of human wisdom, as represented especially by Greece and Rome, in biblical interpretation. The inescapable text is Romans 1.22: "dicentes enim se esse sapientes, stulti facti sunt."[41]

In his commentary on this verse, Marsiglio Ficino joins *stultitia* to

[40] love toward God, parents, fatherland, children, or as Cicero says, justice toward God

[41] Professing themselves to be wise, they became fools.

impietas.[68] The significance of this association is demonstrated by Ficino's gloss on the phrase "omnem impietatem" four verses earlier. Here the word is first defined by negation of the familiar Augustinian terms: "Impietatem, id est, divini cultus praevaricationem."[42][69] Ficino then turns to the significance of "omnem" with some of the same energy that medieval commentators had devoted to the "omnia" of 1 Timothy 4.8. But instead of invoking the fathers, Ficino develops his interpretation of Paul on the authority of Plato. Although the *Euthyphro* might perhaps have been expected in this context, Ficino chooses instead to illuminate Romans by reference to the *Laws:* "Inquit autem omnem impietatem, quia multae sunt species impietatis, quas Plato in decimo legum enumerat latius, et effulminat."[43] Ficino proceeds to paraphrase the conclusion to the first paragraph of *Laws* 10, where Plato identifies three impious types: he who does not believe in the gods; he who believes but denies that the gods care for men; he who affirms both the existence and the providence of the gods, but holds that they can be bribed by offerings and prayers. Responding to this same passage of *pius* Plato[70] in his disquisition on Platonic theology, Ficino points out three ways to *pietas* ("Ad quam certe pietatem causis praecipue tribus inducimur"). The first is *sagacitas,* infused in us by divine providence; the second consists of *rationes philosophicae,* the third of *propheticae atque miracula.*[71] Latent in this passage is the metaphor of a journey "ad pietatem" in which the guidance of the Bible is to be supplemented on Ficino's own example by the wisdom of the ancients.

By making *pietas* stand for a conception of religion as dependent on Plato as on Paul, Ficino articulates a familiar but far from universal attitude of the time. On the contrary: as if in answer, Jacques Lefèvre d'Etaples insists in the preface to his commentary on the Gospels that the word of God is sufficient to eternal life, that the wisdom derived from other sources is superfluous ("Verbum Dei sufficit").[72] Assuming that this claim does not render Lefèvre's own commentary superfluous, the real question remains: how is the sufficient word of God to be interpreted? Obliquely addressing this question in his earlier commentary on the letters of Paul, Lefèvre correlates *pietas* and *puritas* to expound a theory of reading that depends on divine inspiration.[73] In this account of the matter,

[42] Impiety is false worship of God.
[43] Paul refers to all impiety because there are many forms of it, which are enumerated and explained by Plato in the tenth book of the Laws.

pietas is not, however, the end of reading Paul's letters but a necessary precondition of comprehending them: Ficino's goal is Lefèvre's starting point, as the linear metaphor of the journey intersects this Renaissance version of the hermeneutic circle. When Lefèvre repeats this idea later in his preface, he acknowledges another sort of reader: "Qui igitur pie accedent ad haec legenda non Paulus, non quisquam alius, sed Christus et spiritus eius superbonus praestabunt, ut pietate proficiant. Qui vero praesumptuose ac superbe non etiam Paulus, non alius quicumque, sed ille repellet 'qui superbis resistit et humilibus dat gratiam.' "[44][74] This Augustinian division of the world into the humble and the proud establishes two classes of readers, as the moral terms find intellectual correlatives. Those who understand the text must already belong to the city of God; those who do not Lefèvre leaves to divine grace.

For all their evident differences, Ficino and Lefèvre share with their humanist successors patterns of usage that effectively raise *pietas* from the Gregorian viscera and establish its importance in the discourse of mind and spirit. Ficino's *pietas* is closer to the *eruditio* of Erasmus, Lefèvre's to the *spiritus* of Luther, but both stand well apart from the *misericordia* of Gregory and Ambrosiaster. Although different conceptions of *pietas* in Erasmus and Luther are but indications of larger differences, it may be observed by reference to their remarks on 1 Timothy 3.16 how significant the word is for both of them in articulating the religious concerns of the sixteenth century. In the commentary accompanying his Greek New Testament, Erasmus gives the familiar passage a fresh emphasis: "*Pietatem* igitur vocat legem Christi, vacuam ceremoniis, cuius mysterium magnum est, sed quod iam sit *manifestatum* per Christi humanitatem, quod *iustificatum in spiritu et virtute* Dei, nimirum per miracula."[45][75] Specifically dissociated from ceremony, the *pietas* of the pastoral epistle is here considered as implicit authority for reform. It is in this same spirit, moreover, that Luther reads the passage as Paul's plea for simplicity and purity of doctrine. He thus introduces his commentary on chapter 4 by summarizing 3.16: "In proximo loco collegit in quandam summam doctrinam pietatis, ita quod mundus inexcusabilis et omnes, qui errant et pereunt,

---

[44] It is not Paul, nor anyone else who will show those who approach the reading piously how to benefit from such piety, but only Christ and his sublime spirit. But if one should proceed in a presumptuous and proud manner, neither Paul nor anyone else will repel him, but only He who "resisteth the proud, but giveth grace unto the humble."

[45] Thus without reference to ceremonies, he calls piety the law of Christ, whose mystery is great, but which is manifest in the humanity of Christ, justified in the spirit and power of God, truly by miracle.

quia satis declaratum mysterium pietatis, quod praedicari, doceri debet. Hoc ideo urget Paulus, ut conservet doctrinam sanam in ecclesia contra varios et alienos doctores."[46][76] Luther's *doctrina pietatis* thus diverges in implication from the same expression in medieval exegesis in order to commend the necessary union, equally evident in Erasmus, of doctrine and discipline, belief and conduct. Indeed his phrase from later in the same commentary—"pietas ante omnia"[77]—could as well have been written by Erasmus, who would, however, have meant something slightly different by it.

Near the conclusion of his work on theological method, Erasmus concisely expresses his basic orientation toward New Testament scholarship in reflection on Titus 3.9: "Rursum ad Titum, ubi multa monuisset, quae ad pios mores faciunt, etiam atque etiam admonet, ut stultas quaestiones et genealogias et pugnas, quae veniunt ex lege, reiciat."[47][78] Here the phrase "pios mores" stands in sharp contrast to "stultas quaestiones," as Erasmus distinguishes both adjectives and nouns. The adjective *pius* describes conduct and is opposed to what is *stultus*. The contrast in the nouns, moreover, is not between conduct and intellect, but between conduct and false intellect, illustrated here, as commonly in Erasmus, by the "quaestiones" of scholasticism. As he explains several lines later, *pietas* depends on a kind of learning quite different from medieval philosophy: "At si quis magis cupit instructus esse ad pietatem quam ad disputationem, statim ac potissimum versetur in fontibus, versetur in his scriptoribus, qui proxime biberunt de fontibus."[48][79] The phrase "instructus . . . ad pietatem" makes *pietas* the end, instruction in the biblical sources of the faith the means. The unstated terms in this passage—*impietas* as the complement of *stultitia, eruditio* as that of *pietas*—are stated with some frequency elsewhere in Erasmus's work as in that of his contemporaries. Thus he describes Jerome as both *pius* and *eruditus,* terms of praise commonly combined in sixteenth-century dedi-

---

[46] In the last section, he gathered into a sort of summary the doctrine of religion in such a way that the world and all who err and perish are without excuse. After all, the mystery of religion which ought to be preached and taught has been sufficiently declared. Therefore Paul urges this, that one should preserve sound doctrine in the church against various other theologians.

[47] As he had often enjoined the conduct of a pious life, so he warns repeatedly in Titus to resist the foolish questions, genealogies, and disputes which come from legalism.

[48] But if one wants to be directed more toward piety than toward disputation, he should betake himself directly to the source, and stick with those writers who have drunk closest to the source.

cations and letters, just as *impius* and *stultus* predictably meet in satire.[80] Indeed this association is common enough to occasion ironic treatment in the *Praise of Folly:* "Haec quid aliud clamitant, nisi mortaleis stultos esse, etiam pios?"[49][81]

Although the notion that in this world much *stultitia* passes for *pietas* is but one implication of Erasmus's irony, the problem of *ficta pietas* is a recurrent one in his writing and is developed at length in the work quoted above on theological method. After citing Romans 12.15 and 1 Peter 4.8 to define *pietas* in terms of conduct, Erasmus distinguishes conduct from ceremony.

> De caerimoniis nulla umquam mentio. Iam quemadmodum fidei et caritatis comes est animi fortitudo veraque pietas, ita, cum illae languent aut absunt, fervet superstitio. Et quemadmodum sincera pietas animi puritate nititur, ita superstitio caerimoniis sese vendi- tat. Illam spiritus vocabulo frequenter notat Paulus, hanc carnis; nam id sensit, opinor, cum scriberet Galatis: "Sic stulti estis, ut, cum spiritu coeperitis, carne consummemini?" Ab evangelica fide caritateque exorsi ad Iudaismum relabimini? Aliter quidem, sed idem admonet Romanos capite duodecimo, ut neglectis Iudaicis ritibus ad pietatis studium in animo sitae sese convertant.[50][82]

Ceremony, superstition, and ritual are here aligned against faith, charity, and piety, the ways of the flesh against the ways of the spirit, the old law against the new. Erasmus replaces hope in the Pauline triad with *pietas,* but in doing so he finds it necessary to qualify the word twice. Whereas faith and charity stand on their own, *pietas* needs *vera* and *sincera* to assure its opposition to the folly of the Galatians. The reason for these adjectives is evident in the argument that follows. After quoting 1 Timo- thy 4.8 and observing briefly that *pietas* is appropriate to all situations,

[49] What do these things declare, except that mortals are foolish, even the pious?

[50] [In the epistles] there is no mention of ceremonies. As the following of faith and love is true piety and spiritual courage, so when these are weak or absent, superstition heats up. And as sincere piety depends on purity of heart, so superstition promotes itself through ceremonies. The one Paul frequently refers to by the word spirit, the other by the word flesh; for this is what he meant, I think, when he wrote to the Galatians: "Are you so foolish? having begun in the spirit, are you now made perfect by the flesh?" In the faith of the gospel and in love have you begun and have you now fallen back into Judaism? In another place, but in the same sense, he admonishes the Romans in chapter 12 to neglect the Judaic ritual and to turn back to the pursuit of piety in a settled spirit.

Erasmus goes on to consider the threat to *pietas* posed by *simulata sanctimonia* and *falsum pietatis praetextum*.[83] His text here is the warning against false piety in 2 Timothy 3.5, which he aligns with the warning against false wisdom in Colossians 2.23. Erasmus elaborates these passages into a warning of his own against the disturbances that may arise from devotion to appearances, translating the New Testament condemnation of the Pharisees into modern terms and concluding: "Nihil insanabilius esse impietate pietatis imagine personata docet. . . . Ac mox ibidem in factis, non verbis, in affectu, non cultu, in oboedientia, non caerimoniis sitam esse veram pietatem docet."[51][84]

An antidote to the failed leadership of modern Pharisees ("[qui] adeo nihil conducerent ad veram pietatem") is provided by Erasmus in his *Enchiridion,* which invokes *pietas* on almost every page. One of the reasons the word is repeated so often here is that it designates both truth and falsehood: the phrase *pietatis studium* indicates the goal, *persona pietatis* the obstacle.[85] For Erasmus the enemy of *pietas* passes under the same name, but is known by visible signs, whereas true *pietas* as defined in the first six rules of the *Enchiridion* is finally invisible. Relying on the distinction between the letter and spirit of the law, Erasmus expounds the danger of confusing visible observances ("pietas monastica") with *vera pietas.* He summarizes the idea in terms parallel to those in 1 Timothy 4.8: "Non damnantur opera corporalia, sed praeferuntur invisibilia. Non damnatur cultus visibilis, sed non placatur deus nisi pietate invisibili."[52][86] Erasmus pursues this form of definition to its logical conclusion in the sixth rule: "[non] aliunde quam ab uno Christo pietatis exemplum petatur. Hoc est enim unicum archetypum, unde quisquis vel unguem discesserit, a recto discedit atque extra viam currit."[53][87] Here the way and the end of the *Enchiridion* converge: if *pietas* is invisible, it is nonetheless uniquely exemplified by the life of Christ, who is both way and end.

In his succeeding discussion of the thoughts worthy of a Christian,

---

[51] [Paul] teaches that nothing is more incurable than impiety disguised in the likeness of piety. And he goes on in the same place to teach that true piety is in deeds, not in words, in disposition not in ritual, in obedience not in ceremonies.

[52] Physical deeds are not condemned, but the unseen are preferred. Visible worship is not condemned, but God is pleased only by piety that is unseen.

[53] [One's] model of piety should be Christ alone and no other. For he is the sole archetype, and whoever departs from it even in the slightest deviates from what is right and runs outside the true path.

Erasmus elaborates this apparent paradox by arguing from specific allusion to Plato's *Republic* that conduct proceeds from belief. If this understanding of *pietas* by reference to Plato suggests affinity with Ficino, the
conclusion reached in this passage is not in any obvious way at odds with
Luther's principle—"qualis doctrina, talis vita"—either.[88] Luther himself
offers a more expansive statement of this idea in his commentary on the
Psalms: "Nam quando de pietate et impietate agimus, non de moribus,
sed de opinionibus agimus, hoc est de fontibus morum."[54][89] In the
lectures on Romans he pushes *pietas* still farther into the domain of the
invisible, expressing even more sharply than Erasmus the dangers that
pietas poses to *pietas*. His example is not the Pharisees of the New Testament but the Baal worshippers of the Old, as he updates the reference to 1
Kings 19.18 in Romans 11.4. Modern idolators are of two types, he
argues, and both are distinguished by pride in their excessive *pietas*. The
first type is engaged in the worship of graven images, worship according
to the senses: "Deum verum colunt secundum sensum suum proprium,
stultissimo zelo, nimia pietate omnibus Impiis peiores."[55] Here, it
should be noted, *stultitia* is associated not with *impietas* but with exaggerated *pietas*. More threatening, however, is the second type, those who
worship an idol of the mind: "Hic est enim obstinatae mentis opiniosa
pietas et induratae cervicis religiosa sapientia, quae sibiipsa in caput a
seipsa constituta, seipsam sequitur in via Dei, Sibi ipsa Magistra ad
Deum . . ."[56][90] Luther's "opiniosa" stands in implied contrast to truth,
as true *pietas* becomes a function of the true word. Although Luther
repeatedly offers assurance that truth will conquer ("Veritas enim super
omnia vincit"), his identification of *pietas* with the divine word is hardly
an adequate definition for a biblical scholar such as Erasmus concerned
with the problem of interpretation. We both have the same word, Erasmus
argues; the problem is how to understand it ("De sensu scripturae pugna
est").[91]

Luther's answer is blunt: Erasmus's position that some passages of
Scripture are too obscure to penetrate he calls foolish and impious.

[54] For when we deal with piety and impiety, we are dealing not with behavior but
with attitudes, that is, with the source of the behavior.

[55] They worship the true God according to their own ideas with most ridiculous zeal;
with their excessive piety they are worse than the most ungodly.

[56] Here is a case of the opinionated piety of an obstinate mind and the religious
wisdom of a stiff neck, which, set up as head by itself and for itself, follows itself on the
way of God; it is its own teacher toward God . . .

"Stultum est vero et impium, scire, res scripturae esse omnes in luce positas clarissima, et propter pauca verba obscura, res obscuras dictare; si uno loco obscura sunt verba, at alio sunt clara."[57][92] So clear is the essence of Scripture for Luther that he belittles the voluminous commentary erected upon it, with particular animus directed against Erasmus's hero Jerome. Criticizing his adversary for appealing to nonbiblical sources, moreover, Luther adopts a persona defined in deliberate opposition to Erasmian erudition,[93] and insists on the role of the Holy Spirit in the understanding of Scripture.[94] Directly apprehended through the spirit, Scripture is so closely identified with true *pietas* that Luther can further deride Erasmus as one ignorant of both ("ignorantiam scripturae et pietatis"). Hence the dissociation of Erasmus from *pietas* in an amicus-Plato–style compliment: "Multa tibi debemus, sed pietati omnia debemus."[58][95]

As Luther refines this emphasis on the spirit in opposition to the erudition of Erasmus, he relies heavily on Paul, especially the epistle to the Romans. His denial of Erasmus's argument for free will is crucially dependent on the phrase "omnem impietatem" in Romans 1.18. Whereas Ficino had interpreted this phrase by reference to the distinctions of Plato's *Laws,* Luther understands the passage as a general indictment: "omnes homines sunt impii."[59][96] This "omnes" specifically includes the ancient philosophers, whose wisdom Erasmus may appeal to, but whose condemnation Luther finds in Romans 1.22.[97] Still pursuing the significance of "omnem impietatem," Luther develops this argument so that it applies not just to all men but to the whole of each man. It is not only in the passions that *impietas* is to be found, but even in the highest reaches of the mind.[98] Not through any personal wisdom or erudition may men escape this general indictment, but only through the intervention of the Holy Spirit. Thus Luther divides humanity along the lines established by Augustine and reflected in Lefèvre: on the one hand, "Corrigentur autem electi et pii per spiritum sanctum"; on the other, "Nos impium dicimus, quisquis sine spiritu Dei fuerit."[60][99] The definition of *pietas* that

[57] It is absurd and impious to say that things are obscure, because of a few obscure words, when you know the contents of Scripture being set in the clearest light. And if the words are obscure in one place, yet they are clear in another.

[58] We owe much to you, but we owe everything to piety.

[59] All men are impious.

[60] The elect and pious will be set right by the Holy Spirit. / Whoever will have been without the spirit of God, we call impious.

emerges from Luther's reflections on free will is, in the end, not far from the definition presented in his commentary on Titus: "Nulla pietas ergo est nisi in fide et veritate."[61] This meaning of *pietas* thus expresses "nostra doctrina" of justification by faith, affirmed here as the way to eternal life.[100]

In the preface to the 1559 edition of the *Institutes of the Christian Religion,* John Calvin similarly expresses his desire to maintain "puram doctrinam pietatis."[101] Sharing Luther's interpretation of Romans 1.18 as an expression of universal *impietas,* Calvin nonetheless allows that *pietas* may stir in the heart of the individual who acknowledges the fatherhood of God. From this assumption he develops a working definition of the word: "Pietatem voco coniunctam cum amore Dei reverentiam, quam beneficiorum eius notitia conciliat."[62][102] There is nothing here about conduct or wisdom, for Calvin's *pietas* is prior not only to these but even to religion itself.[103] Thus defined, *pietas* cannot possibly be confused with external observances, much less with such practices as the sale of indulgences. Rather it is *pietas* that makes judgment of such practices possible: "At qui penitius discutiunt et verius expendunt secundum pietatis regulam quid tot ac tales ceremoniae valeant, intelligunt primum nugas esse, quod nihil utilitatis habeant: deinde praestigias, quod spectantium oculos inani pompa deludunt."[63][104] In contrast to the *pietas* that is defined as "ad omnia utilis" in 1 Timothy 4.8, these ceremonies are "nihil utilitatis." In the *Institutes* Calvin thus follows the logic and usage of his sixteenth-century predecessors in driving *pietas* backward in the chain of causes and inward to the invisible place of the spirit. The last paragraph of the *Institutes,* finally, admonishes Christians to suffer anything rather than turn aside from *pietas:* "hac nos cogitatione consolemur, illam tum nos praestare quam Dominus exigit obedientiam, dum quidvis perpetimur potius quam a pietate deflectamus."[64][105]

The stresses placed on *pietas* in the religious discourse of humanism and reform thus vary from one writer to the next, from one work of an

[61] Therefore there is no godliness except in faith and truth.

[62] I call piety that reverence joined with love of God which the knowledge of his benefits induces.

[63] Those who more deeply investigate and, according to the rule of piety, more truly weigh the value of so many and such ceremonies, understand first that they are trifles because they have no usefulness; secondly, that they are tricks because they delude the eyes of the spectators with empty pomp.

[64] Let us comfort ourselves with the thought that we are rendering that obedience which the Lord requires when we suffer anything rather than turn aside from piety.

individual writer to another, and even within single works. Yet certain tendencies of usage are clearly observed: definitions of *pietas* may refer to both doctrine and discipline, but ultimately give priority to the doctrinal significance of the word (however various the doctrines); this priority reflects a pervasive distrust of any definition that emphasizes visible observances; thus driven inward, *pietas* tends to become the source of all true thought and right conduct. By insisting on the *impietas* of all mankind, however, reformed theology leaves *pietas* very little room to operate, in marked contrast to scholastic *pietas* that is "ad omnia utilis." The spatial contraction of the word is affirmed by the Spanish humanist Vives, himself a Catholic and follower of Erasmus: "Pietas res est maxime recondita, et quae solius Dei oculis est aperta ac exposita."[65][106] Such restriction on the domain of the word eventually proves decisive in advancing its decline toward irony, but even reformed usage cannot immediately abolish prior definitions that are part of the history of *pietas*. Indeed a variety of earlier applications of the word are collected, recorded, and widely disseminated in the emblem books of the Renaissance.

Iconography

Emblem books were popular all over Europe in the sixteenth and seventeenth centuries, but the most influential of them derive from Italy. Although religious symbols are included, and the discernible religious orientation is Catholic, the broad base of illustration in these encyclopedias of symbolism is classical. Thus the standard icon of *pietas* is Aeneas with his father on his back. From the first edition of Andrea Alciati's prototypical *Emblemata* in 1531 to the elaborately annotated editions that come later, this image appears under the title "Pietas filiorum in parentes." In the Padua edition of 1621, for example, emblem 195 (Fig. 1) bears this title above with verses translated from the *Greek Anthology* below, followed by three pages of commentary.[107] The commentary divides into four parts of unequal length: a brief prose rendering of the visual image, an extended discussion of the epigraph, glosses on specific words from the epigraph, and then almost four columns celebrating

[65] Piety is the most concealed thing, to the eyes of God alone open and exposed.

Pietas filiorum in parentes.
EMBLEMA CXCV.

PER *medios hosteis patria cum ferret ab igne*
   AEneas humeris dulce parentis onus:
Parcite, dicebat: vobis sene adarea, rapto
   Nulla erit, erepto sed patre summu mihi.

FIG. 1.   Andrea Alciati, *Emblemata cum commentariis* (Padua, 1621), Emblem 195, p. 828.

heroic models of *pietas*. This multiplication of authorities, examples, and analogies, which emphasizes similarities rather than differences, serves to place the Vergilian image in a context larger than the *Aeneid*.

The range of illustrations gathered in the commentary, though wide indeed, is limited by the title: not "Pietas" but "Pietas filiorum in parentes." The implicit recognition that the word has other applications as other emblems demonstrate, lends a decidedly classical cast to the selection of explanatory examples. Half of the examples in the commentary are cited from Valerius Maximus's memorabilia.[108] Of the instances not already gathered by Valerius under the rubric "De pietate in parentes," the commentary allots the most space to the son of Iulius Mansuetus, whose battlefield encounter with his father during the civil war of 69 is recounted by Tacitus.[109] Although Tacitus does not invoke the ideal of *pietas* in this passage, the Renaissance commentator nonetheless discovers in the behavior of the son an exemplary instance of *pietas*. The shoulder note reads: "Mira pietas in filio erga parentem."[66] The moral of such examples is clear: "Quare hoc loco monemur, quanta observantia, quantoque amore debeamus prosequi parentes."[67]

Governed by this ethical concern, the diffusion of classical authority in the commentary is countered by patterns of repetition and analogy that link the diverse examples not only to each other but also to the epigraph. Although the translated epigraph diverges from the narrative of *Aeneid* 2, the corresponding paraphrase is recognizably Vergilian in its vocabulary ("Quod hostes Graeci cum vidissent, moti pietate tam insigni . . ."). Later discussion of the epigraph, moreover, calls attention to details of vocabulary by offering alternatives to Alciati's translation of the Greek, which is cited in the commentary for purposes of comparison: "Ἐκ πυρὸς Ιλιακοῦ δοράτων μέσον ἥρπασεν ἥρως/ Αἰνείας, ὅσιον παιδὶ βάρος, πατέρα."[68] Alciati's translation reads: "Per medios hosteis patriae cum ferret ab igne/Aeneas humeris dulce parentis onus."[69] The most striking word in this version is "humeris," as it has no equivalent in the original. Imported from *Ae-*

[66] Wondrous piety of a son toward his parent

[67] Wherefore we are here advised to imitate with regard to our own parents, such great respect and love.

[68] From the fire of Troy and from the midst of enemy spears, the hero Aeneas rescued his father, a pious burden for a son.

[69] From the midst of the enemies of the fatherland, Aeneas carried the sweet burden of his parent on his shoulders from the fire.

neid 2.708 to emphasize the weight of duty shouldered by Aeneas, the word recurs throughout the commentary. In the example of Anapius and Amphinomus, the Sicilian boys who rescue their parents from an eruption of Mount Aetna: "patrem unus, matrem alter humeris sufferentes ab incendii loco."[70] And again in the case of Oppius's son: "Oppium a triumviris proscriptum . . . filius humeris extulit, et incolumem pervexit in Siciliam."[71] The Latin word for shoulders effectively functions as synecdoche for the *pius* hero in these examples, so firmly established is the classic Vergilian image of *pietas*.

In both of these examples the child rescues the parent from danger, "per medios hosteis" in the case of Oppius's son and "ab igne" in that of the Sicilian boys. Although other patterns of rescue occur, escape from fire and enemies dominates, and these variations on the escape of Aeneas invest *pietas* with an almost magical power over adversity. In the words quoted from Seneca: "quid non pietas potest?"[72] Referring here specifically to Aeneas, Seneca extends his discussion to include a version of the Anapius–Amphinomus legend in which the flames part so that the brothers may pass.[110] Although this portion of the passage from Seneca is not mentioned in the commentary on Alciati, the same idea appears in lines on Aeneas quoted from the Renaissance poet Jacopo Sannazaro, who transfers the hero's *pietas* to the fire itself in the expression "pia flamma." Another significantly transferred epithet appears in Claude Mignault's alternative Latin translation of the epigraph. Mignault would replace Alciati's "dulce parentis onus" with "pium filio pondus." The virtue of the son, transferred to the flame in Sannazaro, is here attributed to the weight he carries. All three words—shoulders (usually in the ablative plural, "humeris"), fire ("flamma" as well as "ignis"), and weight (both "onus" and "pondus")—mediate between the emblem and the adjoining commentary. Complete with epigraph and commentary, the emblem creates the impression of a potentially hostile world that can be controlled by allegiance to a patriarchal moral order. The vertical image of order ascends even to the divine, as quotations are offered to recall the fatherhood of God. Sanction for this idea of order is found in book 11 of Plato's *Laws* and chapter 20 of Exodus: the Mosaic promise

[70] One the father, the other the mother, they carried on their shoulders from the fire.
[71] The son carried Oppius, proscribed by the triumvirs, on his shoulders, and led him safely to Sicily.
[72] What is not possible with piety?

of long life in the Land and the Platonic threat of Nemesis are both cited to urge adherence to the prescribed code.

Emblem 195 is repeatedly cross-referenced in emblem 30 (Fig. 2) of the Padua Alciati. This emblem for gratitude shows a parent bird bringing food to its waiting offspring. The first line of the epigraph ("Aerio insignis pietate ciconia nido") identifies the bird as the stork and its distinguishing virtue as *pietas*. The cross-reference via the *Aeneid* to emblem 195 suggested by "insignis" is confirmed at the close of the epigraph by invocation of the famous shoulders ("sed fessa parentum / Corpora fert humeris").[111] The epigraph that begins with *pietas* as the virtue of parents thus concludes with *pietas* as the virtue of children. The commentary specifically acknowledges the filial in an epigram quoted from Joannus Mallarus ("in quo ciconiae pietas extollitur") that begins with Aeneas ("Qui legis Aeneae pietatem in fata parentis, / Cumque humeris olim dulce referret onus") and proceeds to Anapius and Amphinomus before it finally reaches the stork. It may be pointed out as well that in the Augsburg first edition of 1531, the emblem for gratitude (Fig. 3) emphasizes *pietas* as a filial virtue by showing one bird with another on its back, an image that suggests analogy with Aeneas and Anchises. In these emblems, then, the ascending and descending directions of the word are presented as ideally reciprocal.

Although emblem 30 thus expresses an ideal of gratitude, the commentary in the Padua edition is rarely far from satire, calling attention to multiple examples of ingratitude. Especially telling is the quotation from Hesiod's *Works and Days* concerning Zeus's intended destruction of mankind for refusing to return the nurture of parents. Although quoting the passage in Greek, the commentator describes the potential victims of divine wrath in Latin as representatives of a "saeculum impium." Delinquent regard for parents is thus taken as evidence of a general failure to observe the truth of Cicero's "Pietas virtutum fundamentum." Complementing the citations from Hesiod and Cicero are passages from Basil and Cassiodorus. The eighth homily of Basil's *Hexaemeron* is quoted to celebrate the filial devotion of the stork and to shame mankind for failing to attain an equivalent sense of virtue. The passage from Cassiodorus qualifies the prevailing attitude of condemnation by pointing in the direction of Christian redemption. Although the quotation begins with lament ("Proh dolor ..."), it concludes by identifying *pietas* with restoration: the stork restores its parent to life and is itself a harbinger of spring, and its reward is

Gratiam referendam.

EMBLEMA XXX.

AERIO infignis pietate ciconia nido,
    Inueftes pullos, pignora grata fouet.
Taliaq; expectat fibi munera mutua reddi,
    Auxilio hoc quoties mater egebit anus.
Nec pia fpem foboles fallit, fed feffa parentum
    Corpora fert humeris, præftat & ore cibos.

FIG. 2 Andrea Alciati, *Emblemata cum commentariis* (Padua, 1621), Emblem 30, p. 172.

fulfillment of the promise in Exodus 20. The potential Christian significance of such a passage is more than hinted at in versions of this emblem that show a cross in the foreground (Fig. 4). Yet the biblical passage alluded to here is not from the New Testament, but from the Song of Moses in Deuteronomy 32.11: "Sicut aquila provocans ad volandum pullos suos/Et super eos volitans,/Expandit alas suas, et assumpsit eum,/Atque portavit in humeris suis."[73] These verses have evident affinities with Alciati's epigraph, and provide biblical sanction for both of the basic images of "Gratiam referendam," including especially the bird figure that appears in the 1531 book of emblems. But since the eagle of Moses' song is the parent (explicitly analogous to God in the next verse) rather than the child, the passage also endorses the emphasis on the parental role seen in the emblem of the 1621 edition. And in this version of the emblem, *pietas* is domestic rather than heroic, suggesting not rescue but instead a continuing pattern of nurture. The epigraph refers to the parent specifically as "mater." As the ascending and descending dimensions of *pietas* are thus reciprocally portrayed in the emblem books, the dimension of the word that will become the English *piety* remains patriarchal, but here at least the other derivative *pity* gravitates toward the maternal.

In its domestic and maternal dimension, emblem 30 is related to emblem 194, "Amor filiorum." The commentary on this image of the bird nesting in winter focuses at first on exemplars of *impietas,* principally Medea and Procne. This leads eventually to an extended quotation from Lactantius condemning ("maxima est impietas") the practice of exposing infants. The counterexample, the bird that here puts mankind to shame, is the pelican. Although the exposition of "Pelicani avis pietas in suos" is elaborate, ranging over several authorities and somewhat divergent opinions, the meaning of *pietas* is throughout closely related to the meaning of "Amor" in the title. The citations from Greek authorities produce not piety (εὐσέβεια or ὁσιότης) but love (στοργή and φιλοστοργία) as the relevant meaning. The Vergilian analogy, moreover, is not to the heroic Aeneas who rescues his father, but rather to the paternal Aeneas who cares for his son (1.646). The primary image that illustrates this meaning of *pietas* is that of the pelican drawing blood from its own thigh in order to feed its young: "femora etiam vellicat, ut excusso sanguine filii pascantur

[73] As an eagle stirreth up her nest, fluttereth over her young, spreadeth abroad her wings, taketh them, beareth them on her wings.

GRATIAM REFERENDAM

Fig. 3.   Andrea Alciati, *Emblematum liber* (Augsburg, 1531), p. 3.

aliquandiu."[74][112] Variations on this image of *pietas*—the most popular version shows the pelican piercing its own breast (Fig. 5)—recur in other emblem books and iconographies.

Among the most prominent of these is Valeriano Bolzani's *Hieroglyphica,* published in 1556 and subsequently in enlarged versions. The London edition of 1602, for example, considers the pelican under several headings, one of which is "Pietas et amor in filios." The relevant shoulder note is "Pelecanus commendatur a pietate in suos" and the corresponding description in the text reads: "incomparabili paterni affectus charitati, supremaeque miserationi, qua erga filios maxime omnium afficiatur."[75][113] The specifics that support these claims are largely the same as those in the annotated Alciati, although the Valeriano account devotes more attention to the pelican's willingness to endure death for the sake of its offspring: "mortis genere omnium atrocissimi conficitur, tanta in eo charitas, tantus amor, tanta vis pietatis elucescit."[76] Such sacrifice, it is pointed out, may be considered as folly, but folly may also be understood in Christian terms: its sacrifice is an icon of the crucifixion; indeed, some versions of the

[74] It even plucks its thigh, in order to feed its young for some time on the blood drawn.

[75] The pelican is commended on account of piety toward its young/the feeling of incomparable paternal charity, and exalted compassion, whereby the pelican is influenced most of all toward its offspring.

[76] It is consumed by the cruelest death, so greatly do charity, love, and pity shine forth in him.

pelican emblem show a crucifixion scene in the background (Fig. 5). In Valeriano, the pelican that represents foolishness ("insipientia") and piety ("pietas et amor in filios") also represents compassion ("miseratio"), and the corresponding image (Fig. 6) is given significance by reference to both testaments. The line quoted from Psalm 101 (102)— "Similis factus sum pellicano solitudinis"[77]—identifies the pelican with David; the shoulder note identifies this image of *pietas* with Christ.

[77] I am like a pelican in the wilderness.

FIG. 4.   Diego Lopez, *Declaración magistral sobre las emblemas de Andrés Alciata* (Valencia, 1655), Emblem 30, p. 162.

FIG. 5.   George Wither, *A Collection of Emblemes, Ancient and Modern* (London, 1635), p. 154.

The Christian significance of the emblem is developed in greater detail by Filippo Picinelli, whose book of symbols was first published in Italian in 1669 and subsequently in a greatly expanded Latin version edited by August Erath in 1694. Picinelli catalogues a dozen distinct versions of the pelican emblem, and nine of them are said to symbolize Christ. Although the accompanying references range all the way from Isocrates to Ariosto, the preponderance of the literary evidence is patristic and medieval. Chrysostom, Augustine, Gregory, Anselm, and Bernard are among those quoted, often in reference to specific passages from the Bible. The vocabulary that surfaces to describe the emblems here indicates, moreover, the survival of terms cultivated during the Middle Ages. And this is the case even when the evidence comes from a Renaissance contemporary such as Cornelius a Lapide, here commenting on Luke: "Per viscera misericordiae Dei nostri . . . , qui summa miseriae nostrae misertus, ut illi succurreret, sua viscera, id est filium suum unigenitum in eius incarnatione dedit, et quasi in nos effudis."[78][114] The words that define *pietas* in patristic and medieval exegesis of the Bible are here gathered around the emblem of the pelican, whose lacerated viscera come to represent divine *misericordia*. This vocabulary, moreover, is used in Picinelli to describe the pelican as a political emblem, representing the earthly king who would be an image of the divine, willing to pour out his life for his people (Fig. 5).[115]

As the Renaissance emblem books demonstrate, the ways of *pietas* can be traced through many different sources, but they keep returning to Aeneas and Jesus Christ, each proclaimed as *auctor pietatis*. The competing Vergilian and biblical claims on pietas, which vex the life of the poet who would translate the *Aeneid* or rival it by imitation, are visualized in two distinct emblems. The emblem of Aeneas with Anchises on his back represents *pietas* as a virtue that looks upward to traditional authority: in this emblem, the son sustains the father in accordance with *officium, cultus,* and *religio,* ideas captured in the English word *piety.* The emblem of the Christ-like pelican represents an alternative but also complementary understanding of *pietas* in which the parent sustains the child, even

[78] By the compassionate flesh of our God, who endured the greatest of our miseries, that he might succor us, He gave His only begotten Son in the flesh, poured out for us.

FIG. 6.   Valeriano Bolzani, *Hieroglyphica* (London, 1602), p. 201.

with its own blood: this emblem is domestic, even maternal, looking downward in an expression of *affectus, caritas,* and *misericordia,* and corresponds to the English word *pity.* What the static emblems can only suggest by their implied narrative of generational succession, however, is the temporal domain of the word, its engagement with the discourse of history. By turning, then, to the histories and historical epics of Latin literature after Vergil, the divergence of Christian from classical under-standing of pietas may be considered in relation to the prior divergence of imperial from republican conceptions of the ancient ideal.

3
History:
Pietas and Roman Destiny

In the first book of the *Metamorphoses,* Ovid turns to Latin the passage from Hesiod cited in the Alciati commentary (emblem 30) and glossed by the phrase "saeculum impium." In Ovid's version, the defeat of *pietas* and the flight of justice together mark the advent of the iron age. Ovid's phrase—"victa iacet pietas"[1][1]—touches a sensitive nerve in Augustan poetry, which supplies ambivalent answers to the fundamental question: how is the virtue on which Rome is said to be founded engaged in its actual history?[2] Pastoral that describes the golden age finds *pietas* there, in a past imagined to be free of the troubles that perplex the present; heroic looks instead to a figure eventually identified with the emperor who will subdue present troubles and restore *pietas* in a prophesied renewal of the golden age. Suspended between the pastoral vision of ancient *pietas* and the heroic vision of *pietas* to come is the less tractable domain of satire, the "saeculum impium" of the present. The historical crux of such conflicting attitudes is the civil war, which yields in Roman literature after Augustus not ambivalence, but rather sharply polarized historical perspectives, as response to the *Aeneid* is shaped by political imperatives. Velleius Paterculus and the panegyrists who follow him now locate *pietas* in the present age, whose glory and future security are said to be guaranteed by loyalty to the current emperor. Lucan and Tacitus, on the other hand, reject imperial *pietas* as a sham virtue, cultivated by the court to mask the origins of the imperial system in civil strife. When the collapse of the empire finally produces a lasting historical synthesis, Augustine recasts the Roman legends of national origin by discrediting the glory of Aeneas and insisting on the parallels between

[1] Piety lies vanquished.

Romulus and Cain. The opposition of *pietas* to *impietas* in Roman history is thus redefined to distinguish the history of the city of God from the history of the city of man.

Pietas Victrix

However closely identified with Vergil and Rome in the minds of such later writers as Dryden, *pietas* is not obviously reconcilable with a history that must acknowledge Romulus and Remus as well as Aeneas and Anchises, the *impia arma* of civil war as well as the *pia arma* of national defense and foreign conquest. Nor is it obvious to Vergil's younger contemporaries that *pius* is the natural epithet of Aeneas. Carefully distinguishing the golden age of *pietas* from the subsequent age of heroes, Horace closes his sixteenth epode by excluding even the most famous wandering heroes from the isles reserved for the pious.[3] As he here denies the essential premise on which Vergil's epic will be based, so later in the centennial hymn he responds to the epic by describing Aeneas not as *pius* but as *castus* and *clarus*—words entirely apt for a hero who is said to come through his experience "sine fraude."[2][4] Even in poems such as Propertius's elegy 4.1, where Aeneas is granted his Vergilian epithet, he is still a figure of legend with hardly any attributes beyond his famous shoulders. As a walking synecdoche, he passes untouched through the flames of Troy, bears no responsibility for the actions of Romulus, remains disengaged from the historical acts his voyage sets in motion.[5] When the connection between Aeneas and Romulus is admitted in Ovid's *Fasti,* it serves as a prelude to praise of Augustus, thus announcing a specifically imperial pattern of usage and a preoccupation of later Roman literature.[6]

As representative of these tendencies in Augustan poetry, consider the historical complexity of Tibullus's elegy 2.5, which adds to the problem of Romulus that of Jupiter, whose overthrow of Saturn is celebrated in the poem's invocation of Apollo. Although initially presented as victory, the triumph of Jupiter is rendered increasingly suspect, as Tibullus proceeds to structure the poem's historical concerns on multiple versions of the son-father figure, including Messalinus, whom the poem honors, and

[2] unscathed

his father, the poet's patron. But the poem's most famous son appears without his father, and is identified instead as the brother of Cupid. Here Aeneas must make his way into Roman history under the aegis of the god who killed his own father and as the forerunner of Romulus who killed his own brother. The arrival of Aeneas in Italy thus marks the end of the pastoral golden age, but it also inaugurates a heroic vision of Roman history that culminates in the "pia . . . spectacula" of the poem's last lines.[7] A regressive historical vision of sudden retreat from the pastoral ideal yields to a progressive vision that locates a modified version of heroic *pietas* in the prophesied future.

So pronounced is the son-father figure and so frequent are the allusions to the *Aeneid* in the elegy that Vergilian *pietas* is an inevitable topic of critical discussion. Confronting the first mention of Aeneas in the poem, Benedetto Riposati typically finds a thoroughly Vergilian hero: here (in lines 19–22), he says, is the heart of "pius" Aeneas.[8] Yet it should be observed that Tibullus, however successfully he has recaptured the most celebrated moment of Vergil's epic, describes the hero who bears his father from Troy not as *pius* but as sorrowful ("maestus," 21). This dejected Aeneas is characterized by his refusal to believe in a future after the destruction of Troy.[9] In striking contrast to this sad, retrospective figure is the Aeneas who suddenly appears nine couplets later. In the words of the Sibyl: "Impiger Aenea, volitantis frater Amoris, / Troica qui profugis sacra vehis ratibus, / iam tibi Laurentes adsignat Iuppiter agros, / iam vocat errantes hospita terra Lares" (39–42).[3] As in the prior reference, the attention paid to the Lares evokes the hero of Vergil, but again this only emphasizes the absence of the Vergilian *pius* and the substitution here of *impiger*. This Aeneas looks to a Roman future founded on industry, action, labor—on all that is implied by his newly acquired epithet. Tibullus's *maestus* Aeneas expresses one attitude toward history, his *impiger* Aeneas another.

The two glimpses of Vergil's hero are separated by a vision of Rome before his arrival.

(Romulus aeternae nondum formaverat urbis
moenia, consorti non habitanda Remo;

---

[3] Aeneas never-resting, brother of Cupid ever on the wing, whose exiled barks carry the holy things of Troy, now doth Jove allot to thee the fields of Laurentum, now doth a hospitable land invite thy wandering gods.

sed tunc pascebant herbosa Palatia vaccae
    et stabant humiles in Iovis arce casae. . . .
at qua Velabri regio patet, ire solebat
    exiguus pulsa per vada linter aqua.
illa saepe gregis diti placitura magistro
    ad iuvenem festa est vecta puella die,
cum qua fecundi redierunt munera ruris,
    caseus et niveae candidus agnus ovis.
                                (23–26, 33–38)[4]

The pastoral detail of this topos is warm, intimate, small in scale, and as clearly retrospective as Aeneas's view of Troy in lines 21–22. By describing the landscape with reference to modern place names, Tibullus anticipates the day when the humble and primitive will be pushed aside by the urban and monumental. The cost of this historical process is measured by allusion to the story of Romulus and Remus, as the brothers are contrasted to an anonymous pair of pastoral lovers. The holiday meeting of boy and girl that concludes this portrayal of pre-Phrygian Rome in turn sets the stage for the intrusion of Aeneas. This moment is marked not by the articulation of a moral and religious ideal, but rather by an invasion of national energy. The adjective that defines Aeneas's contribution to Roman history is so antithetical to the preceding pastoral as to make Vergil's hero the sponsor of Romulus and the enemy of the values represented by the two lovers. The threat that Aeneas poses to the lovers (who in fact disappear from the poem as soon as he arrives on the scene) is confirmed by the identifying phrase "frater Amoris." As Romulus is to Remus, so is Aeneas to Amor. In fact, as David F. Bright has argued, the fratricide of Romulus is almost made to appear a consequence of Amor's eviction by Aeneas.[10] Further, the following reference to Jupiter should recall the opening of the poem and the similar eviction of Saturn ("Saturno rege fugato," 9). Both victories mark the end of a golden age.

If Aeneas is guilty by association with the parricide of Jove and the fratricide of Romulus, that guilt vanishes in the lines that follow. The

[4] Not yet had Romulus traced the walls of the Eternal City wherein was no abiding for his brother Remus. But still on a grassy Palatine browsed the kine, and lowly cabins stood upon the heights of Jove. . . . But where now spreads the quarter of Velabrum, a small skiff stirred the waters as it plied across the shallows. There oft a lass who would please some rich keeper of a herd was ferried on holidays to her swain, and with her came back the gifts of a thriving farm, cheese and the white lamb of a snowy ewe.

conclusion to the Sibyl's prophecy offers an entirely different evaluation of Aeneas's contribution to Roman history: "iam tibi praedico, barbare Turne, necem"(48).[5] This account has the same shape as the one it replaces, but the pastoral version of history is now to be rewritten as heroic: the idyllic is reconceived as the barbaric, the lovers who inhabit the land before Aeneas are replaced by Turnus, and the successor to Aeneas is not Romulus but Ascanius. The dominant verb tense also changes from imperfect to future, reflecting a dramatic shift in perspective. The poem that up to this point has idealized the past now turns to celebration of the future. But before situating the specific ideal of *pietas* in relation to these alternative historical visions, Tibullus first reflects for the only time in the poem on actual history.

> haec fore dixerunt belli mala signa cometen,
>   multus ut in terras deplueretque lapis.
> atque tubas atque arma ferunt strepitantia caelo
>   audita et lucos praecinuisse fugam:
> et simulacra deum lacrimas fudisse tepentes
>   fataque vocales praemonuisse boves.
> ipsum etiam Solem defectum lumine vidit
>   iungere pallentes nubilus annus equos.
>   (71–78)[6]

Considering the events that provide the background of Vergil's epic, the poet here acknowledges descent from pastoral quiet into public disorder as a pattern that would account for the civil wars, but then he immediately counters this view by removing the civil wars from the domain of the poem's concern: "haec fuerant olim" (79).[7] Treated not merely as past but as distant past, the civil wars have prepared the way for an ordered future prophesied in the poem's conclusion.

The prophecy is in two parts, reaffirming the poem's fundamental

[5] Now, savage Turnus, I foretell thy fall.

[6] These told that a comet should appear, the evil sign of war, and how that thick on earth should fall the stony shower. And they say that trumpets and the clash of arms were heard in heaven, and sacred groves rang with the coming rout. From the images of the gods poured the warm tears; and kine found tongue and spake of the coming doom. Yea, from the very Sun ebbed the light, and the clouded year saw him yoke dim horses to his car.

[7] So was it once.

ambivalence toward Aeneas, and again juxtaposing pastoral and heroic modes. First, the conclusion focuses on the Palilia, which memorializes the birthday of Rome in terms that recall the earlier picture of pre-imperial Italy. The restored pastoral emphasizes the fertility, prosperity, peace, and joy that preceded empire. The holiday honors Pales without reference to the imported Lares; the allusions to Vergil derive not from the *Aeneid* but from the *Eclogues* and the *Georgics;* the son-father relationship is playfully free of the consequence it bears in Vergil's epic (91–92). For the duration of the festival here described, Rome escapes the legacy of Aeneas. But the account of the Palilia is succeeded by a prophecy in which the ideal of *pietas* is finally, if only briefly, asserted. Anticipating a future day of triumph for his patron's son, Tibullus closes with celebration of the empire.

> ut Messalinum celebrem, cum praemia belli
> ante suos currus oppida victa feret,
> ipse gerens laurus: lauro devinctus agresti
> miles "io" magna voce "triumphe" canet.
> tunc Messalla meus pia det spectacula turbae
> et plaudat curru praetereunte pater.
>
> (115–20)[8]

The "laurus" that earlier (63) offers good omens to the humble farmer is here transfigured to grace the brow of the conqueror, as rustic festival is replaced by imperial ceremony.

Theatrical in its grandeur, this celebration of the hero in his triumphal chariot is centered on the son-father figure. But in this climax, the son does not bear the father on his back; rather, the father applauds the performance of the son. Since this performance is still a matter of prophecy, Tibullus effectively situates *pietas* in the future, as the ideal toward which Roman history moves. The implication is that progress toward this future depends on a patriarchal order in which sons earn the applause of their fathers and victors the allegiance of their soldiers. The procession itself rewards the loyalty of the crowd with the spoils of war,

---

[8] that I may tell of Messalinus when before *his* chariot he shall bear the conquered towns, the prize of war, wearing the bay wreath, while his soldiery, with wild bay round their brows, loudly chant the cry of triumph. Then let my dear Messalla afford the throng the sight of a father's love and clap his hands as his son's car passes by.

the concrete evidence of cities conquered. The heroic is here transformed into ritual: the conclusion attaches "pia . . . spectacula" to a progressive idea of history predicated on military success and social order. The end of the poem thus fulfills the initial promise of "laudes" in line 4 and points toward later imperial panegyric. The adjective that qualifies "laudes" in this line is usually taken to be "meas," but there is manuscript evidence for "sacras" and "novas" as well, and the text preferred by the Loeb editor reads "pias": "nunc precor ad laudes flectere verba pias."[9][11] However uncertain its authority, this reading would anticipate the usage of later celebrants of the empire, for whom a dominant meaning of *pietas* will be loyalty.

In Latin literature of the silver age, the pastoral and heroic modes combined in Tibullus's elegy are both adapted to the purposes of panegyric, which attains its greatest literary and political importance in the age of Theodosius. Well before the close of the fourth century, however, apologists had variously attempted to imitate Vergil in accommodating *pietas* to an imperial ideology of rule. The connotations of the word are thereby narrowed to suit the requirements of propaganda, as *pietas* is taken to express a vertical principle of social organization. In its descending aspect it marks the obligation of emperor to people and becomes a synonym for *clementia;* in its ascending direction *pietas* promotes the obligation of people to emperor and signifies political allegiance. This understanding of the word's reciprocal meanings is defined against the background of history that now assumes the shape of redemptive ritual. Turning on some recent event, such as the accession of a new emperor, time is divided into a dark past (*prius*) and a glorious present (*nunc*). The future is cast as an extension of the present, provided that the ideal of *pietas* is not violated. Celebration of the present reign sustains the impulse in Augustan poetry toward *pia spectacula,* but without the alternative historical perspectives that qualify this phrase in Tibullus's elegy. In the first century, the history of Velleius Paterculus, pastorals 1 and 4 of Calpurnius Siculus, and Silius Italicus's heroic poem on the Punic Wars all bring *pietas* into the present to celebrate the imperial peace.

Like Vergil, though without the poet's acute sense of loss and sacrifice, Velleius Paterculus takes Actium as the turning point in Roman history. The past of political turmoil and civil war is succeeded by a present peace that reflects the clemency of the victor: "Victoria vero fuit cle-

[9] Now tune thy song to a loyal paean.

mentissima."[10][12] Contrasted to the cruelty of Antony (2.87), the clemency of Octavian guarantees the restoration of peace, law, religion, and property (2.89). Concentrating attention on the public celebration of the victor's return to Italy, the historian presents the acclaim of the spectators as evidence of national union. By the time Paterculus wrote this endorsement of the new order, however, the empire was already half a century old. The real argument of the later chapters of the history is therefore the confirmation of Tiberius as heir to the glory inaugurated by Augustus.

To accomplish this, Paterculus devotes considerable attention in his account of Augustus's reign to publicizing the bond between the emperor and the stepson who is also his son-in-law. Even the least promising events in the life of Tiberius are therefore turned into moments of ritualized action that connect him with the emperor. Tiberius's retirement to Rhodes, ascribed by others to jealousy of his stepson Gaius, Paterculus takes as evidence of *pietas* ("mira quadam et incredibili atque inenarrabili pietate," 2.99). In this way the historian offers to counter any aspersions that might be cast on Tiberius, as the traditional meaning of filial duty here dovetails with the emergent emphasis on political loyalty. Whereas Gaius and Lucius may, just possibly, be driven by ambition, Tiberius is devoted only to serving his "father," who also happens to be the emperor. Paterculus later supplies Tiberius, now returned to active life and recently named Caesar, with a parallel motivation to explain his journey back to Rome after the German campaign of A.D. 4. "Pietas sua Caesarem paene obstructis hieme Alpibus in urbem traxit"(2.105).[11] Crossing the Alps is seen as a heroic endeavor that demonstrates, again, the incredibly miraculous nature of Tiberius's devotion to Augustus. Again *pietas* expresses the relationship of son to father as a way of validating the relationship of successor to emperor. Superimposed on the bond of kinship is the bond of loyalty, not (as in Cicero) to the state, but now to an individual ruler. This implication of the word is affirmed in the concluding prayer to Jupiter that brings Paterculus's history down to the present reign of Tiberius.

custodite, servate, protegite hunc statum, hanc pacem, hunc principem, eique functo longissima statione mortali destinate suc-

[10] Great clemency was shown in the victory.
[11] Caesar was drawn to the city by his filial affection, though the Alps were almost blocked by winter's snows.

cessores quam serissimos, sed eos, quorum cervices tam fortiter sustinendo terrarum orbis imperio sufficiant, quam huius suffecisse sensimus, consiliaque omnium civium aut pia fovete aut impia opprimite. (2.131)[12]

For all the Herculean grandeur of the imagery, the *imperium* is here defined not (as in Vergil) by looking outward from Rome to the world, but rather by looking inward to the Roman citizenry itself. Some citizens are pious, some impious. The pious are those who share the historian's allegiance to the emperor and devotion to the status quo; the impious are those who might want political change. This pregnant division of the nation into *pii* and *impii* thus discloses the very reason for writing this kind of history: the possibility of disloyalty creates the need for propaganda. The historian of the early empire brings *pietas* into the present in order to endorse and defend the current regime.

The closing prayer also looks to the future, to the "successores" of Tiberius with shoulders strong enough to sustain the empire. This prayer is taken as fulfilled by Calpurnius Siculus. Modelled on Vergil's "Pollio," Calpurnius's first eclogue adapts pastoral conventions to the celebration of the emperor (traditionally assumed to be Nero, but now a matter of dispute), whose succession is said to mark the advent of a new golden age ("Aurea secura cum pace renascitur aetas").[13] Alluding to *Aeneid* 1.234 and 1.295, Calpurnius contrasts the glorious present to the past ruled by *impia Bellona* (1.46–47). The significance of this contrast is implied in veiled references to the civil disturbances, exaggerated by analogy to the civil war of a century earlier, that marred the last years of the Emperor Claudius. In contrast, the new reign, like that of Augustus in Paterculus's history, is personified by Clementia ("insanos Clementia contudit enses," 1.59). Later defending the adaptation of pastoral to panegyric in his fourth eclogue, Calpurnius has the shepherd Corydon explain to Meliboeus: "Dum mea rusticitas, si non valet arte polita/ Carminis, at certe valeat pietate probari" (4.14–15).[13] Corydon de-

[12] Guard, preserve, protect the present state of things, the peace which we enjoy, the present emperor, and when he has filled his post of duty—and may it be the longest granted to mortals—grant him successors until the latest time, but successors whose shoulders may be as capable of sustaining bravely the empire of the world as we have found his to be: foster the pious plans of all good citizens and crush the impious designs of the wicked.

[13] While my rustic performance, though it is not highly polished, surely passes the test of loyalty.

clines the admittedly hopeless task of justifying his praise on aesthetic grounds, offering instead a political defense of his intended poem. The telling word "rusticitas," which defines the poet's limitations by contrast to the refined art of the city, reinforces through traditional association with pastoral the counterclaim to *pietas,* which expresses the poet's loyalty to the new emperor.

These lines also provide a political rationale for writing bad poetry, of which there is generally agreed to be a lot in Silius Italicus's *Punica.* Even less successfully imitative of Vergilian epic than Calpurnius is of Vergilian pastoral, Silius celebrates the Flavian restoration by versifying Livy. Shaping the Augustan historian's material to the ideology of Paterculus, Silius places national disasters, including Cannae, within a framework of optimism justified by the present. The poem's several prophecies locate value in a future represented by Vespasian and his successors, most notably Domitian, who is shown in his triumphal chariot parading victoriously through Rome.[14] The war against Hannibal is offered as a test of Roman character, exemplified above all by Fabius, the opponent of *furor* who dominates the earlier books, and by Scipio, the model of *pietas* whose destiny is identified with Rome and its emperor in the poem's conclusion. Moderating this celebration of national heroes is a host of secondary figures, most pious like Paulus ("mecum erit haec prorsus pietas,"8.328), but some impious like the Capuans of book 11. Attributing their participation in "impia bella" (11.28) to sloth, debauchery, indolence, and luxury, Silius turns his invective against aspects of Roman character better known from the satires of his younger contemporary Juvenal. This unequal division of the nation into *pii* and *impii* in the manner of Paterculus corresponds to a contrived division within Scipio himself, who reenacts the choice of Hercules (15.18–128). Rejecting the Capuan alternative voiced by Voluptas, Scipio makes the choice that guarantees the successful prosecution of his "pia bella" (15.162).

For all the carnage that swells the volume of the *Punica,* the battles are a measure of moral order. Modelled on Aeneas as well as Hercules, Scipio makes his first appearance in a manner that explains his ultimate victory. Just after his father has been speared, Scipio is introduced on the battlefield in Vergilian phrases:

> tunc, rapta propere duris ex ossibus hasta,
> innixum cervice ferens humeroque parentem,
> emicat . . .

> . . . pietasque insignis et aetas
> belligeris fecit miranda silentia campis.
>   (4.466–68, 70–71)[14]

So conspicuously established from the outset, Scipio's *pietas* seals the fate of Hannibal and ensures the glorious destiny of Rome; the subsequent encounter between the two adversaries in book 9 thus portends all that happens later by proclaiming Roman moral superiority ("melior pietate fideque," 9.437). But if victory will belong to the good, the battles that follow do not justify the appropriation of Vergil's "horrida . . . bella" (13.451–52); the testing of *pietas* against *arma* that extends to the last lines of the *Aeneid* is never at issue in the *Punica*. The test of character proposed in Silius's poem is always more apparent than real, as is perfectly demonstrated by the nature of the poem's ending. Far from imitating Vergil, Silius borrows instead the topos that concludes Tibullus's elegy 2.5, later shapes Paterculus's account of Octavian's return to Italy, and (more importantly) celebrates Domitian in book 3 of the poem itself. Silius completes the analogy by showing Scipio in his triumphal chariot receiving the applause and adulation of the crowd, as heroism is transformed into ceremonial display, action into imperial ritual: "ipse, adstans curru atque auro decoratus et ostro, / Martia praebebat spectanda Quiritibus ora" (17.645–46).[15] To stress the poem's political implications, Silius then develops an earlier simile (4.275–78) in order to compare his epic hero to the mythic heroes who defended the Olympian gods against the rebellious Titans (17.649–50). Like the last sentence of Paterculus's history, Silius's conclusion advises against any violation of the divine—and hence of the political—order.

Historical epic thus gives way to panegyric, which by the end of the first century has acquired its exemplary form in Pliny the Younger's consular address to Trajan. In fact, the reign celebrated by Silius Italicus provides Pliny with antithetical material for his panegyric honoring the accession of the new emperor. By contrasting the perceived viciousness and ineptitude of Domitian to the *pietas* and *fortitudo* of Trajan, Pliny

[14] Then in haste he drew the spear from the tough bone, and sped away, bearing his father supported on his neck and shoulders. His youth and his noble defence of his father brought about a wondrous silence on the field of battle.

[15] Scipio himself, erect in his chariot and splendid in purple and gold, gave to the citizens the spectacle of his martial countenance.

creates an enduring model to be imitated by Latin orators clear into the period of the Gothic invasions.[15] In formal panegyric, the *prius . . . nunc* pattern of history proclaims successive reigns to be the new golden age by identifying successive emperors and their subjects with the ideal of *pietas*.[16] In a panegyric from the year 291, for example, the age is celebrated in phrases that distantly suggest the conclusion of Tibullus 2.5. "Quale pietas vestra spectaculum dedit, cum in Mediolanensi palatio admissis qui sacros vultus adoraturi erant conspecti estis ambo et consuetudinem simplicis venerationis geminato numine repente turbastis! Nemo ordinem numinum solita secutus est disciplina; omnes adorandi mora restiterunt duplicato pietatis officio contumaces."[16][17] Initially this passage recognizes the *pietas* of Maximian and Diocletian, but concludes by acknowledging the reciprocal *pietas* of the people who have gathered to express their allegiance. Similarly in Claudian's panegyric on the third consulship of Honorius, a loyal people applaud the embrace of father and son in the familiar triumphal chariot.

> Quanti tum iuvenes, quantae sprevere pudorem
> spectandi studio matres, puerisque severi
> certavere senes, cum tu genitoris amico
> exceptus gremio mediam veherere per urbem
> velaretque pios communis laurea currus![17][18]

The prophecy of Tibullus is here fulfilled at much greater distance than he could have imagined, as Claudian proclaims the golden age in an idiom eager to display its affinities with the Augustan poetry not only of Tibullus but even of Horace and Vergil: "en aurea nascitur aetas, / en proles antiqua redit. Concordia, Virtus / cumque Fide Pietas alta cervice vagantur."[18][19]

---

[16] What a spectacle your piety offered, when in the palace of Milan you both appeared to those who had been admitted to adore your sacred faces, when the sudden presence of your double divinity confused the homage normally addressed to just one. No one observed the usual protocol with regard to the hierarchy of divinities: everyone stopped to adore you, waiting to fulfill the double obligation of piety.

[17] How many youths, how many matrons set modesty aside in eagerness to behold thee! Austere greybeards struggle with boys for places whence to see thee in the tender embraces of thy sire, borne through the midst of Rome on a triumphal chariot decked but with the shade of a simple laurel branch.

[18] Lo! a golden age begins; lo! the old breed of men returns. Peace and Godliness, Love and Honour hold high their heads throughout the world.

In Roman panegyric the *pietas* appropriate to the emperor can encompass a range of excellence, including specifically filial and religious devotion, but the primary meaning that emerges in panegyrical poems and orations is clemency. In Nazarius's panegyric to Constantine of 321, for example: "Itaque non plus ex eo laudis fortitudini tuae datum quam pietati tributum est quod, dum scelestos persequeris, miseros liberasti."[19][20] Here the emperor's *fortitudo* serves the function of *debellare superbos,* his *pietas* that of *parcere subiectis.*[21] Again in Claudian the personified Clementia of Paterculus and Calpurnius is now closely identified with personified Pietas: "nonne vides, ut nostra soror Clementia tristes/obtundat gladios fratresque amplexa serenos/adsurgat Pietas."[20][22] In this passage *pietas* is elevated to describe the age; it is the virtue of subjects as well as emperor. Often enough, however, *pietas* as the virtue of subjects is expressed negatively in Roman panegyric to warn against disloyalty or sedition.[23] In the panegyrics of the later fourth century especially, the supreme antithesis of this virtue is rebellion. Witness the defeat of the usurper Maximus as described in a panegyric addressed to the emperor Theodosius: "Datur debito rebelle agmen exitio, volvuntur impiae in sanguine suo turbae."[21][24] The subsequent restoration of order then offers the panegyrist new opportunities to celebrate the emperor for his achievement and to reproclaim the golden age. In Latin panegyric, then, the *pietas* of subject and emperor sustains—in the words of Paterculus's history—"hunc statum, hanc pacem, hunc principem."

The emphasis on the *pietas* of the present, underlined in Paterculus's conclusion by the repeated demonstrative pronoun, is given a theological significance in the poetry of Claudian's Christian contemporary Prudentius, who celebrates the peace and stability of imperial Rome as necessary preparation for the advent of Jesus Christ.[25] To connect Roman history with the scriptural narrative, Prudentius elaborates Latin *pietas* by reference to Hebraic legend, beginning with Genesis 4. Cain is the type of *impietas* in contrast to the *pietas* of Abel. By his sin (*caedes*

---

[19] Nor has your bravery occasioned any less tribute than your piety, for you have punished criminals even as you have freed the wretched.

[20] Seest thou not how my sister Mercy blunts the cruel sword of war; how Piety rises to embrace the two noble brothers.

[21] The army of rebellion is delivered to its due destruction, the impious battalions roll in their own blood.

impia) Cain is linked to the criminal figures of later biblical history, most notably Absalom.

> taetrum pater ille, sed unum,
> innocuas inter suboles genuit patricidam,
> ausus in auctorem generis qui stringere ferrum
> (a pietas!) signis contraria signa paternis
> egit et unius commisit sanguinis arma.[22][26]

Here the contrast between "pietas" and "sanguinis arma" is defined by the overlapping contexts of parricide and rebellion. To the authority of father and king Prudentius adds that of God by describing David as "pariturae et virginis auctor."[23][27] Against this triple authority stands Absalom, whose condemnation is sealed in a phrase that further identifies David with the fabled pelican: "Abessalon lacerans pia viscera ferro."[24][28] The multiple violations committed by Absalom make him a model of *impietas* analogous to Cain, just as their victims are both types of Christ. As this pattern of contrast is also taken to express the opposition between God's chosen people and their enemies, it can be easily modulated into one between Christians and their pagan persecutors—until the conversion of the empire under Theodosius. At this moment the division of the world into *impii* and *pii* becomes a division in time between past and present, as the emperor and descendant of Aeneas bows before the cross: "iam purpura supplex/ sternitur Aeneadae rectoris ad atria Christi,/vexillumque crucis summus dominator adorat."[25][29]

Prudentius explores the significance of national conversion most fully in *Contra Symmachum,* written early in the fifth century to counter the influence of an eloquent appeal for toleration of the pagan deities made some years earlier by Quintus Aurelius Symmachus. A thoroughly Roman poem that attempts to place the conversion to Christianity in the

[22] In that instance a father begot, among his innocent children, a horrid patricide, but only one, who dared to draw the sword against the author of his being (alas, for filial duty!), set forces in motion against his father's, and fought against his own flesh and blood.

[23] ancestor of the virgin who was to bear a child

[24] Absalom who tears the flesh of his kin with the sword

[25] Now the successor of Aeneas, in the imperial purple, prostrates himself in prayer at the house of Christ, and the supreme lord adores the banner of the cross.

larger context of national history, *Contra Symmachum* adapts the temporal pattern of imperial panegyric to reveal conversion as the natural fulfillment of Roman destiny. Searching the past for analogues of redemption, the poet recalls acts of salvation from external (Jugurtha) and internal (Catiline) enemies to honor Theodosius as the successor of Marius (a less than ideal exemplar from other points of view) and Cicero and, at the same time, to counter Symmachus's appeal to tradition and custom. Personified Roma herself acknowledges this historical pattern in an address to the sons of Theodosius. In her speech impious past yields to pious present, the "miserum . . . saeclum" of Jove, cruelty, and bloodshed to a new age identified with "cultus . . . Christi."[30] The rejoicing that follows conversion proclaims the poem's essential *Romanitas:* "exultare patres videas, pulcherrima mundi/lumina conciliumque senum gestire Catonum/candidiore toga niveum pietatis amictum/sumere et exuvias deponere pontificales" (1.544–47).[26] Although the change in vestments symbolizes rejection of the old religion, the word "pietatis" is itself a measure of continuity with the past. The new age does not jeopardize class privilege, does not threaten the power of the empire, does not even revise the contemporary vocabulary of power. Indeed, the language of the poem's last lines sounds very familiar: "sit devota Deo, sit tanto principe digna/et virtute potens et criminis inscia Roma,/quemque ducem bellis sequitur, pietate sequatur" (2.1130–32).[27] Like Paterculus and Silius before him, Prudentius directs his conclusion to the conditions that must be met to secure the future. Devotion to the Christian God is to be expressed by allegiance to the Christian emperor. The Christian and Roman contexts that coalesce around "pietate" serve to underline the basic argument of the poem: Rome is now a Christian empire, secure in its future if all citizens follow the religion of the emperor.

Confuting right to the end Symmachus's argument for toleration of the pagan deities, Prudentius insists on Rome's conformity to Christianity, but he insists equally on Christianity's conformity to Rome. It is this meeting of Roman history and biblical revelation that sustains the

[26] The fathers were to be seen leaping for joy, the world's noblest ornaments, that assemblage of old Catos eager to put on, with whiter toga, the snowy robe of holiness, and cast off their priestly vestments.

[27] Let Rome dedicate herself to God; let her be worthy of her great emperor, being both mighty in valour and innocent of sin; let her follow in goodness the leader she follows in war.

poem's redemptive and ultimately progressive vision of history. Prudentius emphatically rejects the myth of historical decline (2.272–76). Appropriating the very terms that in Ovid's *Metamorphoses* define the advent of the iron age, Prudentius asserts that *pietas* is not conquered but revealed ("pietas quam prodita caelo") in time. Although shared by the line of writers from Paterculus to Claudian who gravitate toward imperial panegyric, this is a historical view that provokes strong opposition from those who find little in the present to celebrate under the imperial system.

Pietas Victa

Foremost among the poets whose conception of *pietas* derives from nostalgia for the republic is Lucan. Indeed, the hostility to Caesarism articulated by Lucan is present as a subdued countercurrent even in the panegyrical poetry celebrating and defending the later emperors. In Claudian's panegyric on the sixth consulship of Honorius, for example, is this account of Augustus: "pavit Iuleos inviso sanguine manes/Augustus, sed falsa pii praeconia sumpsit/in luctum patriae civili strage parentans."[28][31] Although designed to extol by contrast the clemency of Theodosius, the notion of false *pietas* associated with the founding of the empire recalls the perspective of Lucan's anti-*Aeneid*. The last lines of *Punica* 10 offer a similar perspective: "haec tum Roma fuit; post te cui vertere mores/si stabat fatis, potius, Carthago, maneres" (10.657–58).[29] In the poems of both Silius and Claudian, moreover, celebration is accompanied by admonition; in the prose panegyrics as well, imperial *pietas* functions as a moral restraint on imperial power, a restraint seen as necessary to ensure the continuation of present happiness.

Lucan's much disputed invocation to Nero acknowledges, by contrast, no such restraint and places the emperor in a present that is very far from being happy.[32] The prior description of the demolished and depopulated Italian cities, the unploughed fields overgrown with weeds, identify the

---

[28] Augustus sated the shade of Caesar with his enemies' blood, but he made a false advertisement of piety when, to the grief of his fatherland, he offered the blood of citizens to his father's ghost.

[29] Such was Rome in those days; and, if it was fated that the Roman character should change when Carthage fell, would that Carthage were still standing.

"nunc" (1.24) of Nero's reign as anything but a golden age. Inconsistent with the emerging patterns of panegyric, even more obviously inconsistent with the historical perspective of the narrative itself, this flattery of Nero is best construed as preliminary evidence that the individual glory of the Caesars has been won at the expense of the country whose descent into tyranny is the historical subject of the poem. Lucan's perspective on this subject is defined in a highly emotional passage from book 7 that concludes with the phrase: "Pharsalia tanti/Causa mali" (7.407–8).[30] In this account Pharsalia, not Actium, is the hinge of Roman history, reversing Roman destiny and undoing all the work of the past (7.426–27). The *pietas* that expresses social order for Paterculus assumes in Lucan perverted meanings shown to derive from the *impietas* of civil war.

One of the key words of the poem is the verb *perire,* attached not only to individuals but also to institutions and ideals. Pompey describes himself after Pharsalia: "vivit post proelia Magnus/Sed fortuna perit" (8.84–85).[31] The meaning of the battle is summarized in an earlier phrase: "Hic patriae perit omne decus" (7.597).[32] The disaster is foreseen by the Roman matrons who pour into the temples to lament the commencement of civil war: "Tales pietas peritura querellas/Egerit" (2.63–64).[33] An epic of "pietas peritura," Lucan's *Pharsalia* dismisses the redemptive view of Roman history in a phrase that also gives a negative answer to Priam's cry in *Aeneid* 2: "mortalia nulli/Sunt curata deo" (7.454–55).[34] In this poem, *pietas* is not protected by the gods from the ravages of history. On the contrary, the direction of Roman history is embodied in the figure of Caesar, repeatedly described as a natural force—thunderbolt, fire, wind, tide—not to be withstood even by the gods (3.399–452). Weighing the wrath of Caesar against the wrath of the gods, his men uneasily choose to follow him. At the Rubicon and again on the eve of Pharsalia, Caesar's troops express their uneasiness by appeal to *pietas,* closely connected in book 1 to the values represented by *patria* and the *penates.* "Pietas patriique penates/Quamquam caede feras mentes animosque tumentes/Frangunt; sed diro ferri revocantur amore/Ductorisque metu" (1.353–

[30] Pharsalia is the cause of so great a mischief.
[31] Magnus survives the battle, though his greatness has gone.
[32] All the glory of our country fell there.
[33] Such were the complaints poured forth by patriotism that was soon to pass away.
[34] Man's destiny has never been watched over by any god.

56).[35] The replacement of *pietas patriae* by *ferri amor* confirms the direction of Roman history and identifies this direction with Caesar. The pattern is repeated in book 7: "Tamen omnia torpor/Pectora constrinxit, gelidusque in viscera sanguis/Percussa pietate coit" (7.466–68).[36] Even this natural reaction to civil war has been anticipated by Caesar: "Sed dum tela micant, non vos pietatis imago/Ulla nec adversa conspecti fronte parentes/Commoveant; voltus gladio turbate verendos" (7.320–22).[37] His words clarify the meaning of his ultimate victory: the triumph of Caesar is explicitly the defeat of *pietas,* signified by the bloody standards—"inpia signa" (7.838)—carried from the field of Pharsalia.

In contrast, the poem's representative of the decaying republic seizes upon *pietas* in defeat. Having arrived after Pharsalia on the island of Lesbos, Pompey is moved to find the inhabitants devoted to him: "Tali pietate virorum/Laetus in adversis . . ." (8.127–28).[38] Yet the *pietas* of these lines is confined to the narrow meaning of personal affection; the constriction of the word to this meaning is reflected in the territorial constriction of the republic itself, as Pompey's Rome is confined to the place where he is loved (8.133). This meaning is again revealed when Pompey tries to extend the domain of personal allegiance to include Egypt, where his supporters detect no signs of *vera pietas* (8.573), the adjective here confessing the sincerity absent from the Egyptian welcome. That this sense of the word should define the republican cause after Pharsalia is sure evidence that the forecast of *pietas peritura* has come true.

After the death of Pompey, fragments of an older ideal may be found in Cordus (8.718), who retrieves the body (though not the head) of Pompey, in Pompey's son Sextus (9.147), and in his wife Cornelia (9.180). Yet in none of these figures does *pietas* transcend personal devotion, and in the case of Sextus ("iustaque furens pietate") even this devotion is expressed as *furor.* What has perished is the Ciceronian sense

[35] Fierce as they were with bloodshed and proud of heart, they were unnerved by love of their country and their country's gods, till brought to heel by horrid love of slaughter and fear of their leader.

[36] Nevertheless, a numbness froze each bosom and the blood gathered cold at each heart, from the shock to natural affection.

[37] But while their weapons glitter, no thought of natural affection, no sight of your sires in the front rank of the foe, must weaken your purpose; mangle with the sword the faces that demand reverence.

[38] Cheered in his hour of defeat to find such devotion . . .

of *pietas* as devotion to the republic; once the republic has become an empire, *pietas* is adapted to the end of keeping it an empire. Thus Lucan interprets the legend of Aeneas as an instrument of imperial propaganda by connecting Caesar and Troy. In his speech from the ruins, Caesar claims the legacy of Aeneas: "Gentis Iuleae vestris clarissimus aris/Dat pia tura nepos et vos in sede priore/Rite vocat" (9.995–97).[39] The meaning of such public gestures Lucan then sums up in his account of Caesar's lachrymose reception of Pompey's head: "Quisquis te flere coegit/Impetus, a vera longe pietate recessit" (9.1055–56).[40] By claiming the Trojan inheritance, by weeping over the head of Pompey, Caesar assumes the postures appropriate to securing his own supremacy. For Lucan, however, such posturing is a long way from republican understanding of what *pietas* really is.

Although Cato might be expected to inherit and preserve *vera pietas,* he is not once in the poem identified with this ideal. As Frederick M. Ahl has carefully shown, Cato is characterized instead by his stoic *virtus.*[33] Here conceived to transcend history, *virtus* is distinguished from *pietas,* which belongs to the temporal domain of things that perish. To characterize Cato as *pius* would be to invoke Vergil's Aeneas, who figures in book 9 of the poem as the ancestor of Caesar. It would also mean attaching his hero to an ideal whose definition has been so altered by the events of history as to convey a meaning quite contrary to Catonian idealism. After Pharsalia, *pietas* is perverted to signify allegiance to the commander of the army, the expression *pietas militiae* (4.499) capturing in a phrase the verdict of the civil war. *Pietas* can no longer mean devotion to the *patria* because the *patria* has been taken over by one man ("Omnia Caesar erat," 3.108). As a republican ideal *pietas* is dead. Dead too is Lucan at the hands of Nero, whose crime ("o dirum scelus! o scelus!") is condemned by Statius in *Silvae* 2.7.[34]

The hostility to tyranny expressed in this ode in honor of Lucan is fully developed in the *Thebaid.* Although the fiction is Greek, the poem's theme of fraternal strife in the pursuit of power is profoundly Roman. What Statius says of Lucan might well be said of Statius himself: "tu carus Latio memorque gentis."[41][35] Expressed in the alternative ori-

---

[39] I, most renowned descendant of the race of Iulus, here place incense due upon your altars, and solemnly invoke you in your ancient abode.

[40] Whatever the impulse that forced you to weep, it was far removed from sincere affection.

[41] thou, dear to Latium and mindful of thy race

ginary legends of Aeneas, on the one hand, and Romulus and Remus on the other, the fundamental conflict in Roman history between *pietas* and *impietas* receives epic treatment in this version of the seven against Thebes. Derived from the *Phoenissae* of Euripides, the *Thebaid* weighs in twelve-book detail the implications of the most famous lines from the Greek tragedy, spoken by Eteocles to Jocasta,[36] and given a Roman significance in Cicero's translation. "Nam si violandum est ius, regnandi gratia/Violandum est; aliis rebus pietatem colas."[42][37] Said to quote repeatedly the words of Eteocles as justification for his own ambition, Caesar pushes *pietas* aside, removing the moral obstacle to what Cicero calls "parricidium patriae." Cicero's rendering of Euripides might well be glossed by Lucan's *pietas peritura* or, even more to the point, by Statius's own summary phrase, "nusquam pietas" (3.350).[38]

   This phrase is voiced by Tydeus in calling the Argives to arms. As in Lucan, *arma* and *pietas* are seen in Statius as competing rather than as complementary forces: "arma, arma viri, tuque optime Lernae/ductor, magnanimum si quis tibi sanguis avorum,/arma para! nusquam pietas, non gentibus aequum/fas aut cura Iovis"(3.348–51).[43] There is no possibility here of Vergil's "pietate insignis et armis" (6.403); nor is there any question of whether the gods care for men, but rather a flat denial that men any longer care for the gods. This denial is repeated from a quite different moral perspective by Lycurgus, who makes explicit the association of civil war with violence to the gods: "pergite in exscidium, socii si tanta voluptas/sanguinis, imbuite arma domi, atque haec inrita dudum/templa Iovis—quid enim haud licitum?—ferat impius ignis" (5.683–85).[44] The bitterness of the irony, especially in the word "voluptas," here underlines the threat to civilized order that is fulfilled by book 11, which also completes the poem's tendency to allegorize *pietas*.[39] As the poem moves toward the climactic encounter between the two brothers, the female figure of Pietas—quite distraught by contrast to the joyous personifications of Calpurnius and Claudian—attempts to intervene.

   [42] If wrong may e'er be right, for a throne's sake/Were wrong most right: —be God in all else feared!
   [43] To arms, to arms, ye men, and thou, most worthy ruler of Lerna, if thou hast the blood of thy brave ancestors, to arms! Natural ties, justice, and reverence for Jove have perished from the world!
   [44] March on then to destroy, if kindred murder so delights you, flesh first your arms at home, ay, and let impious fire—what indeed is not lawful?—devour Jove's temple.

Iamdudum terris coetuque offensa deorum
aversa caeli Pietas in parte sedebat,
non habitu, quo nota prius, non ore sereno,
sed vittis exuta comam, fraternaque bella,
ceu soror infelix pugnantum aut anxia mater,
deflebat, saevumque Iovem Parcasque nocentes
vociferans, seseque polis et luce relicta
descensuram Erebo et Stygios iam malle penates.
(11.457–64)[45]

The place of *pietas* could hardly be more vividly displayed than it is here. Isolated from the impious world and from its gods as well, *pietas* is defined by the spirit of sister and mother, as a feminine virtue opposed to the strife of men. The effect of her appearance on the battlefield is to identify the ideal she represents with the spirit of peace (11.473–76). For a moment the pattern of *pietas victa* is reversed, and the Greek warriors hesitate, just as the soldiers of Lucan's Caesar hesitate in deference to *pietas* at the Rubicon and again on the night before Pharsalia. Yet here also *pietas* is easily overcome by the call of *arma*. Voiced by the fury Tisiphone, the appeal to arms captures the essential liability of *pietas* as a force in history: it is ultimately unheroic, even antiheroic. Tisiphone penetrates to the heart of the matter when she contemptuously describes Pietas as "numen iners pacique datum" (11.485).[46] As such, she is helpless to prevent the resumption of battle:

Tunc vero accensae stimulis maioribus irae:
arma placent, versaeque volunt spectare cohortes.
instaurant crudele nefas; rex impius aptat
tela et funestae casum prior occupat hastae.
(11.497–500)[47]

[45] Long time, offended alike by earth and the company of the gods, had Piety been sitting in a remote region of the heavens, with unwonted dress and troubled countenance, and fillets stripped from off her hair: she bewailed the fraternal strife, as though a hapless sister or anxious mother of the fighters, and loudly chiding cruel Jove and the guilty Fates protested she would leave heaven and the light of day, and descend to Erebus, for already she preferred the abodes of Styx.

[46] sluggard, peace-devoted deity

[47] Then verily are they kindled to yet more fiery wrath; battle pleases, and the armies, changed once more, are willing to look on. They begin anew the savage work: the impious monarch aims his dart, and first dares the fortune of the deadly spear.

Reminiscent of Vergil's "furiis accensus et ira/terribilis" (12.946–47), these lines express the very non-Vergilian idea: "arma placent." In a world thus defined, in a realm governed by the "rex impius" Eteocles, Pietas can only return to exile, a historical leftover alienated from the domain of power. In her absence, the Romulus–Remus theme in Roman literature receives an especially horrific statement as the two brothers kill each other in an orgy of *furor* (11.537–38), leaving Creon to assume the tyrant's role.

The triumph of *furor* over *pietas* evident in the broad design of the poem is also apparent in particular episodes. The figures of *pietas* in the poem are killed ("Invida fata piis," 10.384), overcome by the more powerful force of *arma*. Those who do survive are female, and they survive only to bury the dead. Creon's refusal to allow funeral rites, reminiscent of Caesar's *impietas* after Pharsalia, lends a genuine dignity to the midnight encounter of Antigone and Argia, who defy the new ruler in attempting to secure the rites of burial. Like Lucan's Cordus, they represent what is left of *pietas* after the slaughter is over, confronting by then a situation in which *pietas* is effectively against the law. Their only recourse is to an outsider bound to them by no ties of kinship or nation. Called upon to remedy the dismal situation in Thebes, Theseus enters the poem very much in the manner of Tibullus's Messalinus and his successors in imperial panegyric (12.519–22). Neither Theban nor Argive, Theseus turns his weapons against Creon without incurring the guilt of civil war, and guarantees burial of the dead without, conversely, embodying any ethical norm beyond the *clementia* that Paterculus had claimed for Octavian. Whereas the events of the poems have already driven Pietas into exile, Clementia (12.482) lives to be embodied in Theseus, who is the ultimate beneficiary of *pietas victa*. Although the distinction between *pietas* and *clementia* is eroded in later imperial pane-gyric, Statius significantly holds to the difference. By declining to identify Theseus with the ideal that fraternal strife has destroyed, basing the restored order of the poem's conclusion on *clementia* instead, Statius indicates how civil war leads to political dependency. The Theban and Argive women must beg for the intervention of Theseus, for unlike *pietas, clementia* is not an obligation, but a gesture that strength has the option of making to weakness. As Ronald Syme has written: "Clemency depends not on duty but on choice or whim, it is the will of a master not an aristocrat's virtue. To acquiesce in the 'clementia Caesaris' [implies] a recognition of despotism."[40] Although the *clementia* of Statius's Theseus cannot be directly equated with that of Caesar, neither can his role in the last lines of the poem support the claim that the "*Thebaid* is an epic not of sin but of redemption, a chronicle not of evil but of triumphant good."[41] Such a conclusion is no more accurate applied to Statius than it would be applied to Tacitus, who chronicles the age in which the *Thebaid* was written.

Whereas Statius's poem emphasizes the fatal consequences of *pietas* sacrificed to the *arma* of ambition, Tacitus insists, with a good deal more subtlety, on the ways in which the word has been abused in the armed pursuit of power and corrupted by the power thus attained. The traditional understanding of *pietas* is prominent in Tacitus's early celebration of his father-in-law Agricola: "hic . . . liber honori Agricolae soceri mei destinatus, professione pietatis aut laudatus erit aut excusatus."[48][42] The book itself thus manifests what it celebrates in the career of Agricola. When the exemplary figure himself dies, he is honored by both his daughter and her husband. In his peroration, then, Tacitus connects past to future in a chain of devotion. He looks first to the dead, "Si quis piorum manibus locus" (46.1),[49] and then to the living, who by admiring and imitating the deceased express their own *pietas:* "admiratione te potius et immortalibus laudibus et, si natura suppeditet, similitudine colamus: is verus honos, ea coniunctissimi cuiusque pietas" (46.6).[50] As implied criticism of the late Emperor Domitian and as implied celebration of the new dynasty, the *Agricola* conforms to the pattern of imperial panegyric. As a prologue to the *Histories* and *Annals,* on the other hand, the *Agricola* defines the ideal from which Roman civilization under the principate has fallen. With each successive work, as Tacitus probes to the very origins of the imperial system, the prospects for *pietas* in his vision become dimmer and dimmer.

The *Histories* of Tacitus concerns the turmoil of the period that followed upon the death of Nero, and has been aptly described by Syme: "Detesting civil strife and suspicious of power and success, Tacitus achieves a sombre and savage impartiality in the portrayal of the crime and violence of the year 69. Tacitus is harsh and bitter, offering no consolation anywhere. His despair is engendered by the contrasts be-

[48] This book is dedicated to the vindication of my father-in-law Agricola: its plea of filial duty will commend or, at least, excuse it.

[49] If there be any habitation for the spirits of the just

[50] Let reverence rather, let unending thankfulness, let imitation even, if our strength permit, be our tribute to your memory: this is true respect, this is kinship's duty.

tween word and fact, between ambitions and achievement, by the tragic vicissitudes of men and governments."[43] One of the specific "contrasts between word and fact" is between the word *pietas* and the specific facts that claim its endorsement. In the *Histories* the traditional distinction between foreign and civil war, the one pious the other impious, is insistently blurred. Far from providing an obstacle to civil war, *pietas* here becomes an accepted part of the rhetoric advocating and defending campaigns against other Roman forces. The *pietas* that panegyric regards as an imperial virtue is claimed by all the pretenders to empire in the year 69. Each such claim is based on the force of *arma*, as the meaning of the word is narrowed to that advanced by Lucan's Vulteius and Scaeva: *pietas militiae*. Thus Vitellius praises his rapacious, jealous, and riotous soldiers: "transgressus in castra ultro pietatem militum conlaudavit."[51][44] And again: "Multa cum exultatione in urbem revectus frequenti contione pietatem militum laudibus cumulat" (3.36).[52] Thus Otho addresses his own mutinous soldiers in a speech analogous to Caesar's in book 5 of the *Pharsalia* and ironically suggestive of the first epic simile of the *Aeneid*. "Tumultus proximi initium non cupiditate vel odio, quae multos exercitus in discordiam egere, ac ne detrectatione quidem aut formidine periculorum: nimia pietas vestra acrius quam considerate excitavit" (1.83).[53] Otho manages to proclaim the victory of *pietas* over *furor* by simply exchanging the names: *furor* is "nimia pietas." But Tacitus himself calls things by their real names. In a passage from book 3 replete with echoes of Vergil and Horace that effectively fulfills the prophecy of Statius's Lycurgus, for example, Tacitus recounts the burning of the temple of Jove: the temple that no enemy could capture now succumbs to the fury of Rome's own princes. Tacitus here offers *furor principum* (3.72) to explain the decline of Rome, originally founded (he says) on *pietas hominum* (4.53). From the *pietas* of men to the *furor* of princes, the pattern of Roman history is that of *pietas victa* and the blame is placed squarely on the imperial system.

Yet Tacitus perceives *pietas* to be not merely conquered but, more

[51] Then he went to the camp and took occasion to praise the loyal devotion of the soldiers.

[52] In high exultation he rode back to the city, and in a crowded assembly extolled to the skies the devoted loyalty of his soldiers.

[53] The recent disturbances owed their beginning not to any greed or hate, which are the sentiments that drive most armies to revolt, or even to any shirking or fear of danger; it was your excessive loyalty that spurred you to an action more violent than wise.

important, drained of real meaning and turned into a fake virtue disguising the abuses of imperial power, most fully displayed in the *Annals.* Witness the *pietas* ascribed to Nero. Shocked by his mother's assumption of imperial prerogatives in the presence of foreign ambassadors, Nero averts scandal with an ostentatious gesture of filial duty (*species pietatis*). As a sequel, the emperor plots his mother's murder, complete with a plan for a temple and altars in her honor: "additurum principem defunctae templum et aras et cetera ostentandae pietati" (14.3).[54] In the *Annals,* the show of piety replaces the thing itself, as publicized virtue becomes a shield for the enactment of crimes long recognized as impious. Language has become disguise, as *pietas* involves saying, in Swift's words, "the thing which was not."

Responsibility for this development is traced to the origins of the imperial system. Reflecting on the character of Augustus and his significance in Roman history, Tacitus acknowledges divergent opinion. On the one hand: "pietate erga parentem et necessitudine rei publicae, in qua nullus tunc legibus locus, ad arma civilia actum, quae neque parari possent neque haberi per bonas artis" (1.9).[55] On the other: "pietatem erga parentem et tempora rei publicae obtentui sumpta" (1.10).[56] The catalogue of specific crimes that follows this assertion, however, leaves no doubt where Tacitus stands: Augustan *pietas* was a cover for *cupido dominandi* (1.10). In this sense, then, rather than in the sense claimed by Paterculus, Tiberius is indeed the true heir of Augustus. As emperor, Tiberius extols the *pietas* of a senate he distrusts (3.51) and commends the *pietas* of Sejanus at the very moment his subordinate's treachery has been discovered (4.40). As camouflage for the true motives of government, this word assumes in the *Annals* the silent quotation marks of irony.

The subversion of Vergilian *pietas* evident in Lucan, Statius, and Tacitus provides the relevant background for reconsidering Lactantius's attempt to redefine the word in explicit opposition to Vergil. In book 1 ("De Falsa Religione") of the *Divine Institutes,* Lactantius condemns the false *pietas* of the Roman poets, citing two examples from the

[54] The sovereign, naturally, would assign the deceased a temple and the other displays of filial piety.

[55] Filial duty and the needs of the country, which at that time had no room for law, had driven him to the weapons of civil strife—weapons which could not be either forged or wielded with clean hands.

[56] Filial duty and the critical position of the state had been used merely as a cloak.

Aeneid, and in the next breath compares their celebration of the pagan deities to their adulation of monarchs ("panegyricis mendacibus adulantur").[45] Lactantius thus aligns himself against the tradition of panegyric and against Augustan imperialism; instead of *Romanitas,* Lactantius offers *humanitas* as the standard by which *vera pietas* may be known. Indeed, he argues that *pietas* is what makes us human. "Hominem vero quia nudum fragilemque formavit, ut eum sapientia potius instrueret, dedit ei praeter caetera hunc pietatis affectum ut homo hominem tueatur, diligat, foveat, contraque omnia pericula et accipiat, et praestet auxilium" (6.10).[57] Negations of this idea ("Impium, quod violatur humanitas," 6.19) serve to explain why neither Aeneas nor Augustus can be taken as a measure of *pietas,* why *pietas militiae* is finally an oxymoron. By taking literally and without exception the biblical prohibition against killing (6.20), Lactantius attaches *pietas* to the ideal of *humanitas,* as that word is in turn defined by *iustitia:* "Nam ipsa humanitas quid est, nisi iustitia? quid est iustitia, nisi pietas? pietas autem nihil aliud est, quam Dei parentis agnitio" (3.9).[58] For all the circularity of this definition, the meaning is clear: the parent relevant to a true understanding of *pietas* is neither Anchises nor Julius Caesar but the Christian God.

When Lactantius in turn evokes the Ovidian depiction of the golden age, he affirms its essential truth. Rather than ridicule this poetic fiction in the manner of Prudentius, Lactantius perceives in this evidence a historical pattern consonant with Christian conceptions of time: here the Saturnian golden age is understood as the period before worship of the false gods had begun. Lactantius then blames the son of Saturn for all that follows. Citing *Aeneid* 8.320 ("Arma Iovis fugiens et regnis exsul ademptis"), the Christian apologist argues that Jupiter set an example of *impietas* for mortals to imitate: "ipse propemodum parricida exemplo caeteris esset ad violandam pietatem" (5.5).[59] Through this primal conflict of *arma* and *pietas,* Jupiter becomes the type of the *impius tyrannus* (5.6): "Universa igitur mala, quibus humanum genus seipsum

[57] But, because God made man uncovered and weak that He might instruct him rather by wisdom, He gave him, besides the others, this affection of piety, in order that man might kindly regard his fellowman and love him and cherish him and take him in against all dangers and furnish him help.

[58] But that very humanity, what is it if not justice? And what is justice if not piety? And piety is nothing other than the acknowledgment of God as parent.

[59] Jupiter himself, a near-parricide, was an example to others for violating piety.

invicem conficit, iniustus atque impius deorum cultus induxit. Nec enim poterant retinere pietatem, qui communem omnium patrem Deum tanquam prodigi ac rebelles liberi abnegassent" (5.8).[60] If the attempt to explain the Christian idea of the fall in terms of pagan myth is awkward, the correspondence between the Hebraic and Roman legends of *pietas victa* is obvious enough. As Prudentius is the Christian heir to the redemptive vision of Roman history, so Lactantius adapts to Christian ends the alternative vision of Lucan, Statius, and Tacitus.

Augustine

In the very process of articulating this regressive view of history, however, Lactantius expresses a wish for a new golden age, characterized by a list of virtues that includes and colors *pietas:* "Quam beatus esset, quamque aureus humanarum rerum status, si per totum orbem mansuetudo, et pietas, et pax, et innocentia, et aequitas, et temperantia, et fides moraretur" (5.8).[61][46] By identifying *pietas* with *pax* and detaching it from *arma,* he not only corrects Vergil but also anticipates Augustine, whose *City of God* stands at the end of the double tradition of Roman history. The Augustinian synthesis converts the two patterns of this history to describe the two cities of God and man: the redemptive pattern of panegyric he ascribes to the *civitas piorum,* the regressive pattern of satire to the *civitas impiorum.* After depicting the destruction of the impious in book 21, Augustine turns in the last book of the *City of God* to the reward of the pious. In the process he answers the rhetorical question raised in book 4—"Nam quo modo ibi esset vera felicitas, ubi vera non erat pietas?" (4.23)[62]—by moving from history to eschatology. "Sic enim erit inamissibilis voluntas pietatis et aequitatis, quo modo est felicitatis. Nam utique peccando nec pietatem nec felicitatem tenuimus, voluntatem

[60] Therefore, all the evils with which the human race weakens itself in turn, have been brought on by the unjust and unholy worship of the false gods. For they could not retain piety who had denied as perfidious and rebel children the common father of us all, God.

[61] How blessed and how golden would be the condition of human affairs if, throughout the whole world, meekness and devotion and peace and innocence and fairness and temperance and faith should tarry.

[62] For how could true happiness exist where there was no true piety?

vero felicitatis nec perdita felicitate perdidimus" (22.30).[63] Projected beyond time, the "inamissibilis" *pietas* of Augustine's heavenly city is not just redefined but in the end regained.

   As Augustine approaches this conclusion, he lends specificity and weight to the ideal of *pietas* by identifying it with figures from Hebraic and Roman history. The word in turn comes to control the significance of other abstractions and to signify the true faith as expressed in the supreme commandment of Matthew 22.37–40. Commenting on this passage, Augustine writes: "Hic est Dei cultus, haec vera religio, haec recta pietas, haec tantum Deo debita servitus" (10.3).[64] In contrast to this definition of *pietas* as love of God and neighbor, *impietas* is defined as love of self (14.28). The *civitas piorum* is characterized by *humilitas*, producing such phrases as *humilis pietas* (10.19) and *pia humilitas* (14.13); in contrast, the *civitas impiorum* is the city of pride, frequently associated with blindness, insanity, and discord—with the very ideas conveyed by Vergil's *furor*. That *pietas* must be qualified by *vera*, however, confesses the strength of the pagan claim on the word, a claim that Augustine is at pains to disallow. He proceeds to do this by denying the ideal of Rome painted in *Aeneid* 6, promoting instead the counter view of Sallust and Lucan, and emphasizing the Romulus myth of Roman origins to make explicit the analogy between Romulus and Cain. The premises of this "stereoscopic" design are evident in the opening paragraphs.[47] In announcing his topic, Augustine makes clear that the history of the city of God on earth is one of pilgrimage "inter impios"—thus identifying in the very first sentence the enemy and also the audience of the work. Characterizing this audience in the first section, he establishes the basic cluster of associations that *impietas* will carry right to the end: "Et nunc ingrata superbia atque impiissima insania eius nomini resistunt corde perverso . . ." (1.1).[65] His purpose, then, is to persuade the *impii* to embrace *vera pietas* (2.29).

   Augustine begins to refute the arguments of paganism even in his preface, where he juxtaposes parallel quotations: James 4.6 ("Deus superbis resistit, humilibus autem dat gratiam") and *Aeneid* 6.853 ("Par-

----

[63] For the desire for godliness and righteousness will be as impossible to lose as the desire for happiness. For surely in sinning we retained neither godliness nor happiness, but though we lost happiness we did not lose the desire for happiness.

[64] This is the worship of God, this is true religion, this right piety, this the service due to God only.

[65] And now, in thankless pride and most wicked madness, they perversely oppose that name . . .

cere subiectis et debellare superbos"). Similar except in their respective subjects, God in the New Testament and Rome in the *Aeneid,* these two passages illustrate for Augustine the distinction between the two cities. Placed against the authority of the Bible, Vergil's line is read by the Christian apologist as an illustration of the very pride that God resists in the verse from James. The pride that expresses itself in the pagan poet as a usurpation of divine prerogative expresses itself historically as a passion for rule, a passion well documented by Rome's own historians. To express this passion Augustine has only to modify a phrase from Tacitus, but the *libido dominandi* of Augustine's Rome belongs to a larger construct of distinctions. Thus Augustine repeats the passage from James (11.33) to distinguish the loyal from the fallen angels, adding a commentary on the passage that affirms the affinity between Satanic pride and Roman power. The model for Roman history is, in effect, provided by the fallen angels, whose ambition and desire produce the turbulence that characterizes the city of man. When, on the other hand, Augustine repeats *Aeneid* 6.853, he discredits Vergil's definition of imperial *pietas* by denying that Rome ever battered down the proud or spared the humble (1.6). Tireless in his efforts to show how the facts of Roman history have failed to conform to the ideal pattern outlined in *Aeneid* 6, Augustine points specifically to the evidence of civil war, seen through the eyes of the author most antithetical to Vergil. Appropriating Lucan's "Bella . . . plus quam civilia" to characterize early Roman conquests, Augustine takes familial violence as the essential theme of Roman history. The true founder of Rome is not Aeneas but Romulus.

Compared to Paris, whose adultery is the determining event in Trojan history, Romulus determines the pattern of Roman history by killing his brother. Aeneas—"pius totiens appellatus" (1.3)—is merely the link between Trojan adultery and Roman fratricide. As the son of the goddess who provoked the adultery of Paris, as the offspring of an adulterous pair, Aeneas escapes the punishment inflicted on his city for the crime of Paris only to found a new line intent on the self-punishment of civil war. Nor is such self-destruction prevented by the pagan gods, who are so weak as to require the protection of Aeneas in the famous exodus from Troy. Passing over the image of Aeneas with his father on his back, Augustine makes the critical point of this episode the acknowledged defeat of the Trojan gods. In a later passage he develops the point by arguing that the pagan gods were really only men. This serves to explain the primal case of defeated deity, Saturn at the hands of Jupiter, whose act of parricide Augustine understands as a case of *impius* son killing *impius* father (7.18). In its more extended sense, *parricidium* is the word that Augustine had already invoked to describe the murder of Remus (3.6). Drawing the obvious but telling comparison between Romulus and Cain (15.5), Augustine names fratricide as the founding act both of Rome and of the larger *civitas impiorum*.

This archetypal relationship between Cain and Romulus allows Augustine to sustain further comparison between Hebraic and Roman history. Stressing the importance of Genesis 4.17, for example, he notes with evident satisfaction that whereas Abel was a wanderer, a pilgrim on earth, Cain built a city. This, in turn, suggests analogy with the founders of other earthly cities, Babylon as well as Rome. According to Augustine's reading of Genesis 11, the founder of Babylon was the giant Nimrod, whose "superba . . . impietas" (16.4) is most powerfully imaged in the Tower of Babel: "ab illa superbia aedificandae turris usque in caelum, qua impia significatur elatio, apparuit civitas, hoc est societas, impiorum" (16.10).[66] The Roman connection is later made explicit when Augustine describes Rome as a new Babylon in the West whose true ruler is Satan (16.17, 18.41). In contrast to Cain and those who take after him are the pilgrims who comprise the *civitas piorum*. Since the church itself is understood as an image of the slain Abel, persecution of Christians is a reenactment of Cain's sin (18.51), and persecution is therefore an act that serves to distinguish the two cities. And yet Augustine emphasizes that in this world the two cities cannot always be so easily distinguished, and the inevitable mingling of pious and impious means that there are Christian heretics who belong to the city of man (18.51) just as there are Roman emperors who belong to the city of God (5.21–26).

It follows, then, that God has granted earthly power to citizens of both cities, to Nimrod as well as Hezekiah, to Domitian as well as Constantine. For Augustine the biblical type of the *impius rex* is Jeroboam I: "instituit idolatriam in regno suo et populum Dei secum simulacrorum cultu obstrictum nefanda impietate decepit" (17.22).[67] His *impietas* is readily assimilated to *nefas*, as this description directs attention to the

[66] By men's arrogance in building a tower to reach the sky, a symbol of impious self-exaltation, the city or community of the ungodly was revealed.

[67] He not only established idolatry in his kingdom, but with abominable impiety beguiled God's people to follow him into bondage to the cult of images.

violation of the covenant given in Exodus 20, and especially the first two commandments. Jeroboam's crime is against God, but it is magnified by his earthly power; his *impietas* is reflected in the idolatry of the people he rules and is imitated by many of his successors ("verum etiam successores eius et impietatis imitatores . . . ," 17.22). As with the Hebraic kings, so with such Roman emperors as Nero, who combines effeminate *luxuria* with tyrannical *crudelitas*. Like Jeroboam, Nero also has many imitators ("pessimi atque improbi reges," 5.19) who belong to the *civitas impiorum* and whose ultimate destruction, assured from the beginning, is detailed in book 21.

The contrasting portrait of the ideal king is most fully developed around the figures of David and Theodosius. Their *pietas* is a function of sin and repentence. Consider Augustine's characterization of the penitent David.

> Regnavit ergo David in terrena Hierusalem, filius caelestis Hierusalem, divino multum testimonio praedicatus, quia et delicta eius tanta pietate superata sunt per saluberrimam paenitendi humilitatem ut prorsus inter eos sit de quibus ipse ait: "Beati quorum remissae sunt iniquitates et quorum tecta sunt peccata." (17.20)[68]

As king in the terrestrial and son in the celestial Jerusalem, an idealized David would have a claim on both imperial and republican meanings of the Latin word, but Augustine instead associates David's *pietas* with Christian humility, its constant companion in the *City of God*. *Pietas* is the power of penitence to conquer not nations or armies, but the "delicta" here acknowledged and translated into "peccata" by the pendant quotation from Psalm 32. Also among the blessed is the emperor Theodosius, whose idealized portrait in book 5 is, like that of David, organized by the paradox of humility and sublimity. Where praise of Theodosius for outlawing paganism might have been expected, Augustine instead focuses attention on the emperor's most publicized failing, the massacre at Thessalonika. Repentance for this "gravissimum scelus"

---

[68] Now David reigned in the earthly Jerusalem, being a son of the heavenly Jerusalem, greatly extolled by the divine testimony because his sins were overcome by such great piety, through a most salutary humility of repentance, so that he assuredly belongs among those of whom he himself says: "Blessed are they whose iniquities are pardoned, and whose sins are covered."

assures his final reward: "aeterna felicitas, cuius dator est Deus solis veraciter piis" (5.26).[69]

Augustine thus lends his authority to a conception of *pietas regia* that involves the ideal monarch in the affairs of this world. "Illi autem qui vera pietate praediti bene vivunt, si habent scientiam regendi populos, nihil est felicius rebus humanis quam si Deo miserante habeant potestatem" (5.19).[70] This is an ideal that will elicit many responses in medieval and Renaissance discussions of governance, where *pietas* distinctly bears the traces of its engagement with Roman history. What Dryden, across barriers of time and language, will call "pious times" signifies a golden age of peace, order, and happiness, in opposition to the iron age fury of rebellion or civil war. This golden age is to be guaranteed by the *pietas* of both monarch and subject. Defined by humility and clemency, modelled by David and Theodosius, the *pietas* of the true king is opposed to the pride and cruelty of the tyrant, whose model is Nimrod. The corresponding *pietas* of the subject is understood as loyalty to the ruler, in contrast to impious Titans and fallen angels, as both Vergilian and Augustinian versions of the idea are conveyed to the political writers of Latin Christendom.

[69] eternal happiness, which God grants only to those of the true religion

[70] But if those who are endowed with true religion and live good lives know the art of ruling the nations, there is no greater blessing for mankind than for them, by the mercy of God, to have the power.

4

Governance:
Royal and Ecclesiastical Pietas
in the Middle Ages

In his *Res Gestae* Augustus describes a golden shield presented to him and adorned with the words *virtus, clementia, iustitia, pietas*.[1] Reflecting on these imperial virtues, M. P. Charlesworth observes that *pietas* is the most difficult to define of the four. "Pietas," he writes, "is the inward and spiritual link of the imperial system. In the ruler it is a feeling of duty and love towards the Roman people, their traditions and their religion; in the ruled it is the affectionate loyalty of subjects to one whom they regard as head of the family."[2] Although the failure of such a definition to admit the realities of imperial rule creates the ironic possibilities exploited by Tacitus, the political significance of the word survives the indignity of association with such emperors as Caligula and Nero, finally outlasting the empire itself. Thus Cassiodorus can write on behalf of the Ostrogothic King Theodoric: "Pietas siquidem principum totum custodit imperium."[1][3] This version of the relationship between *pietas* and *imperium* is subjected to a host of stresses over the next millennium as the vocabulary of the ancient world is adapted to the political conflicts of the Middle Ages, eventually and above all the conflict between church and state. A word with both political and religious meaning, *pietas* figures prominently in the correspondence between sacerdotal kingship and imperial papacy, even as a term of address that may be accorded or withheld as circumstances dictate. With specific reference to this conflict, the political history of the word in post-classical Latin may be outlined by tracing its association with four other words that express for the Middle Ages the responsibilities of governance: *iustitia, cura, pax,* and *clementia*. Overlapping without duplicating the list on the imperial

[1] Piety is the guardian of all princely power.

shield, these terms and certain near synonyms (*aequitas, sollicitudo, tranquillitas, misericordia*) provide lexical coordinates for understanding the political significance of *pietas* in medieval Latin and explaining its limited success in negotiating the transition to the modern languages.

Iustitia: From Antiquity to the Middle Ages

The long and close connection of *pietas* and *iustitia* reflected in Vergil's characterization of Aeneas has acquired by the early Middle Ages expressly royal associations. The most influential version of this conjunction is given by Isidore of Seville: "Regiae virtutes praecipuae duae: iustitia et pietas. Plus autem in regibus laudatur pietas; nam iustitia per se severa est."[2][4] Although the balance between the two terms eventually tilts decisively toward *iustitia,* the importance of *pietas* in the political discourse of the early Middle Ages is unmistakable. From the beginning of the Carolingian period the word is recurrent in the royal correspondence,[5] as protocol derived from late imperial Rome urged those with petitions or praise for the monarch to refer to him as *vestra pietas.*[6] In a letter written about 775, for example, Cathulfus addresses Charlemagne as "Domino regi piissimo," affirms divine sanction for his rule in a phrase that observes the analogy between divine and royal ("mira pietas et magna clementia Dei"), and concludes with an expression of personal humility in the face of so virtuous a king: "Placuit mihi rustico verbo, quam vis sicut sum ignarus, tamen vobis scribere, in vestram pietatem confidens."[3][7] Apologies aside, Cathulfus knows the vocabulary appropriate for a letter to the king that includes substantial comments on the nature of kingship.

This was a favorite subject of Carolingian writers, including Alcuin. Written over the years 793–801, Alcuin's letters on kingship repeatedly emphasize the importance of *pietas.* At the same time they disclose the potential difficulties of applying the ancient word to latter-day political circumstances. In the closing of a letter to the Mercian king, Alcuin identifies "divina pietas" as the source of all goodness: "Divina te in

---

[2] There are, above all, two royal virtues, justice and piety; but piety is more praised in kings, because justice by itself is strict.

[3] It has pleased me to write you in plain words, inexperienced as I am, but trusting in your piety.

omni bonitate pietas florere faciat."[4][8] In offering political wisdom to Charlemagne himself, Alcuin wonders just how high "inaestimabilis pietas" might exalt the throne,[9] speculation consistent with the specific advice of another letter, which claims *pietas* as the ideal by which true kings will be remembered and rewarded.[10] In effect, Alcuin endorses the aphorism of Cassiodorus that makes *pietas* the moral and spiritual foundation of royal power. Yet when he explains the actual operation of this preeminent royal virtue, he does not treat *pietas* as a self-contained political ideal. "Disce diligenter illorum exempla, a patre auctoritatem, a matre pietatem. Ab illo regere populum per iustitiam, ab ista compati miseris per misericordiam."[5][11] Expressing the conjunction of Isidore's key terms metaphorically by reference to the responsibilities of parenthood, Alcuin renders *iustitia* a function of paternal authority and maternal *pietas* the source of mercy. This adaptation in turn yields two important and influential distinctions: between action and character, and metaphorically between masculine and feminine aspects of governance. Whereas *iustitia* indicates a way of acting, *pietas* refers to a quality of character that generates a complementary way of acting, indicated by the word *misericordia*. Although this inward turning of *pietas* to define character rather than to judge action underlines a major tendency in the history of the word's usage, more immediately pertinent is the identification of *pietas* with the mother in contrast to the *iustitia* of the father.

In this respect Alcuin's conception of royal governance derives from Gregory, who had used the same parental metaphor in remarking on the kind of man who ought to rule ("Curandum quippe est ut rectorem subditis et matrem pietas, et patrem exhibeat disciplina").[12] Poised earlier in the *Pastoral Care* against *rectitudo* and later against *iustitia*, *pietas* is a feminine principle for Gregory just as it is later for Alcuin.[13] As a royal virtue, then, the *pietas* of the early medieval period moves away from the patriarchal and heroic context of the *Aeneid*. The word that connotes nobility to Vergil must now reflect the Christian humility of the king under God; the word defined for Vergil by the son-father relationship is now defined by the relationship of mother and child to express

[4]   May divine piety cause you to prosper in all goodness.
[5]   Study carefully the models of paternal authority and maternal piety. From the one learn to rule the people with justice, and learn through the other through mercy to have compassion on the wretched.

the obligations of the king to his people. The uses of *pietas* in Alcuin's account of kingship thus mirror the larger problem raised by this series of letters: how are the ethics of Christianity to be reconciled with the practice of power? The problem is one of more than theoretical importance during (and for some time after) the reign of Louis the Pious (Ludovicus Pius). The panegyrical, biographical, and historical works that survive from this reign demonstrate the importance of *pietas* as an ideal of royal governance, but at the same time provide evidence for the connotation of political weakness that attaches itself to the term by identification with a monarch perceived to be excessively lenient, especially to his own son.

The recipient of an instructional tract by Smaragdus of St. Mihiel, who addresses the king as "iustissime ac piissime rex,"[14] Louis is also the subject of a lengthy panegyrical poem by Ermoldus Nigellus, who misses few opportunities to extol the king's "pietas inmensa."[15] The contextually established meaning of the royal epithet is here so broad as to include all Louis's good deeds, but the emphasis falls on his mercy to the conquered: it is principally by moderating the claims of justice that the king fulfills the promise of the poem's frequent Vergilian tags. The *pietas* that Ermoldus celebrates during the life of Louis, Theganus then extols in his honorific biography of the late "piissimus princeps."[16] Theganus's portrayal of Louis as ideal ruler reinforces the panegyrist's conception of the emperor's denominative virtue: "piissimus imperatorum, quod . . . pepercit inimicis suis."[6][17] If the phrase "pepercit inimicis" is more suggestive of the Bible than of Vergil, Theganus is nonetheless quite explicit in contrasting the perfect prince to the "Infelix Theseus" of *Aeneid* 6.618, quoting the lapidary injunction: "Discite iustitiam moniti et non temnere Divos."[7][18] Behind this injunction are the injustice and impiety that define for the ninth century the figure of the tyrant, in contrast to the "piissimus princeps" who is the subject of the life. In Theganus's biography as in Ermoldus's poem, then, Louis the Pious exemplifies the ideals of rule as they had been drawn by Alcuin.

In another biography of Louis, however, the problems latent in Alcuin's account of royal *pietas* begin to surface. In this life by an anonymous admirer of the king, *pietas* is defined throughout as *clementia* ("Imperator vero clementissimus natura . . .").[19] This character of the

[6] the most pious of emperors, because he spared his enemies
[7] Be warned; learn to be just and not to slight the gods!

emperor is affirmed, for example, by his response to the fortuitous deaths of several enemies; rather than exulting in the plague that claimed their lives, he prays for God's blessing upon them, eliciting the admiration of his biographer.[20] Although it might be said that clemency toward enemies already dead is a meager, or at least a convenient, expression of *parcere subiectis,* the tears that Louis sheds on this occasion are consistent with the biographer's sense of the emperor's character, succinctly summarized on the eve of death: "ultra humanum modum natura mitissimus, fortitudine magnanimus, pietate cautissimus."[8][21] In this summation the cardinal virtue complementing *pietas* is not justice but fortitude, which only partially moderates the force of "mitissimus"—the superlative form of the adjective that describes the yoke of piety in Ambrose and links *pius* to *misericors* in Augustine. Exactly what the other superlative "cautissimus" might mean here is not immediately certain, but it does indicate some restriction on the association of the emperor's *pietas* with the meek and mild *mitis* of the Gospels. As if to counteract any connotation of weakness in the word that Alcuin had followed Gregory in identifying with the feminine, the biographer here makes a determined effort to emphasize the strength of the emperor named "the Pious."

In what has been considered a sequel to the anonymous life, the question of royal weakness is more directly raised by Nithard. Book 1 of Nithard's history of Louis's sons narrates the rebellion of Lothair (Lotharius) against his father, concluding with the son's submission to paternal authority at Worms in 839. In asking forgiveness the son appeals to the very qualities taken by the anonymous biographer to define Louis's character. As Nithard recounts the emperor's response: "Idem autem, ut pius ac clemens pater, et delicta postulanti indulsit, et gratiam roganti concessit."[9][22] Though the indulgence is conditional—the son is prohibited from any further rebellion against the father and from any attempt to violate the territory granted to his half-brother Charles— Lothair waits only until his father's death a year later to invade Charles's territory, an event which Nithard relates in book 2. The inference that a prince who is "pius ac clemens" may entail disorder upon his realm is

[8]   By nature gentle beyond human measure, great-hearted in courage, most cautious in piety

[9]   Yet like a pious and lenient father, he both indulged the crimes and granted the request of his son.

certainly justified by the narrative evidence. The very ideal represented by Louis becomes now a cause of political instability.

This is underlined by a contemporary annalist, who reiterates the ablative phrase "solita pietate"[10][23] to establish the constant motive of Louis, which is not always recommended by the consequences. In the chronicler's account of an earlier reconciliation between father and son, for example, the emphasis falls on the king's vulnerability: "ibique filium suum, qui taliter seductus fuerat, ad se venire fecit, ac solita pietate, quae contra se facta fuerant, omnia illi indulsit."[11][24] The danger is manifest in the result, as the struggle between *pius pater* and *impius filius* is repeated in the narrative of events that leads to Worms. In this version of that reconciliation, the emperor is portrayed as "paternae pietatis non immemor" in relation to a son who returns "ad imperatoris clementiam."[12][25] Although the criticism of the emperor here is subdued, the definition of his famous virtue by *clementia* and its illustration in the portrait of an overindulgent father indicate a perception of discrepancy between the historical facts and the royal ideals of the time. The political failures of Ludovicus Pius are traced directly to his cognomen.

Narrowed by association with Louis to the meaning of *clementia* or *misericordia*, *pietas* continues to complement *iustitia* in the royal education tracts written for the benefit of Louis's filial successors by Jonas of Orleans and Sedulius Scotus. Sedulius's *On Christian Rulers*, composed for the grandson of Louis the Pious before he became King Lothair II in 855, is particularly notable because it attempts to restore some of the diminished authority of the word by appeal over the head of Louis to the ancient example of Antoninus Pius. Interweaving biblical and Vergilian quotation, Sedulius insists on the importance of *pietas* as the necessary restraint that prevents just wrath from becoming the irrational fury of revenge. "Nam sicut debellare superbos, ita et parcere subiectis, iustum et misericordem dominum oportet. Unde et Antoninus imperator dicebat malle se unum civem servare, quam mille hostes occidere."[13][26] Sedulius here connects "debellare superbos" to *iustitia*, "parcere subiectis" to

[10] by his customary piety

[11] He had his delinquent son come to him there, and by his usual piety forgave all the deeds done against himself.

[12] not unmindful of paternal piety / to the clemency of the emperor

[13] For it is just as necessary for a just and merciful ruler to spare his subjects as it is to vanquish those who are arrogant. In this regard the emperor Antoninus asserted that he preferred to spare one citizen than to kill a thousand enemies.

pietas, which he follows Jonas in explaining by the synonym *misericordia.* Having remarked upon the exemplary case of Antoninus, Sedulius then discovers the emperor's biblical counterpart in David: "At patientis virtute mansuetudinis sanctus David praeditus, etiam inimicis suis saepe pietatis affectu pepercit."[14][27] Thus calling upon Hebraic as well as Roman history to illustrate the text of Vergil, Sedulius defines *pietas* as a royal virtue whose operation is conveyed by the verb *parcere.* Whereas Vergil's *pietas* can (as in 2.536 and 4.382) include an idea of *iustitia* severe enough to admit revenge, the ideal of governance later built on the Vergilian vocabulary sharply distinguishes the two terms, increasingly so after the reign of Louis the Pious.

The longer-term consequences of Louis's reign are emphasized by the ninth-century bishop Hincmar of Rheims, who (in contrast to Sedulius) finds battering down the proud more to the point of a king's responsibility than sparing the conquered. Drawing his scriptural authority from the gospel story of Christ throwing the money-changers out of the temple, Hincmar urges the monarch to take a hard line against those in violation of divine and human laws, against (that is) "profanam insolentiam atque impietatem."[15][28] Although the bishop duly recites the Isidoran formula,[29] he also discovers in the effects of Louis's reign an argument for revising its emphasis. Most forcefully in his "De regis persona et regio ministerio," Hincmar addresses the problem illustrated by what he regards as Louis's undue lenity to his son. His argument centers on a passage from Coelestinus, which reads in part: "Etenim talis frequenter est pietas, ex qua nascatur impietas."[16][30] Amplifying his exposition of this idea by further quotation from Gregory and Augustine, Hincmar considers the analogous case of David and Absalom. The moral to be drawn from the biblical narrative is expressed as advice to contemporary rulers: "sit pietas, sed non plus quam expediat."[17][31] Retrospectively, this practical limitation corrects the "pietas inmensa" of Ermoldus's poem and goes a long way toward explaining the phrase "pietate cautissimus" in the anonymous biography of Louis the Pious. Prospectively, Hincmar's words anticipate the unflinching critique of

---

[14] Blessed David, endowed with the virtue of patient compassion, often spared even his enemies with tender mercy.
[15] profane arrogance and impiety
[16] For indeed, from such constant piety may impiety be born
[17] Let there be piety, but not more than may be useful.

royal *pietas* to be found a century and a half later in Peter Damian's dissertation on monarchical duty.

The first chapter of this tract is titled "Quod iustitiae rigor regna conservet," and the title accurately reflects the argument. Here Isidore's formula for royal virtue is openly challenged. Seizing upon the notion that *pietas* may beget *impietas* ("Inordinata sane pietas nutrit impietatem"), Damian develops the idea in a sustained medical simile that reasserts Hincmar's warning against paternal indulgence.[32] In his second chapter, Damian extends this hard line on the evidence of the biblical house of Eli, who honored his sons before God. Hincmar had used the same example, quoting commentary on Eli and his sons from Gregory's *Pastoral Care* to the effect that Eli had been misled by *falsa pietas*.[33] This, says Damian in chapter 3, is too often the case: "Multi nempe falsae pietatis errore decepti."[18][34] After citing a dozen more biblical texts, he succinctly expresses his main point in the form of a rhetorical question: "Inordinata nempe pietas principis, quid est aliud, quam confusio plebis?"[19][35] Underlining the argument in the last two chapters, Damian directs attention to its practical implications.[36] Chapter 4 is therefore concerned with the choice of advisers, whose prudence should help the king avoid *frivola pietas;* chapter 5 sums up the duties of the prince with a warning against *noxia pietas*.[37] Isidore's caution against undue severity in the pursuit of justice is then replaced by the countercaution against excessive *pietas;* where Cassiodorus had written, "Pietas . . . custodit imperium," Damian advises the prince "semper iustitiam custodire."[38]

Without recourse to Damian's adjectives, John of Salisbury would also restructure the relationship between *iustitia* and *pietas* by developing the distinction between the king's two bodies present in the letters of Alcuin.[39] In John's account *pietas* refers to the character of the man, *iustitia* to the obligations of the office. Elaborating this view from the evidence of the *Aeneid*, he argues that the *pietas* of a hero must be transformed into the *iustitia* of a king. Yet the author of the *Polycraticus* is not so sanguine as to believe that even this innate quality always translates into responsible governance. On the contrary, he acknowledges that public responsibility may become private opportunity, corrupting the character of the man. The relevant example is from Lucan:

[18] Truly, many are deceived by the error of false piety.
[19] Indeed, what is the excessive piety of a prince if not the disorder of his people?

"exeat aula,/Qui vult esse pius."[20][40] When John turns his attention specifically to the received formula of Isidore, he therefore updates the complementary terms, retaining *iustitia* but finding alternatives to *pietas: misericordia, moderatio, patientia,* and especially *clementia.* Thus in book 4, on the authority of the prince in relation to the law, John writes: "sic clementiam temperat rigor iustitiae."[21][41] By reversing the expected subject and object, and replacing *pietas* with *clementia,* John thus acknowledges what has become obvious by the twelfth century: in contrast to *iustitia, pietas* has acquired associations that have begun to limit its political usefulness.

Cura: The Perspective of the Church

Although the recommended balance between royal *iustitia* and royal *pietas* depends on who is doing the recommending and under what political circumstances, the complementary relationship of the two terms is so often repeated that its aphoristic force long outlives thoughtful discussion of its meaning. Indeed this formula is encountered in discourse by and about royalty as long as Latin is the language of politics.[42] It is no surprise, then, to discover Isidore quoted in the last of the great medieval encyclopedias, the thirteenth-century *Speculum* of Vincent de Beauvais. Here the model of the ideal king is David ("pius ac iustus rex"),[43] and his modern counterpart is the French king, Philip the Fair, tellingly described in the wake of military victory: "ille tamen ut mitis et pius vitam condonavit omnibus. Et si enim servebat in eo contra rebelles severitas, maior etiam vigebat in eodem clementia in subiectos, cuius intentio semper erat, 'Parcere subiectis, et debellare superbos.' "[22][44] In "mitis et pius" the encyclopedia brings together the attributes of Christian ("mitis sum") and Vergilian ("sum pius") hero. The meaning of this compound is then defined by *clementia* in contrast to *severitas,* terms that gloss the quotation from *Aeneid 6,* and situate this idealization well within the political framework defined by earlier adapters of Isidore.

[20] Let him depart from court who desires to be righteous.
[21] and so temper mercy with the strictness of justice
[22] Gentle and pious, he gave life to everyone. And even if he was severe with rebels, yet was he even more merciful toward his subjects; his motto always was "to spare the humbled and to tame in war the proud."

But other passages in the *Speculum* elevate alternative imperial and royal figures who exemplify another dimension of *pietas* that derives from ecclesiastical definition of the word's political meaning. As applied by church leaders to secular rulers, *pietas* had become by the time of Vincent's *Speculum* a common term in developing the analogy between divine and human governance, argumentatively expressed in Salvian's *Governance of God:* "Igitur si stulte atque impie creditur quod curam rerum humanarum pietas divina despiciat, ergo non dispicit: Si autem non despicit, regit."[23][45] The perfect prince is one who shoulders the divine analogy and thus deserves to be celebrated as *piissimus et Christianissimus* or *pius et religiosus*. From the fourth to the thirteenth century, this ideal had been washed by tides of conflict and accommodation, its meaning shaped to ecclesiastical purposes by strong bishops and popes in confrontation with secular power. Assuming the stance of the biblical prophet—Nathan opposite David, Samuel opposite Saul—church leaders had promoted a conception of the *pius princeps* as one who serves the perceived interests of the church, so that *cura subiectorum* tends to become *cura ecclesiae*.

The chief exemplar of this ideal is described in the *Speculum* as the "piissimus et Christianissimus Constantinus." Before the reign of the first Christian emperor, according to the encyclopedic account, the state was the embodiment of *impietas* in contrast to the *pietas* and *sanctitas* of the church. To illustrate, acts of cruelty by a succession of emperors are recited and juxtaposed to the sufferings of early Christian martyrs. Maximinus, for example, is described as *crudelissimus tyrannus,* his deeds summarized in a chapter titled "De impiis edictis Maximini contra Christianos." As the most famous victim of this emperor, St. Catherine exemplifies the Christian character celebrated in a chapter titled "De pietate Christianorum in paganos." With the conversion of Constantine, however, the conception of the ideal prince as one who protects the church is fully realized in the imperial character: "Imperator Maximus Constantinus qui primus pietate morum ornavit Imperium . . ."[24][46] From the perspective of the church, then, *pietas* is a political expression of pastoral *cura,* often conveyed in action by the verb form *curare*.

The only subsequent Roman emperor who approaches the legendary

[23] If it is foolish and irreverent to believe that divine Love disdains the care of human affairs, then He does not disdain them. If He does not disdain them, He rules them.
[24] The Emperor Constantine the Great, who first adorned the imperium with piety of character

status of Constantine is Theodosius I. The model emperor of Augustine's *City of God*, Theodosius is later accorded elaborate praise by Sozomenus, whose panegyric is translated in Cassiodorus's tripartite history. Although *pietas*—"quae est verus ornatus imperii"—is not the only virtue of Theodosius here, it is quite emphatically the most important: "omnemque virtutem habens et praecipue pietatem."[25][47] As Theodosius's claim on the word grows in clerical tradition alongside Constantine's, the determining event is the moral debacle of 390: the repentant Theodosius provides later writers with the classical historical exemplum of imperial submission to the authority of the church. As the instrument of this repentance, the letter of rebuke that Ambrose wrote to Theodosius is a text often cited in the later ecclesiastical explanation of the two powers. Writing as Nathan to David, a role that he had explored in his letters for several years before the massacre of Thessalonika provided the occasion for direct accusation of the emperor, Ambrose bases his letter on the conjunction of religious and political value inherent in his conception of *pietas*.[48] His warning to the emperor is clear: "pietatis studio vincis impetum naturae."[26][49] Elaborating this admonition, the bishop emphatically reminds Theodosius of the virtue that defines the imperial character. "Suadeo, rogo, hortor, admoneo: quia dolori est mihi, ut tu qui pietatis inauditae exemplum eras, qui apicem clementiae tenebas, qui singulos nocentes non patiebaris periclitari, tot periisse non doleas innocentes. Etsi in praeliis felicissime egeris, etsi in aliis quoque laudabilis, tamen apex tuorum operum pietas semper fuit."[27][50] The studied use of the past tenses here confirms the imperial virtue and mourns its violation. Once penitence had been performed, however, Ambrose found opportunity in a subsequent letter to reproclaim the virtue of Theodosius ("pius es, imperator . . .") and to describe his political role in sacerdotal terms: "Opto tamen tibi etiam atque etiam incrementa pietatis, qua nihil Dominus praestantius dedit; ut per tuam clementiam Ecclesia Dei sicut innocentium pace et tranquillitate gratulatur, ita etiam reorum absolutione laetetur. Ignosce maxime his qui non ante

[25] possessing every virtue, but chiefly piety

[26] conquer by love of duty your natural impetuosity

[27] I urge, I ask, I beg, I warn, for my grief is that you, who were a model of unheard-of piety, who had reached the apex of clemency, who would not allow the guilty to be in peril, are not now mourning that so many guiltless have perished. Although you waged battles most successfully, and were praiseworthy also in other respects, the apex of your deeds was always your piety.

peccarunt."[28][51] That *pietas* here means what the church says it means sets a precedent eagerly followed by later church authorities, including Gregory VII and Innocent III, who will assume the role not of Nathan but of the priest-king Melchizedek.

Already in the fifth century the sacerdotal conception of the imperial character comes to be matched by an imperial conception of the papacy that claims *pietas* as an expression of its own authority.[52] By setting ecclesiastical over imperial *pietas* in formulating his doctrine of the two powers, Pope Gelasius I articulates the clerical view that the terrestrial kingdom is the natural servant of the celestial.[53] Inheriting and developing this idea, Gregory the Great encourages the extension of ecclesiastical power in this world, but insists also on the corresponding responsibilities of power, expressed in letter after letter on the subject of pastoral care. For example, in a letter expounding passages from Paul that bear on the question of power, Gregory concerns himself with the necessary balance between *iustitia* and *pietas,* and illustrates his understanding of the idea by reference to the parable of the Good Samaritan, whose healing oil is called *oleum pietatis.*[54] The medical comparison is one that Gregory returns to more than once as he extends the vocabulary of rule to the clerical domain, enlarging his conception of pastoral care until it overlaps the imperial *cura subiectorum.*[55] And when the *cura* of Constantinople fails, Gregory has no qualms about reminding the emperor of his duties: "Piissimus atque a Deo constitutus dominus noster inter ceteras augustorum ponderum curas pro conservanda quoque sacerdotalis caritatis rectitudine studio spiritali invigilat, videlicet pie veraciterque considerans neminem recte posse terrena regere, nisi noverit divina tractare, pacemque reipublicae ex universalis ecclesiae pace pendere."[29][56] Such elaborate formality is not without purpose, for it acknowledges the divinely sanctioned power of the emperor and at the same time his responsibility for peace, including the peace of the church; indeed, imperial care is all that justifies the otherwise increasingly hollow formula of *vestra pietas.* Although

[28] Yet I hope that you will experience even more and more an increase of piety, for God can give nothing more excellent than this, that through your clemency the church of God, as it rejoices in the peace and tranquillity of the innocent, may even so be gladdened by your pardoning of the guilty. Pardon especially those who have not offended before.

[29] Our most pious and divinely ordained lord, among other concerns of reverence and gravity, by the integrity of his sacerdotal love watches over spiritual devotion, piously and truly considering that no one can justly rule on earth, unless he knows how to manage things divine, to esteem the peace of the universal church as well as the peace of the state.

Gregory reserves this formula for letters to the emperor in the East, declining to use it as a term of honor for his Saxon and Merovingian contemporaries, this is a fine point of decorum that his papal successors will necessarily abandon as their Western orientation increasingly tends to make the denizens of Constantinople the real barbarians.

In the papal correspondence over the next two centuries, control of the word is itself an assertion of ecclesiastical power. Responding to the edict against icons of 726, Gregory II abandons the decorous formality of his papal namesake and bluntly accuses Leo the Isaurian of both religious heresy and political arrogance. Prior emperors, Gregory asserts, deserved to be called "pius," but not Leo: "ubi est Christi amator ac pius imperator, qui de more in senatu sedere debet, et eos qui recte loquuntur munerari, eosque qui aliena a veritate blaterant amandare, cum tu, imperator, vacilles ac barbaros imiteris?"[30][57] The appeal here to Roman values lends classical weight to the phrase "pius imperator" and thus widens the rift between the Latin West and the Greek East. Hardly more conciliatory is the strong ninth-century pope, Nicholas I, who extends the accusation of barbarism against the East by ridiculing the reigning emperor's imperfect Latin. How can Michael claim to be emperor of the Romans if he cannot command the language of Rome?[58] The emperor's failure to grasp the language specifically includes a failure to understand the essential imperial virtue. "O imperator . . . non agnoscitis quam a priorum imperatorum pietate in hac re differatis."[31][59] Like Leo, Michael III is cut off from the virtue of prior emperors, and thus from the ideal represented by Constantine.[60] Although Nicholas extends Michael the courtesy of addressing him as "piissimus" and asks that his letter be accepted by "vestra pietas," the general tone of the letter is more like that of Elijah to Ahab than of Nathan to David.[61]

With the growing hostility of the papacy toward Constantinople, *pietas regia* is transferred to the formerly barbarian kings of the West. The attendant obligations of royalty are spelled out in concrete detail in the papal correspondence with the Frankish kings. Having crowned Charles emperor (reportedly in the words "Karolo, piissimo Augusto a Deo coronato, magno et pacifico imperatore, vita et victoria"),[62] Leo III

---

[30] Where is the lover of Christ and pious emperor, who by custom ought to sit in the senate, reward those who speak honestly, and dismiss those who babble away at odds with the truth, while you, emperor, resemble a barbarian staggering this way and that?

[31] O emperor, in this matter, you do not even know how far you are from the piety of previous emperors.

makes a point of addressing the emperor tactfully ("si placet pietati vestrae . . .") in order to remind him of his responsibility to the church: "curam quam erga tranquillitatem sanctae Dei Ecclesiae vestra serenitas semper gerit."[32][63] Designated *iugum pietatis* in a letter written eight years after the coronation,[64] this obligation to protect the church from its enemies eventually grows into an ideology of church-state relations that draws its precedents from the correspondence of Ambrose, Gelasius, and Gregory I.[65] This historical perspective, the justification of present policy by former example, is characteristic of the papal correspondence well before the period of the reform movement and the investiture contro-versy, but it is Gregory VII who assumes the mantle of Ambrose with most alacrity. Endorsing and expanding the claims of his predecessors and supporting his arguments with the authority that descends from the correspondence with Theodosius, Gregory argues that the secular pow-ers have failed the responsibilities of *cura* and that only a monarchical papacy can save the situation. In a letter of January 1075 concerning the corruption of the imperially chosen clergy, for example, Gregory ob-serves that he can find no secular rulers who prefer the honor of God to their own, or justice to lucre. Under such circumstances, he contends, the pope must act to restrain the rage of the impious ("impiorum sevitiam") and protect ecclesiastical rights: "oportet nos, quandoquidem non est princeps qui talia curet, religiosorum tueri vitam."[33][66] By acting in fact, Gregory provokes the conflict with Henry and then defends his action by assuming the role of Samuel opposite Saul. In the process he claims the superior authority of the church in highly inflammatory phrases. Again referring to kings and princes who prefer their own honor and wealth to the justice of God, Gregory draws a sharp distinc-tion between regal and episcopal power: "Illam quidem superbia hu-mana repperit, hanc divina pietas instituit."[34][67] That *pietas*—with its long history as an ideal attribute of monarchy—is here identified exclu-sively with the spiritual power is of the utmost significance. Whereas Gelasius had allowed *pietas* to designate both powers, and the *vestra pietas* formula had long been used in addresses to both papal and impe-rial authorities, Gregory here attempts to remove the word from the

[32] the care which your serenity always bears toward the tranquillity of the holy church of God

[33] It is proper for us, since princes do not care about such things, to watch over the life of the clergy.

[34] Indeed, human pride discovered their domain; divine piety established ours.

discourse of secular power, discourse which now describes the realm of
superbia. The two cities of Augustine are thus equated by Gregory with
church and state.

Yet it is clear even from the writing of Gregory's own supporters that
his usage anticipates the future better than it describes the present. For
participants on both sides of the investiture controversy, *pietas* retains its
power to define the ideal character of the monarch. Thus Manegold of
Lautenbach, who argues forcefully and originally on Gregory's behalf
that kingship is an office and those who hold it can be deposed without
having any right of nature violated, nonetheless asserts a traditional
ideal of kingship when he writes:

> Regalis ergo dignitas et potentia sicut omnes mundanas excellit
> potestates, sic ad eam ministrandam non flagitiosissimus quis-
> que vel turpissimus est constituendus, sed qui sicut loco et
> dignitate, ita nichilominus ceteros sapientia, iusticia superet et
> pietate. Necesse est ergo, qui omnium curam gerere, omnes
> debet gubernare, maiore gratia virtutum super ceteros debeat
> splendere, traditam sibi potestatem summo equitatis libramine
> studeat administrare.[35][68]

Far from portraying a divided society, Manegold emphasizes the universal obligation of the king: "qui omnium curam gerere, omnes debet
gubernare." Asserting this ideal as part of a larger argument to show
that the king forfeits his power when he strays into tyranny, Manegold
supports the position of Gregory from assumptions significantly more
traditional than those of the pope himself. Indeed Manegold shares with
Gregory's opponents the fundamental assumption that the power of
kings and emperors derives as much from God as does the power of the
pope. This point was not overlooked by Henry IV. Writing in 1093 after
Gregory had died, Henry claims divine sanction for his rule in terms very
similar to those Gregory had used to deny it. The king's power, he

---

[35] Therefore, as the royal dignity and authority exceeds all other earthly powers, so
every shameful and wicked man is not to be appointed to its service just because of his
rank and status, but only those others who excell in wisdom, justice, and piety. It is
necessary, therefore, for him who must bear the care of all, who must govern all, to
outshine others in virtue, to take pains to administer his inherited power with maximum
justice.

maintains, is a function of *divina pietas,* and as ruler he obliges himself to fulfill the responsibilities that this entails.[69]

Even so, the authority of the church to determine whether or not a particular king is living up to the ideal of *pietas* as defined by *cura* had been powerfully asserted by the conflict between Henry and Gregory. By the time of Innocent III the role of the pope in making and unmaking emperors was a fact of political life, and Innocent himself has no hesitation in explaining obligations to various kings. He seems never to tire of quoting Matthew 16.18, of expounding the importance of Melchizedek, of retailing his own version of Gelasius's theory, or of reminding secular rulers that priests anoint kings and not kings priests.[70] Innocent is thus the heir of Gregory in asserting the primacy of the ecclesiastical power, which he claims is as superior to the secular as spirit is to matter and as heaven is to earth. When necessary, moreover, he too can batter down such allegedly proud rulers as the heretical Raymond of Toulouse ("Proh dolor: quae cor tuum superbia tumefecit . . ."), who becomes for Innocent the antithesis of the ideal ruler, a modern Nimrod, an embodiment of the irrational against the reason of God and his earthly vicar: "Impie, crudelis, et dire tyranne."[36][71] In contrast, Innocent proclaims the pope-made emperor Otto IV as the ideal protector of the spiritual power in this world: "regalem deposcimus excellentiam quatenus clericos et Ecclesias dilligas et honores, manuteneas et defendas, ut devotus ac pius princeps in omnibus comproberis."[37][72] Although Otto conspicuously fails to live up to such high expectations, Innocent's characterization reveals not only the durability of the *pius princeps* in the ecclesiastical definition of political power, but also the success of the church in conferring the word upon—and withholding it from—secular authority. Yet this success does not last. The short-term triumph of papal over imperial *pietas* has the long-term effect of encouraging the development of a secular political order not based on any such ideal.[73] Gregory's division of the world into the realms of *superbia* and *pietas* not only violates the vastly greater subtlety of Augustine's division, but it also anticipates the later restriction of *pietas* to the sphere of the church and much later the devolution of the word's significance to "churchliness." Indeed, the ecclesiastical exposition of *pietas* by reference to the obligations of *cura*

[36] O impious, cruel, and horrible tyrant

[37] We ask your royal eminence to esteem the clergy and the church, to maintain and defend its honors, so that you will be confirmed as a devout and pious prince in all things.

already suffers from declining credibility by the end of the thirteenth century, as the political vocabulary of Aristotle begins to displace the terms sanctioned by Vergil and Augustine.

Pax: The Perspective of the State

In his correspondence with Otto IV, Innocent describes the ideal ruler as one devoted to "vera pax et firma concordia inter Ecclesiam et imperium."[38][74] By thus characterizing the *pius princeps* with reference to *pax,* Innocent expresses an ideal of governance traditionally exemplified by Antoninus Pius. As early as the *Augustan History* Antoninus is compared to Numa, whose distinguishing moral characteristic in Plutarch's life is εὐσέβεια: "qui rite comparetur Numae, cuius felicitatem pietatemque et securitatem caerimoniasque semper obtinuit."[39][75] As the successor and antitype to Romulus, Numa evokes the aura of a peaceful reign, here serving to enhance the reputation of Antoninus, who will in turn do the same for later emperors and kings. Indeed, the peace and tranquillity of his reign is one of the explanations commonly given for his cognomen: "rempublicam gubernavit adeo tranquille et sancte, ut merito Pius et pater patriae nominatus sit."[40][76] This frequently quoted judgment from the universal history of Orosius is borrowed by John of Salisbury to proclaim Antoninus as the model ruler, and the same phrase emerges modified only slightly by Hugh of Fleury for inclusion in the thirteenth-century *Speculum:* "ita tranquillus erat, ut merito Pius appellatus sit."[41][77] This conception of the ideal monarch proves particularly appealing to those who favor imperial over papal authority, from Sedulius Scotus in the ninth century to William of Ockham in the fourteenth.[78]

Before the time of Ockham perhaps no work illustrates this perspective better than an anonymous polemic on the necessity of preserving the unity of the church, written between 1090 and 1093 against the claims of the papacy.[79] Arguing that the pope has no authority to depose kings,

[38] genuine peace and steadfast concord between church and state

[39] He is justly compared to Numa, whose good fortune and piety and tranquillity and religious rites he ever maintained.

[40] He governed the state so peacefully and conscientiously that he deserved to be called Pious and named father of his country.

[41] Because he was peaceful, he deserved to be called Pious.

the author reconsiders the texts, beginning with Ambrose and Gelasius, that had provided support for the Hildebrand position. He accuses the papacy of misrepresenting the precedents, which he argues reveal no such rights as those claimed. The secular power is divinely sanctioned, therefore legitimate and independent of the spiritual power. The real threat to peace, then, is the papacy itself, which has attempted to usurp the power of the secular authority. Because "Christus pax est," the disturbance caused by Gregory represents a violation of "sacramentum pietatis." With respect to the excommunication of Henry IV, the author is quite specific: "videtur non esse officium pietatis nec signum concordiae et unitatis."[42][80] The pope therefore bears responsibility for the resultant disturbances that have set people against people, son against father, father against son, and brother against brother.[81] For such crimes Gregory is brought under the indictment of Cyprian, who is quoted to the effect that being against peace means being against Christ and his church. Even more to the point, the author brings the pope under the indictment of Scripture, including 1 Timothy 2.2–3, twice quoted to make it quite clear that the real threat to Christendom is the Hildebrand party, "qui . . . faciant praelia, seditiones et homicidia."[43][82] By citing not only patristic but also scriptural authority against the alleged usurpations of the papacy, the author forecasts the manner of political argument in the fourteenth century.

The major political writers of this period differ in various ways, and these differences have often been studied, but the desire for peace is everywhere expressed. Dante speaks for his age when he writes: "inter alia bona hominis potissimum sit in pace vivere."[44][83] Marsilius of Padua seconds this belief in the *Defender of Peace,* which begins with an epigraph from Cassiodorus on civil tranquillity, followed in the first paragraph by a sequence of biblical passages on the theme of peace. Two of these same passages are repeated by William of Ockham to support his conception of the state, and John Wycliffe not only devotes whole sermons to the true meaning of peace, but also argues in his tract on papal power that the greatest threat to the peace of the world comes from the church.[84] This view is widely shared among writers in search of alternatives to the papacy as the institutional focus of the political order,

[42] This does not appear to be an action of piety nor a sign of concord and unity.
[43] which is the cause of battles, rebellions, and murders
[44] Among other human blessings the greatest is to live in peace.

especially so in France where the conflict between Philip the Fair and Boniface VIII had greatly strengthened the state at the expense of the church. Responsive to this situation, Jean of Paris and Pierre Dubois lend the theme of peace a flavor that is in some passages national as well as secular. For all the differences that separate Dante from Marsilius, Ockham from Wycliffe, Jean from Dubois, they all express profound concern for peace combined with variable degrees of antipapalism. Considered collectively, moreover, they share a political vocabulary in transition from Vergil and Augustine to the Latin Aristotle. As if accepting Gregory's challenge, proponents of secular power simply relinquish *pietas* to the popes. Consigned with increasing frequency to the exclusive domain of the spiritual power, such recurrent phrases as *piae causae, pii usus,* and *opera pietatis et misericordiae* are taken to delimit ecclesiastical authority, in contrast to secular authority defined by Aristotelian *iustitia* and *prudentia.*

Although *pietas* is still visible in the late medieval lexicon of political discourse, its inherited affinity with *pax* and *tranquillitas* has now the ring of unreality or anachronism. Witness this passage from part 2 of Dante's discourse on monarchy, which characteristically points back to Rome.

> Quod autem Romanus populus bonum praefatum intenderit, subiciendo sibi Orbem terrarum, gesta sua declarant. In quibus, omni cupiditate submota, quae rei publicae semper adversa est, et universali pace cum libertate dilecta, populus ille sanctus, pius et gloriosus, propria commoda neglexisse videtur, ut publica pro salute humani generis procuraret. Unde recte illud scriptum est: Romanum Imperium de fonte nascitur pietatis.[45][85]

For all its eloquence, this passage has few parallels in the political writing of the fourteenth century, which shows less interest in propounding historical analogies than in freeing itself from the heavy hand of their traditional implications.[86] When Dante himself dissects the various precedents commonly advanced in support of papal supremacy, he reserves

---

[45] That the Roman people did pursue this good when they made the whole earth subject to them is proved by their deeds, for putting aside all greed as always incompatible with the commonwealth, and seeking universal peace with liberty, this holy, pious, and glorious people seemed to neglect its own interests in order to promote the public interest for the salvation of mankind. Hence it is truly said: "The Roman Empire springs from the fountain of piety."

his strongest animus for the decretalists ("Hi sunt impietatis filii"), likened to hypocrites whose drapery of traditions only disguises their true nature. In the very next paragraph Dante describes himself, by contrast, as *pius filius* ("pius in Christum, pius in Ecclesiam . . ."), a character consistent with the reverence he maintains for the office, as distinct from the person, of supreme pontiff.[87]

This reverence is not shared by Marsilius of Padua. Although he acknowledges that religion is one of the causes of civil peace when it promotes "opera pietatis et misericordiae," Marsilius finds the papacy guilty of abusing its claim on these virtues. "Hiis autem sic sumptis sub quadam pietatis et misericordiae specie (prima quidem, ut ex charitate sollicitari et curare de omnibus videantur, secunda vero, ut omnibus misereri posse ac velle credantur), privilegiis et concessionibus principum fulti, praecipue imperiali sede vacante, titulum hunc consequenter extenderunt episcopi Romanorum."[46][88] Acknowledging the clerical definition of *pietas* by reference to *cura*, Marsilius declares such words to be a mere front for the pursuit of power. Later repeating the accusation that the popes have acted "sub specie pietatis" or "sub ficta specie pietatis ac misericordiae," Marsilius attaches the word to the idea of religious fraud, now said to be customary in the Vatican: "more solito curam plebis et pietatem praetendens."[47][89] By identifying the popes with the false doctors of 2 Timothy 3.1–5, who are among other things "sine pace," Marsilius lays the foundation for the charge of papal rebellion and usurpation. "Sed proh dolor, quod propter hanc speciem pietatis in tantum homines seduxerunt ut iam violenta freti potentia, quam sub specie pietatis obtinuerunt gratis in parte, plurimum vero latenter usurpaverunt, et nunc patenter atque violenter usurpant, devitari non possunt, violentiam Christi fidelibus inferentes."[48][90] Thus are the popes identified, finally, with heresy and sedition.[91]

---

[46] Having thus assumed these powers under a guise of piety and mercy (piety, that they might seem to have care and solicitude for all men by the motivation of charity; mercy, that they might be thought to have the power and the desire to take pity upon all men), the Roman bishops, supported by the privileges and grants of rulers, and especially when the imperial seat was vacant, then extended this title.

[47] pretending as usual to be pious and solicitous for the people's welfare

[48] But, sad to say, they now wield violent power, obtained partly through gift, because their specious godliness has enabled them to deceive so many men, but mainly seized through usurpations, at first hidden, but now flagrant and violent; and hence the Christian believers, made the objects of such men's violence cannot turn away from them.

Condemning the papacy as the great disturber of the peace, the antipapal writers of the fourteenth century pin their hopes for restored tranquillity on different secular rulers. Although the names vary with time and place, there are marked similarities in the descriptions of this ideal figure, who is now less often characterized as the *pius princeps*. The *pietas* of Isidore's formula is shouldered out by its companion *iustitia,* greatly enhanced in its importance by the rediscovered texts of Aristotle. Book 5 of the *Ethics* provides fourteenth-century writers with a mine of citations to this effect, including: "In iustitia autem simul omnis virtus est. . . . Haec quidem igitur iustitia, non pars virtutis, sed tota virtus est."[49][92] Aquinas had drawn from such passages the inference that justice is the main concern of the prince ("enim princeps institutus est ut custodiat iustitiam"), and this view is firmly asserted in the fourteenth century.[93] With Aristotle and Aquinas behind him, Jean of Paris (for example) characterizes the ideal prince as the guardian of justice.[94] Developing this conception of the ruler with reference to a specific jurisdictional dispute between church and state, Jean draws a revealing distinction between the domains of spiritual and secular power. At issue is legal right to unclaimed legacies, and he argues that this is a problem pertaining more to the prince than to the pope: "magis videtur pertinere ad iustas causas quam ad pias causas."[50][95] Although the issue is a narrow one, the definition of distinct spheres of power—the temporal designated by *iustitia,* the spiritual by *pietas*—has general significance and wide application. For Jean himself the significance of this distinction is spelled out in a later account of temporal power: "Et ideo sine rectore Christo est vera et perfecta iustitia que ad regnum requiritur cum regnum ordinetur ad vivere secundum virtutem moralem acquisitam cui accidit quod perficiatur per ulteriores virtutes quascumque."[51][96] The accumulation of bold assumptions here—that the essential requirement of monarchy is justice, that justice is an acquired virtue independent of other moral assets, that morality can be independent of theology— effectively dismisses the traditional formula, as *iustitia* rises with the

[49] Justice alone contains all virtue. Thus justice in this sense is not part of virtue, but is coextensive with virtue.

[50] The problem seems to pertain more to issues of justice than to those of piety.

[51] Therefore, the true and perfect justice a kingship requires exists without the reign of Christ, since kingship is ordered to the life of acquired virtue, to which it is accidental that it be perfected by any other virtue whatsoever.

ascendance of Aristotle while *pietas* falls into the category of "ulteriores virtutes."

That Jean develops his arguments by frequent reference to Augustine renders them all the more forceful; similarly, Pierre Dubois supports his quotations from Aristotle with frequent references to Scripture. Dubois's plan for a united and peaceful Europe is grounded on two quotations, one from the Bible ("Quia omne regnum in se divisum, desolabitur") and the other from Aristotle ("Omnis virtus unita fortior est seipsa dispersa et divisa").[97] The ideal ruler to oversee a united Christendom is described, however, not as *pius princeps,* but as *prudentissimus princeps.*[98] Although this is a formula of address dating at least as far back as the age of Innocent III, the notion of *prudentia* as a virtue defining kingship is strongly promoted by the Latin versions of Aristotle. Book 3 of the *Politics* claims *prudentia* as the characteristic virtue of the ruler, the quality necessary if he is to function as the guardian of justice. As Marsilius expresses the idea in his character of the perfect prince as *defensor pacis:* "Sunt autem futuri principantis perfecti habitus intrinseci duo, separationem non recipientes in esse, videlicet prudentia et moralis virtus, maxime iustitia."[52][99] In Dubois, the authority of this prudent prince is extended over the pious work so long directed by the papacy: "pio proposito subsidii Terre Sancte."[53][100] The right of *prudentia* over *pietas* is thus affirmed in Dubois's ideal conception of a peaceful—and secular—European polity.

A yet more powerful, if more gradual case is made against the authority of *pietas* by William of Ockham. In an early work opposing the temporal power of the papacy, Ockham advances a narrow definition of *pietas:* "Alia est sollicitudo compassivae pietatis, qua quis de relevanda proximi indigentia est sollicitus, sicut sunt illi, qui faciunt eleemosynas et tenent hospitalitatem."[54][101] As this identification of *pietas* with almsgiving plays its part in Ockham's quarrel with John XXII, the effect is not only to confine the term but to confine the power of the pope as well. In his later attack on Benedict XII, Ockham invokes this meaning of the word to explain the pope's eighth error ("Iste error omnem utilitatem

---

[52] The man who is to be a perfect ruler should have two intrinsic habits which cannot exist separately, namely, prudence and moral virtue, especially justice.

[53] the pious undertaking for the benefit of the Holy Land

[54] Another care of compassionate piety is that which is anxious to relieve the want of one's neighbor; such are those who give alms and preserve hospitality.

spiritualem includit"): "non est aliud quam homines ab operibus misericordiae et pietatis retrahere."[55][102] The traditional association between *pietas* and *misericordia* is here attached to the domain of the
spiritual power, which in the person of the pope is perceived to have
neglected its responsibility to the poor. The understanding of the word
to designate a specific responsibility of the church is also brought to bear
on Ockham's argument that the English clergy are obliged to use the
wealth of their churches to aid Edward III even over Benedict's express
objections. At issue in this context is whether ecclesiastical resources are
better diverted to the king or used for the very charitable purposes that
Ockham had already accused the pope of neglecting. In effect, the issue
is between two dimensions of *pietas,* which Ockham underlines by quoting Cicero's definition of the word. Effectively setting this classical definition against its evolved meaning, Ockham leaves the papacy in a narrow
bind between obligation to the poor and allegiance to the secular state.

> magis pium est defendere patriam quam pascere pauperes: tum
> quia, secundum Tullium in sua Rhetorica, per pietatem "patriae
> benevolum officium et diligens tribuitur cultus," et per consequens
> pietas directe ad patriam se extendit; tum quia bonum commune
> est "melius et divinius" quam bonum unius, primo Ethicorum; ex
> quo infertur quod bonum totius patriae est melius et divinius quam
> bonum pauperum illius patriae; ex quo concluditur quod magis
> pium est subvenire toti patriae quam pauperibus patriae. Constat
> autem quod clerici de bonis ecclesiae subvenire tenentur pau-
> peribus; ergo multo magis, cum facultates laicorum non suppe-
> tunt, regi debent pro defensione patriae et publicorum iurium
> subvenire.[56][103]

[55] This is nothing other than to draw men back from acts of mercy and piety.

[56] It is more pious to defend one's native land than to feed the poor: thus, according
to Cicero in his Rhetoric by piety is meant "the feeling which renders kind offices and
loving service to one's country," and as a result piety is extended to the fatherland; then,
because the common good is better and more divine than the good of one, according to
the first book of the Ethics, it may be inferred that the good of the whole country is better
and more divine than the good of the poor of that country, and from this it may be
concluded that it is more pious to relieve that whole country than to relieve just its poor. It
is agreed, moreover, that clerics are bound to use the goods of the church for the relief of
the poor; it follows, then, how much more—when lay resources are lacking—should they
come to the aid of the king in defense of the country and the laws of the state.

The only choice here is between *pietas* that would restrict the church to what Ockham calls "utilitas spiritualis," and *pietas* that would lead directly to subordination of the church to secular power.

Still later in his *Dialogus* on papal power, Ockham himself chooses for the church the first of these alternatives. In the process of doing so, however, he effectively withdraws the term *pietas* from discussion of both secular and ecclesiastical power. Developed by analogy to his secular counterpart, the ideal character of the ecclesiastical ruler is defined by Aristotelian *prudentia* and biblical *sapientia*.[104] Although the sphere of the church remains distinct from that of the king, the spiritual ruler is held to the same wisdom as the secular ruler and is likewise responsible for public tranquillity. In effect, there is no distinct term to sanction the political authority of the church. Whereas Jean of Paris delineates the separate domains of *iustitia* and *pietas,* and Pierre Dubois asserts the right of *prudentia* over *pietas,* Ockham shoves the separate domain of *pietas* clear off the political map. When, finally, the student of the *Dialogus* attempts to bring *pietas* back into the discussion, he receives what amounts to a reprimand: "pietas autem utilitatem includit."[57][105] Political discussion, the master indicates to the student, is not a matter of the pious, but of the just and the prudent, the useful and the necessary.

Although the vocabulary of the Latin Aristotle does not suddenly or completely evict *pietas* from the political lexicon of the fourteenth century, the example of Ockham is indicative of a significant shift in emphasis. This reorientation of the vocabulary that diminishes the importance of *pietas* relative to *iustitia* and *prudentia,* is evident even where Vergil and Augustine remain political authorities. Dante, whose poetic allegiance to Vergil gives him a bias in the matter that is especially evident in the *Commedia*,[106] creates an image of the universal monarch that deemphasizes *pietas* in favor of *iustitia:* "Iustitia potissima est in mundo, quando volentissimo et potentissimo subiecto inest: huiusmodi solus Monarcha est; ergo soli Monarchae insistens iustitia in mundo potissima est."[58][107] Similarly Wycliffe, who follows Bernard and Bede and ultimately Augustine in celebrating David as the ideal ruler by virtue of his *pietas, humilitas,* and *mititas,* describes the Old Testament king as "pru-

[57] Piety, moreover, obstructs usefulness.

[58] Justice is most powerful in the world when it resides in the most willing and able being; the only thing being of this nature is the monarch. Therefore, justice is the most powerful in the world when it resides solely in the monarch.

dentissimus rex."[108] Conceded to the ecclesiastical power as a measure of political weakness rather than strength, *pietas* declines during the late Middle Ages in favor of Aristotelian *iustitia* and *prudentia*, and in the early Renaissance this decline will appear relative to translations and derivatives of Senecan *clementia* as well.

Clementia: From the Middle Ages to the Renaissance

Although writers in the different European vernaculars respond in different ways to the task of translating *pietas*, by the fourteenth century the essential meaning of the word to be rendered in the modern languages is *clementia*. From the late imperial period onward, *clementia* is the most common synonym for *pietas* in the discourse of rule.[109] The question of how Antoninus Pius earned his cognomen occasions comment not only on the tranquillity of his reign, but also on his clemency. Thus Marcus Aurelius writes to his wife, Antoninus's daughter: "non enim quicquam est, quod imperatorem Romanum melius commendet gentibus quam clementia. haec Caesarem deum fecit, haec Augustum consecravit, haec patrem tuum specialiter Pii nomine ornavit."[59][110] These words are quoted to good effect in the *Augustan History* and thereafter the name Antoninus Pius becomes a byward for clemency.[111] Although the identification of Antoninus's essential virtue with the *clementia Caesaris* effectively erases the republican sense of the word, it conforms easily to the celebration of the imperial system.[112] Witness the panegyrist Claudian, who imagines Theodosius to address his son Honorius in words frequently quoted throughout the Middle Ages: "Sis pius in primis; nam cum vincamur in omni / munere, sola deos aequat clementia nobis."[60][113] Yet by the time these words are cited in John of Salisbury's *Polycraticus*, an important connotative distinction between the two terms has emerged: whereas *clementia* suggests mercy that proceeds from strength, *pietas* has come to convey a sense of vulnerability, of mercy that proceeds

[59] For there is nothing which endears a Roman emperor to mankind as much as the quality of mercy. This quality caused Caesar to be deified and made Augustus a god, and it was this characteristic, more than any other, that gained your father his honourable name of Pius.

[60] Above all fail not in loving-kindness; for though we be surpassed in every virtue yet mercy alone makes us equal with the gods.

from weakness or excessive indulgence. The resultant preference for *clementia* and its vernacular derivatives is advanced in the early Renaissance by appeal to Seneca, whose essay on clemency is a favored text, especially of English writers from Gower in the fourteenth to Elyot in the sixteenth century.

Writing in French early in his career, Gower calls attention to a Senecan aphorism—"Nullum tamen clementia ex omnibus magis quam regem aut principem decet"[61][114]—which he translates: "Senec le dist q'a Roialté/Plus q'a nul autre affiert pité."[115] Taking *pité* to translate Senecan *clementia*, Gower then uses the same word to render *pietas* in developing the authority of Constantine and Cassiodorus on the subject of royal governance. In effect, Gower would have the word signify both *pitié* and *piété* in the manner of Italian *pietà*. Yet a few lines later the comprehensive *pité* is supplanted by the more confined *mercy*, which is the word now summoned as the complement to *justice*. Gower proceeds, moreover, to describe the ideal king as "joust et debonnere," acknowledging *débonnaireté* as the prevailing word for translating *pietas* into early modern French.[116] Whereas *iustitia* survives the transition to the vernacular intact, Gower's French shows that the vernacular derivative of *pietas*—in this case *pité*—has strong competition for a place in the European vocabulary of rule.

This may be further illustrated from book 7 of *Confessio Amantis,* an English poem with Latin chapter titles and glosses. Largely devoted to the "governaunce of Kinges," book 7 includes a section on "Iustitia" (9) and a sequel on "Pietas" (10). Near the conclusion of chapter 10, Gower offers a summary that starkly juxtaposes the *pietas* of Cassiodorus with that of Isidore.

> And every governaunce is due
> To pite, thus I may argue,
> That pite is the foundement
> Of every kinges regiment.
> If it be meddled with justice
> They two remeven alle vice
> And ben of vertue most vailable
> To make a kinges regne stable.[117]

[61] Yet of all men none is better graced by mercy than a king or a prince.

The marginal Latin glosses make clear the intended equivalence of Latin *pietas* and English *pite,* which is here asked to carry the considerable burden of meanings that attend the Latin word in medieval political discourse. The conception of *pite* as the foundation of government reflects the *Variae* of Cassiodorus ("Pietas siquidem principum totum custodit imperium"), while the notion of *pite* as the complement of *justice* suggests the formula of Isidore. On the one hand, *pite* is the unique "foundement" of government; on the other, it is a dependent of justice.

   Gower elaborates the political implications of the word by theological analogy, taking *pite* in the manner of medieval exegetes to express the incarnation:

> It is the vertue of pite,
> Through which the highe mageste
> Was stered, whan his sone alight
> And in pite the world to right
> Toke of the maide fleshe and blood.
>   (190)

Developing the significance of the divine analogy for royal education, Gower retreats from the absolute value here attached to the word by subsequently joining the second to the first person of the trinity, "pite" to "justice," in defining the office of the king. "Justice, which doth equite,/Is dredful, for he no man spareth./But in the lond, where pite fareth,/The king may never faile of love"(191). Yet this affirmation of Isidore is itself later qualified in terms that suggest Peter Damian's critique of the formula.

> But pite how so that it wende
> Maketh that god is merciable,
> If there be cause resonable,
> Why that a king shall be pitous.
> But elles if he be doubtous
> To fleen in cause of rightwisnesse,
> It may be said no pitousnesse,
> But it is pusillamite . . .
>   (210)

In this portrayal of the king as image of both divine attributes, *pite* becomes a negotiable virtue whose significance is a function of circumstance. In the lines immediately following these, Gower even warns of the dangers "if pite mesure excede," dangers considered three centuries earlier in Damian's attack on *inordinata pietas*.

The state of the English political vocabulary is thus shown to be quite unsettled in Gower, and not much has changed by the time of Thomas Hoccleve's *Regement of Princes*. This early fifteenth-century poem also considers the traditional royal virtues, which are designated in Latin subtitles. A total of 45 stanzas is devoted (albeit with some digressions) to the topic "De pietate," which Hoccleve defines as "good wille of debonair hert." This section is followed by another twenty stanzas under the rubric "De misericordia," which Hoccleve translates as "mercy." The very structure of the work suggests both affinity and difference between the two English words *pite* (often *pitee* in Hoccleve's spelling) and *mercy*, which (he observes) "ben negheboures so nygh."[118] Between these two neighbors, Hoccleve grants priority to *pite*, which as the source of mercy retains its theological dimension, traceable to the patristic *pietatis auctor:* "But our lord god, of pite the auctour" (433). As in Gower the development of the theological analogy complicates the political use of the word, for divine ideas are not easily applied to earthly situations.

> Pitee availith mochil, but naght there;
> for bet it is to sle the mordreman,
> Than suffre hym regne, for he hath no fere
> His hand to use forth as he by-gan;
> And in my conceit, feele wel I can,
> That of suche pitee, is the abstinence
> Of gretter pite, for the consequence.
>
> (453)

Attempting to solve the problem of the absolute versus the relative, the poet creates the additional category of "gretter pite," but this only serves to emphasize the difficulty. Whereas the Latin *pietas* had managed to hold together religious and political ideas, the tension between these two aspects of the word becomes very evident in English translation.

As Gower and Hoccleve explore the possibilities of accommodating Christian ideals to the reality of rule and at the same time the Latin vocabulary to English, their invocation of pietas in the form of *pite* is attended by qualification and uncertainty that portends the ultimate division into *pity* and *piety*. In the sixteenth century Sir Thomas Elyot offers a more resolute attempt to stabilize the political vocabulary in the *Boke Named the Governour*. This is well indicated by the title of chapter 7 in book 2: "That a governour ought to be merciful, and the diversity of mercy and vain pity." Introducing this chapter Elyot sets up the familiar terms of opposition: "The vice called cruelty, which is contrary to mercy, is by good reason most odious of all other vices."[119] Whereas the medieval Latin writers repeatedly affirm the opposition of *crudelitas* to *pietas*, in translation Elyot opts for the term *mercy*, which he takes to be the appropriate translation—not, as in Hoccleve, of *misericordia*—but of *clementia*. He therefore offers this definition: "And if ye ask me what mercy is, it is a temperance of the mind of him that hath power to be avenged, and it is called in Latin *clementia*, and is always joined with reason" (119). Here translating a passage from Seneca ("Clementia est temperantia animi in potestate ulciscendi"), Elyot distinguishes *mercy* from *pity* as Seneca had distinguished *clementia* from *misericordia*. "For he that for every little occasion is moved with compassion, and beholding a man punished condignly for his offence lamenteth or waileth, is called piteous, which is a sickness of the mind, wherewith at this day the more part of men be diseased. And yet is the sickness much worse by adding to one word, calling it vain pity" (119). Adding the adjective *vain* to *pity* as Damian had added the adjective *frivola* to *pietas*, Elyot continues with an attack on contemporary vices—all placed at the door of "vain pity." "And this may well be called vain pity; wherein is contained neither justice nor yet commendable charity, but rather thereby ensueth negligence, contempt, disobedience, and finally all mischief and incurable misery" (120). In effect, Elyot uses the Senecan distinction to express fears summed up in Damian's rhetorical question: "Inordinata nempe pietas principis, quid est aliud, quam confusio plebis?" Elyot's *pity* captures in English the dominant meaning and the negative connotation of Latin *pietas* as it had developed in later medieval discourse of governance. His chosen alternative is *mercy*, which he would have translate into English the authority of Seneca's *clementia*.

Eliot's *Governour* was published in 1531 and from a European perspective immediately overshadowed by posthumous publication in the next year of Machiavelli's radical approach to many of the same problems. In the Italian of *The Prince*, the derivative *pietà* comprehends the meanings that Gower and Hoccleve had attempted to combine in the form *pite*, but its dominant sense is the meaning indicated by Elyot's *pity*, with some differences as well as similarities in connotation. Although he most frequently invokes *pietà* in opposition to *crudeltà*, Machiavelli summons this conventional opposition only to undermine it. In chapter 17, which bears a Latin title beginning "De crudelitate et pietate . . . ," Machiavelli acknowledges the traditional vocabulary by admitting that every prince would rather be thought "pietoso" than "crudele."[120] He nevertheless goes on to discuss the limits of *pietà* in a way that suggests Peter Damian more than it does Vergil, referring to "quali, per troppa pietà, lasciono seguire e' disordini, di che ne nasca occisioni o rapine" (17).[62] For historical example, Machiavelli turns to the Second Punic War, attributing the rebellion against Scipio in Spain to "troppa sua pietà" (54). The key word here is "troppa": there is room in politics for *pietà*, Machiavelli implies, provided it is not excessive. But the further implication is that there is room for *crudeltà* on the same condition. Thus when Machiavelli later takes up the familiar question of what qualities make a good prince, he actually collapses the traditional opposition of pietas to cruelty in his portrait of Ferdinand of Aragon. Ferdinand's "pietosa crudeltà" turns the medieval tradition of contrasting king and tyrant into a distinction without meaning, now replaced by a distinction between success and failure.[121]

Taking up the same traditional pair of terms in the *Discourses*, Machiavelli first offers the equations inherited from the Latin between *pietas* and success, *crudelitas* and failure: "Donde e' pare che e' sia meglio, a governare una moltitudine, essere umano che superbo, pietoso che crudele."[63][122] Whatever the precise force of "meglio" here, the conclusion conforms at least accidentally to moral order. But this comforting view is subverted in the contrast between Scipio and Hannibal that follows. Again taking Scipio as his exemplar of *pietà* opposite the *crudeltà* of Hannibal, Machiavelli reveals these two tactics to have an equal chance of success. No longer an ideal, but merely a method, *pietà* is judged according to its effectiveness and found to be neither more nor less useful than *crudeltà*. In sum: "modi tutti contrari"—"medesimo

[62] those who, from excess of tenderness, allow disorders to arise, from whence spring bloodshed and rapine

[63] Whence it would seem that a multitude is more easily governed by humanity and gentleness than by haughtiness and cruelty.

effetto" (3.21).[64] In the ensuing discussion, then, Machiavelli returns to the issue raised by chapter 17 of *The Prince,* correlating *pietà* in the ruler with *amore* in his subjects, *crudeltà* with *timore.* Once expressed in this way, the balance tilts decidedly away from *pietà.* "il più delle volte è più seguito e più ubbidito chi si fa temere che chi si fa amare" (3.21).[65]

Not content to abolish the moral distinction conveyed by the inherited Latin vocabulary, Machiavelli also deliberately denies the distinction drawn by his predecessors between *vera pietas* and *species pietatis.* Consider section 1.53–54 from the *Discourses,* which elaborates on a passage in book 5 (5.25.2–3) of Livy's history concerning conflict between plebians and patricians.[123] The problem raised by this passage for Machiavelli is the same as that later illustrated in the contrast turned comparison between Scipio and Hannibal: "governare una moltitudine." Although Livy does not invoke *pietas,* the passage nevertheless suggests to Machiavelli the situation described in Vergil's first simile, where the *pietas* of the leader prevails over the *furor* of the mob. As Machiavelli interprets this situation, the instructive point is the tendency of the mob to shrink at the sight of age, honor, dignity. In the attendant commentary, then, the emphasis falls not on virtue, but rather on the appearance of virtue. In the process Vergilian *pietas* is translated not as *pietà,* but rather as *reverenza* (1.54): "Per tanto, quello che é preposto a uno esercito, o quello che si trova in una città, dove nascesse tumulto debba rappresentarsi in su quello con maggiore grazia e più onorevolmente che può, mettendosi intorno le insegne di quello grado che tiene, per farsi più riverendo" (1.54).[66][124] The emphasis on the idea of "rappresentarsi," even on attire, is then repeated in a parallel example cited from Florentine history, leading to this conclusion: "Conchiudo, adunque, come e' non è il più fermo né il più necessario rimedio a frenare una moltitudine concitata, che la presenza d'uno uomo che per presenzia paia e sia riverendo" (1.54).[67] The reiterated "presenzia" effectively eliminates any concern for the actual character of the ruler provided he can make

[64] completely contrary methods, same effect

[65] Generally he who makes himself feared will be more readily followed and obeyed than he who makes himself beloved.

[66] Therefore whoever is at the head of an army, or whoever happens to be a magistrate in a city where sedition has broken out, should present himself before the multitude with all possible grace and dignity, and attired with all the insignia of his rank, so as to inspire the more respect.

[67] I conclude, then, that there is no better or safer way of appeasing an excited mob than with the presence of some highly respected man of imposing appearance.

the right impression on the populace. And the phrase that designates the right impression—"farsi . . . riverendo"—does not include *pietà*. Although respect for superiors is one dimension of the Latin *pietas,* that implication is attracted in Machiavelli's Italian to *reverenza,* leaving *pietà* to its uneasy marriage of convenience with *crudeltà.*

To defend the traditional ideas against this attack, the anti-Machiavels of the later sixteenth century are at the considerable disadvantage of having to designate the old ideas with new words. Whereas Machiavelli takes full advantage of the negative political connotations that have accrued to the Latin *pietas* by using the Italian derivative *pietà,* his respondents prefer to invoke derivatives from the more assured connotations of *clementia.* This is abundantly evident in Innocent Gentillet's anti-Machiavel polemic of 1576. In full flight backward to Edenic pre-Machiavellian days, Gentillet attempts to recover the idealizing vocabulary of the Latin *specula.* Witness the initial proclamation of idealistic purpose in the preface.

> les Princes qui se sont gouvernez par douceur et clemence conjointe à justice, et qui ont usé de moderation et debonnaireté envers leurs sujets, ont tousjours grandement prosperé, et longuement regné. Mais au contraire, les Princes cruels, iniques, perfides, et oppresseurs de leurs sujets, sont incontinent tombez eux et leur estat en peril, ou en totale ruine, et n'ont gueres long temps regné, et le plus souvent ont finy leurs jours par mort sanglante et violente.[68][125]

Of the words adduced to reassert the correlation between political morality and political success, *clemence* becomes the most important, growing in significance over the course of the tract to define the essential character of Gentillet's prince. A second word to note is *débonnaireté,* already observed in the anglicized French of Gower and commonly associated with *clemence.*[126] Calling upon *moderation* here as well, Gentillet is attempting to find some suitable combination of words to complement

[68] Princes who have governed themselves agreeably, with clemency joined to justice, and who have shown moderation and goodness toward their subjects, have always greatly prospered and ruled long. But on the other hand, cruel, evil, perfidious princes, oppressors of their subjects, have by such excess brought themselves and their power in peril or to complete ruin, have hardly ruled long, and have most often ended their days in bloody and violent death.

the stable term *justice*. Although Gentillet is clearly aware of the larger Latin significance of *pietas,* he nonetheless finds himself casting about for French equivalents from different roots.[127]

When directly faced with Machiavelli's text, Gentillet usually renders Italian *pietà* with French *clemence*. Responding specifically to chapters 17 and 18 of *The Prince,* for example, he affirms Senecan *clementia* as the antithesis of *crudelitas*. Developing the importance of this, he defines the word "en sa plus ample signification": "elle comprend non seulement misericorde et douceur envers les delinquans, mais aussi bonté et debonnaireté en moeurs, popularité et facilité à s'accommoder au peuple, et à tous ceux à qui l'on a à commander, et aussi humanité et affabilité officieuse envers tous hommes" (396).[69] In effect, *clemence* has replaced any derivative of *pietas* as the comprehensive term in characterizing the perfect prince. Concluding his idealization with a statement of the advantages that a prince of this character brings to his people, Gentillet then repeats the connection between *clemence* and *débonnaireté*.

> Or quand les sujets imiteront ceste vertu excellente de clemence et debonnaireté, il est certain que le corps de la chose publique en sera beaucoup mieux composé, et sera plus tranquille et mieux reiglé. Car les hommes s'adonnans à ceste vertu, s'adonneront aussi quand et quand à justice, temperance, charité, pieté, et à toutes les autres vertus, qui ordinairement acompaignent la clemence, dont resultera un estat public comme parfait. (400)[70]

In this context, "pieté" is one virtue among others said to accompany "clemence," and its narrowed force is suggested by contiguity with "charité." Used elsewhere in the work to summon religious authority for the argument, *piété* is the quality said to be conspicuously absent from the thinking of Machiavelli. Charging his Italian rival with teaching the prince to be an atheist and "contempteur de toute pieté" (18), Gentillet

[69] It comprehends not only mercy and kindness toward the criminal, but also goodness and amiable manners, popularity and ease of accommodating oneself to the people and all those one has to command, as well as humanity and dutiful affability toward all men.

[70] When subjects imitate this excellent virtue of clemency and goodness, it is certain that the body politic will be much more harmonious, tranquil, and ordered. For men giving themselves over to this virtue give themselves as well to justice, temperance, charity, piety, and all the other virtues which customarily accompany clemency, and the result is a near perfect state.

counters with nostalgia for the days of "nos anciens Rois [qui] par leur pieté et justice ont obtenu ce nom et titre tant honnorable de Treschrestiens" (16).[71] Here is the old formula intact, but the meaning is not quite the same: as *clemence* has risen to a dominant position in the political vocabulary of Gentillet, *piété* is left to function as a synonym for *religion*. Attempting to recover a golden age of political language before it had been corrupted by Machiavelli, Gentillet must conjure with new terms and with old ones whose implications have changed. His own answer to the "meschancetez et impietez" (148) of Machiavelli is itself evidence that the French vocabulary is still in the process of selecting the vernacular terms that will articulate political ideals.

Whereas *iustitia* is welcomed into the political vernacular, *pietas* is displaced from the center of modern discourse on government by terms from less ambiguous roots. The distinctions between the derivatives of *pietas,* on the one hand, and *mercy* and *clemency* in English, *reverenza* in Italian, *clemence* and *débonnaireté* in French are still in a state of flux in the sixteenth century. This unsettled condition of the political language is nowhere more important than in Renaissance epic, whose heroes represent contemporary princes even as they trace their origins to the example of *pius* Aeneas.[128] As Aeneas could achieve his political destiny only by disengaging himself from Dido, so his Renaissance descendants will negotiate settlement with hers, but on terms that will have to acknowledge feminine claims on the ideal represented by the Vergilian hero.

[71] our ancient kings who by their piety and justice obtained the name and title so honorable of Treschrestiens

5

Love:
Dido and Pietas in the
Early Renaissance

In Renaissance literature the story of Dido and Aeneas is retold in two basic versions: as a temptation narrative in which erotic love distracts the hero from his public duty; and as a narrative of abandonment in which the erotic is subordinated to a conception of love based on mutual fidelity. Both versions respond to *Aeneid* 4, the first from Aeneas's perspective, the second from Dido's. Although the Renaissance Aeneas can appeal to pietas in the classical sense of duty, Dido has a more contemporary claim based on the evolved meaning of compassion. How the union of hero and heroine might be arranged in relation to either of these definitions varies as the story is recast in literary modes other than the heroic: Ovidian, pastoral, and Petrarchan conventions all contribute to rethinking Vergil's subordination of *amor* to *pietas* in *Aeneid* 4.[1] Boccaccio's Ovidian *Elegia di Madonna Fiammetta* translates the love of Dido from ancient Carthage to fourteenth-century Naples; the narrative of David and Bathsheba in Remy Belleau's *La Bergerie* reconsiders the pietas of Aeneas by analogy to the pietas of the biblical shepherd who became king; the dizains that Maurice Scève gathers under the emblem "Dido qui se brusle" invert the roles of Dido and Aeneas in a manner typical of the love poetry that derives from Provençal. In these representative works, heroic conventions are set against alternative traditions that would revise the terms of conflict between male and female inherited from Vergil. When, therefore, the Dido and Aeneas story is directly imitated in the Renaissance epics of Ariosto and Tasso, appeal to pietas can provide no simple or consistent answer to the claims of love.

Ovidian Narrative: Fiammetta

In the Latin of the later empire and especially in Christian literature, the imagery associated with *pietas* is often feminine. In his *Confessions* Augustine finds a model of *vera pietas* in his own mother, a pattern readily adapted to describe the Virgin Mary, the *mater pietatis* of medieval religious lyric and eventually the subject of Michelangelo's *Pietà*.[2] The maternal image of pietas endorsed by Gregory and Alcuin (though it creates difficulties that finally tend to limit the political usefulness of the term) serves to fix the word in the meaning of compassion and to affirm *crudelitas* and its derivatives as natural antonyms. Although the politically evolved meaning of maternal pietas can coexist in the Renaissance emblem books with the patriarchal definition imaged from the *Aeneid,* these potentials of the word tend to conflict in the literary vocabulary of love. In contemporary lyric and narrative, moreover, the feminine identity of pietas now acquires an erotic dimension differentiated from the maternal even as it challenges the dominance of Vergilian definition. As a feminine principle, as an ideal assumed or defined by Renaissance heroines, pietas has a subversive place in the Western lexicon, potentially undermining the very norms of political order that the word is elsewhere reiterated to assure.

The symbolic focus of this challenge is Dido, whose case against Aeneas is reopened by writers of the fourteenth century, most insistently by Boccaccio.[3] In his Latin works this takes the form of correcting Vergil, who is accused of indulging poetic license in fictionalizing the historically chaste queen to express the distracting power of erotic love. Not only would Boccaccio remove the infamy undeservedly cast on her widowhood, but he would even regard her as a figure of exemplary virtue, chastity, and constancy on the model of Penelope.[4] In his vernacular fiction, however, Boccaccio takes a different and more consequential approach, accepting the outcome of Vergil's fourth book but allowing this verdict to emerge from the heroine's point of view. The female narrator of the *Elegia di Madonna Fiammetta* directly asserts her affinity with Dido: "Vienmi poi innanzi, con molta più forza che alcuno altro, il dolore dell'abandonata Dido, però che più al mio simigliante il conosco quasi che altro alcuno."[1][5] Boccaccio thus invites discussion of the

---

[1] After these the grief of forsaken Dido entered with greater force and deeper consideration into my mind, because her condition did of all others most resemble mine.

compatability of pietas and love by proclaiming against the *Aeneid* the example of the *Heroides*—in ways that serve to complicate rather than to simplify the original story.

Supplementing the allusions to epistle 7 with reference to the incest narratives of Phaedra and Myrrha, Boccaccio summons to the *Elegia* Ovidian heroines who have in common the wish to overthrow or redefine *pietatis nomen* in order to satisfy erotic compulsions that this traditional value would prohibit. In the relevant passage of the Cinyras and Myrrha story from *Metamorphoses* 10, for example, *pietas* is repeated as prohibition before it is finally wrenched by Myrrha into conjunction with *amor:* "gentes tamen esse feruntur,/in quibus et nato genetrix et nata parenti/iungitur, ut pietas geminato crescat amore."[2][6] Whereas in the narrative frame *pietas* is a fixed idea, even enshrined in the stars, in Myrrha's soliloquy it is a negotiable term. In this regard, as in others, Myrrha's story has much in common with Phaedra's letter in *Heroides* 4, which is not surprising as they share a common source in the first version of Euripides' *Hippolytos*. The later adaptation of this play by Seneca in turn provides a source for Boccaccio's *Elegia di Madonna Fiammetta,* which repeats basic elements of the incest plot without the incest itself.[7]

When Fiammetta falls adulterously in love with Panfilo, allusions to both Myrrha and Phaedra are invoked to suggest that in this Ovidian world the object of one's passion, even if not incestuous, is still a matter of chance. Witness the words of Venus, who appears before Fiammetta in book 1 to claim her as votary: "Pasife similmente avea marito, e Fedra, e noi ancora quando amammo" (963).[3] To take Phaedra and her mother as prime examples of women who did not let marriage interfere with passion is to render Venus's subsequent distinction between Fiammetta and Myrrha less than fully meaningful. "Bastiti solamente, o giovine, che di non abominevole fuoco, come Mirra, Semiramís, Biblís, Canace e Cleopatra fece, ti molesti" (964).[4] Venus to the contrary, Fiammetta does not consider herself lucky; later she even names some of the same figures of classical legend, including "scelerata" Myrrha, to measure her pain.[8] Though less criminal than Myrrha (she also names Byblis and Canace in this context), Fiammetta believes her-

[2] And yet they say that there are tribes among whom mother with son, daughter with father mates, so that natural love is increased by the double bond.

[3] Pasiphae likewise had a husband, and Phaedra, and I myself when I loved.

[4] Let this suffice, young lady, that you are not molested with such abominable and wicked lust as Myrrha, Semiramis, Biblis, Canace and Cleopatra.

self to have suffered more. In effect, Boccaccio transfers the more obvious argumentative sophistry of Ovid's Myrrha and Phaedra to Venus, leaving Fiammetta to voice the fatal urgency of passion in the manner of Dido.

Like Dido, Fiammetta is abandoned in order that her lover may fulfill the demands of pietas, specifically in this case to his father, whose death is said to be imminent. The conflict is expressly between pietas and love:

> e cioè solamente il pensare che di me far due non posso, com'io vorrei, acciò che ad Amore e alla debita pietà ad un'ora satisfare potessi qui dimorando, e là dove necessità strettissima mi tira per forza, andando. Dunque non potendosi, in afflizione gravissima il mio cuore misero ne dimora, sì come colui che da una parte traendo pietà, è fuori delle tue braccia tirato, e dall'altra in quelle con somma forza da Amore ritenuto. (972)[5]

When she recovers from the initial shock of hearing this speech, Fiammetta gropes her way toward an understanding of the word that has come between herself and her lover: "Ma poi che per lungo spazio ebbi pianto amaramente, quanto potei ancora il pregai che più chiaro qual pietà il traeva delle mie braccia mi dimostrasse" (972).[6] This puts the question very precisely: "qual pietà"?[9] Given the range of possible meanings historically conferred on the word, this question raises in a concretely realized fictional situation the problem that writers from Cicero to Dante had already so variously addressed.

The answer forthcoming is classical. Panfilo defines the word as filial duty ("ubidienza filiale," 972). Beginning to see the position that this definition puts her in, Fiammetta responds by attempting to develop an alternative sense of the word that will secure Panfilo's love. After restating the problem from his point of view ("da pietà tirato e da amore . . ."), she reminds him of his frequent professions of love: "se le tue parole per

---

[5] If only I could make two of myself as I would like, so that I might at one time fulfill the laws of love and of piety, staying here and going where strict necessity draws me by force. I cannot suffer any more, for my wretched heart is drawn in one direction by piety, thus taking me out of your arms, while on the other side with great force of love is still retained in them.

[6] But after I had a long time bitterly lamented, I begged him as much as I could to tell me more clearly what piety it was that drew him from my arms.

addietro sono state vere, con le quali me da te essere stata amata non una volta, ma molte hai affermato, niun'altra pietà a questa potenza dee potere resistere" (973).[7] She then draws her ideas of pietas and love together in a lateral, reciprocal relationship: "Dunque, se io più t'amo, più pietà merito, e perciò degnamente antiponmi, e di me essendo pietoso, di ogni altra pietà ti dispoglia che offenda questa, e senza te lascia riposare il tuo padre" (974).[8] To combat rival meanings and to show the depth of her feeling, Fiammetta supports her appeal with a vision of her own death designed to compete with that of Panfilo's father. "Dunque, la pietà del vecchio padre preposta a quella che di me dei avere mi sarà di morte cagione, e tu non amatore, ma nemico, se così fai" (974).[9] This argument brings to the lover's role an obligation surpassing the *pietà* owed to the father, which is now recharacterized as "iniqua pietà." Duty to him would constitute "pietà giusta" if Panfilo could in fact prevent his death, but as he cannot, it would signify "maggior pietà" to let the old man die in peace without the son's intrusion (974).

The more Fiammetta presses her argument the more her concept of *pietà* becomes engaged with a specific set of circumstances. As such its meaning effectively becomes negotiable, but not finally to her own advantage because Panfilo excels her in pitting definition against definition. Thus he tentatively accepts her contingent explanation of *pietà* only to raise another specific contingency. Reminding her that their love is adulterous, he distinguishes the *pietà* due his father, which belongs to the realm of public and legally guarded relationships, from their secret and illicit affair, which he now describes as "pietà . . . occulta" (976). His partial concession to her usage obscured by the condemning adjective, Panfilo then completes the pattern of argument from classical *pietas* that Aeneas had inflicted on Dido: affirming obligation to all that is signified by the father, Panfilo denies any obligation to love outside the legal sanction of marriage. So it is that Fiammetta can only retreat to Dido's argument for delay by conjuring up the perils of a journey in bad weather, but as in *Aeneid* 4 the argument is to no avail. Abandoned,

[7] If all your words have been true, with which you have not once but many times affirmed that you love me, no other piety should be as powerful and as hard to resist.

[8] If therefore I love you more, I deserve more pity, so preferring me worthily, and being compassionate towards me, forget all other piety which would injure this, and let your father go to his rest without you.

[9] Shall therefore the love of thy old father be preferred to that which you ought to have for me? If so it will be the cause of my death, and you are no lover but an enemy.

Fiammetta listens as Panfilo's farewell speech promises return: "per quello indissolubile amore che io ti porto, e per quella pietà che ora da te mi divide, che il quarto mese non uscirà che, concedendolo Iddio, tu mi vedrai qui tornato" (979).[10] But the promise contains a denial of the very terms on which Fiammetta has staked reconciliation: whereas for Fiammetta *pietà* is a function of *amore,* for Panfilo the two terms are irreconcilable alternatives. The word that she would use to unite them, he uses to mark their separation: "pietà . . . da te mi divide."

After the departure of Panfilo in book 2, Fiammetta's narrative records her response through six more books and an envoi, in which she attempts to elicit the *pietà* of her reader by appealing to the tragic example of Dido: "E certo io nel primo partire di Panfilo sentii per mio avviso quel medesimo dolore, che nella partita di Enea" (1068).[11] If Fiammetta equals Dido in grief, however, she does not approach the depth of the queen's fury; rather, she converts her anger into willful self-deception that keeps her dependent on Panfilo's promise of compassion.[10] Accommodated to the rhetoric of the *Heroides, pietà* now defines a response less to love than to suffering. The relationship implied by her continued invocation of the word is based not on equality but on condescension. And even that is an illusion, as Fiammetta implicitly recognizes by deciding to follow Dido and commit suicide. Like Myrrha and Phaedra she is stopped by her nurse, a figure straight from Seneca's Euripides and thus a reminder of the illicit. Although quite capable of literary comparison, the nurse speaks for the actual world, as distinct from the poetic world of Vergil and Ovid inhabited by Fiammetta. Her presence sets the narrative of adultery against the classical narratives of incest, but at the same time it sets this highly literary world against the social world of fourteenth-century Naples. In both ways the nurse prevents Fiammetta's arguments from engaging the desired sympathy. Indeed, at various points in her complaint, Fiammetta is hardly sympathetic with her own arguments. She is even capable of recognizing that her situation might accurately be described as a case, not of being forsaken by *pietà,* but of forsaking *pietà* herself. "Dove abandonàsti tu la pietà debita alle sante leggi del matrimonio? Dove la castità, sommo onore delle donne,

[10] By that indissoluble love which I bear you, and by that piety which now separates me from you, four months shall not pass but (God willing) you will see me here returned to you again.

[11] And certainly at the first departure of Panfilo I felt (in my opinion) the very same grief as she did at the sailing of Aeneas.

cacciasti allora che per Panfilo il tuo marito abandonasti? Ove è ora verso te la pietà dell'amato giovine?" (1037).[12] By attaching the word to the marital bond and defining it as chastity, Fiammetta uses it in self-condemnation very much in the manner of Myrrha, who calls herself "inpia virgo" and lowers her head in shame when her father describes her as "pia."[11]

Yet Fiammetta is no more capable than Myrrha of acting on the meaning she here acknowledges. It is to explain this gap between under-standing and will that Fiammetta retails her dream of the pastoral golden age.[12] Calling forth the Senecan version of the classical topos, Fiammetta would situate herself outside of historical time before "empio furore" and, above all, before Amor ("il duca e facitore di tutti li mali"). In this vision, then, "il dissoluto amore" (1025) is aligned with the impietas of the iron age.[13] Fiammetta's personal situation is thereby assimilated to a traditional historical pattern that provides an explana-tion that relieves her, if not of affliction at least of responsibility for it. If women are thus shown to be defenseless against this symptom of the iron age, Fiammetta's own passion is nonetheless offered in the conclud-ing address to her book as a warning to other women. Even in the course of advising them to flee the inconstancy of men, however, Fiammetta cannot resist contemplating the possibility that her book will be read by Panfilo's new love, who will understand her grief and be stung by a guilty conscience even to the point of restoring Panfilo: "Oh, quanto felice pietà sarebbe questa . . ." (1079).[13] That the last appearance of *pietà* in the narrative should be in a hypothetical statement suspends the meaning of the word not only between "pity and holy piety"[14] but also between writer and reader, momentarily imagined to be rivals for the love of Panfilo. Throughout the narrative Fiammetta in fact addresses her audience as "pietosissime donne," varying this formula (as in the envoi) to "innamorate donne" and thus anticipating the audience of ladies in love imagined in the *Decameron*. In Boccaccio's greatest work it is the realistic perspective of the nurse that prevails, whereas Fiam-metta's compensatory vision of a golden age of pietas untouched by the sufferings of love proves hard to find even in Renaissance pastoral.

[12] Where did you abandon that love and piety which was due to the holy laws of matrimony? Whither did you banish your revered chastity (the chief honor and ornament of women) when for Panfilo you abandoned your husband? Where is now the pity of the beloved youth toward you?

[13] Oh what happy piety this would be . . .

Pastoral Narrative: Bathsheba

The enduring connection of pietas to pastoral, taken for granted by Fiammetta, is affirmed in the neo-Latin poetry of the Renaissance.[15] The fifth of Petrarch's bucolics, addressed to Cola di Rienzo and titled "Pietas pastoralis," even turns on how *pietas*—the virtue of both shepherds and rulers—should be understood. The shepherd Apicius argues that its meaning is uncertain ("varia est pietas"), thus introducing a dialogue on the subject that is not resolved until the Davidic figure of Rienzo is announced as the realized ideal of the pastor as king.[16] Later Renaissance writers find this figure a natural for Arcadia, where love turns out to be a problem for rural and royal pastors alike. Pastoral lament for lost or unrequited love assumes, moreover, a male point of view the very reverse of the Ovidian, even giving voice to antifeminist complaint. A good example is Mantuan's fourth pastoral, where the catalogue designed to prove female iniquity ironically overlaps with Fiammetta's list of women who suffered for love. The list includes Byblis and Myrrha, Semiramis and Phaedra in a line of women that Mantuan's shepherd traces to Eve ("quae crimina non sunt/feminea temptata manu?"). This catalogue is then followed by an alternative one of men whose heroism is defined by the descent to Hell and back, and first in this list that leads up to Jesus is "pius Aeneas." A third catalogue including Samson makes clear the relationship between the first two, as love is shown to be a potentially dangerous emotion even for the pastor-king ("rex qui pastor erat").[17] This is, in turn, the premise of Remy Belleau's David and Bathsheba narrative, in which pastoral and heroic, classical and Christian models of pietas collide. Here David is tempted by the brother of Aeneas.[18]

Belleau's narrative opens with a clash of classical and biblical worlds, as Amor flies down to Judea. The passage recounting his flight shares certain general features with Mercury's descent to the sandy shore of Libya in *Aeneid* 4 (252–61), where Vergil carefully anticipates the first sight of Aeneas building Carthage. Although Belleau does not use the Vergilian vocabulary (even as transmitted through such contemporary translations as DuBellay's), his lines pointing to Amor's first sight of David offer a similar perspective.[19] Vergil compares Mercury to a bird, Belleau compares Amor to a falcon; Mercury sees "Aenean fundantem . . . ," Amor sees "ce grand Roy . . . bastissant." And yet with evident differences of intent: Mercury will recall Aeneas from love, while

Amor will distract David with love; Aeneas forsakes building Dido's city, David his own; Aeneas comes to himself and his destiny, David will be distracted from himself and his. These differences thus serve to underline the larger similarity, for by introducing Amor into the domain of Jehovah, Belleau offers classical mythology as a surprising analogical context for understanding the *pietas* of the scriptural hero.

The lines that follow draw out the latent parallel with the other great figure of *pietas* in the ancient world: Belleau's vocabulary of city and wall, race and blood now does suggest the basic concerns of Aeneas as embodied in the opening lines of Vergil's poem, even though here it is the race of Jesse that is in question:

> Il sçait que de Jessé et le sang et la race
> Doit perir une fois, et tomber sous l'audace
> Des forces de Satan, et sous l'impiété,
> Ministres de sa proye et de sa cruauté.
>
> (345)[14]

By assimilating the Old Testament narrative to the paradigm of the fall, Belleau invokes the primal impietas of Satan. Characterized in the traditional terms accorded the tyrant, here emphasized by the rhyme ("impiété," "cruauté"), Satan is contrasted not only to the pastor-king of the Old Testament but also to his descendant in the New. By further analogy the "forces de Satan" define the tempter role of Amor, whose "flamme" and "force" will test the character of David. As the boy discloses his intentions, he affirms the temptation as a test of power, pitting "ma loy" against the law of God ("ce Dieu qu'il retient et loge en sa pensee," 345).

Proud of his prior successes ("Depuis le siecle d'or," 345), Amor then offers proof of his power by citing specific cases. Each example is organized around a particular city and serves to illuminate the situation of David, who (according to the Augustinian tradition) always overcomes weakness with pietas.[20] The design and emphasis of this illustrative list is of considerable interest, as four cities with significant histories are now identified and set in implied contrast to the city of David: Babylon, Sodom, Troy, and Gaza. The Babylon of Belleau's example is

[14] He knows that the blood and race of Jesse must one day perish, and fall under the impiety and the audacity of Satan's forces, ministers of his prey and cruelty.

the city of Semiramis, a figure frequently encountered in such lists.[21] As Belleau describes her, Semiramis assumes the character of her city, "Babylon la superbe." Given the venerable contrast between Jerusalem and Babylon, and the identification of the latter not only with pride but also with impietas (Boccaccio, for example, describes her city by naming Nimrod), the example seems carefully chosen. Indeed, the emphasis on the walls of the city—"ses murs les tesmoins/De ma puissance" (345)[15]—recalls by way of contrast the initial sight of David building Jerusalem ("bastissant/De la sainte cité le mur"). In effect, Amor is taking credit for the building of this *civitas impiorum* where Semiramis has honored with incest the "grandeur" of his name. The attention devoted to Babylon is matched by that given to the Gaza of Samson and Delilah. Characterized in heroic terms, Samson surrenders his power and becomes with the loss of his hair one who lives the life of a slave ("vie esclave"). Here the word used earlier to express the intention of Amor with respect to David—"de le rendre esclave aux rigueurs de ma loy" (345)[16]—is repeated. The contest between the law of God and the law of Amor is thus defined by the opposition of Jerusalem (pietas) to Babylon (impietas), its relevance to the situation of David addressed by reference to events in Gaza.

Between Babylon and Gaza, Belleau has squeezed Sodom and Troy. Sodom has a long history of identification with impietas and its destruction or fall ("ruine") here reverberates with the destruction envisioned in the case of Samson.[22] Of greater interest here, however, is the example from Greco-Roman mythology, for the reference to Troy formulates the problem of love as originally confronted by another shepherd who on Mount Ida chose beauty over power and wisdom. As Hallett Smith has described the significance of this choice, with specific reference to Renaissance pastoral: "It is only beauty, of the three ideals represented by the goddesses, which has any significant power in a pastoral life."[23] Belleau provides a case in point, but with a significant twist. Although the attraction of Bathsheba is precisely that of beauty ("en beauté/Surpasser les beautez de toute la cité," 346), the adjective that repeatedly describes her is "chaste" and she is remarkably compared, not to Venus, but to Juno: "imitant le port et les graces divines/De la chaste Junon" (348).[17] If

[15] Its walls are witnesses of my power.
[16] to make him a slave to the rigors of my law
[17] imitating the look and divine grace of the chaste Juno

David is like Paris, he is also potentially like the impious Ixion, endangered by affront to the power of the gods.[24] From the perspective of pastoral the attraction of Bathsheba's beauty is as natural as the choice of Paris; but from the perspective of the heroic it is a temptation with, the references to Troy and the power of Juno both suggest, potentially disastrous consequences. In this situation, then, the struggle is between pastoral and heroic, between the two identities of David as both shepherd and king, and ultimately between two definitions of pietas.

At the moment he first sees Bathsheba, David is drawn to traditional type:

> David, ce grand Prophete,
> David choisi de Dieu pour son divin poëte,
> Son chantre, son guerrier, brave, vaillant, facond,
> Et qui en pieté n'eut jamais de second.
>
> (348)[18]

In the last line cited here, Belleau brings together the Roman and Hebraic strands of the poem, acknowledging David as unrivaled exemplar of pietas. Given the framework of classical myth already established, and the specific reference to the matter of Troy, the hyperbole of "jamais de second" seems quite calculated to affirm David's superiority to Aeneas and to suggest *Aeneid* 4 as the appropriate classical analogue for understanding the story of David and Bathsheba. As in Vergil's narrative, love at first prevails. Although Belleau finds no word as effective as the "uxorius" spoken by Vergil's Mercury (4.266), the significance of this initial triumph is spelled out in the very terms of Amor's earlier promise: "S'en est rendu captif, esclave et serviteur,/Elle dame et maistresse, et Amour son seigneur" (349).[19] The effect is not just to make David unmindful of his kingdom, but even to turn him into a tyrant ("ce tyran meurdrier"). The tradition of using pastoral conventions to describe the ideal ruler here reveals the perversion of rule in the traditionally ideal king. The recipient of extraordinary divine favor, the pastor become king is now reduced to an adulterous assassin (354). Identifying David as

[18] David, the great prophet, David chosen by God as his divine poet, his singer and warrior, brave, valiant, eloquent, and who for piety has no rival

[19] He is made a captive, slave and servant, while she is lady and mistress, and Love is his lord.

murderer, Belleau elicits from the biblical narrative a countertypology that would lead back to Cain as type of impietas.

But this effect produced by love in turn becomes a cause, as Vergilian pietas yields by the end of the poem to the Augustinian, and David finally assumes his medieval character of sincere penitent. Responding to the words of the prophet Nathan, David—both shepherd and king in Nathan's allegory—confesses his sin and in so doing indicts "Amour."

> Tantost en s'accusant il accuse l'Amour,
> Abhorre son peché, deteste le beau jour
> Qui premier luy fit voir les vives estincelles
> De l'oeil qui le ravit en ses pinces cruelles.
> Amour n'est plus son hoste, et n'a plus rien au coeur
> Que de la main de Dieu la justice et la peur.
>
> (357)[20]

David as model of pietas finally overcomes erotic desire and can therefore be said to have accomplished what his classical counterpart accomplishes in *Aeneid* 4. But in the concluding characterization of David, he becomes a specifically Christian rather than a classical hero. Amor's paradox of "Roy"/"esclave" is thus replaced by the Christian paradox of the lowly king: "Voyez d'un pauvre Roy l'audace retranchée,/Et de la main de Dieu l'ame prise et touchee" (358).[21] As the humility of the shepherd ("pauvre") is joined to the eminence of royalty ("Roy"), pastoral and heroic converge to portray David as supreme exemplar of penitence. The dialectic of love and pietas in Belleau's poem is resolved, finally, by reconfiguring the basic terms in penitential sequence as sin ("peché") and remorse ("regrets"). The consequences of this particular sin are manifest in the suffering and humiliation—not of the female, as in Boccaccio—but rather of the male figure of pietas. By his suffering, then, David is restored to the penitential role he had assumed since the time of Ambrose: his love for Bathsheba is reduced to the category of sin, his pietas removed from its initial Vergilian to its final Augustinian

---

[20] So much does he abhor his own sin that, accusing Love, he detests the beautiful day which first caused him to see the living sparks from the eye that ravished him in its cruel pincers. Love is no longer his host, and he no longer has in his heart anything but justice and the fear of the hand of God.

[21] See the arrogance of a poor king suppressed, his soul taken and touched by the hand of God.

context. The priority granted Augustine's definition thus makes possible a specifically religious resolution to this Hebraic version of the Dido and Aeneas story.

Petrarchan Lyric: Délie

Unlike Aeneas, David will not be pursued by the curse of Dido. Yet reverberations of Dido's rage, especially her furious attempt to deny Aeneas his mother (4.365–67), will be often heard in love poetry from the fourteenth century forward: Dante, *Rime* 80; DuBellay, *Olive* 91; Ronsard, *Amours de Marie* 14; Samuel Daniel, *To Delia* 18; and somewhat more obliquely, Spenser, *Amoretti* 56, and Sidney, *Astrophil and Stella* 44.[25] The irony is that in these poems her words will be directed by suffering males against the inaccessible female, thus reversing the Vergilian roles of Dido and Aeneas. Commenting on this situation as expressed in Ronsard's "Petite pucelle Angevine," for example, Belleau affirms the desired nuance of *pitié* by association with "douceur": "Il se plaint en ceste Chanson des cruelles rigueurs de sa Dame, qui ne peuvent s'amollir par pitié ny par douceur, faisant une comparaison du fier naturel d'elle à une roche pendante sur la mer."[22][26] In this vein the Renaissance sonnet not only expresses the cruelty of the lady in imagery derived from Dido's curse, but will also amplify the cruel mistress trope in the language of the governance tracts, thus revealing the political dimension of the lover's distress in the face of the loved one's emotional and psychological power. To express this power Spenser coined the English word "Tyranesse,"[27] negatively defined by the absence of *pity,* which like Ronsard's *pitié,* takes its meaning from the *pietà* of Petrarch and his predecessors.

Adopted as a favored term by the poets of the *dolce stil nuovo,* the Italian *pietà* derives from the Latin by way of Provençal *pietat.* In Italian love poetry, the word belongs to a feminine order that effectively overturns the *pietas* of the Vergilian heroic and places the male in the position of Dido. According to Cino da Pistoia, "Pietate" descends not from God or father or king, but from the personified feminine figure of Mercè

---

[22] He complains in this song of the cruel rigors of his lady, which won't be softened by pity or sweetness, making a comparison of her natural haughtiness to a rock hanging over the sea.

("Perchè Pietate da Mercè discende").[28] The power of the female who withholds her *pietà* is evident in Gianni Alfani's "Donne, la donna mia a d'en disdegna," which includes a not unusual expression of humiliation: "Ond 'i ' vi dico ch' i' m'ucciderei,/se 'l su' dolce valore/non avesse pietà del mi' dolore."[23][29] Such power over the suppliant male generates a surrounding political vocabulary that is often quite explicit, as in the valedictory of Dante's *Rime* 89, where the poet bids farewell with a sustained analogy between *bella petra* and Florence ("vota d'amore e nuda di pietate"), between the female and the tyrannical state. The negation of both "amore" and "pietate" in this poem is expressed by the condition of exile and bondage, as the cruelty of Florence is finally overmatched only by that of the lady.

But the word that thus connotes sexual humiliation may also signify spiritual humility, as *pietà* is also sought by Dante in Beatrice and ultimately in the Virgin Mary of *Paradiso* 33.[30] The ambiguously carnal and spiritual significance of the word in Renaissance love poetry turns on the female figure as mistress and mother. Consider, for example, Petrarch's sonnet 285, which is expressly concerned with divine and earthly meanings of *pietà:*

> Né mai pietosa madre al caro figlio
>   né donna accesa al suo sposo diletto
>   die' con tanti sospir, con tal sospetto
> in dubbio stato sì fedel consiglio,
> come a me quella che 'l mio grave esiglio
>   mirando dal suo eterno alto ricetto
>   spesso a me torna co l'usato affetto,
> et di doppia pietate ornata il ciglio,
> or di madre, or d'amante. Or teme or arde
>   d'onesto foco, et nel parlar mi mostra
>   quel che 'n questo viaggio fugga o segua,
> contando i casi de la vita nostra,
>   pregando ch' a levar l'alma non tarde.
>   Et sol quant' ella parla ò pace, o tregua.[24][31]

---

[23] Whence I say that I would kill myself, if her sweet virtue did not have pity of my grief.

[24] Never did a pitying mother to her dear son or a loving wife to her beloved husband give with so many sighs, with such anxiety, such faithful counsel in a perilous time, as she gives to me, who, seeing from her eternal home my heavy exile, often returns to me with

The several patterns of doubling on which the sonnet depends yield at the end of the octave, the phrase "doppia pietate." Reflecting the "dubbio stato" of line 4, it is commonly translated as "double pity." Yet the phrase refers diversely to the "pietate" of "madre" and "donna," a distinction marked in the opening lines and repeated in the "or . . . or" construction of line 9. The possibilities of "doppia pietate" are thus organized along two axes: one vertical, "pietate" descending from mother to son; the other horizontal, "pietate" defining a love relationship both ardent and chaste. The basic figure is given new force in the pronoun "nostra" of line 12, as subject and object are joined in a Dantean pilgrimage that ascends toward the last poem of the collection, addressed to the Virgin Mary ("il Fonte di pietate," 366.42). On the way of this pilgrimage *pietà* acquires a finely nuanced range of meanings emphasizing the spiritual, the "pietà celeste" (360.58) that promises the lover peace. That such *pietà* is not finally attained, or that the ambivalences of the cycle as a whole are still present in the concluding poem to the Virgin, has frequently been argued, and it is evident that as this ambivalence is reflected in the word *pietà* itself, it is shared by Petrarch's many imitators.[32]

The doubled image of *pietà* as mistress and mother is especially complex in poems where it is the mother of Aeneas rather than the mother of Jesus who is invoked. Consider, then, Maurice Scève, whose *Délie* includes as one of its emblems Dido on her funeral pyre. In the verses ("Non de Venus les ardentz estincelles") dedicating his series of poems "A Sa Délie," Scève portrays Venus as mother to Amour and Cupido ("Enfantz jumeaulx de toy, mere Cypris").[33] Seen in the light of the dedication, dizain 74, in which the poet compares himself to Venus's son Amour, is of particular interest.

> Dans son jardin Venus se reposoit
> Avec Amour, sa tendre nourriture,
> Lequel je vy, lors qu'il se deduisoit,
> Et l'apperceu semblable a ma figure.

---

her usual affection and with her brow adorned with double pity, now that of a mother, now that of a lover. Now she fears, now she burns with virtuous fire; and in her speech she shows me what in this journey I must avoid or pursue, telling over the events of our life, begging me not to delay in lifting up my soul. And only while she speaks do I have peace—or at least a truce.

> Car il estoit de tresbasse stature,
> Moy trespetit: luy pasle, moy transy.
> Puis que pareilz nous sommes donc ainsi,
> Pourquoy ne suis second Dieu d'amytié?
>   Las je n'ay pas l'arc, ne les traictz aussi,
> Pour esmouvoir ma Maistresse a pitié.[25]

The poet is like "Amour" in all ways but one, and that one is his capacity to attain "pitié." The significance of this is evident by comparison with 101, where the mistress is in turn compared to Venus.

> Sur le matin, songeant profondement,
> Je vy ma Dame avec Venus la blonde.
> Elles avoient un mesme vestement,
> Pareille voix, et semblable faconde:
> Les yeulx riantz en face, et teste ronde
> Avec maintien, qui le tout compassoit.
>   Mais un regret mon coeur entrelassoit,
> Appercevant ma Maistresse plus belle.
> Car Cytarée en pitié surpassoit
> Là, ou Delie est tousiours plus rebelle.[26]

The first six lines indicate the exactness of the similarities, an emphasis repeated in 120, where Jupiter himself cannot distinguish Délie from Venus until she herself denies the identification ("Delie suis, dit elle, et non Déesse," 120.9). In 101 the only difference between them is expressed in the last four lines, but the difference is again the point: Venus has the "pitié" wanting in the mistress. The attendant irony of the two comparisons depends on the ambiguity of erotic and maternal contained in this one word and perfectly captured in the figure of Venus as mother.

To attempt resolution of this ambivalence by looking to other poems

[25] Venus was resting in her garden with Love, her tender child, whom I saw as he amused himself, and his form resembled mine. For he was very low in stature, I very small: he was pale, I paralyzed. Since we are thus alike, why am I not a second god of love? Alas, I have no bow, nor the arrows to move my mistress to pity.

[26] Toward morning, dreaming deeply, I saw my lady with Venus the blond. She had the same dress, like voice and similar eloquence. The eyes laughing back and forth, her face round with a countenance that gave shape to the whole. But a sigh escaped my heart, seeing my Lady to be the more beautiful, for Venus surpassed her in pity, whereas Délie is always more resistant.

in the collection is only to discover additional semantic possibilities. For example, as 28 answers 27, the word is literally colored by Délie's blush, which the poet first interprets as a sign of hope: "Je croy *pitié* soubz honteuse doulceur" (27.6).[27] But in the response, this carnal thought is questioned: "Ay je peu veoir le vermeil de la honte / Ardoir la face a son honnesteté? / Et croire encor, que la pitié luy monte / Sur le plus cher de sa grand' chasteté?" (28.1–4).[28] As "pitié" is thus distinguished from both "honnesteté" and "chasteté" it acquires a connotation at odds with the poet's own aspirations to attain it. Indeed, he is twice compelled to counter the idea of "pitié" as a code word for erotic love by adding the adjective "honneste," most notably in 346 where the word comes especially close to signifying pietas both in the classical sense of duty and the Christian sense of holiness:

> A si hault bien de tant saincte amytié
> Facilement te deburoit inciter,
> Sinon debuoir, ou honneste pitié,
> A tout le moins mon loyal persister,
> Pour unyment, et ensemble assister
> Lassus en paix en nostre eternel throsne.
> (346.1–6)[29]

Here "honneste" appears necessary to secure a connotation for "pitié" consistent with "saincte" on the one hand and "debuoir" on the other.

Although the frustrated poet of *Délie* does not directly imitate the curse of *Aeneid* 4.365–67, in number 45 his appeal for *pitié* does evoke a harsh landscape similar to the one envisioned in Dido's words: "Ma face, angoisse a quiconques la voit, / Eust a pitié esmeue la Scythie" (45.1–2).[30] Here the meaning of *pitié* is revealed by contrast to image patterns that express the cruelty of the mistress as harsh, hard, barbaric, Scève's Scythia taking the place of Dido's Caucasus and Hyrcania. Such a passage lies directly in the background of the poems grouped under the emblem

[27] I think of pity under ashamed kindness.
[28] Have I been able to see the blush of shame burn the face of her purity? and to believe still that pity rises to the height of her great chastity?
[29] To a good so high of love so holy you should be easily incited, if not by duty or honest pity, then at least by my loyal persistence, in order to join as one there in peace on our eternal throne.
[30] My face, anguished to whoever sees it, would move Scythia to pity.

"Dido qui se brusle" (emblem 13, poems 114–22) and its motto "Doulce la mort qui de dueil me delivre."[31] Although the relationship between emblem and poem in *Délie* is a difficult question, in this particular instance it is clear that the emblem itself faithfully represents *Aeneid* 4.642–65 and that its emphasis on suffering and martyrdom is indeed relevant to the poems that follow. But, as Dorothy Gabe Coleman has pointed out, the emblem provides the emotional background for a "paradoxical reversal of values."[34] Specifically, it can be observed that Dido is identified with the male figure, as her burning and death find resonance in the emotional state of the lover, who is also a martyr to love: "Croire fauldra, que la Mort doulce soit, / Qui l'Ame peult d'angoisse delivrer" (114.9–10).[32]

As the image of flame is developed in this sequence of poems, it effectively subverts the meaning of the attached motto: there will be no deliverance by fire; as a result, the lover is actually in a situation worse than Dido's. Far from fulfilling the promise of the emblem, the "feu despiteux" of 115 becomes another way of expressing the lady's cruelty. Yet remarkably, this poem begins with an oxymoron that describes her "regard" as "severement piteux."

> Par ton regard severement piteux
> Tu *m'esblouis* premierement la veue:
> Puis du regard de son feu despiteux
> Surpris le Coeur, et l'Ame a l'impourveue,
> Tant que despuis, apres mainte reveue,
> J'ars de plus fort sans nouvelle achoison.
>   Ce mesme temps la superbe Toison
> D'ambition, qui a tout mal consent,
> Toute aveuglée espandit sa poison
> Dessus le juste, et Royal innocent.[33]

The initial phrase shares its paradoxical terms with the governance literature, in which *severitas* is understood as what *iustitia* becomes in the

[31] Sweet the death which delivers me from grief.

[32] It is necessary to believe that death may be sweet, which can deliver the soul from anguish.

[33] By your look severely kind, you first stun my view; then from the look of its fire unkind surprise the heart and the soul unexpectedly, so much that since, after many looks back, I burn stronger without fresh cause. At the same time the proud wool of ambition, consenting to all evil, entirely blind, spreads its poison over just and innocent royalty.

absence of *pietas*. This is particularly worth noting as the last four lines of the poem are overtly political, concluding with a reference to royal justice. As in Dante's *Rime* 89, politics here serves as complex analogy for love, the two experiences linked by the phrase "Ce mesme temps." Whereas in 101 Délie is "rebelle," here her power over the lover, paradoxically "piteux" and "despiteux," is implicitly contrasted to the national power of the just king.

The cruelty emphasized in this sequence is thus set against pity in a way that both parallels the contrast between tyrant and king in the governance literature and reverses the inherited roles of Dido and Aeneas. As in Boccaccio's Ovidian narrative and Belleau's pastoral, so in Scève's *Délie* pietas is host to contemporary meanings that compete with those anchored by Vergil's epic.[35] The rival possibilities of the word thus revealed are variously enacted in the chivalric narratives of Ariosto and Tasso.

Heroic Poetry: Alcina, Angelica, Bradamante

The story of Ruggiero's temptation by Alcina in canto 7 of *Orlando Furioso,* like the later story of his entanglement with Angelica in cantos 10 and 11, sustains the poem's extended analogy between Ruggiero (assumed ancestor of Ariosto's patron) and Aeneas (assumed ancestor of Vergil's patron). In different but mutually illuminating ways, these two episodes comment on the disengagement of *pietas* from *amor* in *Aeneid* 4 by situating the Dido and Aeneas story against the conventions of Renaissance love lyric.

The encounter with Alcina is generally shaped to the Vergilian model, most obviously recalled in the description of the hero's dress, which mirrors the Tyrian garb of Aeneas (4.261–64).[36] The description of Alcina meanwhile elicits from the *Aeneid* the dimension of Dido that Vergil had drawn from Homer's Circe, but is here assimilated to the vocabulary of Renaissance love poetry and thus to an idea of pietas at odds with the heroic.

> Sotto due negri e sottilissimi archi
> son duo negri occhi, anzi duo chiari soli,
> pietosi a riguardare, a mover parchi;

> intorno cui par ch'Amor scherzi e voli,
> e ch'indi tutta la faretra scarchi,
> e che visibilmente i cori involi . . .
>   (7.12.1–6)[34]

Here, in effect, is the answer to the perpetual complaint of the Petrarchan lover, a woman who does not withhold *pietà*. Alcina has suitably Petrarchan eyes, at once "negri" and "chiari," but here those eyes are "pietosi a riguardare," in contrast (for example) to the paradoxical "regard severement piteux" of Scève's Délie. As "pietosi" yields to the more direct and explicit "Amor," the hero is placed in a situation where the conventions established by Homer and Vergil are joined to those of Petrarch.[37] Ruggiero could hold off the "empii" (6.79.8) who had attacked him on the road past Alcina's palace, but he is helpless in the face of the sexual temptation that distracts him from his immediate goal, Logistilla's house (in Harington's allegorical interpretation "the court of vertue, of temperance, of pietie,")[38] and his long-range goal of union with Bradamante.

The eventual rescue of Ruggiero indicates, however, that this version of the love story is finally even more prejudicial against Dido than it is against Aeneas, who is now restored by Melissa to his heroic role. In the shape of Atlante she performs the function of Vergil's Mercury, confronting the overdressed Ruggiero with an austere version of the heroic (7.57) and exposing Alcina's erotic pietas to contempt and shame. Far from the Petrarchan mistress of 7.12 or even the Cleopatra of 7.20, Alcina is now reduced to a mere prostitute: "Che ha costei che t'hai fatto regina, / che non abbian mill'altre meretrici?" (7.64.1–2). Harington's play on *queen/ quean* successfully captures the idea in Elizabethan English: "What good hath this great Queene unto the done / But many other queans can do the same?" (7.54.1–2) Her true nature thus revealed, Alcina can be perceived as a false version of the Petrarchan mistress because, among other indications, she is not inaccessible. She may therefore be profitably contrasted to the very inaccessible Angelica, chained Andromeda-style to a rock by the sea orc in canto 10. But even in contrasting the apparent Petrarchan

---

[34] Beneath two of the thinnest black arches, two dark eyes—or rather, two bright suns; soft was their look, gentle their movement. Love seemed to flit, frolicsome, about them; indeed, Love from this vantage point would let fly his full quiver and openly steal away all hearts.

heroine to a true stone lady, it will be apparent that the subordination of male to female characteristic of the Renaissance lyric provides no basis for the reconciliation of pietas to love. What it does provide is a progressive reduction of the Vergilian heroic.

This episode (specifically connected to the Alcina story at 10.108) begins with another stylized description of the female, who evokes in the hero conflicting thoughts: "Pietade e amore a un tempo lo traffisse" (10.97.3).[35] In the following verses *pietà* and *amore* are triangulated with *crudeltà*, as Ruggiero uses his magic shield to fend off the monster whose cruelty is responsible for Angelica's plight. In this understanding, then, his pietas is more than compassion for her suffering; realized in action, his compassion updates and elevates the heroic virtue of Aeneas to the exalted conception of chivalric duty. Yet in the aftermath of this triumph (and across the division between cantos 10 and 11), the struggle between "Pietade e amore" is resumed and redefined, as Ruggiero considers his situation in regard to the naked Angelica now riding along behind him (11.2.1–4). His pietas soon supplanted by furor ("libidinosa furia," 11.1.4), he becomes a decidedly un-Vergilian figure of low comedy: in one of the poem's most absurdly ludicrous moments, he is prevented from any further involvement with Angelica by inability to shed his armor in time. Tangled not only in desire but also in his own gear, he is frustrated in every way, as Angelica uses the very ring that had saved him from Alcina—and sent to him by the readily forgotten Bradamante (11.2.5)—to escape. In his ensuing lament, the hero resorts to the rhetoric of the Petrarchan lover, casting Angelica ("Ingrata damigella") in the role of "crudel" (11.8.8). The metamorphosis of his role from dragon-slayer to frustrated lover matches hers from distressed maiden to cruel mistress of the true *bella petra* type. Ruggiero's first sight of her as a figure of stone is thus affirmed in a way that Orlando would understand very well.

As this episode comments on the earlier encounter with Alcina, so the incompatibility of pietas and love disclosed here is in turn qualified by the experience of still other episodes. Most obviously pertinent is the story of Norandino and Lucina, whose capture by the land orc causes her to be chained like Angelica to a rock. This story begins with Norandino's courtship of Lucina, and at first Norandino's "amorosa rabbia" (17.38.3) does not seem that far removed from the "libidinosa

[35] He was pricked with compassion and love.

furia" of Ruggiero. But once married to her, Norandino is characterized by a spirit that conquers all obstacles to save her (17.48); when she is chained to the crag, Norandino refuses even the wish of the orc's wife that he save himself and abandon Lucina.

> Così la moglie ancor de l'Orco priega
> il re che se ne vada, ma non giova;
> che d'andar mai senza Lucina niega,
> e sempre più constante si ritruova.
> In questa servitude, in che lo lega
> Pietate e Amor, stette con lunga pruova
> tanto . . .
>
> (17.62.1–7)[36]

This description recalls Ruggiero's emotions in the very similar context of canto 10, but radically alters the nuance of the same paired words, here revealed by the context to be complementary rather than contradictory. When the narrator—the story is told by one of Norandino's men—finishes, the listening knights draw this conclusion: "e conchiudon ch' amore e pietà immensa / mostrò quel re con grande esperimento" (17.69.3–4).[37] Norandino and Lucina exemplify what is impossible for Aeneas and Dido, and so long delayed for Ruggiero and Bradamante. Indeed, the reconciliation of love and heroism in Norandino serves as a not entirely favorable comment on the retarded progress of the poem's Vergilian hero.

The achievement of this episode is, moreover, extended two cantos later in the poem's most detailed response to the Dido problem. In canto 19, Ariosto rewrites *Aeneid* 4 as pastoral romance, with Angelica in the role of Dido and the quite unlikely Medoro now in the role of Aeneas. Recasting the Vergilian tragedy of intractable opposition between *pietas* and *amor,* Ariosto reconciles the two terms in an episode that renders heroic compatible with pastoral, things lofty with things humble, even pagan with Christian. Left for dead on the field of battle, Medoro is discovered by Angelica, who has taken refuge in the home of shepherds

---

[36] Orcus' wife, too, begged him to be gone, but all in vain: he refused to leave without Lucina, and his constancy grew only firmer. It was a long time that he endured this servitude, bound thereto by Devotion and Love . . .

[37] concluding that the king had given proof of outstanding love and devotion

from the amorous pursuits of the poem's greatest heroes. Now dressed as a shepherdess ("avolta in pastorale et umil veste," 19.17.2), she is presented as a natural object for the revenge of Amor, whose role in this poem—though benign in the consequence—is very similar to his role in Belleau's David and Bathsheba narrative. Whereas in the later poem, Amor will use Bathsheba to reach David, here he uses Medoro to reach Angelica, as her heart is first stirred by pity for him.

> insolita pietade in mezzo al petto
> si sentì entrar per disusate porte,
> che le fe' il duro cor tenero e molle,
> e più, quando il suo caso egli narrolle.
> (19.20.5–8)[38]

The pastoral home of "pietade" provides the background for the emergence of "amoroso fuoco" (19.26.8). But the Vergilian *furor,* though suggested, is never fulfilled, as the potentially tragic analogy between Angelica and Dido is rendered as a comedy of reconciliation. Vergil's "coniugium vocat; hoc praetexit nomine culpam" (4.172)[39] even becomes the occasion for one of the most beautiful stanzas in the entire poem, beginning famously: "Angelica a Medor la prima rosa / coglier lasciò . . ." (19.33.1–2).[40] Similarly, Vergil's "nunc hiemem inter se luxu, quam longa, fovere / regnorum immemores turpique cupidine captos" (4.193–94)[41] is transformed into "e più d'un mese poi stèro a diletto / i duo tranquilli amanti a ricrearsi" (19.34.3–4).[42] Love is here tranquillity rather than fury, and pietas—far from being in conflict with love—is the anteroom to the cave of its celebration. By the time the analogy with Dido and Aeneas is made explicit (19.33–35), the *Aeneid* has become a countertext.

> nel mezzo giorno un antro li copriva,
> forse non men di quel commodo e grato,

[38] An unaccustomed sense of pity stole into her breast by some unused door, softening her hard heart, the more so when he related his story to her.
[39] She calls it marriage and with that name veils her sin.
[40] Angelica let Medor pluck the first rose . . .
[41] Now they spend the winter, all its length, in wanton ease together, heedless of their realms and enthralled by shameless passion.
[42] And the tranquil lovers passed more than a month there in pleasurable enjoyment.

> ch'ebber, fuggendo l'acque, Enea e Dido,
> de' lor secreti testimonio fido.
>
> (19.35.5–8)[43]

Here "forse" unravels the Vergilian allusion in the very process of making it. The *pietas* of Aeneas is discovered after the union in the cave to be incompatible with *amor;* the *pietà* of Angelica leads to the cave where it is consumed in *amore.* Vergil's narrative works by exclusion, renunciation, and sacrifice, Ariosto's by inclusion, expansion, fulfillment, even indulgence.

Yet the larger difference is that the Latin poet tells the Dido story only once, while Ariosto tells it by reference to Petrarchan conventions in canto 7, again as pastoral in canto 19, and again as Ovidian complaint in the framing story of Bradamante. Oft forgotten, if not finally forsaken, Bradamante has all too frequent occasion to lament Ruggiero's shortcomings, which are measured against her understanding of what *pietà* ought to mean.

> Misera! a chi mai più creder debb'io?
> Vo' dir ch'ognuno è perfido e crudele,
> se perfido e crudel sei, Ruggier mio,
> che sì pietoso tenni e sì fedele
>
> (32.37.1–4)[44]

Here asserting the meaning that her marital status had prevented Fiammetta from securing against Panfilo's "ubidienza filiale," Bradamante describes Ruggiero in the vocabulary of the *Heroides.* Although the occasion of this lament turns out to be a false alarm, the Ovidian configuration of synonyms and antonyms—"perfido"/"fedele": "crudel"/"pietoso"—governs the episodes that test the hero's constancy.[39] Casting herself in the role of Ovid's Dido, who had hurled at Aeneas the charge of *impietas* ("non bene caelestis inpia dextra colit," 7.130), Bradamante has disappointment and anger enough to call Ruggiero "pergiuro, empio e superbo" (42.28.4), the very terms that with differ-

---

[43] At noontide a cave would shelter them, doubtless no less handy and hospitable than the one which offered Dido and Aeneas shelter from the rain and proved a trusty witness to their secrets.

[44] Ah me, whom shall I ever trust now? Every man must be faithless and cruel if you, my Ruggiero, are faithless and cruel, you whom I held to be so good and true.

ent meanings describe the adversary Rodomonte. As Ruggiero earns the negation of his Vergilian epithet by inconstancy, so Bradamante asserts against the heroic definition of pietas an Ovidian meaning that affirms the earlier passage in which Aeneas is relegated to Hell for abandoning Dido (34.14).

As descendant of Aeneas, Ruggiero thus has to contend with competing demands on his inherited virtue, even as his stature is rendered doubtful by overt references to the Vergilian original. Though praised as "il pietoso figliuol" (43.149.8) of Anchises, Aeneas is grouped with Achilles and Hector as heroes whose fame has been exaggerated ("Non sì pietoso Enea . . . / . . . come è fama," 35.25.1–2). Reduced in the phrase itself, the ancient meaning that "pietoso" evokes by reference to Aeneas is further reduced in the larger context represented by the different versions of the Dido story. Ruggiero's variously futile attempts to maintain a heroic conception of pietas yield control of meaning to Alcina, Angelica, and Bradamante. The hero submits to Alcina, is eluded by Angelica, in the process proves unfaithful to Bradamante, and in the most satisfying revision of *Aeneid* 4 is displaced by the humble Medoro. Although differently conceived according to different literary conventions in each instance, pietas repeatedly touches the concerns of love in ways that diminish the latter-day Aeneas. Change in the meaning of the word is at once cause and effect of change in the perception of Vergil's hero.

Heroic Poetry: Armida

Whereas Ariosto's epic draws on a range of literary conventions to offer different perspectives on the question of love and heroism, Tasso's heroic poem attempts to purge pietas of the specifically erotic implications it has acquired in Renaissance literature, and to reclaim simultaneously its Vergilian and Augustinian authority. Commenting on the *Aeneid* in his discourses, Tasso abstracts from the poem the character of Aeneas as "un perfetto cavaliero" without acknowledging any evident distinction between *pietas* and *pietà*: "Si trova in Enea l'eccellenza della pietà."[45][40] The Dido episode does not, apparently, qualify this judgment, although Tasso does consider it necessary to defend love as a legitimate subject of

[45] One finds in Aeneas the excellence of piety.

epic.[41] The kind of love he has in mind, and the attitude toward love that prevails in his own poem, is then summed up in a phrase: "Sempre fu e sarà virtù la pudicizia."[46][42] In the poem itself, consideration of *pietà, amore,* and *pudicizia* is initiated by Armida in canto 4, developed in the episode of Rinaldo's willing imprisonment on Armida's island in canto 16, and not completed until the poem's last canto.

Sent as an agent of the infernal powers to distract the Christian army from its heroic endeavor, Armida carries out a deliberate rhetorical strategy designed to appeal, not to any imagined weakness in the Christian leader but precisely to his strength: "ricovro al pio Goffredo, e in lui confido;/tal va di sua bontate intorno il grido."[47][43] Having taken the measure of her audience, Armida weaves around herself a tale of dispossession and desired restoration significantly parallel to the larger action of the poem: she has been evicted (she says) from her rightful inheritance by an evil uncle. As her fiction calls to mind the Christian hope of paradise regained (4.40.3–4), so it is also classical in its Vergilian emphasis on the restoration or renewal of the kingdom (4.41.7–8). Like the larger narrative, her own also depends on pietas: "la fé, ch'ho certa in tua pietà, mi giove" (4.42.3).[48]

From the beginning of her story, Armida defines Goffredo's *pietà* in ways that will suit her purposes. She first invokes a traditional context of understanding the term that depends upon the distinction between kin ("congiunti") and foreigner ("le straniere genti"), a distinction that produces a correlative contrast between *pietà* and *furor.*

> e s'altri aita a i suoi congiunti chiede
> contra il furor de le straniere genti,
> io, poi che 'n lor non ha pietà più loco,
> contro il mio sangue il ferro ostile invoco.
> (4.40.5–8)[49]

What is remarkable here is that Armida's situation reverses the expected correlations; having found "furor" in her own family, she appeals out-

---

[46] The virtue of modesty always was and always will be.

[47] I make my recourse to the worthy Godfrey, and trust in him. So much the report of his goodness is noised abroad.

[48] The certain faith that I have in your human kindness may comfort me.

[49] And where another asks aid of his kin against the fury of foreign peoples, I (since pity has no more place in them) against my own blood invoke the hostile steel.

side it—and outside her religion—to the "pietà" of the stranger king.
She then effectively alludes to the ideal of rule outlined by Anchises in
Aeneid 6.

> né la tua destra esser dèe meno avezza
> di sollevar, che d'atterrar altrui;
> né meno il vanto di pietà si prezza,
> che 'l trïonfar de gl' inimici sui . . .
>
> (4.41.3–6)[50]

Both "sollevar" and "atterrar" are relevant to her purposes, as she goes
on to place herself in the class of Vergil's "subiectis," her uncle in the
class of "superbos" ("i superbi e gli empi"). Appealing to Goffredo's
characteristic virtue in stanzas 61–62, Armida ("io misera fanciulla,
orba, innocente") then situates Goffredo's pietas in opposition to the
impietas of her uncle ("il tiranno"). Appealing, that is, to Goffredo's
characteristic virtue, Armida tests the ideal against the situation she has
created, making Goffredo's claim to pietas ("il titolo di pio") dependent
on a positive reply and corresponding action.

It is not surprising that Armida's narrative throws the leader of the
Christians into a quandary: "Goffredo il dubbio cor volve e sospende/
fra pensier vari . . ." (4.65.3–4).[51] As he clearly recognizes, he is
being forced to choose between different conceptions of the ideal he
represents: "pietoso affetto/ . . . che non dorme in nobil petto"
(4.65.7–8).[52] The dilemma, the problem of living up to the complex
meaning of the word, is deferred without being resolved in his promise
to her:

> Ben ti prometto (e tu per nobil pegno
> mia fé ne prendi, e vivi in lei secura)
> che, se mai sottrarremo al giogo indegno
> queste sacre e dal Ciel dilette mura,
> di ritornarti al tuo perduto regno,
> come pietà n'essorta, avrem poi cura.

---

[50] Nor should your arm be less accustomed to raise up others than to cast them
down; nor hold itself less honored by the reputation of mercy than by triumphing over its
enemies.

[51] Godfrey revolves and suspends his doubtful mind among conflicting thoughts.

[52] the passion of pity, that never slumbers in the noble breast

Or mi farebbe la pietà men pio,
s'anzi il suo dritto io non rendessi a Dio.
(4.69)[53]

Goffredo takes the primary significance of the word to express what is due from the king to God. The impossibility of acceding to Armida's request is then captured in the paradox of "pietà men pio." The choice that Goffredo makes, and the priority he grants to the *pietà* invested in the mission to recover Jerusalem, is aided considerably by his suspicion (as in "timeo Danaos") of heathen deception: "Teme i barbari inganni" (4.65.5).[54] Without this ethical clue, the choice could hardly have been so easy. Even so, the episode raises in vigorous form the liability of claiming this multifaceted virtue. The paradox—that an act of *pietà* can make the hero less *pio*—suggests that the different implications of the ideal, even though recognized, cannot always be harmonized.

This is especially evident in the sequel, as Goffredo's own knights take up the cause of Armida, reconfiguring the encounter between dispossessed queen and idealized king along the lines of *Aeneid* 4.365–67: "Se mercè da Goffredo or non impetra,/ ben fu rabbiosa tigre a lui nutrice,/ e 'l produsse in aspr'alpe orrida pietra" (4.77.4–6).[55] Casting Goffredo in the role of Aeneas abandoning Dido, the Christian knights acknowledge their leader's pietas as a way of abusing what they take to be his narrowly Vergilian conception of the ideal. He thus becomes in their characterization "crudel" (4.77.8), his cruelty defined in the rock and animal metaphors of Dido's curse. Their alternative proposal, to which Goffredo reluctantly agrees, is not to choose, but to have both Armida and Jerusalem, or in their terms, love and pietas. Although these are not the terms of the problem as it had been presented to Goffredo, the knights change the problem by changing the vocabulary in which it is formulated. Witness Eustazio, who burns "di pietade e d'amore" (4.78.2). Now redefining the situation according to

[53] I promise you firmly (and you may take my word as the honored pledge for it, and live secure in it) that if ever we free from the unworthy yoke these walls so holy and beloved of Heaven, then we will make it our care to restore you to your lost kingdom, as pity encourages us to do. At present pity would make me less religious, if I did not rather render God his due.

[54] He fears the deceptions of barbarians.

[55] If she does not get aid from Godfrey now, surely a raging tigress was his nurse and among rugged mountains the forbidding rock ridge brought him forth.

the conventions of the love lyric, the knights inevitably transfer *pietà* to the female. Indeed, the knights now become her suppliants, seeking in her face "un raggio di pietà" (4.89.6),[56] as she in effect tortures them with their own definition of this virtue: "e in foco di pietà strali d'amore/tempra . . ." (4.90.7–8).[57] The judgmental last stanza of the canto indicates the significance of this shift in meaning, as the arms of the poem's first line are displaced by arms of another sort:

> anzi pur furon l'arme onde rapille,
> ed a forza d'Amor serve le feo.
> Qual meraviglia or fia, s'il fèro Achille
> d'Amor fu preda, ed Ercole e Teseo,
> s'ancor chi per Giesù la spada cinge,
> l'empio ne' lacci suoi talora stringe?
>   (4.96.3–8)[58]

Here, by allusion to the loves of Achilles, Hercules, and Theseus, the ever-present Amor reacquires the epithet "empio" that he has in Fiammetta's vision.

This episode provides the relevant background for consideration of the Dido and Aeneas story as rendered in canto 16. The carved doors of Armida's palace tell the stories of heroes disabled by Amor, stories similar to those alluded to in the last stanza of canto 4, Hercules actually figuring in both. The most detailed narrative is that of Antony, whose situation in the lap of Cleopatra ("in grembo a lei," 16.7.2) anticipates the first glimpse of Rinaldo ("in grembo a la donna," 16.17.8). The fundamental polarity of the canto is provided by the intrusion of Carlo and Ubaldo into the pastoral setting of the garden, the world of knighthood—"dura," "casto," "rigida," "costante"— discovering the world of love—"dolcissimi," "tenera," "allettatrici," "lusinghiere" (16.16–17). The contrast between the physical softness and dissipation of love and the mental strength and emotional control

---

[56] one ray of pity
[57] and in the fire of pity tempers the arrows of love
[58] These were the weapons by which she seized them and made them slaves of love perforce. Now what kind of marvel will it be if fierce Achilles was the prey of Love, and Hercules and Theseus, if even him who buckles on the sword for Christ the impious fellow catches in his toils?

of knighthood is reflected in the two mirrors, the mirror of love in stanza 20 and the mirror of arms in stanza 30. In the first instance the mirror is a crystal that Rinaldo wears at his side, "estranio arnese" (16.20.1)[59]—"estranio" because it replaces his sword. Yet it is not Rinaldo but Armida who actually looks in this mirror (16.20.5–8, 21.1–2), and as she does he looks at her, so that both see the same thing ("un solo oggetto," 16.20.6). The meaning of this vision is first cast in political terms, his servitude in relation to her power, and then in religious terms, her self-glorification and his glorification of her. As an earthly paradise quite different from Milton's ("Hee for God only, she for God in him"), Armida's garden is a place of disarming, where male is subject to female and neither appears subject to God. The implications of the first mirror are still more directly drawn out in the second, where Rinaldo looks at himself in the mirror of the shield (16.30). What he sees is described in a series of contrasts with "ferro." The adjectives—in particular, "delicato," "lascivie," "effeminato"— represent love as seen from the perspective of arms. What the intrusion of Ubaldo and Carlo onto the island suggests, and the contrasting mirrors confirm, is the irreconcilability of the two modes of perception. The differences here are fixed without obvious prospect of accommodation, and yet from this point of maximum separation the poem moves to modify its own rigid categories by appeal to *pietà*.

The process is already latent in the description of the second mirror, for the vocabulary of this stanza recalls the initiation of Ruggiero's awakening from the chains of Alcina in *Orlando Furioso* 7.53. Through Ariosto the passage looks back to *Aeneid* 4.262–64, where Aeneas is confronted by Mercury. The effect is to place Rinaldo in the situation of Aeneas on the verge of renewing the quest for the city, and thus to redefine the role of Armida to make her less a temptress (4.86) and now potentially an abandoned heroine. As Ariosto's Bradamante can think Ruggiero to be "pergiuro, empio e superbo," so Armida now also adopts the stance of a figure from the *Heroides:* "Che temi, empio, se resti?" (16.40.7)[60] Her appeal is especially powerful as it is expressed in stanza 46:

> Aggiungi a questo ancor quel ch'a maggiore
> onta tu rechi, ed a maggior tuo danno:

[59] strange armor

[60] Impious creature, what can you fear if you pause?

t'ingannai, t'allettai nel nostro amore;
empia lusinga certo, iniquo inganno,
lasciarsi côrre il virginal suo fiore;
far de le sue bellezze altrui tiranno;
quelle ch'a mille antichi in premio sono
negate, offrire a novo amante in dono!

(16.46)[61]

The irony of the fourth line here articulates the view of her held by Carlo and Ubaldo, but the clear import of her speech is that the real impietas is Rinaldo's, for he now becomes the tyrant. The final lines, moreover, suggest how differently this pastoral episode is conceived from the Medoro–Angelica story in *Orlando Furioso* 19 (especially 19.33). The mutuality achieved in Ariosto is lost (or at least deferred), the Vergilian emphasis restored, as Armida now aims Dido's Hyrcanian tigers at Rinaldo: "te l'onda insana / del mar produsse e 'l Caucaso gelato, / e le mamme allattâr di tigre ircana" (16.57.2–4).[62] The first step toward detaching pietas from its erotic associations is thus taken by placing the female back in the role of Dido as defined by Vergil.

This alteration of Armida's character nonetheless serves in turn to modify that of Rinaldo, creating possibilities for love unsuspected in the vision of the two mirrors. Unlike Ruggiero, Rinaldo does not represent a version of the pious heroic, but, as his conduct in the battle for Jerusalem amply demonstrates, descends rather from Achilles and Turnus. Thus when Armida describes him as "uomo spietato" (16.57.5),[63] she refers rather to his treachery in love, negatively repeating an understanding of pietas by now conventional to the abandoned heroine. Her appeal on this basis for his fidelity cannot challenge his pietas because in this rather schematic poem pietas is not his, but Goffredo's characteristic. On the contrary, it is love that creates the possibility of pietas for him, exactly reversing the situation in *Orlando Furioso* 19. Rinaldo cannot leave Armida, as Ruggiero does Alcina, nor can he stay with her as Medoro

[61] Add yet to this what you hold as your greater shame, your greater hurt: I entrapped you, I allured you into my love—surely a wicked deception, iniquitous deceit, to make another the tyrant of her beauties, to let him pluck the flower of her virginity; that which to thousands of old had been denied as their reward, to offer as a gift to a new lover!

[62] The raging ocean wave and frozen Caucasus gave birth to you, and the dugs of the Hyrcanian tigress gave you milk.

[63] heartless man

does with Angelica. Instead, his response is described in terms of a redefined *pietà*.

> Non entra Amor a rinovar nel seno,
> che ragion congelò, la fiamma antica:
> v'entra pietade in quella vece almeno,
> pur compagna d'Amor, benché pudica;
> e lui commove in guisa tal, ch'a freno
> può ritener le lagrime a fatica.
>
> (16.52.1–6)[64]

Distinguished from "Amor" in ways it is not at the end of canto 4, the meaning of "pietade" is here governed by the adjectives that describe it: "pur" and "pudica." A highly distilled emotion, this "pietade" nevertheless creates or acknowledges a personal relation. The direction suggested by "pur" and "pudica" is confirmed two stanzas later as eros is pushed still farther into the past and morally distanced by the word "colpe" in his address to her.

> ma che? son colpe umane, e colpe usate:
> scuso la natìa legge, il sesso e gli anni.
> Anch'io parte falii: s'a me pietate
> negar non vuo', non fia ch'io te condanni.
> Fra le care memorie ed onorate
> mi sarai ne le gioie e ne gli affanni;
> sarò tuo cavalier, quanto concede
> la guerra d'Asia e con l'onor la fede.
>
> (16.54)[65]

Here are terms for negotiation: Rinaldo asks to find in Armida the "pietate" that he has discovered in himself, as the term now seems even

---

[64] Love does not enter to kindle the old flame anew in his breast, which reason hardened; pity at least, in place of that, finds entrance there—pity, companion of Love, though chaste; and moves him in such fashion that he can scarcely hold his tears in check.

[65] But what of that? They are human faults, and familiar. I find their excuse in the customs of your country, your sex and your age. I too have partly been at fault; if I do not want sympathy denied to me, it shall not be that I condemn you. In joy and in sorrow you will be among my dear and cherished memories; I shall be your knight, as far as the war with Asia permits, and fealty with honor.

to connote forgiveness. On the basis, then, not of *amore* but of *pietà*, he would be reconciled both to her and to the world of public virtue, here expressed in the last two lines: "sarò tuo cavalier." Armida answers in contempt for this moral speech: "odi il pudico / Senocrate d'amor come ragiona!" (16.58.5–6).[66] Nonetheless a vocabulary of possible reconciliation, including even the disgusted "pudico" of her reply, is here articulated to wait upon events.

The actual moment of departure reveals how the struggle between heroism and love has been internalized and redefined.

> Or che farà? dée su l'ignuda arena
> costei lasciar così tra viva e morta?
> Cortesia lo ritien, pietà l'affrena,
> dura necessità seco ne 'l porta.
>   (16.62.1–4)[67]

The appeal of Armida, formerly "allettatrici e lusinghiere" (16.17.2), is now identified with "cortesia" and "pietà," while the appeal of arms, once "rigida e costante," is now a matter of "dura necessità." The conflict—the Dido problem—is not solved, but it is rephrased. This attempted use of the multivalent *pietà* as a vehicle of mediation between public and private worlds is repeated in the conclusion of the Rinaldo–Armida plot (canto 20). After the battle for Jerusalem is won, Rinaldo recovers Armida in a tearful scene of reunion. Although curious in a number of details and deleted in *Gerusalemme Conquistata,* this resolution places her in clear subjection to him (20.136), not only in religion, as the scene presumes her conversion (20.135), but also in understanding. Her tears are a Petrarchan distillation of love and disdain ("amore e sdegno"), whereas his reaffirm the terms achieved at the end of canto 16: "l'affetuoso pianto egli confonde, / in cui pudica la pietà sfavilla" (20.134.3–4).[68] The adjective "pudica" would hardly be intelligible here if pietas had no history of association with erotic love. It would hardly be necessary if Rinaldo were a different type of character from the one revealed by the events of war.

[66] Hear how the chaste Xenocrates marshals his reasoning concerning love!

[67] Now what shall he do? Should he leave her on the barren sands, thus half alive, half dead? Courtesy restrains him, Pity bridles him, harsh necessity drags him along with her.

[68] He mingles his own tender sorrow, through which a quiet pity gleams.

6
War:
Turnus and Pietas in the
Later Renaissance

The strength and persistence of Dido's challenge to the pietas of Aeneas is matched by that of Turnus. This chapter, then, is concerned with the significance of pietas as it figures in expressions of heroism, with specific reference to the duty of war. Its focus is the moment in Renaissance epic when the hero stands over his defeated opponent, faced with the choice that had confronted Aeneas as he looked down at Turnus. In this scene, the evolved connotations of pietas—compassion, clemency, peace—necessarily perplex the characterization of the hero on the model of Aeneas; indeed, to follow the revisions of *Aeneid* 12 in Renaissance epic is inevitably to raise the larger problem of contradiction between classical heroism and Christian ethics. Although a direct approach to this problem is exemplified in Vida's *Christiad,* more subtle are the climactic encounters between Ruggiero and Rodomonte in *Orlando Furioso,* and Argantes and Tancredi in *Gerusalemme Liberata,* where the heroic vocabulary is accommodated to the crusade fiction that takes as its initial premise the contrast of Christian pietas to heathen impietas. Traditional divergence between the meaning of pietas as it describes the ruler and the meaning of the same word when applied to the hero creates an additional pattern of division: Spenser's distinction between "a good governour and a vertuous man" is very much to the point of *pity* in book 2 of *The Faerie Queene* and *impiety* in books 5 and 6 of *Paradise Lost.*

Aeneid XIII

How a word that has evolved toward clemency, compassion, and peace to characterize the "good governour" can still signal the character of the hero in arms is a problem that Renaissance poets naturally address by appealing to the example of Aeneas. That the Vergilian model raises more problems than it solves, however, is evident from the apparent necessity of rewriting the ending of the *Aeneid* to make the "vertuous man" responsive to medieval as well as to classical conceptions of pietas. Uneasiness with Vergil's ending, which has a long life in the commentaries on the poem, is eventually expressed by the addition of a thirteenth book, which ends not with the death of Turnus but with the apotheosis of Aeneas. Completed in 1428 but influential down to the end of the sixteenth century, the added book of Maffeo Vegio (Maphaeus Vegius) exaggerates the rage of Turnus and directs the *pietas* of Aeneas toward the goal of peace: even as Turnus is identified with the fury of war, here not heroic but savage, so Aeneas is identified with the life of the community after the war is over.[1] Although he does not spare Turnus, Aeneas does show at least ritual clemency by returning the body to Daunus for proper burial. Aeneas now becomes a teacher of *pietas,* a role sequential to that of warrior: "at bello vos, et praestantibus armis/Discite me et pietate sequi" (98–99).[1] The postwar settlement is confirmed by marriage to Lavinia, and after nine days of feasting, Aeneas marks with a plow the boundaries of the new city. Before his apotheosis, then, Aeneas makes the transition from hero in war to ruler in peace, as Vegio solves the problem of *arma* and *pietas* by placing them in temporal sequence.

The impulse behind this unraveling of Vergil's "pietate insignis et armis" is also evident in Lodovico Dolce's vernacular epic on the matter of Troy, which combines the *Iliad* and the *Aeneid* into a single poem accompanied by allegorical commentary. Identified in the allegory with pride (and described as "orgoglioso"), Dolce's Turnus has good reason to acknowledge the *pietà* of his rival.

> Io sò che lode altissima acquistasti
> D'esser in fatti in ver di tutti pio:
> Hor similmente in me mostra pietate,
> Nè ti vinca superbia, ò crudeltate.[2][2]

[1] And you [who followed me] in war and glorious arms, learn to follow me also in piety.

[2] I know that you have won highest praise for true piety in every deed; now in the same way show your piety toward me, nor let yourself be conquered by pride or cruelty.

The self-interested rhetoric of Turnus's supplication speech celebrates the essential virtue of Aeneas in terms more medieval than classical. Situated between "superbia" and "crudeltate," on the one hand, and "pietate" on the other, Dolce's Aeneas discovers his characteristic virtue narrowed to the idea of pity. This carefully calculated appeal is initially successful ("Et era Enea per moversi à pietade . . . ," 531). To render explicit what is not explicit in the *Aeneid,* Dolce not only connects the hero's *pietà* to the decision of the poem's final scene but also defines it in terms more emotional than moral. Whereas the emphasis of Vergil's last scene falls on the character of Aeneas, thus raising for later interpreters the question of whether his action is consistent with his essential virtue, in Dolce's adaptation the derivative "pietate" designates not an attribute of character or a state of being but rather an emotional response to someone else's state of being. As a result the range of potential claims on his virtue is drastically expanded beyond the bounds of kinship and nationality, and the emphasis is shifted from the character of the hero to the rhetoric of the claimant. The ethos of Aeneas gives way to the pathos generated by Turnus, a shift of emphasis that begins to suggest how resolutions to the battle scenes in Renaissance epic will diverge from the Vergilian model.

Dolce does not change Vergil's plot to the point of sparing Turnus. The girdle of Pallas is discovered and Turnus is finally killed. The commentary explains with some care that this act does not diminish the pietas of Aeneas; but then, as if to justify his denial that killing Turnus in any way jeopardizes the character of the hero, Dolce extends the narrative on the model of the thirteenth book. Assenting to the prior request of his adversary, couched in terms that echo the request of Priam to Achilles in Dolce's *Iliad,* Aeneas surrenders the body of Turnus to Latinus for burial. Dolce then adds a canto describing the marriage of Aeneas and Lavinia, the founding of Rome, and ultimately the deification of the hero turned king. Dolce's allegorical interpretation of these events endows Aeneas with the virtues of a Christian prince: "Per Enea . . . si discerne la candidezza, e la pietà d'un religiosissimo, e Christianissimo Principe" (526).[3] In Dolce's version, then, Aeneas not only retains the pietas of "a vertuous man" but emerges by the end of the poem as the model of "a good governour."

[3] Through Aeneas, we discern the purity and the piety of a most religious and Christian prince.

The thirteenth book is also preserved in the Scots translation of Gavin Douglas, whose version of Turnus's supplication speech at the end of book 12 perfectly illustrates the evolved affinity between pietas and the injunction to spare the humble. The words of Vergil's Turnus ("oro . . . Dauni miserere senectae") become in the Douglas translation: "Have rewth and mercy of Kyng Dawnus the ald."[3] Aeneas responds in a way that emphasizes the critical role of the suppliant's rhetoric and especially of his vocabulary, his "wordis": "And mor and mor thir wordis, by and by,/Begouth inclyne hym to reuth and mercy" (12.14.127–28). The phrase "reuth and mercy" is answerable not only to the plea of Turnus, but also to the character of Aeneas as Douglas describes him. In the Scots poem "sum pius Aeneas" is translated "Rewthfull Ene am I" (1.6.125). Just how consciously Douglas addresses the problem of translating the Latin *pietas* is well indicated by his informative note on this passage:

> for [Aeneas] was that man quhilk, by the common voce, was clepit Eneas full of pyete. And for that Virgill clepis hym swa all thro this buyk, and I interpret that term, quhylys, for *rewth,* quhils, for *devotion,* and quhilis, for *pyete* and *compassion;* tharfor ye sall know that pyete is a vertu, or gud deid, be the quhilk we geif our dylligent and detfull lawbour to our natyve cuntre, and onto thaim beyn conionyt to us in neyr degre: and this vertu, pyete, is a part of justyce, and hes ondyr hym twa other vertues; amyte, callyt frendschip, and liberalyte.[4]

Remarkable for its comprehension, this definition attempts to bring together classical and Christian, ancient and medieval conceptions of pietas. After listing the vernacular words that he has called up to translate the Latin, Douglas then repeats the standard Ciceronian definition as modified by the neo-Platonism of Landino. Yet for all this elaboration, the meanings that predominate in the translation itself are those that precede the first semicolon: *rewth, devotion, compassion,* all meanings of the English word *pyete.* Thus in book 12 when Aeneas hesitates, inclining to grant Turnus mercy, he is seen as acting in accordance with the virtue he represents. When he chooses to kill his adversary, Aeneas is described in terms hitherto reserved for Turnus himself: "full of furour," "Full brym of ire" (12.14.142, 143).

The problem of the hero's fury is then addressed by Douglas in his version of the thirteenth book. The Scots translator cannot spare Turnus any more than Vegio or Dolce can, but like them he can and does attempt to affirm or reestablish the hero's pietas. The crucial phrase is Vegio's "Discite me et pietate sequi." Whereas Thomas Twyne, for comparison, translates the "pietate" of this passage as "godlinesse," Douglas has: "Lern forto follow me and to be meik,/yhe contyrfyt my reuth and piete eik."[5] By conflating *Aeneid* 13 with Matthew 11.29 ("discite a me, quia mitis sum, et humilis corde"), Douglas adapts Vergilian to Christian heroism, the nobility of Roman *pietas* to the humility of its Christian counterpart. By doubling pietas to produce both pity ("reuth") and piety ("piete"), Douglas brings together the two *auctores pietatis* of the ancient world, as his translation of *Aeneid* 13 overlaps with the Geneva translation of the Gospel: "learne of me, that I am meke and lowlie in heart."

The Renaissance heroes who take this advice bear a double allegiance: they must be like the classical prototype, Aeneas, but must at the same time adhere to the ethical ideals of Jesus Christ. The problem thus defined in adaptations and extensions of the *Aeneid* is directly addressed in an original poem by Marco Girolamo Vida. Writing in purified Renaissance Latin, Vida adapts Vergilian form, style, and vocabulary to the story of the Gospels. Here the Roman definition of *pietas* is associated with Pontius Pilate. Speaking to Joseph of Arimathea after the crucifixion, Pilate places the trial of Jesus within a Vergilian framework that identifies the Roman officials with "pietas" and the Jewish rabble with "crudelis . . . furor." Although there is obvious verbal hand-washing in this passage, especially in the avoidance of the singular pronoun, Pilate speaks in the traditional vocabulary.

> Et nobis pietas colitur, sanctique penates.
> Sed nihil invita tandem profecimus urbe.
> Crudelis vicit gentis furor. ite, sepulcro,
> Muneribusque pii exanimum decorate supremis.[4][6]

Even in the passive, the combination of subject and verb here recalls the advice of Cicero's *Republic,* while the reference to the Penates suggests Vergil. But in this context Roman *pietas* is shown to be inadequate to the situation, as the passage effectively reshapes the first simile of the *Ae-*

---

[4] We, too, cherish piety and hold the gods to be holy. But at the last I could do nothing with this stubborn city; the mad blood-thirstiness of the people triumphed. Go and reverently honor the dead man with burial and the last rites.

neid: here cultivation of *pietas* does not enable the heir of Cicero and Vergil to cope with mob *furor.* Moreover, as the conflict is translated into judicial terms, Pilate as representative of Roman *pietas* stands in judgment over the incarnation of a new definition of the same word. The verdict in Pilate's favor stands only to be revised by subsequent events.

The crucifixion itself is narrated in book 5 of the *Christiad,* where the meaning of the event is dramatized with reference to the angels. Eager to imitate those who had thrown Satan and his defeated ("debellatos," 5.598) cohorts into the abyss, the angels seek revenge for the crucifixion of Jesus. But it is not *debellare superbos* that is called for, as God acts to prevent the revenge of the angels by sending forth allegorical representations of the ideals truly relevant to the situation. First of these is Clementia (5.628), but she is joined by others: "Addunt se comites Pietas, Paxque aurea. it una / Spesque, Fidesque, piique parens placidissima Amoris" (5.640–41).[5] Clementia, Pietas, and Pax thus complement the three theological virtues in disarming the angels of wrath (5.643–44). The military solution offered by the angels is dismissed by God as "insania ferri" (5.651), words that repeal in this Christian epic the action that concludes its Vergilian model.

In Vida's poem Christ is the exemplar of true *pietas,* most clearly in the Harrowing of Hell, where he is immediately recognized ("tua ingens / Haec pietas," 6.261–62). But as the poem moves toward its conclusion, the heroic mercy of redeeming the patriarchs is succeeded by royal mercy in the person of Peter. In Christ's words:

> Interea Petre te (nulli pietate secundum
> Novi etenim) his rerum summam, clavumque tenentem
> Praeficimus cunctis, ultro qui nostra sequuti
> Imperia. hoc te praecipuo insignimus honore.
> Tu regere, et populis parcens dare iura memento.
> Summa tibi in gentes iam nunc concessa potestas.
> Iamque pios tege pace. voca sub signa rebelles.
>
> (6.662–68)[6]

[5] Holiness and golden Peace came in her company. Hope and Faith also went, and the gentle mother of holy Love.

[6] Meanwhile, Peter, since I know that your piety is second to none, I put you in complete command of all who follow our sway, and you shall hold the key of highest office. I mark you out with this signal honor. Remember to rule and give judgment to the

In this revision of Anchises's commission to Aeneas, the heroic gives way to the royal, and the goal of *pietas* becomes peace. But the words of instruction do not end here, as the passage continues by advancing the idea of just wrath against those who neglect the summons of *pietas* and threaten the congregations of the faithful ("piorum," 6.671). Thus complementing *pietas* with *iustitia,* Vida renders the traditional royal virtues responsive to a division in the world parallel to the two cities of Augustine, a line of thought that had long since been developed to justify war against the infidel. Although Christ is himself identified with both *pietas* and *pax,* Peter faces the difficulty of living these ideals of rule in the world.

How he will succeed where Pilate so signally failed is explained by the ending of the poem, which anticipates a new golden age: "toto surgit gens aurea mundo,/Seclorumque oritur longe pulcherrimus ordo" (6.985–86).[7] In this vision of a world governed by God, the vexations of rule and the hostilities of war simply disappear: "Assurgunt reges pavidi, tibi sceptra, tibi arma/Deponunt, longeque tremunt, et numen adorant" (6.780–81).[8] Vida thus solves, or at least escapes, the problems attendant upon *pietas* as royal and heroic ideal by assimilating both "good governour" and "vertuous man" to Christian eschatology. In this historical design rulers will simply lay down their arms before the Christ who replaces Aeneas as exemplar of *pietas.* This solution will not, however, prove adequate to the problems posed by *Orlando Furioso* and *Gerusalemme Liberata,* where hero and ruler, Aeneas and Christ, will have to coexist.

Ariosto

The adaptations of the *Aeneid* that follow in the tradition of the commentaries make a moral issue of the inherent conflict between pietas and arms. But in another, and highly developed sense of the word, pietas

---

people with mercy. The highest power has now been given you over the nations. And now protect the faithful by peace and summon the recalcitrant to your banners.

[7] A golden race arose upon all the earth, and by far the fairest succession of ages began.

[8] Affrighted kings rise up and for you lay down their sceptres and their arms and at a distance tremble and worship your godhead.

subordinates ethics to culture, as the word functions to distinguish Christian from heathen. And in this sense, the ancient conception of *pia arma* comes to be closely identified with the heroic endeavor of the crusades. In the propaganda directed against the infidel, the basic terms of governance are repeated to proclaim religious and cultural difference: tyranny and cruelty become the province of the heathen enemy, justice and pietas the attributes of Christian crusaders, and especially of the leaders, princes by birth and heroes by deed. Victory over the heathen becomes the model par excellence of the pious heroic.

In proclaiming the first crusade at Clermont in 1095, Pope Urban II lamented that the land where Christ once walked had fallen into the hands of the heathen ("in manus impiorum").[7] Urban thus holds out the promise of remission of sins to those who will undertake this great work ("haec pietatis opera") against the *impii* (41–42). Supporting this call to arms by citing Matthew 10.34 ("non veni pacem mittere, sed gladium"), the pope blesses the idea of holy war and in the name of *pietas* asks the cooperation of the princes whose stories are gathered in the popular crusade narrative written by William of Tyre. In William's account, the basic terms of the pope's request are repeated in a letter attributed to Daimbert urging the cooperation of the prince of Antioch:

> Tu autem, si quid pietatis habes, et nisi paternae gloriae vis esse degener filius, qui, tyrannica crudelitate clausum, ab impia manu domnum apostolicum Gregorium de urbe Roma eripuit (unde memorabile saeculis omnibus nomen emeruit) omni occasione remota, festina venire; et terrae regnique tui cura in militibus tuis prudentioribus sapienter disposita, sanctae ecclesiae miserabiliter laboranti misericorditer succurre (405–6).[9]

The vocabulary here appeals at once to the spirit of filial duty, compassion, and care, to hatred of tyranny and cruelty, and finally to religious loyalty. All of these values are summed up in the word *pietas,* the ideal modelled in William's history by Godfrey of Bulloigne: "piissimus et

[9] Therefore, if you have any loyal compassion for me and if you would not fall below the glorious reputation of your father (who rescued the apostle Gregory from the city of Rome when the holy man was imprisoned by the tyrannical cruelty of wicked men, and who should be remembered for that deed forever), lay aside all excuses and come to me at once. Wisely commit the care of your kingdom and lands to some of your reliable warriors and mercifully come to the help of holy church in her pitiful struggles.

misericordissimus dux Godefridus" (472).[10] The presentation of Godfrey in book 9, chapter 5 elaborates the character of the hero on the
model of the ecclesiastical *pius princeps:* "dominus Godefridus, vir
religiosus, clemens, pius ac timens Deum, iustus" (371).[11] In opposition to Godfrey, the heathen king of Damascus is emphatically characterized as "perfidus et impius Damascenorum rex" (535).[12]

The lines thus drawn between Christian *pietas* and heathen *impietas*
eventually find their way into the literature of Ronscevalles. In the enor-
mously popular narrative of Charlemagne and Roland ascribed to
Turpin (and now commonly known as "Pseudo-Turpin"), the heroic
Roland is "animo pius" and is characterized so as to deserve the author's
apostrophe: "O virum per omnia laudabilem, pietate redundan-
tem."[13][8] The Saracen enemies of Roland represent *impietas* and con-
tinue to do so in the popular narratives of Pulci and Boiardo, which
provide the immediate inspiration for *Orlando Furioso*. Much more
fully than any predecessor, however, Ariosto's poem repeatedly tests the
material supplied by the popular romances against the example of Vergil.[9] The Vergilian vocabulary, often refracted through such later Roman
poets as Ovid and Statius, undermines the clichéd identification of *pio*
with *cristiano;* yet at the same time the medieval implications of the
word also subvert the classical Roman understanding of the Vergilian
ideal, above all in passages that reflect—and revise—the climactic struggle between Aeneas and Turnus.

Ariosto's rewriting of Vergil's ending in the last stanzas of canto 46
responds not only to the tradition of discontent with *Aeneid* 12 but also
to earlier passages in *Orlando Furioso* itself. The extended passage that
bears most directly on the problems raised by Vergil's ending centers on
the figure of Medoro. In cantos 18 and 19 Medoro plays in succession
four roles from the *Aeneid:* Euryalus opposite Cloridano's Nisus, Aeneas
to Dardinello's Anchises, and then Turnus to Zerbino's Aeneas, before
he enters the cave to play Aeneas opposite Angelica's Dido. Telescoped
in this way, the Vergilian episodes are explored with specific and repeated attention to the potential meanings of *pietà/pietas*, as Ariosto
offers a sustained consideration of the pious heroic. Although Medoro

[10] Most pious and merciful Duke Godfrey
[11] Lord Godfrey, a religious, merciful, pious, just and God-fearing man
[12] the perfidious and impious king of Damascus
[13] O man praiseworthy in all things, overflowing with piety

inevitably changes to suit the roles he plays, he is characterized with sufficient consistency to exclude two common implications of the word, one contemporary and one ancient. First, he is not a Christian, so that to whatever extent he comes to embody pietas he excludes the use of the word as shorthand to signify the true faith. Second, he is not a noble, so that to express pietas through him is to deny the ancient identification of this ideal with the aristocracy, to deny more generally the assumption that this is a virtue that implies social or political eminence. The compatibility of heathen religion and plebian status with pietas leads to larger areas of compatability in the narrative, eventually symbolized by the love between Medoro and Angelica.

Yet the narrative begins by defining a relationship between *pietà* and the heroic ethos that is anything but idealized. The night raid becomes the occasion for exposing in graphic and often grotesque detail the aftermath of battle. Adapting incidents diversely from Homer, Vergil, and Statius, Ariosto treats this traditional episode with a skeptical irony that is evident from the moment night falls. The set-piece episode begins with a set-piece of poetic description: "venìa la notte tenebrosa,/...et acquetò ogni cosa;//dal Creator accelerata forse,/che de la sua fattura ebbe pietade" (18.161–62).[14] In the very process of describing night as a sign of divine "pietade," and thus placing the whole episode under the initial sanction of this divine attribute, the truth of the description is shadowed by the word "forse," which intrudes between creator and creation and syntactically distances the creator from the quality attributed to him. The succeeding lines, a survey of the field that night has turned over to thieves and wolves, create a grim landscape to illustrate "sua fattura" and thus to underline the irony of "forse" (18.162.3–8). The skepticism directed toward a creator who would permit the carnage displayed in this lurid description extends as well to those more directly responsible; hostility to the heroic is never far beneath the surface of the next twenty stanzas.

Thus as Medoro and Cloridano reenact the story of Nisus and Euryalus, they engage in the traditional slaughter of unarmed, often sleeping victims, a slaughter summed up in the words "empia strage" (18.181.5).[15] But this is hardly a massacre of innocents, as the scene is

[14] Dark night descended bringing a lull—hastened on, perhaps, by the Creator, who had pity on his creatures.
[15] pitiless butchery

unredeemed by any sign of virtue on the part of the victims, most of whom are killed in various acts of excess, self-indulgence, and debauchery: when Grillo's head is sliced off, he becomes a fountain spurting as much wine as blood. The ironic climax of this episode comes in the apostrophe of stanza 179, which parodies the manner (though not the precise words or sense) of Vergil's famous "Fortunati ambo" (9.446–49). Instead of extolling Medoro and Cloridano as Vergil had immortalized Nisus and Euryalus, however, Ariosto transfers the apostrophe to a pair of victims, a duke and an anonymous camp follower ("una dama") killed in the act (18.179.5–8). The field of heroism, however much it may validate or create distinctions of rank by day, is seen by night to erode even more fundamental distinctions than those of personal status: "in un vermiglio stagno/giaccion poveri e ricchi, e re e vassalli,/e sozzopra con gli uomini i cavalli" (18.182.6–8).[16] To compare this passage with its probable source in the *Aeneid* (11.633–35) is to discover just how forcefully Ariosto has rendered Vergil's perception of the barbarism that underlies the heroic.

The levelled field of this episode would seem to erase all possibility of classical *pietas*. But in fact it is against this background of "orrida mistura" (18.183.1) that Medoro emerges as the poem's finest example of Vergilian idealism. With a striking shift in tone, marked by the prayer to the moon (184), Medoro and Cloridano abandon killing in order to carry out their original intention of recovering their commander's body. Ariosto turns the moment of their success into an emblem of pietas: "Fu il morto re sugli omeri sospeso/di tramendui, tra lor partendo il peso" (18.187.7–8).[17] Specifically labelled "opera pia" in the preceding line, the action of the two boys looks back through Statius to Vergil. The passage in Ariosto shares with its classical predecessors an understanding of pietas that involves a subordination of strength to principle, self to superior, safety to duty. As the narrative develops from this point, however, Ariosto significantly revises the end of the Latin night raid, first by isolating Medoro from Cloridano and then by allowing him to survive the event. When Cloridano runs away at the approach of the Christian enemy, Medoro is placed still more obviously in the situation of *Aeneid*

---

[16] Here poor men and rich, kings and vassals lay together in a crimson bog, men and horses all entangled.

[17] After heaving the dead king onto their shoulders, sharing his weight equally

2: "il grave peso . . . su le spalle" (19.3.3).[18] When he is then confronted by Zerbino, the verse elaborates the meaning of their respective roles:

> Or Zerbin, ch'era il capitano loro,
> non poté a questo aver più pazïenza.
> Con ira e con furor venne a Medoro,
> dicendo: "Ne farai tu penitenza."
> Stese la mano in quella chioma d'oro,
> e strascinollo a sé con vïolenza:
> ma come gli occhi a quel bel volto mise
> gli ne venne pietade, e non l'uccise.
>
> (19.10)[19]

Zerbino, portrayed in other episodes as entirely honorable, here represents the form of heroism whose consequences are displayed in the earlier night scene. Associated with the forces of wrath and madness, he expresses precisely the powers that threaten *pietas* in the *Aeneid*. The congruence of Italian and Latin in "ira" and "furor" underscores the Vergilian context, suggesting at least as much as any other passage Aeneas standing over Turnus in the poem's last scene. But in a stunning reversal of Vergil's conclusion, Medoro—in the place now of Turnus—is spared because "ira" and "furor" give way to "pietade." The last line of the stanza polarizes the two forms of the heroic described in this episode, rendering in the phrase "e non l'uccise" the meaning of "pietade." In effect, Ariosto reads Vergil's last scene from the perspective of the evolved meaning of the Latin *pietas*.

The reprieve that Medoro has won by his looks is then confirmed by his words, which elaborate the meaning of the ideal.

> Il giovinetto si rivolse a' prieghi,
> e disse: "Cavallier, per lo tuo Dio,
> non esser sì crudel, che tu mi nieghi
> ch'io sepelisca il corpo del re mio.

[18] the heavy burden on his shoulders
[19] Now Zerbin, their captain, could stand this no longer. Fuming with rage he approached Medor and shouted: "You shall pay for this!" He reached out and grasped his golden curls and tugged him forward petulantly—but when he laid eyes on the youth's handsome face he took pity on him and did not slay him.

Non vo' ch'altra pietà per me ti pieghi,
né pensi che di vita abbi disio:
ho tanta di mia vita, e non più, cura,
quanta ch'al mio signor dia sepultura.

E se pur pascer vòi fiere et augelli,
che 'n te il furor sia del teban Creonte,
fa lor convito di miei membri, e quelli
sepelir lascia del figliuol d'Almonte."
Così dicea Medor con modi belli,
e con parole atte a voltare un monte;
e sì commosso già Zerbino avea,
che d'amor tutto e di pietade ardea.

(19.11–12)[20]

Whereas Turnus appeals to the son-father relationship that is the foundation for definition of *pietas* in the *Aeneid,* Medoro appeals to the principal relationships that the word had come to govern in Christian Europe: man to God and subject to king. The remarkable expansion of the meaning here, as Ariosto virtually recapitulates the history of the word, is all the more remarkable because Medoro is not asking for his own life, but only for the right to bury Dardinello. It may be recalled how severely the refusal to allow burial of the enemy dead condemns Lucan's Caesar (whose "inpia signa" are therefore said to drip with blood), and how the attempt of Cordus to secure at least a pauper's funeral for Pompey forecasts the night raid in the *Thebaid,* where the role of tyrant ("rex impius") is transferred from Caesar finally to Creon. It is Creon, then, one of the "tiranni atrocissimi" catalogued in canto 17 of *Orlando Furioso,* whom Medoro specifically refers to here, forcing Zerbino to choose between pietas and impietas.

Although this episode rewrites the ending of the *Aeneid* in telling ways, it nonetheless does not come at the end of the poem, and therefore repre-

[20] Now the boy entreated Zerbin, saying, "For the sake of your own God, sir knight, be not so cruel as to prevent my giving burial to the body of my king; further pity than this I do not crave nor would I have you think that I long to live. I care for my life only so far as it will enable me to bury my lord, no further. But if you are a man possessed like Creon the Theban, and needs must fatten the beasts and birds, give them my corpse to feast upon, but let that of Almont's son receive burial." Thus spoke Medor; his manner and his words could well have swayed a mountain. Zerbin was so touched by them, he blazed with love and pity.

sents but a partial or provisional response to the Turnus problem. In the actual ending, Ruggiero confronts Rodomonte in an encounter that does not provoke the kinds of questions raised by the conclusion of the *Aeneid*. Ruggiero is provided with more than enough justification for killing Rodomonte, to whom he does in fact offer mercy. His offer silently refused, Ruggiero's hesitation endangers his own life, when Rodomonte attempts to stab him in the back. Far from playing the role of helpless suppliant in the manner of Turnus, Rodomonte declines that role and thereby closes off any possibility of an alternative ending.[10] Ariosto has significantly altered the immediate context of the climactic struggle, as well, for Rodomonte's challenge comes not in the course of battle but rather as an intrusion upon a wedding feast. By interrupting the celebration of Ruggiero's long-delayed union with Bradamante, Rodomonte by his very appearance casts a long shadow over the resolution to the poem, whose final note is not marriage but death.[11] The questions raised by Ariosto's ending concern not the morality of victory but rather its tenuousness. Everything seems to be resolved when out of nowhere a powerful and disruptive force appears that is only just overcome.

What does Rodomonte represent? What other manifestations of this power are found in the poem? Rodomonte is described in the penultimate stanza as "empio Saracin" (46.139.8). At first glance the epithet appears redundant, since "empi" is elsewhere used alone to signify the Saracen enemy. Yet *empio* is preeminently the epithet of Rodomonte, whose words and actions lend a particularity to the adjective that makes it more than a national or religious label. This is nowhere more evident than in canto 16, where "l'empio re, capo e signor degli empi" (16.26.2)[21] enters the Parisian citadel. Although he displays a titanic strength in this episode, tearing down buildings with his bare hands, his acknowledged "gran valor" is surpassed by a "gran crudeltade" (16.25.7). His indiscriminate wrath allows for no mercy even to the innocent and no respect even for temples of worship. Compared to a cannon ("bombarda," 16.27.5), the strength of Rodomonte is analogous to the power of artillery that elsewhere in the poem signifies the end of chivalry. Not surprisingly, therefore, he shares his epithet with Cimosco, "l'empio re" (9.42.4) of canto 9, possessor of gunpowder, "che né virtù né cortesia / conobbe mai" (9.63.7–8).[22] Rodomonte and Cimosco are joined under this epithet by

[21] the impious king, master and chief of all the wicked
[22] who had never found a use for the knightly virtues

the multiplied figure of "l'empio gigante." What defines the impious heroic here and throughout the poem is strength or power out of proportion to moral worth.

Indeed the lament over the invention of gunpower in canto 11 interrupts the narrative of Bradamante pursued by just such a giant figure (11.19.4), who surfaces again under the name of Caligorante (15.58.5), and who is aptly portrayed as "l'empio Tifeo" (26.52.4) on the shield of the Avalos. As type of impietas, Typhoeus brings to the poem a rich cluster of associations, all suggesting disproportion on a cosmic scale.[12] The size of Typhoeus—taller than mountains, his head brushing the stars, according to Apollodorus—is stressed by later mythographers, who treat him effectively as the last of the Titans. Ariosto's younger contemporary Natalis Comes, for example, typically assimilates Typhoeus ("tanta magnitudinis corporis fuisse dicitur") to his narrative of the rebellion against Jove, which concludes with moral exegesis and admonition: "sine religione ac Deorum metu, nihil neque iustum, neque pium, neque sanctum fieri potest."[23][13] Similar warnings commonly derive from the biblical narrative of the Tower of Babel, the giants of classical myth having long been construed as counterparts to the legendary giants of Genesis. As the most famous of these, Nimrod had been held responsible by Augustine and generations of successors for building Babylon and Babel. The giant figure represents, then, disproportionate size and strength in uncontrolled rebellion against divine authority and order, rebellion correlative to the moral disorder that Augustine calls "superba . . . impietas."[14]

Both Typhoeus and Nimrod serve to deepen the meaning of Rodomonte's character, the first obliquely, the second quite directly. In a Vergilian simile that illuminates the relationship between "l'empio re" and the other "empi" attacking the gates of Paris, Rodomonte is compared first to a tiger among the herd, then to a wolf among goats and lambs. But Ariosto adds to the simile an allusion to the Typhoeus myth: "o 'l lupo de le capre e de l'agnelle / nel monte che Tifeo sotto si frange" (16.23.3–4).[24] While this appears to place goats and sheep in a particular locale, there are enough variants of the myth to render "monte" quite uncertain; what is not uncertain is the effect of associating, however obliquely, Rodomonte and Typhoeus. In the preceding stanza, moreover, Rodomonte is described as "il Saracin robusto" (16.22.2), a phrase that

[23] Without religion and fear of the gods, nothing just, pious, or holy is possible.
[24] as the wolf treats the goats and ewes up on the mountain which crushes Typhoeus

echoes Olympia's description of Cimosco (9.28.1), and recalls the Vulgate description of Nimrod ("robustus venator coram Domino," Genesis 10.9). Nor is this choice of adjective likely to have been merely fortuitous, as the comparison of Rodomonte to Nimrod has already been established in canto 14: "Rodomonte non già men di Nembrotte/ indomito, superbo e furibondo" (14.119.1–2).[25] Whereas the shield of the Avalos expresses, with more than a little hyperbole, the containment of impietas, the shield of Nimrod is brandished by Rodomonte in uncontained imitation of the legendary giants. Here and elsewhere, Rodomonte exemplifies a version of the heroic—"indomito, superbo e furibondo"—the heroic in monstrous form, out of control and out of scale. And this sense of a hero out of proportion to his world is expressed in time as well as space: as Nimrod and Typhoeus, Rodomonte extends his impietas into the legendary past; as "bombarda" he extends it indefinitely into the future. In sum, the "empio Saracin" of the poem's conclusion represents a power more sinister and less vulnerable than the analogy with Turnus, or even Mezentius, would suggest. Nor is the challenge of Rodomonte truly turned back in the last stanza because the prophecy of 41.61 predicts the ultimate death of Ruggiero at the hands of the "empi e malvagi" (41.61.8). As the poem thus repeats and revises the conflict between Aeneas and the various avatars of Turnus, even the final version of this episode comes to seem provisional.

The incompleteness of the victory that closes *Orlando Furioso* is particularly remarked later in the sixteenth century by the French poet Philippe Desportes. His poem "La Mort de Rodomont et sa descente aux Enfers," subtitled "Partie imitée de l'Arioste, partie de l'invention de l'auteur," responds to the conclusion by treating Ariosto's poem as Maffeo Vegio had treated Vergil's. The portion of the original imitated by Desportes (*Orlando Furioso* 46.101–40) establishes Rodomont as a figure even more like Mezentius than he is in Ariosto. As "le contempteur des dieux," his designated characteristics are "arrogance" and "insolence" as well as strength; the "empio Saracin" of Ariosto becomes "Rodomont impiteux," "Rodomont, tout brûlant de fureur et de rage."[26][15] In the face of death he refuses to appeal for mercy and leaves the world blaspheming, Ariosto's last lines becoming in French "l'âme en blasphemant, or-

[25] Rodomont was every whit as dauntless, proud and rabid as Nimrod
[26] pitiless Rodomont/Rodomont all burning with fury and rage

gueilleuse et despite /. . . prend fuite" (342).[27] Thus far Desportes follows Ariosto fairly closely, even exaggerating Saracen furor and impietas. But the invented extension of the narrative is very inventive indeed. Instead of emphasizing the hero's pietas, or apologizing for Roger, Desportes celebrates the poem's final victory without a hint of Christian guilt or any suggestion that killing Rodomont endangers the hero's virtue. Indeed, Desportes makes Bradamant the reward for the victory, a reward that she herself relishes in language that resembles "Angelica a Medor la prima rosa / coglier lasciò" of *Orlando Furioso* 19: "Et souhaitte en son coeur de voir la fin du jour, / Pour cueillir le doux fruit de si parfaite amour" (342).[28] Whereas Ariosto's poem ends with Ruggiero in the arms of his enemy, Desportes places him in the arms of his bride.

Meanwhile, the body of Rodomont is left for the crows and ravens: mediated by Ariosto, Desportes's response to the last request of Turnus is to make a point of denying it. Rodomont does not receive the burial that Turnus receives in the additions to the *Aeneid,* nor does the verse suggest that he deserves it. But Desportes is not finished with Rodomont. His body left for the birds, the Saracen's soul goes to Hell, and in this context the French poet directly addresses the problem of pietas. Once in Hell, Rodomont's plan is to take over the place. As Proserpina and Pluto rally the infernal armies against this threat, Hell is defined as above all a place "sans pitié." As Proserpina expresses it to her infernal subjects:

> Encor que la pitié n'ait point icy de place,
> Resistez par pitié contre cil qui pourchasse
> De m'oster la couronne et se faire empereur
> De ces lieux pleins d'effroy, de silence et d'horreur.
>
> (344)[29]

The irony of the situation is underlined by verbal repetition. Whereas the absence of *pitié* defines the nature of Hell, it is *pitié* that is now required to defend it. Moreover, the second instance of the word here suggests the incomplete separation of French *pitié* from Latin *pietas,* as the meaning

[27] the soul, proud and scornful, cursing took flight

[28] And wishes in her heart for the end of the day, to pick the sweet fruit of so perfect a love

[29] Though pity has no place here, resist by pity he who would rob me of my crown and make himself emperor of this place full of fright, silence, and horror.

appears to include the late classical sense of the word as loyalty to the ruler. As the ironies multiply, the word is again repeated in the speech of Pluto to his "braves soldarts": "Et si n'avez pitié de mes gemissemens, / Prenez au moins pitié de vos cruels tourmens" (346).[30] Here making the word self-referential, Pluto promises to relieve their punishments in exchange for support. And the speech gets results, as all the famous pagans of Ariosto's narrative come forth competing for the honor of leading the troops against Rodomont. In the bumbling that follows, Rodomont falls into Lethe and escapes back to the world. The comedy of Desportes's invention (comparable in some ways to that of Byron in *The Vision of Judgment*) alleviates the gravity of Ariosto's ending through caricature of the impious heroic in Rodomont and ironic definition of the pious heroic here sought among the denizens of Hell. If the first thrust of Desportes's extension is to tidy up Ariosto's ending, the second is to render it less threatening. Rodomont is returned to the world as a comic caricature of the Typhoeus–Nimrod–Mezentius figure that he is in Ariosto's poem.

However comic, Desportes's rewriting of Ariosto's ending to include a scene in Hell acknowledges at least indirectly the satanic power of impietas in the original poem. The French poet thus responds to the tenuousness of victory in *Orlando Furioso* 46, just as Ariosto himself had responded to the moral ambiguity of victory in *Aeneid* 12. The challenge left by Vergil's ending is how to save the character of Aeneas without saving Turnus. Ariosto's solution is to allow Ruggiero to act as Lactantius (for example) thinks Aeneas should have acted, and then to pursue the consequences. The hero offers mercy to the conquered, thereby fulfilling the evolved understanding of pietas, while the rejection of this offer allows him to kill Rodomonte, the poem's most exalted version of impietas. By thus having it both ways, Ariosto answers Vergil (and Lactantius) but leaves unanswered, or incompletely answered, the threat of impietas generated in his own narrative. The problem forecast in the prophecy of canto 41 and evidently recognized by Desportes is that the adversary power— " 'l nimico empio / de l'umana natura" (11.22.1–2)[31]—will live to fight another day.[16]

---

[30] And if you have not pity of my plaints, at least take pity of your own cruel torments.

[31] the Evil One, enemy of human kind

Tasso

In *Gerusalemme Liberata* the adversary power lives to fight again under the banner of the infidel, and yet here the opposition of pietas to impietas yields a conclusion so ambiguous that Tasso drastically changed it for *Gerusalemme Conquistata*. Indeed, from the beginning the difficulties of reconciling the pietas of Aeneas with the pietas of Christ, the pietas of the hero with the pietas of the king, are exemplified in the characterization of Goffredo: "Canto l'arme pietose e 'l capitano / che 'l gran sepolcro liberò di Cristo" (1.1.1–2).[32] The poem's initial affirmation condenses into two lines the basic issues raised by pietas in Renaissance epic. The situation of "pietose" at the very center of the first line raises a question of meaning that is considered from multiple perspectives over the course of the poem's twenty cantos. Although Vergil's "Arma virumque cano" is distinctly heard behind the words of Tasso, the replacement of "virum" with "capitano" nudges Goffredo away from Aeneas as "vertuous man" and toward the idea of a "good governour" in a manner that parallels the allegory of Dolce, who describes Aeneas after his victory over the Latians as "nobilissimo Capitano" (526).[17] Not the precise equivalent of Spenser's "good governour," but rather a word that attempts to bridge the distinction between hero and governor, "capitano" introduces an idea of power that is more than heroic. Whether, then, the potential oxymoron of "arme pietose"—itself a condensation of Vergil's "pietate insignis et armis"—can be held together depends on the political power vested in Goffredo, who is perilously situated in this opening couplet between the heroic duties of war and the religion of Christ, between the means and the end of heroism.

The word that indicates the means is itself of ambiguous status in the first line. In one sense "arme" appears to refer to the personal arms of Goffredo, but in another the word may be metonymy for the soldiers under his command, in which case the conjunctive syntax initiates a pattern of opposition specified even before the end of the poem's first stanza. From these opening lines the rest of the stanza multiplies the contrary forces that Goffredo must control as governor or defeat as hero.

[32] I sing the reverent armies and the captain who liberated Christ's great sepulcher.

> molto egli oprò co 'l senno e con la mano,
> molto soffrì nel glorïoso acquisto:
> e in van l'Inferno vi s'oppose, e in vano
> s'armò d'Asia e di Libia il popol misto;
> il Ciel gli diè favore, e sotto a i santi
> segni ridusse i suoi compagni erranti.
>
> (1.1.3–8)[33]

After coupling " 'l senno" of rule with "la mano" of heroism, these lines place Goffredo in relation to the cosmic struggle between Hell and Heaven. Yet this broad division between what will emerge in the poem as pagan impietas and Christian pietas is undermined by the concluding characterization of his men: "i suoi compagni erranti." The moral order of the first line gives way to a principle of disorder and error in line 8. To reread the whole stanza from the perspective of the last line is to call in doubt the several conjunctions, as the patterned design of reconciled antitheses is threatened by the emergent opposition between "compagni" and "capitano," vertical hierarchy by lateral dispersal, power by rebellion. Goffredo, then, must contend not only with the infernal armies of Asia and Africa ("molto . . . oprò"), but also with the derelictions of his own followers ("molto soffrì"), all too ready to dispute what is later called his "titolo di pio" (13.67.1).

Throughout the poem "il pio Goffredo" bears the epithet of the ideal king in opposition to "l'empio tiranno" (11.26.3) Aladine, ruler of "gli empi pagani" (1.8.6). In the poem's early conflicts, however, *pietà* comes to be closely identified with defeat in battle; rather than restraining the force of arms, pietas lends gravity and ceremony to scenes of death in arms. In canto 3, for example, the classic image of pietas, as modified by the Medoro episode of *Orlando Furioso* (18.187–88), is recast to mark the death of the Christian crusader Dudone.

> né in parte alcuna de gli estremi uffici
> il corpo di Dudon restò fraudato.

[33] Much he wrought with his wit and with his hand; much he suffered in the glorious conquest. And vainly Hell opposed herself to it, and vainly the combined peoples of Asia and Libia took up arms. Heaven granted him favor and brought back under the holy standards his wandering companions.

> Su le pietose braccia i fidi amici
> portârlo, caro peso ed onorato.
>
> (3.54.3–6)[34]

The emblematic nature of this scene is underlined by the phrase "caro peso," which could readily serve to translate the "dulce onus" of Alciati 195 and suggests as well "il grave peso" of *Orlando Furioso* (19.3.3). In this context the adjective "pietose," asserted in the poem's opening line to characterize "arme," governs a complex of ideas organized around the personal consequences of war. In effect, "pietose" designates not what happens during war, but what happens after it, as the Vergilian emblem of *pietas* is attached in a new way to the Ciceronian synonym *officium*. The "estremi uffici" performed here lend this scene a ritualistic as well as emblematic force that significantly complicates the idea of "arme pietose."

Definition of this initial phrase is even more vividly achieved in the sarcophagus-like portrait of Sweno in canto 8.

> Chiusa la destra, e 'l pugno avea raccolto,
> e stretto il ferro, e in atto è di ferire;
> l'altra su 'l petto in modo umile e pio
> si posa, e par che perdón chieggia a Dio.
>
> (8.33.5–8)[35]

One hand on his sword, the other on his chest "in modo umile e pio," Sweno brings together arms and *pietas* not so much in reconciliation as in unresolved juxtaposition: one hand is closed to strike, the other (apparently) open in expression of ultimate defenselessness and humility. Whereas the first two lines here express power and situate the warrior in relation to the world, the two following define the warrior's relationship to God, and it is this relationship that attracts to "umile" the adjective "pio." While this traditional combination of words would seem to fit Sweno for the city of God, the supplication of divine pardon suggests that, in truth, the left hand knew all along what the right was doing. Augustine and many eminent successors had taken *pietas* to express the

---

[34] Nor was Dudon's body in any respect deprived of its last rites. His loyal comrades bore him off in their reverent arms, a treasured and honored burden.

[35] He had his right hand closed and his fist clenched and his sword clutched tight and is in the act of striking; the other is folded on his breast in humble and reverent fashion, and seems that it would ask God for forgiveness.

supreme commandment of Matthew 22.37–40, but in these lines duty to God and duty to neighbor are clearly at odds with one another. Only if the Islamic adversary is excluded from the category of neighbor can Sweno be taken unambiguously to represent "arme pietose."

As it happens, of course, that is effectively what occurs in the first half of the poem, as the infidel is shown to be the enemy of pietas. Consider, for example, the battle between Argantes and Ottone in canto 6. Not content just to kill the Christian, Argantes tramples his victim with his horse, thus provoking Tancredi to an inconclusive battle that will be resumed in canto 19 as the poem's most obvious imitation of *Aeneid* 12 and *Orlando Furioso* 46. Cast in the Turnus–Mezentius–Rodomonte role, Argantes is characterized by an attitude toward arms that is expressed very early in the poem:

> impaziente, inessorabil, fèro,
> ne l'arme infaticabile ed invitto,
> d'ogni Dio sprezzatore, e che ripone
> ne la spada sua legge e sua ragione.
> (2.59.5–8)[36]

The phrase "d'ogni Dio sprezzatore" becomes in a later stanza "feroce ed empio" (2.90.7); like Rodomonte, Argantes is marked by "il furor pazzo" (2.91.2)[37] of Nimrod, and his power is ultimately traced to Satan (7.99). Yet for all this, Tasso's impious hero never assumes the proportions of Ariosto's character, retaining much more of Vergil's Turnus, to whom he is repeatedly compared. Thus his role in the pagan council of canto 10 opposite Orcano's Drances tends to keep Argantes within the boundaries of Vergil's character. In the final encounter with Tancredi, moreover, he is addressed not as a giant but as a killer of giants. By the time the climactic battle takes place, Argantes—*empio* though he is—is seen to belong to the same order of nature as his Christian rival.

In the climactic battle itself the crucial moment is actually doubled, as Tancredi not once but twice offers Argantes the opportunity to surrender (19.21 and 25) and thus to spare himself. But Tancredi's "pietà" (19.26.2)

[36] Impatient, unrelenting, fierce, in arms unwearying and invincible, a despiser of every God, and one who bases on the sword his reason and his law

[37] insane rage

is refused by reappeal to arms. The offer of *parcere subiectis* thus rejected in the manner of Rodomonte, the final act of *debellare superbos* follows, as Tancredi now enacts the *furor* that overcomes Aeneas.

> Infurïossi allor Tancredi, e disse:
> "Così abusi, fellon, la pietà mia?"
> poi la spada gli fisse e gli rifisse
> ne la visiera, ove accertò la via.
> Moriva Argante, e tal morìa qual visse;
> minacciava morendo, e non languia.
> Superbi, formidabili e feroci
> gli ultimi moti fûr, l'ultime voci.
>
> (19.26)[38]

The simultaneous identification of Tancredi with *furor* ("Infurïossi") and *pietas* ("la pietà mia") brings into sharp focus the problem posed by Vergil's ending. Tasso exploits the word that signifies the possibility of mercy to the conquered, but like Ariosto also provides additional grounds, including self-defense, for denying mercy. Indeed, Tasso exaggerates the hero's furor, which exceeds anything in Vergil and Ariosto, and goes well beyond what is necessary to kill his antagonist: "gli fisse e gli rifisse / ne la visiera."[18] As the fury that characterizes Argantes in the battle of canto 6 is here transferred to Tancredi, difference between the two is effectively erased: "Al fin isviene; e 'l vincitor dal vinto / non ben saria, nel rimirar, distinto" (19.28.7–8).[39] Tasso's treatment of the climactic battle will not easily sustain an interpretation that makes impietas the equivalent of pagan, pietas of Christian.

The role of Rinaldo in the last two cantos underlines this conclusion. Although Rinaldo certainly has redeeming virtues, pietas is not one of them. On the contrary, the Christian hero represents another version of the impious heroic, variously modelled not only on Homer's Achilles, but also on Vergil's Turnus, Lucan's Caesar, and Ariosto's Rodomonte. Like Rodomonte, Rinaldo is compared to a wolf (*Orlando Furioso*

[38] Thereupon Tancred grew furious, and said: "Thus, villain, do you abuse my pity?"—then thrust and thrust again his sword into the visor, where it made the way certain. Argantes died, and as he lived he died: dying he uttered threats, and did not languish. Ferocious, fearsome and proud were his final words, his final gestures.

[39] At last he faints; and looking upon them the victor could not well be distinguished from the vanquished.

16.23, *Gerusalemme Liberata* 19.35), as Rodomonte scaling the walls of Paris now becomes Rinaldo scaling the walls of Jerusalem. In a sequence of stanzas beginning at 20.53, moreover, the force of Rinaldo, initially compared to that of earthquake and thunder, eventually touches the very limits of nature: "Poi ch' eccitò de la vittoria il gusto/l'appetito del sangue e de le morti/nel fèro vincitore, egli fe' cose/incredibili, orrende e monstruose" (20.54.5–8).[40] In the next stanza the word "monstruose" is specified in a comparison to a triple-tongued snake that serves to associate Rinaldo with the serpent figure of *Aeneid* 2. Only after this monstrous hero has vanquished all that stands in his way does the imagery of furor diminish, but even as it does, the range of comparison is extended to include Lucan's Caesar (3.362–66). No more "pietose" than the arms of Caesar, the arms of Rinaldo express only fury and wrath ("arme impetuosa fère," 20.59.8).

The concurrent Homeric parallel justifies the expressions of admiring awe that accompany the recitation of Rinaldo's exploits, but the analogy with Achilles also complicates the larger structure of Vergilian parallels. On the model of Turnus, Rinaldo is Latian (Rutilian), on that of Achilles he is Greek, but in no case is he a Trojan, as that identity is reserved for the infidel in Tasso's revision of *Aeneid* 2: Aladine's "Noi fummo" (19.40.7) is only the most obvious reference to the last night at Troy in cantos 19 and 20. Led by Rinaldo, the Christians become descendants of Ariosto's Saracens, Lucan's imperialists, and Vergil's Greeks. The bearers of "arme pietose" are thus identified by the poem's end with the forces of furor. The effect is to erode altogether the distinction between the pious and impious heroic. Thus in the Rinaldo-led attack on the temple of Solomon (19.38), the church is profaned to punish those who had profaned it. Here "l'empio pagano" (19.38.7) is a victim of divine justice administered by Christians whose pietas is asserted in a sentence that attaches it to wrath: "l'ira ne' cor pietosi" (19.38.6). Later, when the two armies battle over Raimondo, the contrast between furor and pietas is thus without referent: "Quinci furor, quindi pietoso affetto/pugna . . ." (19.45.5–6).[41] When the last battle cries are sounded, both armies are asked by their leaders to defeat the "empi." In the words of Goffredo: "Ite, abbattete gli empi . . ."

---

[40] When the taste of victory roused in the fierce victor his appetite for blood and death, he accomplished things incredible, horrid and monstrous.

[41] On this side rage, on that side pitying affections, wage the fight.

(20.19.5)[42]; in those of the pagan Emireno: "assecura le vergini da gli empi . . ." (20.26.3).[43] By canto 20 the word central to the poem's first line is defined entirely by point of view, expressing nothing fixed with reference to the external world.

This is confirmed by Tasso's own second thoughts, which run in the direction of drawing precisely the kind of contrast that fails to emerge from *Gerusalemme Liberata*. The climactic battles in Vergil and Ariosto are rewritten by others; Tasso rewrites his own. In *Gerusalemme Conquistata*, he revises the battle between Argantes and Tancredi, and adds stanzas to the poem's ending evidently designed to remove the ambiguities that characterize the conclusion of the earlier poem. In the recasting of Tancredi's victory over Argantes, Tasso adds two details of particular interest. First, in the initial offer of surrender, Tancredi gives his pagan adversary the chance to become a Christian and thus to save himself in more ways than one, a chance which Argantes furiously rejects.[19] Second, when the final offer is rejected, the words of Tancredi's response are significantly modified from *Gerusalemme Liberata* to emphasize, not furor but pietas: "Turbossi allora il pio guerriero e disse: / 'Giusta pietate è il non usarla or teco' " (23.105.1–2).[44] This attempt to reconcile the act with the Vergilian ideal is consistent with the subsequent elaboration on the treatment of the body. Two stanzas of the earlier poem are expanded into fourteen, in which the body of Argantes is restored to his wife, lamented ("Non ti spero veder mai più risorto, / per mia pietosa cura"), and honorably buried.[20] All this by way of trying to assert the value that is called in doubt by the conclusion of *Gerusalemme Liberata*.

In both the original and the revised version, the poem concludes by shifting attention back to Goffredo. The very last stanza of the *Liberata* shows Goffredo, still bloody from battle, bearing his arms into the temple.[21] Here they are hung as trophies of victory in the poem's final attempt at reconciling pietas and war. If arms hanging in a church serve only to recall "arme pietose" as oxymoron, it is notable that this stanza occasions no reference to the poem's governing ideal. The Christian victor is here—not "il pio Goffredo"—but "il sommo duce" (20.144.6), nor are the "arme sospende" (20.144.7) of the poem's penultimate line

[42] Go, smite the infidel.
[43] Safeguard my virgins from the infidel.
[44] Agitated, the pious warrior then said: "You do not avail yourself of just piety."

now described as "pietose." The final image of Goffredo praying at the holy sepulcher while wearing "il sanguinoso manto" (20.144.5) completes the unravelling of the poem's first stanza. Sustained by the allusions in the last two cantos that align the Christian crusaders with traditional figures of impietas, this ending is heavily revised in the *Conquistata* to reassert the claim of "arme pietose." Remarkably, this phrase is deleted from the first line in revision, and replaced by: "Io canto l'arme e 'l cavalier sovrano."[45] The moral definition of the poem's subject is delayed until the seventh stanza, where it is adapted to praise of Pope Clement VIII: "e de' pietosi eroi l'imprese e l'armi" (1.7.8).[46] From this beginning, the *Conquistata* attempts to do for the *Liberata* what Vegio and Lodovico Dolce had done for the *Aeneid:* to reclaim pietas from the web of ambiguity in which engagement with arms has entangled it. In the end, this means affirming the nominative virtue of "il pio Goffredo."

Compare, then, the last stanza of the original poem with its revision, no longer the last stanza in the new poem:

> Così vince Goffredo; ed a lui tanto
> avanza ancor de la diurna luce,
> ch'a la città già liberata, al santo
> ostel di Cristo i vincitor conduce.
> Né pur deposto il sanguinoso manto,
> viene al tempio con gli altri il sommo duce;
> e qui l'arme sospende, e qui devoto
> il gran Sepolcro adora, e scioglie il vóto.
>
> (20.144)[47]

> Così vinse Goffredo: e 'n cielo, intento
> a mirar la vittoria, è fermo il sole.
> E poi nel giro suo più tardo e lento
> non par ch'ad altra gente indi sen vole.
> È già tranquillo il mar, sereno il vento,
> l'aria più chiara assai ch'ella non suole:

[45] I sing of arms and of the sovereign knight.

[46] the deeds of pious heroes and arms

[47] So triumphs Godfrey; and daylight enough is left him yet to lead the victors to the city now liberated, to the holy house of Christ. And not yet having laid aside his bloody mantle, the commander in chief comes to the temple with the others; and here hangs up his arms, and here devoutly adores the great Sepulcher, and discharges his vow.

tanto col vincitore il ciel s'allegra,
e la natura, dianzi afflitta ed egra.
(24.132)[48]

The differences are obvious enough. Goffredo has here achieved victory
as clear and unclouded as the day that celebrates it. The natural images
of furor, wind and sea, observe a halcyon calm of the sort that characterizes the reigns of Plutarch's Numa and Orosius's Antoninus Pius. The
adjectives "tranquillo," "sereno," and "chiara" express the nature of
Goffredo's triumph over disorder, which parallels that of the imperial
figures in Roman panegyric. Entirely without the shadows cast over the
conclusion of the *Aeneid, Orlando Furioso,* or Tasso's own *Gerusalemme Liberata,* this stanza anticipates the last lines of the new poem:
"E 'l duce, di pietà sublime esempio,/donò le spoglie e sciolse i voti al
tempio (24.137.7–8).[49] Whereas in the final couplet of the earlier
poem, Goffredo represents arms, here he represents pietas: "di pietà
sublime esempio." For all the Vergilian allusions, the "pietate insignis et
armis" of Aeneas comes completely undone in Tassonian epic. The
phrase "arme pietose" of the original first line divides into its component
parts, and ultimately into two poems.

Spenser

As the epics of Ariosto and Tasso demonstrate, *pietà* is a richly
polysemous word: its dominant implication varies from duty to devotion
to mercy without necessarily excluding the alternatives. Its meaning directed by different literary conventions within the Italian poems, *pietà* is a
challenge to the English translator, who does not rely exclusively on *pity*
or *piety* to render the meaning of the original. In his translation of *Orlando Furioso* 19.10–12, for instance, where Ariosto has Italian derivatives of the Latin in each of the three stanzas, Sir John Harington does not

[48] Thus conquered Godfrey: and the victory is mirrored in the sky, which holds the
sun, slowed in its circular path, though not apparent to other people over whom it passes.
And already peaceful is the sea, calm the wind, the air much clearer than usual, so greatly
does heaven rejoice in the victory, and nature too, that before was afflicted and sick.

[49] And the leader, the supreme example of piety, yields the spoils and performs his
vows in the temple.

choose any English derivative even once. Rather, the English equivalents are "pardon," "compassion," and "mercie" (19.7.8, 19.8.3, 19.9.2). Of these *mercy* especially is preferred to *pity*, which is nonetheless the usual word of choice where the Italian *pietà* bears some negative connotation. Thus *pity* is the word that Sir Edward Fairfax chooses to translate the lament of *Gerusalemme Liberata* 9.32: "vana e folle pietà" (9.32.3) becomes "O foolish kindnes, and O pitie vaine."[22] The latter phrase echoes not only Elyot's *Governour*, but also book 2 of *The Faerie Queene*, where both *pity* and *vain* are accorded close scrutiny.[23] Given the still incomplete separation of *pity* from *piety* in sixteenth-century English, given also Spenser's manifest interest in etymologies and deliberate cultivation of archaism, the uses of *pity* in the most Vergilian book of the poem bear significantly on larger issues of interpretation.

How the heroic mind may be touched by *pity* is viewed as problematic from the very beginning of the poem because the word itself is both true and false: *vera pietas* in Una is matched by *species pietatis* in Duessa. In the first instance, *pity* is a mark of humanity and civilized conduct, fulfilling the sense of the Latin word so strongly emphasized by Lactantius. Taking the apologist's conception one step farther, Spenser even confers the English derivative on a humane animal, for it is *pity* that calms the rage of the lion that would attack Una. "Forgetfull of the hungry rage, which late / Him prickt, in pittie of my sad estate."[24] This contrast between "rage" and "pittie," an evolved version of Vergilian *furor* and *pietas*, is here assimilated to a difference in power, as *pity* moderates the imbalance between physical strength and weakness. Similarly, *pity* is the mark of emerging civility in the Satyrs in their encounter with Una: "They in compassion of her tender youth, / And wonder of her beautie soveraine, / Are wonne with pitty and unwonted ruth, / And all prostrate upon the lowly plaine, / Do kisse her feete, and fawne on her with count'nance faine" (1.6.12.5–9). In this passage "pitty" is joined with "compassion" and "ruth," a semantic cluster that again mediates between strength and weakness; here, however, the issue is complicated not only by the parallel distinction between barbarism and civility, but also by the phrase "beautie soveraine," which expresses the authority of truth in political terms: the Satyrs bow down before her. Fulfilled at the end of the next stanza where she is worshipped "as Queene" (1.6.13.9), this passage that first engages *pity* as an expression of their power over her ends as an expression of her power over them. The word is from the beginning engaged with the problem of mediation, is accommodated to a political vocabulary, and varies markedly in connotation from one context to another.

Although the word can thus signify positively in relation to Una, *pity* is first spoken in the poem by Duessa, her phrase "in pitty of my state" (1.2.26.3) closely matching Una's later "in pittie of my sad estate" that expresses the moderation of the lion's rage. But more is involved here than a renewal of the struggle between true and false meaning; the word recurs in a range of contexts that makes such simple distinctions impossible to sustain. Consider, for example, the success of Duessa's rhetoric before the Queen of Night. "Her feeling speeches some compassion moved / In hart, and chaunge in that great mothers face: / Yet pittie in her hart was never proved / Till then: for evermore she hated, never loved" (1.5.24.6–9). The same vocabulary that in the next canto will express a movement toward truth, here belongs to the mother of darkness, and is an emotion provoked in the service of revenge. Duessa's words thus belong to a context not entirely different from that which elicits Guyon's vow and suggests its Vergilian background: "Go gather up the reliques of thy race, / Or else goe them avenge" (1.5.24.2–3). But the question here is not Priam's—whether there is pietas in Heaven—but rather whether it exists in Hell. The answer, of course, is that it does. And therein lies the problem, as the trial of Duessa in book 5 well illustrates.

Most at issue in books 2 and 5, which James Nohrnberg has called the "Books of the Governors,"[25] *pity* is carefully related to such alternatives as *clemency, compassion,* and *mercy,* even as it is distinguished from them. In the trial of Duessa, whose "allure" is said to be "compassion" and "pitie" (5.9.38.9, 39.8), judgment will ultimately be passed by a queen whose name signifies *mercy.* The first speaker for the defense, and evidently an effective one, is Pittie. Even Arthur is moved: "With the neare touch whereof in tender hart / The Briton Prince was sore empassionate" (5.9.46.1–2). But Zele counters this response in rebuttal, with accusations of *Murder, Sedition, Incontinence, Adulterie,* and *Impietie* (5.9.48). Thus identified, Duessa is accused of crimes that writers from Damian to Elyot had declined to forgive in the name of pietas. Implicitly commenting on this tradition, the queen acts "With piteous ruth" (5.9.50.2), an apparent redundancy that serves to emphasize the several terms of opposition to "just vengeance" (5.9.50.5). At the same time, however, this subjective use of "piteous" in combination with "ruth" is revealed as imperfectly consonant with the very name of Mercilla. In the succeeding canto this dissonance will be corrected, and *mercy* will emerge as the appropriate term of judgment, its affinity with *clemency* affirmed without any reference to *pity*.

The distinction that emerges in this canto, indeed in this book, between personal feeling and official duty, is expressed in the very organization of the poem, as the fate of Duessa is postponed across the canto division. It is not until the fourth stanza of canto 10 that the execution of Mary Queen of Scots is actually acknowledged, in a passage so oblique that the action is easily missed on first reading: "And yet even then ruing her wilfull fall, / With more then needfull naturall remorse, / And yeelding the last honour to her wretched corse." (5.10.4.7–9) Reverting to the conventional device of those who rewrite the ending of the *Aeneid*, Spenser adds the ritual of conferring "honour to her wretched corse" while stressing Mercilla's "mercies rare, / And worthie paterns of her clemencies" (5.10.5.6–7). To think of the trial as a judicial version of the decision rendered against Turnus by Aeneas may in fact be helpful in considering episodes from *The Faerie Queene* that are more obviously parallel. Not only does the trial amplify the significance of Aeneas's hesitation, but it also reveals the moment of decision to be an aspect of governance rather than of heroism, a political rather than a personal act. Whereas Servius could express this only as paradox, crediting Aeneas with *pietas* for both personal feeling and political necessity, Spenser distinguishes *pity*—said to be an "allure" and expressed in Mercilla's tears as a "passion" (5.9.50.9)—from the *mercy* that expresses her "Royall" (5.10.5.6) or public character.[26]

If *pity* can be "allure" and "passion" to the "good governour" of book 5, so can it be also to the "vertuous man" of book 2, most remarkably so in canto 12. The setting of the Bower of Bliss, with its evident resemblance to Armida's gardens and Alcina's island, suggests the temptations of Ruggiero and especially Rinaldo. Although the lure of the unheroic is indeed evident here, as Verdant reclines in the lap of Acrasia (2.12.76.9), what tempts Guyon is not ease but distress: the most traditional of all knightly duties, the rescue of the distraught maiden, is presented as a distraction from the heroic endeavor. And the siren cry is *pity:* "And as they went, they heard a ruefull cry / Of one, that wayld and pittifully wept" (2.12.27.2–3). The word "pittifully" here characterizes the rhetoric of tears that elicits from Guyon the natural response, until he is restrained by the Palmer:

For ill it were to hearken to her cry;
For she is inly nothing ill apayd,
But onely womanish fine forgery,
Your stubborne hart t'affect with fraile infirmity.
                                              (2.12.28.6–9)

The emotion involved in "pittifully" is thus assimilated to the convention of female temptation. The "seemely Maiden" (2.12.27.6) becomes a
figure of "womanish fine forgery," and the response she would elicit is
now called "foolish pitty," a phrase falling somewhere between the
frivola and *noxia pietas* of Peter Damian. As the Palmer explains the
danger:

. . . when she your courage hath inclind
Through foolish pitty, then her guilefull bayt
She will embosome deeper in your mind,
And for your ruine at the last awayt.
                                              (2.12.29.1–4)

This passage provides a succinct reminder of semantic evolution: the
Latin word that names the capacity of Aeneas to overcome feminine
temptation names in English derivative the feminine temptation itself. As
it has evolved through literary conventions alternative to the heroic,
pietas in the form of *pity* has become in Spenserian epic the problem
rather than the governing virtue. Yet the problem is no simple one, as
more detailed consideration of *pity* in the first half of the second book
may indicate.

   If the pejorative "womanish" represents a rejection of pietas personified as feminine, it will be recalled that book 2 begins with Amavia, who
also personifies the word. Actually, the "Pittifull spectacle" (2.1.40.1,9)
of Ruddymane's bloody hands is the book's first image of *pity,* which is
then personified as female in the maternal "Lady, which the image art/
Of ruefull pitie" (2.1.44.4–5). Thus imaged and personified, *pity* occasions Guyon's quest for "dew vengeance" (2.1.61.7) that is finally completed with "rigour pittilesse" (2.12.83.2) in the Bower of Bliss. The
organizing motive of the second book is disclosed to have affinity with
the tradition of commentary and revision founded on *Aeneid* 12, and
Guyon's encounter with Pyrochles in canto 5 in particular bears more

than passing resemblance to the situation of Aeneas and Turnus. In fact, the Pyrochles episode belongs to a sequence of cantos that depend on derivatives of *pietas,* as Spenser considers the Turnus problem from a succession of different perspectives. In these episodes the diadic possibilities of Vergil's "pietate insignis et armis" repeatedly yield to triadic structures in which *pity* negotiates its way toward the midpoint between extremes of conduct in arms.

Medina's intervention in the battle of canto 2 is an immediate case in point. The battle of Huddibras and Sans-loy is cast in the conventional terms of furor: "horrible assault, and furie fell" (2.2.20.4). Guyon, whom they attempt to attack before falling out between themselves, figures here as likely peacemaker, and almost literally as mediator. Yet his attempt to "pacifie" (2.2.21.9) the two furious knights requires shield and sword, "meanes" (with play on words, 2.2.21.9) contradicting ends, the role of hero proving inadequate to that of governor. In the end he can sustain neither role, as the "double . . . prayse" (2.2.25.9) that Guyon here wins does not succeed in ending the battle. On the contrary, once engaged in the battle he is assimilated to the condition of Huddibras and Sans-loy. The repeated "triple" replaces the repeated "double" of the previous stanza: "A triple warre with triple enmitee" (2.2.26.3). It is in this context that Medina intervenes.

> Whilst thus they mingled were in furious armes,
> The faire *Medina* with her tresses torne,
> And naked brest, in pitty of their harmes,
> Emongst them ran . . .
>
> (2.2.27.1–4)

The three knights are now "mingled" and placed in opposition to Medina, male in opposition to female, plural to singular, "furious armes" to "pitty." The emergent hierarchy of values here is expressed in familiar terms: "furious armes" identified with "cruell discord," "pitty" with justice and peace ("just conditions of faire peace," 2.2.27.9).

This conventional disposition of pietas and furor provides the context for consideration of the revenge motive that initiates and underlies Guyon's quest.

> And were there rightfull cause of difference,
> Yet were not better, faire it to accord,

Then with bloud guiltinesse to heape offence,
And mortall vengeaunce joyne to crime abhord?
O fly from wrath, fly, O my liefest Lord:
Sad be the sights, and bitter fruits of warre,
And thousand furies wait on wrathfull sword;
Ne ought the prayse of prowesse more doth marre,
Then fowle revenging rage, and base contentious jarre.

                                                (2.2.30)

Medina's argument—even "rightfull cause" does not justify "fowle revenging rage"—bears not only on the conduct of Guyon but also on that
of his prototype in the last lines of the *Aeneid*. This answer to the
problem posed by Vergil's ending—"fly from wrath"—is, moreover,
similar to that found in allegorical interpretations of the *Aeneid* as early
as Fulgentius, whose moralized version of the flight from Troy ("vir enim
pius superbiae voces et malorum poenas effugit ac pavescit") offers significant precedent for the advice of Medina. As the allegorized *Aeneid*
turns the poem inward, so Spenserian allegory turns from an outer war
that can never be won to an inner war that can be. Referring to the life of
virtue, Medina instructs the knights: "Brave be her warres, and honorable deeds,/By which she triumphes over ire and pride" (2.2.31.5–6).
Not only does this passage turn the idea of *debellare superbos* inward,
thus rebutting the persistent identification of pietas with *parcere subiectis,* but it also creates a scenario in which the end of war actually is
peace. "Be therefore, O my deare Lords, pacifide,/And this misseeming
discord meekely lay aside" (2.2.31.8–9). In this context, for which the
closest "Vergilian" analogue is the thirteenth book, the word "meekely"
is at least worth noticing as the adverbial form of Christ's distinguishing
virtue in Matthew 11.29. The Geneva Bible's "meke and lowlie in heart"
is the apparent antidote to the "ire and pride" of the impious heroic:
apparent because subsequent cantos subject even this conclusion to further scrutiny, as Spenser's poem continues to rewrite itself.

   That "meekely" may be hard to distinguish from weakly, for example,
is brought immediately to attention with the introduction of Braggadocchio in canto 3. Here the final encounter between Aeneas and Turnus
is recast as parody of the battle in canto 2. Medina's expression "Vaine is
the vaunt, and victory unjust" (2.2.29.8) is now surprisingly elaborated
to elicit from the Turnus problem the dimensions, not of pietas and
furor, but of cowardice and vanity. The word *vain* occurs more times in

book 2 than in any other of the poem partly because it is the epithet of Braggadocchio, who appears at the beginning of the canto "puffed up with smoke of vanitie" (2.3.5.3) as a result of finding Guyon's horse. In imitation of the pious hero he confronts Trompart, who holds up "pitious hands" (2.3.6.9) in his role as suppliant. More than parody of a traditional epic situation, however, this encounter reveals that the ethical positions advanced by Medina in the previous canto can readily be fulfilled by those with only a spurious claim on the heroic. Braggadocchio does exactly what Lactantius would have Aeneas do and the result is peace and concord, the very values espoused in the extensions of the *Aeneid* that turn the hero into a king. Medina's statement in stanza 31 ("But lovely concord, and most sacred peace / Doth nourish vertue, and fast friendship breeds," 2.2.31.1–2) effectively becomes the basis for the reconciliation of Braggadocchio and Trompart: "So happy peace they made and faire accord" (2.3.9.1). As they make fast friendship, the "highest prayse" (2.2.31.4) of Medina is turned to "fine flattery" (2.3.9.8). In the course of four stanzas Spenser comically subverts the response to *Aeneid* 12 that would have Aeneas show his *pietas* as *pity,* by acknowledging the ease with which exactly that reaction to the "pitious" can be performed by Braggadocchio.

What is missing from this scene is not only *vera pietas* but also *vera furor,* the force of which is allegorized in canto 4. Guyon's encounter with Furor proceeds from the same kind of circumstance that provides the recurrent starting point for episodes in this book. That is, some instance of real or apparent distress provokes the hero's impulse to pity; in this case it is the sight of Furor dragging Phedon by the hair while Occasion tags along provoking Furor to further vengeance and wrath. But by engaging Furor out of compassion for Phedon, Guyon only injures himself: "To overthrow him strongly did assay, / But overthrew himselfe unwares, and lower lay" (2.4.8.8–9). This draws into a narrow compass the implication often marked in imitations of the conclusion to the *Aeneid,* as Spenser's lines transform the climactic struggle into psychomachia. The very act of the pious hero in attempting to kill his adversary is inevitably to succumb to him: to overcome furor is to become furious. The intervention of the Palmer, explaining that Furor—"cursed cruell wight" (2.4.10.6)—can never be killed, only controlled, reveals the significance of the allusion (2.4.14–15) to the binding of *furor impius* in *Aeneid* 1.[27] But because Furor is bound, not killed, because this is not the end of book 2, much less of the whole poem, it is hardly surprising to find Furor unbound in the very next canto, thus making way for the encounter between Pyrochles and Guyon.

This encounter is less an imitation of the confrontation between Turnus and Aeneas than a deep response to the problems raised by it and already considered in cantos 2 through 4. The accusation that Pyrochles makes in provoking battle with Guyon is one that declines to distinguish the hero from his empty imitation, Guyon from Braggadocchio. After condemning Guyon as one who fights "With silly weake old woman" (2.4.45.5), referring to Occasion, Pyrochles labels Guyon a coward (2.5.5.3–4). In this second look at the problem addressed as parody in canto 3, Pyrochles denies the metonymy of arms and heroism that Braggadocchio takes for granted: "Thereby thine armes seeme strong, but manhood fraile" (2.5.5.6). That Guyon cannot be taken to illustrate this principle is then proved in battle, and Guyon's victory is emblematically expressed in the classic posture already assumed by many a victor in Renaissance epic: "Then on his brest his victour foote he thrust" (2.5.12.6). It is at this point that the second and more difficult test begins, and like Aeneas, Ruggiero, and Tancredi, Spenser's hero hesitates, in this case long enough to make a considerable speech. "Fly, O *Pyrochles*, fly the dreadfull warre, / That in thy selfe thy lesser parts do move, / Outrageous anger, and woe-working jarre" (2.5.16.1–3) Closely parallel to Medina's advice to Guyon himself, these words elicit from Pyrochles a revealing reply: he asks for *mercy* by declaring the motive of his attack in precisely the terms that Guyon has been acting on (or responding to) throughout this book: according to Pyrochles, his double motive was the relief of distress and vengeance on those causing it. He attempts, that is, to cast the mother-son figure of Occasion–Furor in the role of Amavia–Ruddymane and himself in the role of Guyon. Challenged in this way, Guyon responds by repeating Pyrochles's word *mercy* (2.5.18.3) in giving assent to the release of Furor and Occasion.

That this word does not conform to the action described is revealed by the sequel. Immediately set upon by Furor, Pyrochles calls to Guyon for help. The situation that emerges shares certain features with the battle in canto 2 between Huddibras and Sans-loy. Whereas in that instance Guyon intervenes with his sword and thus becomes as furious as they, here Guyon remains deliberately outside the battle: "Ne would with vaine occasions be inflamed" (2.5.21.7). But if Guyon does not intervene with his sword, he is nonetheless asked to respond to Pyrochles's distress.

> The knight was greatly moved at his plaint,
> And gan him dight to succour his distresse,
> Till that the Palmer, by his grave restraint,
> Him stayd from yielding pitifull redresse;
> And said, Deare sonne, thy causelesse ruth represse,
> Ne let thy stout hart melt in pitty vayne:
> He that his sorrow sought through wilfulnesse,
> And his foe fettred would release agayne,
> Deserves to tast his follies fruit, repented payne.
>
> (2.5.24)

In this repetition of the basic challenge to the hero in the first half of book 2, Guyon's word *mercy* is corrected by the Palmer, whose word is *pity*. Alienated from the meaning it has in canto 2 by the attributive "vayne," *pity* as motive for heroic action is here called seriously in doubt. How does "pitty vayne" function here? Is the adjective meant as always qualifying "pitty"? Or is pity vain only by reference to these particular circumstances?[28] The closest the passage itself comes to defining the phrase is in the parallel "causelesse ruth." And if "cause" is taken in the sense of reason, then the vocabulary suggests a disengagement of the qualities reflected in the division between the Palmer and Guyon, the reason of the one opposite the pity of the other. That is to say, *pity* is not to govern but to be governed: hence the importance of the verb "represse." What this passage urges is recognition not of difference but of similarity, even analogy between *pity* and *furor,* which is also described as "vaine" (2.4.7.4) and is also not to be killed but only repressed or constrained (2.4.15.2). Instead of the polarized disposition of furor and pietas inherited from Vergilian epic, canto 5 explores the restraint of both furor and pietas in the temperate mind.

If this is to be considered as a resolution to the problem of *pity* in book 2 of *The Faerie Queene,* it must be set against Spenser's repeated adaptations of Vergil's first simile. In canto 2, where its appropriateness is indicated by the "troublous seas" and "raging windes" (2.2.24.1,2) that characterize the furor of the battle between Huddibras and Sans-loy, the "pitty" (2.2.27.3) of Medina is expressed in the manner of Vergil's Neptune.

> Yet she with pitthy words and counsell sad,
> Still strove their stubborne rages to revoke,

> That at the last suppressing fury mad,
> They gan abstaine from dint of direfull stroke,
> And hearken to the sober speaches, which she spoke.
>   (2.2.28.5–9)

Here language itself—"words" and "speaches"—suppresses "fury mad," evidently a quite deliberate attempt to capture the precise nuance of the Latin *furor*. But if order emerges from disorder here, the passage does not express anything so permanent as a vision of history. Indeed, the temporal markers suggest rather a narrative in which the relationship between the order of speech and the disorder of "stubborne rages," between pietas and furor, is ever subject to revision, a suggestion confirmed by alternative versions of the same simile.

In a comparable context, the Vergilian simile is evoked by Phaedria in canto 6, but with a significant shift in vocabulary. Like Medina in canto 2, Phaedria intervenes "atweene" two knights, here Guyon and Cymochles at the "extremities" (2.6.36.2). First she appeals to "pittie" (2.6.33.2) in a passage that suggests analogy with "love" (2.6.33.1) and the amorous otium of Acrasia's realm, and recalls the traditional antithesis between pietas and cruelty (2.6.32.6). But as temptation gives way to a sustained and powerful critique of the heroic, the language changes.

> Therewith she sweetly smyld. They though full bent
> To prove extremities of bloudie fight,
> Yet at her speach their rages gan relent,
> And calme the sea of their tempestuous spight,
> Such powre have pleasing words: such is the might
> Of courteous clemencie in gentle hart.
> Now after all was ceast, the Faery knight
> Besought that Damzell suffer him depart,
> And yield him readie passage to that other part.
>   (2.6.36)

In this simile of calming the stormy sea, as in Vergil's, the power of speech is contrasted to that of force. Though bearing the legacy of Vergil's "pietate gravem . . . virum" (1.151), Phaedria is now identified, not with *pietas*, but rather with *clementia*. The preference for "clemencie" here is remarkable not only because of the Vergilian background of the passage, but also because the poem here expresses a sententia usually dependent on the resonance of pietas both in Italian and in English: as in Tasso's "pietoso affetto / . . . che non dorme in nobil petto" (4.65.7–8), and famously in Chaucer's "For pitee renneth soone in gentil herte."[29] The shift from "pittie" at 33.2 to "clemencie" at 36.6, in a line whose antecedents promise a derivative of *pietas,* has the effect of avoiding the ambiguities attendant upon "pity." Like *mercy, clemencie* commands ready assent in the poem, whereas *pity*—commonly on the tongues of the poem's more dubious figures, including Duessa—argues semantic and moral uncertainty. The very use of the word *clemency* here is a measure of how seriously Spenser entertains Phaedra's argument.[30] This adaptation of Vergil's simile confirms a basic tendency of Spenser's vocabulary to distinguish *pity* from *mercy* and here *clemency.* The latter two are fit terms of governance and self-governance, while the former must itself, like *furor,* be governed.

So governed, as Guyon is by the **Palmer** in canto 12, for example, *pity* has its uses and place. Or to express this more positively: *pity* may be a form of excellence in the ideal figure who is at once "a vertuous man" and "a good governour." There is a glimpse of this figure to be had in the British Numa of canto 10. In Spenser's chronicle of British monarchs, the demise of "*Brutus* sacred progenie" (2.10.36.1) in fraternal strife leads to the emergence of a new ruler eventually described as "The gracious *Numa* of great *Britanie*" (2.10.39.6). The traditional associations that attend this classical figure are introduced in lines that again suggest the first simile of the *Aeneid.*

> Then up arose a man of matchlesse might,
> And wondrous wit to menage high affaires,
> Who stird with pitty of the stressed plight
> Of this sad Realme . . .
>
> (2.10.37.1–4)

This is not, obviously, passive imitation, as Spenser has significantly modified Vergil's description of the man who arises to quell disorder (the "discord" and "factions" of the previous stanza) to suit difference of circumstance: the public man of the Latin simile is already known by his *pietas,* whereas Spenser's man of "might" and "wit" is moved to public service by his *pity.* Although the Vergilian context lends weight to the political use of the word here, even without it *pity* is untouched in this stanza by the negative connotations that it often has elsewhere in book 2. Indeed "pitty" for the "Realme" is even consistent here with the killing of several enemies in the interest of establishing "civill governaunce" (2.10.38.8), significantly rhymed here with "valiaunce" (2.10.38.6), as the roles of hero and king are combined in one figure. In the "pitty" of this distant and idealized figure, celebrated by comparison to Plutarch's Numa rather than to Vergil's Aeneas, pietas survives, even as it survives in the form of "Pietie" to characterize the host of good angels who serve the perfect hero-king of *Paradise Lost*.

Milton

Historically, *clemency* and *mercy* displace derivatives of the Latin *pietas* to express political ideals in English, and this historical process is reflected in the vocabulary of *The Faerie Queene*. But such displacement does not occur in the negative, as *impious* and *impiety* do not just survive, but indeed thrive as terms of opprobrium for rebels and tyrants. This aspect of the word's history is reflected in Milton's war in Heaven, where the nature of Christ as hero and king is revealed by antithesis to Satan, who "with ambitious aim / Against the Throne and Monarchy of God / Rais'd impious Warr in Heav'n and Battel proud / With vain attempt."[31] The adjective here bears traditional associations that deprive Satan of whatever glory his exploits might seem to win, for "impious Warr"—as in the Latin *impia bella*—here signifies civil war with the additional political connotation of disloyalty. This is specifically the sense in which Abdiel uses the word in answering Satan's complaint that submission to the Son as well as the Father is too much to ask:

> O argument blaspheamous, false and proud!
> Words which no eare ever to hear in Heav'n
> Expected, least of all from thee, ingrate,
> In place thy self so high above thy Peeres.
> Canst thou with impious obloquie condemne
> The just Decree of God, pronounc't and sworn,
> That to his onely Son by right endu'd
> With Regal Scepter, every Soule in Heav'n
> Shall bend the knee, and in that honour due
> Confess him rightful King?
>
> (5.809–18)

Here "impious" is opposed to "just" in the manner of biblical usage, as well as parallel to "blaspheamous, false and proud," thus combining implications of the word developed in relation to both monarchy and deity. One main sense of *impious* as it is attached to Satan, then, is political and places him in opposition to the idea of "a good governour" or "rightful King."

When Abdiel repeats the word in urging Satan not to pursue his plan of rebellion, the phrase "impious rage" (5.845) suggests as well the recurrent adversary of the pious hero. Describing Satan as "Proud" (6.131) and "vain" (6.135), Abdiel reminds him that there are angels "who Faith/Preferr, and Pietie to God . . ." (6.143–44); when speech fails, he initiates war with the phrase: "This greeting on thy impious Crest receive" (6.188). The angels thus fall out into two camps, which like the two cities of Augustine are respectively identified with impietas and pietas. As Augustine's *civitas impiorum* is the city of pride, so pride is the idea that characterizes Satan, who bears the diminishing epithet "vain" that Spenser had given to Braggadocchio, along with the "impious" that he shares with the Titan figures of Italian poetry. Initially visualized as a giant in the literary mold of Rodomonte, Satan is the natural culmination of the impious heroic in Renaissance epic. And yet, the essential argument of books 5 and 6 is that there can be nothing truly heroic about impietas. Although the climactic encounter repeated from earlier epics is here stripped to its essentials, the expected battle between the impious Satan and Christ, the incarnation of pietas and true "King anointed" (5.777) of Christian theology, simply does not happen, or at least does not happen on the model of *Aeneid* 12.

One reason it does not happen is that Milton's Christ, like Aeneas in the thirteenth book, is more than a hero; like Vida's Christ, he is an agent of peace whose ultimate mission is to repair and restore. In God's own words: "For thee I have ordaind it, and thus farr/Have sufferd, that the Glorie may be thine/Of ending this great Warr, since none but Thou/Can end it" (6.700–703). These lines, as Stella Revard has suggested, express an idea already present in God's identification of the Son with peace in book 3: "O thou in Heav'n and Earth the onely peace/Found out for mankind under wrauth" (3.274–75).[32] As in the extensions of the *Aeneid* that show Aeneas transformed into the peaceful ruler of a restored kingdom and ultimately into a deity, so in *Paradise Lost* Christ claims this role from the beginning. As a result the final battle becomes rather the last phase of a trial, in which Christ as king administers "punishment" (6.807) of the guilty. And this punishment or "doom" (6.817) must be expressed in the only terms the "cursed crew" (6.806) understands.

> Or I alone against them, since by strength
> They measure all, of other excellence
> Not emulous, nor care who them excells;
> Nor other strife with them do I voutsafe.
> (6.820–23)

These lines indicate, then, the second reason there is no final combat on the model of *Aeneid* 12: the poem undermines the possibilities of the impious heroic even as it moves toward a final contest of strength. In thus defining his own role, Christ also defines that of his enemies in ways that never allow Satan the individual dignity of Turnus, or even of Rodomonte or Argantes: "I alone against them." There is no single combat, and therefore no moment directly correspondent to the scene that concludes the *Aeneid*.[33]

Indeed there is no real battle in any traditional sense at all; the "idle weapons" (6.839) are "idle" because they are utterly useless in such an encounter as this. As in Spenser, the battle here turns inward: "as in thir Soules infixd/Plagues . . ." (6.837–38). At the moment of victory, then, the adjectives that describe the enemy express their inward condition: "Exhausted, spiritless, afflicted, fall'n" (6.852). It is at this point in the *Aeneid* that Turnus is allowed to speak, at this point in the Pyrochles episode of *The Faerie Queene* that the defeated begs the victor for mercy, at this point in Ariosto and Tasso that the defeated specifically declines to speak, refusing to make the gesture that would win reprieve. In Milton there is neither speech nor declining of speech; without announcement or appeal Christ checks his Vergilian "terrour" (6.824) and "wrauth" (6.826) short of destruction: "Yet half his strength he put not forth, but checkd/His Thunder in mid Volie, for he meant/Not to destroy . . ." (6.853–55). The final act of the battle is not destruction but collapse, as the "fall'n" condition of the adversaries is now dramatized: "headlong themselves they threw/Down from the verge of Heav'n" (6.864–65). Their last moment in Heaven recapitulates and emphasizes the choice they had made to follow Satan.

From the moment Christ engages his adversaries—"Hee on his impious Foes right onward drove" (6.831)—the battle is notable for the absence of any reference to Satan. Although the word "impious" here corresponds to the "empio" summoned, for example, to describe Rodomonte in the final battle with Ruggiero, the striking difference is between the singular and plural nouns to which the adjective is attached. Although Satan is the progenitor of the impious heroic, he is not permitted to embody its characteristics in the final battle. Nor are his plural surrogates finally allowed to sustain the heroic. Compared to "Goats or timerous flock" (6.857), they participate in the metamorphosis of impietas that leads ultimately to the hiss of book 10. The reduction achieved by recasting the one as many and the many as goats reveals Milton's response to the problem that originates with Turnus but grows to gigantic proportions in Renaissance adaptations. For Milton the compatibility of pietas and war is never at issue; what is at issue is impietas and war, and what the war in Heaven reveals is that there is nothing truly heroic about it. In the end the attempt to diminish God has only diminished the "rebellious" (6.786) and "Godless" (6.811) who subjected themselves to the pride and vanity of Satan. As this is expressed in the choral harmony that celebrates creation in book 7:

> Who can impair thee, mighty King, or bound
> Thy Empire? easily the proud attempt
> Of Spirits apostat and thir Counsels vaine
> Thou hast repelld, while impiously they thought
> Thee to diminish, and from thee withdraw
> The number of thy worshippers.
>
> (7.608–13)

In these reflections on the meaning of the war in Heaven, impietas is shown to be not only self-diminishing but even to have an effect the reverse of that intended: "Who seekes/To less'n thee, against his purpose serves/To manifest the more thy might: his evil/Thou usest, and from thence creat'st more good" (7.613–16). Conventionally described by size disproportionate to merit, the impious hero is in Milton ultimately dwarfed as well as degraded.

The division of the angels on the model of Augustine's two cities connects the distinction between pietas and impietas to the largest issues in the poem. Fighting alone, Christ fights against the many fallen angels but also for the many good angels. The battle is a form of sacrifice, and in this sense the encounter with Satan that does not happen in book 6 does happen in book 12.[34] The crucifixion as described in lines 412–14 is paradoxically reversed in the following lines, where the final battle is rewritten: "But to the Cross he nailes thy Enemies, / The Law that is against thee, and the sins / Of all mankinde" (12.415–17). Defeating Sin and Death, the "two maine armes" (12.431) of Satan, Christ transforms even as he fulfills the role of "Victorious King" (6.886). But this image of kingship is not to be found in the courts of the world, where Belial (1.490), Nimrod (12.33–42), and others of the impious rule. This includes the Bacchus of the invocation to book 7, who will nonetheless be compared to David and Aeneas, to Christ and Augustus, as one of several heirs to ancient pietas in the poetry of John Dryden.

7
Heredes Pietatis: Pietas and Piety in the Work of John Dryden

The most prominent of Vergil's English translators, John Dryden finds more than two hundred occasions outside the twelve books of the *Aeneis* to invoke pietas: in relation to love and war in his heroic plays, to history and governance in his public poems. Given this frequency it is not surprising that his usage is variable both in meaning and connotation. His predominantly Vergilian sense of pietas is shadowed by the Ovidian, and both are assimilated to a Christian vocabulary (initially Protestant, later Catholic) influenced both by the revolutionary claims on the word made by the Puritans and by the dismissal or neglect of the term by contemporary English theorists of the social contract. Dryden's specific remarks on *pietas* in the preface to the *Aeneis* thus reflect concerns already deeply embedded in his original poetry, at once informed by the example of Vergil and now informing his translation. Endeavoring to make the Roman poet speak "such *English,* as he wou'd himself have spoken, if he had been born in *England,* and in this present Age,"[1] Dryden tests the virtue of Aeneas against the history of seventeenth-century England. Whereas Dryden's *Aeneis* situates this virtue in time, his Ovidian *Fables Ancient and Modern* reconsiders it on the assumption that "Mankind is ever the same, and nothing lost out of Nature, though every thing is alter'd."[2] Taken together with the *Aeneis,* this gathering of ancient and modern writers offers an opportunity to review the uses of pietas in Western literature from Dryden's perspective at the close of the seventeenth century.[3]

The Heroic Plays

In a well-known passage from the preface to *The Conquest of Granada*, Dryden is quite emphatic in stating that his model is epic, quoting the first two lines of *Orlando Furioso* to introduce his contention that "an heroick Play ought to be an imitation, in little, of an Heroick poem."[4] Referring to the epic machinery a few paragraphs later, he provides a convenient list of authors whose works define for him the heroic mode: "*Homer, Virgil, Statius, Ariosto, Tasso,* [and] our *English Spencer.*" The preeminent importance of Vergil in this list has generally been recognized, and the importance of piety specifically stressed in Reuben Brower's valuable article on "Dryden's Epic Manner and Virgil."[5] Yet the Vergilian meaning is repeatedly pressured by its successors and derivatives, as Dryden's plays provide material virtually sufficient to reconstruct the history of the word. The conflict between classical and Christian cultures in *Tyrannick Love* dramatizes contention over its true significance, in effect *vera pietas;* the subsequent division of *pietas* into meanings distinguished by the English words *piety* and *pity* complicates the conflict of Vergilian and Ovidian plots in *Aureng-Zebe;* the fate of Vergilian *pietas* is dramatized in the tragedy of *Don Sebastian,* the now obsolete virtue of the hero replaced by the apparent *piety* of the Mufti, whose hypocrisy illuminates a distinctly modern meaning.

Dryden's appreciation of the conflict inherent in the word is well introduced by his early play *Tyrannick Love.* The play's historical basis is provided by the often embellished story of St. Catherine's persecution at the hands of the Roman emperor Maximin, who had long since acquired the status of *exemplum impietatis* in the conventionally moralized histories of the Roman Empire.[6] In his presentation of Maximin, Dryden combines in one figure multiple versions of impiety to set against finely nuanced definitions of piety dramatized in Catherine, Berenice, and Porphyrius. As a hero of the Nimrod–Mezentius–Rodomonte type, Maximin is characterized by "his impiety to his false Gods."[7] As a tyrant, he is known by his frequently mentioned cruelty. As a son he is without known ancestry, and though a father he will die without heirs.

The contours of the impious character are carefully drawn. Although war initially serves to establish Maximin's heroic scale, love emerges as the real challenge, tested—as the paradoxical title suggests—against power. In the central encounter between Maximin and Catherine, the character of the tyrant in love is revealed in the manner suggested by

Dryden's principal source, Herodian (in Politian's translation): "ira et furore instinctus Maximinus."[1][8] The reply of Catherine to Maximin's egocentric declaration of love captures this sense of his character in the traditional vocabulary: "Nor threats nor promises my mind can move:/ Your furious anger, nor your impious Love" (3.1.88–89). The syntactic parallelism of "furious" and "impious" provides ample literary reference for fixing Maximin in opposition to ethical, political, and religious definitions of pietas. In the ensuing exchange, the tyrant attempts less to deny the charge of impiety than to circumvent it by conjuring with the primitive association of piety and purity, turning the "Act" of love into a form of expiation.

> The Love of you can never impious be;
> You are so pure—
> That in the Act 'twould change th' impiety.
> Heav'n would unmake it sin.
> (3.1.90–93)

But his sophistic appeal to the religious is answered by her definition of "true piety":

> I take my self from thy detested sight:
> To my respect thou hast no longer right:
> Such pow'r in bonds true piety can have,
> That I command, and thou art but a Slave.
> (3.1.94–97)

Here the meaning of the play's title is fully disclosed, as Dryden exploits the historical parallels between the vocabularies of governance and love. A variation on the frustrated lover–cruel mistress trope of Renaissance love poetry, this passage reveals the tyrant in one domain as slave in the other. The paradox of "impious Love" is thus answered by the Christian paradox of "pow'r in bonds" that is for Catherine "true piety."

Catherine's definition of *piety* does not admit pity or compassion. But there are difficulties attendant upon such an exclusive definition that render it more partial or provisional than Catherine's adjective "true" would allow. Witness Dryden's dramatization of semantic history in her

[1] Maximinus, incited by wrath and fury

subsequent encounter with Maximin's wife Berenice. Offered a plan that would save both of their lives, Catherine must now struggle with the two principal derivatives of Roman *pietas* in a "doubtful conflict" entirely characteristic of Dryden's heroic plays.[9]

> Madam, my thoughts are with themselves at strife;
> And Heav'n can witness how I prize your life:
> But 'tis a doubtful conflict I must try
> Betwixt my pity and my piety.
> Staying, your precious life I must expose:
> Going, my Crown of Martyrdom I lose.
>
>   (4.1.507–12)

Here the importance of the conflict is expressed in a judicial metaphor that forces Catherine to choose between ascending and descending dimensions of pietas, between (in effect) love of God and love of neighbor. That her choice must be rendered in public makes "Mankind" an interested party distinct from "Heav'n": "But I am plac'd, as on a Theater,/ Where all my Acts to all Mankind appear,/To imitate my constancy or fear" (4.1.537–39). In these circumstances Catherine defends her choice of piety in a brief discourse on "Religion" that allows her to exit, leaving the means of saving Berenice to God and thus preserving her own prospective crown of martyrdom. Cut off from *pity, piety* is here narrowed to a religious meaning that is finally otherworldly. As exponent of this meaning, the character of Catherine is likewise narrowed to represent but one of the play's several "patterns of piety."[10]

Unlike Catherine, whose Christianity is thus defined in the oppositional manner of Jerome, Berenice regards her new faith in the complementary manner of Ambrose as the fulfillment of classical idealism. She therefore expresses her objections to any plan for her own safety that would involve rebellion against the emperor her husband. Declining to save herself and her newly discovered faith at the expense of the classical virtue that defines the bond between subject and monarch, Berenice validates a Roman conception of pietas. And appropriately so, since she is identified in the play's first scene as a descendant of Antoninus Pius. "The Race of *Antonin's* was nam'd the Good:/I draw my pity from my Royal Blood" (1.1.273–74). Thus connected by blood to an eminent exemplar of imperial pietas, Berenice poses against Maximin an understanding of the ideal different from that revealed in Catherine and explained by traditional reference to the "Good" emperor's "pity." The choice of *pity* rather than *piety* to render the virtue of Antoninus— indeed the substitution of "the Good" for the more obvious "the Pious"—again acknowledges the complexity of the word's history by articulating through Berenice a larger conception of its meaning than appears in Catherine.

But Maximin can understand Berenice's appeal to her paternal lineage only as an expression of family pride.

> Still must I be upbraided with your Line?
> I know you speak it in contempt of mine.
> But your late Brother did not prize me less,
> Because I could not boast of Images.
> And the Gods own'd me more, when they decreed
> A *Thracian* Shepherd should your Line succeed.
>
> (1.1.275–80)

What Maximin perceives as a distinction of class is revealed in his very words as something much more significant. The phrase "Because I could not boast of Images" indicates the filial as well as the national bond: the Roman funeral masks ("Images") signifying duty and honor to forefathers have no place in the experience of a provincial shepherd.[11] His counterclaim of divine favor, moreover, only makes Maximin a parody of David, the shepherd who became king, and of all shepherds who claim the symbolic ancestry of Abel. Murderer of his brother-in-law, the legitimate heir to the empire, Maximin is shown not to have been a true shepherd anymore than he is now a true monarch: just as Berenice's lineage is traced to an icon of pietas, so that of Maximin is gathered to the impietas expressed in fratricide.

A Roman, Berenice is also a Christian, and thus falls under Maximin's later decision "no Christians life to spare" (5.1.177). The failure of *parcere subiectis* in this instance is dramatized by the posture of prayer that Berenice assumes, provoking Maximin to sign her death warrant with the most contemptuous irony: "How much she is to piety inclin'd! / Behead her while she's in so good a mind" (5.1.429–30). The depreciation of her "piety" is matched by his contempt for those who would appeal on her behalf for "pity" (5.1.514), including his own daughter Valeria. "Away, thou shame and slander of my blood. / Who taught thee to be pitiful or good?" (5.1.518–19). The phrase "pitiful or good" echoes

Berenice's earlier stress on her own descent from Antoninus, but if Valeria has been taught by her stepmother's example, she is compelled finally to acknowledge her father's blood just before she dies, leaving him without issue. Having ridiculed her pity, Maximin is now denied her piety: "I would in vain be pious, that's a grace / Which Heav'n permits not to a Tyrant's race" (5.1.555–56). On the one hand, this would appear to mean that as a tyrant's daughter she has no claim on the play's central virtue in any of its dimensions; on the other, it suggests that piety toward such a father and tyrant must be vain because undeserved, precisely the issue raised between Aureng-Zebe and his father in Dryden's later play.

But whereas Aureng-Zebe's father finally abdicates in favor of his son, Maximin must be killed, and it is clear that no female exemplar of pietas can accomplish this without denying what she represents. The logical candidate to abolish tyranny is therefore Porphyrius, who early attempts to argue the case for Brutus, only to be countered by Berenice: "You see the Gods adjudg'd it Parricide, / By dooming the event on *Caesar's* side" (2.1.55–56). Echoing her categories, Porphyrius later recoils at further thought of such violation: "He's both my Father and my Emperour!" (4.1.579). This recognition of pietas from a male figure is necessary to the resolution, for it establishes Porphyrius as the one qualified to assume power (after a convenient rebellion of the soldiers has disposed of Maximin). When Porphyrius accepts the acclaim of the soldiers, he carefully acknowledges the limitations of power, submitting his imperial claim to the senate and disavowing the rule of force in repudiation of civil war (traditionally *impia bella*). These gestures clearly distinguish him from Maximin, who kills to assume power and recognizes no limits once he has it. The tyrant's sense of imperial omnipotence, insistently confusing the divine and human realms, offers power and will as the essential attributes of the divine and hence of the emperor. Porphyrius, on the other hand, reveals a Christian vision of the divine nature when he appeals to Catherine on behalf of Berenice: "Your equal choice when Heav'n does thus divide, / You should, like Heav'n, still lean on mercy's side" (4.1.513–14). Substituting *mercy* for Catherine's word *pity,* Porphyrius takes an important step from personal feeling toward public responsibility.

The effect of these lines, then, is to distinguish Porphyrius not only from Maximin, but also from Catherine, the extremes of impietas and pietas in the play. For both tyrant and saint the problematical quality is pity, ironically so as the moment of death approaches. Self-empowered to "do all things" and "nothing ill" (5.1.375), Maximin would finally spare Catherine as if his "will" were identical with "Fate" (5.1.384–85). The announcement by Valerius that denies this assumption—"Your pity comes too late" (5.1.385)—provokes the tyrant to punctuate his reply by killing the messenger (stage direction: *Kills him, then sets his foot on him, and speaks on*). Unlike the hero of Vergilian epic who hesitates over his fallen adversary, Maximin—in the manner of Argantes's "d'ogni Dio sprezzatore"—voices the ethic of the impious heroic in his last words: "And shoving back this Earth on which I sit, / I'le mount—and scatter all the Gods I hit" (5.1.634–35). Whereas Maximin's death is thus presented as war, Catherine's is recounted as love, for she becomes the bride of God: "Aetherial musick did her death prepare; / Like joyful sounds of Spousals in the Air" (5.1.390–91). Excluded by death from the resolution, Maximin and Catherine are centrifugal forces who in radically opposed ways reject the essential bond that would connect them to the new order that emerges under the aegis of Porphyrius and Berenice.

Replacing Maximin in his roles both as ruler and as husband, Porphyrius expresses the limits of the first by reference to the second: "In Peace or War, let Monarchs hope or fear; / All my ambition shall be bounded here" (5.1.663–64). Berenice reciprocates by confining her "Empire" to the "heart" (5.1.670) of Porphyrius, as they effectively reconcile imperial and romantic dimensions of the epic plot in a way that Maximin and Catherine never could. This final subversion of the play's title is achieved by progressive refinement of what Dryden in his preface variously calls "Examples of Piety," or "patterns of piety," or "lively images of piety." In the end the framing conflict between pagan and Christian is displaced by a centering reconciliation of classical and Christian piety, as conversion secures rather than breaks the bonds of social and political order.

In *Aureng-Zebe* a much finer point is put upon the question of piety, as the conflict of cultures characteristic of the earlier heroic plays is replaced by conflict within one ruling family. Porphyrius's words "He's both my Father and my Emperour" might serve as an appropriate epigraph for consideration of this play about the Indian succession. In the first scene Porphyrius's line is inverted to define filial obligation as understood by the Emperour: "Subject and son, he's doubly born my slave."[12] Against the Emperour who speaks these words and the son spoken of stands Aureng-Zebe, whose "piety" has been stressed by Reuben Brower: "in the emphasis on 'piety' in the character of Aureng-Zebe, we feel that Dryden was emulating Virgil quite directly."[13] Yes, but not only Vergil, for the pietas of

the title character is here elaborated in a context that points to Latin literature after Vergil. Although the play ends with Aureng-Zebe and Indamora
triumphant and united, this success is achieved largely because the several
forces aligned against them eventually foil one another. The conclusion
hardly invalidates the power of Indamora's own words: "Piety is no more;
she sees her place / Usurped by monsters and a savage race" (3.1.461–62).
The pattern of *pietas victa,* here focused with reference to the political
implications of the ideal by the verb "Usurped," creates a vision of history
that suggests Lucan ("pietas peritura") or Statius ("nusquam pietas").

The immediate context of Indamora's weighty pronouncement is threatened fratricide. In the India of the play, conflict among sons is both anticipated and institutionalized, the younger sons killed by state law at the
moment of the elder's succession. Yet from the beginning the rights of
primogeniture are disallowed in favor of alternative and competing conditions for rule. This struggle of principles as well as personalities is quickly
narrowed to Morat and Aureng-Zebe, whose filial piety distinguishes him
from this younger as well as the two older brothers in the eyes of the
nobility. As this opinion is voiced by Arimant: "He sums their virtues in
himself alone, / And adds the greatest, of a loyal son" (1.1.106–7). In opposition to Aureng-Zebe, his fraternal rival stakes his claim to the throne
on force, necessarily exercised against his own brother. In the passage at
hand, Indamora condemns Morat by enlarging upon the Romulus–
Remus theme of Roman literature in ways that suggest the parallel story
of Cain and Abel. Appealing beyond "Nature" to "heaven," she raises the
fratricide theme as one of divine justice: "How can our prophet suffer you
to reign, / When he looks down, and sees your brother slain?" (3.1.465–
66). The answer to this is provided, after plot reversal has brought
Aureng-Zebe to power, by a conclusion that promises abolition of institutionalized fratricide: "Our impious use no longer shall obtain; / Brothers
no more by brothers shall be slain" (5.1.411–23). Although Morat refuses to accept a new order based on pietas, preferring to die rather in the
manner of Maximin, Aureng-Zebe's refusal to enact the part of Romulus
establishes the triumph of the ideal he represents.

The final victory of pietas is gained at the expense of parricide as well
as fratricide. The exclamation of Assaph Khan in the first scene—
"Rebels and parricides!" (1.1.37)—underlines the play's correlation of
political with familial strife. Like Shakespeare's Edmund and Dryden's
Achitophel, Morat would dismiss the claims of age and law ("Birth-
right's a vulgar road to kingly sway," 5.1.66), and assert instead the

rights of power. The ultimate realm of the power struggle in the play is the heart of Indamora. Not only are father and both sons in love with her, but both the Emperour and Morat are already married, the Emperour to Nourmahal, who in turn lusts after her stepson Aureng-Zebe. The Vergilian ideal thus contends with its Ovidian and Senecan negation. The passage of the play most clearly indebted to Seneca is the exchange between Nourmahal and Aureng-Zebe in 4.1. After proclaiming it "impious" even to listen to her, Aureng-Zebe effectively translates words of Seneca's Hippolytus, concluding with a close rendering of the latter's "sum nocens, merui mori;/placui novercae" (683–84): I, too, deserve to die, because I please" (4.1.130).[14] Nourmahal's reply to this is fully in the idiom of Myrrha's "pietas geminato crescat amore" in *Metamorphoses* 10, although the argument itself is closer to that of Phaedra in *Heroides* 4: "Iuppiter esse pium statuit, quodcumque iuvaret,/et fas omne facit fratre marita soror."[2][15]

> Custom our native royalty does awe;
> Promiscuous love is Nature's general law:
> For whosoever the first lovers were,
> Brother and sister made the second pair,
> And doubled, by their love, their piety.
>
> (4.1.131–35)

Nourmahal's attempt to dress her "love" as "piety" thus draws her within the circle of heroines named by Venus in Boccaccio's elegy. As the literary descendant of Phaedra and Myrrha, Nourmahal argues from nature against convention and like them would deny the distinction between familial and erotic affection.

Against Nourmahal's abuse of the word *piety,* Aureng-Zebe characterizes the term as a test of civilization in a way that complements Indamora's vision of *pietas victa.* Whereas she argues the evidence for the symbolic exile of "piety" in the manner of *Metamorphoses* 1, Aureng-Zebe would preserve "piety" by exiling those like his stepmother.

> Hence, hence, and to some barbarous climate fly,
> Which only brutes in human form does yield,

[2] Jove fixed that virtue was to be whatever brought us pleasure; and naught is wrong before the gods since sister was made wife by brother.

And man grows wild in Nature's common field.
Who eat their parents, piety pretend;
Yet there no sons their sacred bed ascend.
To veil great sins, a greater crime you choose;
And, in your incest, your adultery lose.

(4.1.136–40)

Indamora's "monsters" become Aureng-Zebe's "brutes," as he recasts
her distinction between nature and Heaven into one between nature and
law. Obliterated by Nourmahal's confusion of the two terms, this distinction becomes for Aureng-Zebe the measure of civilized order.

As the meaning of *piety* is at issue in the play, so too is that of *pity*.
The political importance of the word is carefully established by
Melesinda in an exchange with Morat that depends on the opposition
of *pity* to *cruelty* made familiar by chapter 17 of *The Prince*. Morat's
view of power as self-interest is disposed against Melesinda's view of
power as a stewardship of divine pity: "And those, who stewards of his
pity prove,/He blesses in return with public love" (3.1.427–28). She
then develops this idea in terms that suggest the Davidic ideal—with all
its contemporary relevance: "If exiled, Heaven restores him to his
throne" (3.1.430). Her contrast between the ideal monarch and the
tyrant is enhanced by the larger context of the play, which invokes still
older conceptions of the word she uses. Consider, for example, the
terms in which Indamora invites Morat to acknowledge the possibility
of Aureng-Zebe as king: "Pity for you had pierced his generous mind./
Pity does with a noble nature suit" (3.1.476–77). Dryden's version of
"For pitee renneth soone in gentil herte" must compete, however, with
the inherited idea of "foolish pity" here voiced by Nourmahal. Rejected
by Aureng-Zebe and therefore ready to welcome his death, she complains to Morat: "What foolish pity has possessed your mind,/To alter
what your prudence once designed?" (4.1.170–71). Recalling in a couplet the shift from *pietas* to *prudentia* in the Latin vocabulary of governance, Nourmahal appeals to the same line of argument that informs
the "foolish pitty" identified by Spenser's Palmer with "womanish fine
forgery." But Nourmahal's self-interested view is not sustained by
events: in this version of the heroic love story, passion is a test of
personal capacity. Whoever wins the love of Indamora will rule. Thus it
is that Berenice's words to Porphyrius from the conclusion of *Tyrannick Love* ("And in no Empire reign, but of your heart") are modified

to suit Aureng-Zebe: "There, there's my throne, in Indamora's heart" (2.1.479).

In Aureng-Zebe and Indamora public obligation and erotic love are finally reconciled. But the world in which this reconciliation takes place is described in terms that diminish the importance of the event. The resolution to the love plot must be dovetailed with the resolution to the political plot, which necessitates the more fundamental reconciliation between father and son. From the beginning such a resolution is rendered difficult by the character of the Emperour, who makes the piety due patriarchal institutions hard to maintain. In the paradoxical and disaffected words of Indamora: "But piety to you, unhappy prince, / Becomes a crime, and duty an offence" (2.1.189–90). For Aureng-Zebe this notion of a world in which piety has become a crime is assimilated to the play's thematic concern with the vanity of human wishes.

> How vain is virtue, which directs our ways
> Through certain danger to uncertain praise!
> Barren, and airy name! thee fortune flies,
> With thy lean train, the pious and the wise.
> Heaven takes thee at thy word, without regard,
> And lets thee poorly be thy own reward.
> The world is made for the bold impious man,
> Who stops at nothing, seizes all he can.
>
> (2.1.502–9)

Aureng-Zebe's division of the world into "pious" and "impious," which could be traced back through Augustine to the age of Augustus, more immediately anticipates the unequal division of *Absalom and Achitophel:* the "lean train" of the "pious" here provides analogy for the "small but faithful Band" of the later poem. The world here described is the natural realm of the "impious man," a reduced and domesticated but still threatening version of the impious hero so at home in Renaissance epic.

In the ending of *Aureng-Zebe* the "impious man" does not prevail. As emperor, Aureng-Zebe replaces his father, who confesses his cruelty and receives in exchange the pity of his son (4.2.188). The play is thus resolved in favor of pietas, as fratricide, parricide, rebellion, tyranny, and incest cancel one another in action and are thus all defeated. The accumulated weight of impietas in the play is, nonetheless, considerable, thus expressing a concern that surfaces with increasing frequency in Dryden's later poetry, as he assesses the capacity of his own age to accommodate the ideal of pietas. This is the central problem not only of Dryden's *Aeneis,* but also of his greatest post-Revolution play, *Don Sebastian* of 1689.

In one of his most interesting prefaces, Dryden directly identifies the title character with "piety." "In the drawing of his character I forgot not piety, which any one may observe to be one principal ingredient of it; even so far as to be a habit in him."[16] This statement bears directly on Dryden's later discussion of the play's moral dimension. After locating the "general Moral of it" in the last four lines, which concern the parent-child relationship, Dryden refers to "another Moral, couch'd under every one of the principal Parts and Characters, which a judicious Critick will observe" (71). Dryden does not, however, give even so judicious a critic as Earl Miner much help in developing this idea. Miner observes in his notes to the play: "Although the moral purpose of drama was a commonplace in England from Jonson to the eighteenth century, Dryden is unusual in claiming that each character embodies a moral. It is not easy today to penetrate the moral intended in each of the characters and parts."[17] Yet the specific comment on the character of Don Sebastian would certainly seem to suggest that "piety" is the "moral" that the hero embodies. The importance of this is suggested by Dryden's further remark: "I have given the same to *Sebastian* and *Almeyda;* and consequently made them alike in all things but their Sex" (71). If this is true, then the Sebastian–Almeyda version of the heroic love story involves two characters who represent the same "moral." Although Dryden concludes his preface by citing "my Old Master *Virgil*" (72), it is necessary to observe that his account of "piety" in the preface does not point toward a narrowly Vergilian definition. In fact, Dryden's comments on the "piety" of Don Sebastian generally indicate religion as the appropriate domain of definition: "This being presuppos'd, that he was Religious, the horror of his incest, tho innocently committed, was the best reason which the Stage cou'd give for hind'ring his return" (68). In the very act of defining the pietas of his hero, Dryden thus calls attention to one of the most traditional of impietas plots, already developed in *Aureng-Zebe.*

Whereas in *Aureng-Zebe* the several dimensions of impietas ultimately subvert one another, in the later tragedy the two versions of pietas cancel one another in the end, sending Don Sebastian and Almeyda into exile and leaving the last word of the play to Dorax. A complex figure derivative from the malcontent of Renaissance drama, Dorax is uneasily assimilated to Dryden's prefatory remarks emphasizing the "moral" embodied in each character. Early in the play he serves to establish the idealized character of Sebastian—"Brave, pious, generous, great, and liberal"—from the perspective of injured merit.[18] When reconciliation with Sebastian becomes possible, Dorax hesitates out of concern for his rival Enriquez: "But pitty is my Friend, and stops me short . . ." (4.3.650). Dorax is here identified with a virtue of considerable importance in the play: Don Sebastian himself earlier refers to "noble pity" (2.1.425) in an abbreviated version of Indamora's "Pity does with a noble nature suit." In effect, Don Sebastian and Dorax bring together these two principal English derivatives of the Latin word. But the reunion of *piety* with *pity* is not finally sustained, nor do Sebastian and Dorax represent the play's only versions of these complementary terms, which are effectively negated by the play's tyrant Muley-Moloch.

As a weak representation of tyranny, Muley-Moloch shares certain characteristics with the Emperor of *Aureng-Zebe;* as ruler who falls in love, he shares with Maximin a negative version of the David–Bathsheba plot. Referred to in the play as "tyrant," Muley-Moloch is described as "cruel" and later identified by Almeyda with all that is "impious" in a passage remotely suggestive of Priam's cry to the gods in *Aeneid* 2 and more immediately comparable to the complaint of Indamora in act 3 of *Aureng-Zebe.*

> But is there Heav'n? for I begin to doubt;
> The Skyes are hush'd; no grumbling Thunders roul.
> Now take your swing, ye impious; Sin unpunish'd;
> Eternal providence seems overwatch'd,
> And with a slumb'ring Nod assents to Murther.
> (3.1.294–98)

Almeyda's refusal to save Sebastian by submitting to tyrannic love completes the pattern initiated by the emperor, whose rhetorical question—"What's Royalty but pow'r to please my self?" (2.1.46)—is contained by the discovery of love itself as tyranny. "Death, must I beg the pity of my Slave? / Must a King beg? Yes, Love's a greater King; / A Tyrant . . ." (2.1.56–57). Like Maximin, Muley-Moloch is at once tyrant and slave, and can neither give nor receive pity.

Remarkably, Don Sebastian shares this language with Muley-Moloch,

characterizing Almeyda as "Tyrant" (2.1.559) in resisting consumma-
tion of their love, attended as it is by prophecies of incest. As Dryden
here develops the incest plot, the reluctance of Sebastian and Almeyda to
surrender their love is cast in decidedly heroic terms. Near the end of the
play, Sebastian himself expresses this:

> one moment longer,
> And I shou'd break through Laws Divine, and Humane;
> And think 'em Cobwebs, spred for little man,
> Which all the bulky herd of nature breaks.
> The vigorous young world was ignorant
> Of these restrictions, 'tis decrepit now;
> Not more devout, but more decay'd, and cold.
> All this is impious; therefore we must part . . .
>
> (5.1.628–35)

Like Ovid's Myrrha, Sebastian here entertains an argument that would
dissolve the conflict between pietas and love only to admit that the
argument is itself "impious." Yet Sebastian's version of this argument
entails a striking vision of historical decline that is fully vouched for in
the comic subplot of the play and in the running commentary on mankind offered by Dorax. The point of contact between the serious and the
comic plot is the character of the Mufti, and it is around him that English
derivatives of *pietas* multiply. These words reflect the play's stringent
satire of religious hypocrisy, what Dorax calls "Vice and Godliness"
(3.1.413), a phenomenon recognized even by the political hypocrites of
the play. Referring to Almeyda, Muley-Moloch says: "I wou'd view the
Face/That warm'd our *Mufti's* Zeal:/These pious Parrots peck the fairest Fruit:/Such Tasters are for Kings" (1.1.421–24). The "pious Pleasures" (1.1.581) of the world and the flesh establish the character of the
Mufti, who nonetheless confronts the invasion of his own domesticity
with cries of impietas. Discovering Antonio with his wife, the Mufti
invokes this word in self-protection: "O thou Villain, what horrible
impiety art thou committing? What, ravishing the Wife of my Bosom?"
(3.2.127–28). However appropriate the word might be spoken by someone else, in the mouth of the Mufti its impotence is readily apparent,
especially given the inflated adjective. While the Sebastian–Almeyda
plot presents conflicting patterns of piety, the comic subplot is busy
undoing the very power of the word itself.

Here the word becomes attached not only to expressions of religious hypocrisy, but to expressions of political hypocrisy as well. Far from being the heroic or noble virtue that it is in the *Aeneid,* and that it still is in the characters of Sebastian and Almeyda, the subplot reveals a popular "piety" that makes the mob vulnerable to the depredations of both priests and politicians. In the words of the Mufti: "the piety of the People must be encouraged; that they may help me to recover my Jewels, and my Daughter" (4.2.221–23). The daughter herself has already asserted this sense of the word earlier in the same scene when she mistakes her father for Antonio: "No Sir, you get more by pious Fools than Raylers, when you insinuate into their Families, manage their Fortunes while they live, and beggar their Heirs by getting Legacies when they dye" (4.2.41–44). Covering her own violation of filial obligation by focusing attention on her father's abuse of his faithful, Morayma crystallizes the decline of the word in her phrase "pious Fools." In the satire of the play, the conventional distinction of fool from knave has been assimilated to that between pious and impious. As satire, the play finally has no place for the heroic figures of Almeyda and Don Sebastian.

Dorax as satirist within the play recognizes this condition of the world in his acerbic commentary on political and religious practice.

> Why then no Bond is left on human kind:
> Distrusts, debates, immortal strifes ensue;
> Children may murder Parents, Wives their Husbands;
> All must be Rapine, Wars, and Desolation,
> When trust and gratitude no longer bind.
>
>   (2.1.307–11)

Although he does not use the word *piety,* which is increasingly left to the Mufti to define, Dorax here offers a vision parallel to the satire of *Amphitryon,* Dryden's other great post-Revolution play, which concludes with Jupiter's vision of the world that awaits the newborn Hercules: "Monsters, and Monster-men he shall ingage,/And toil, and struggle, through an Impious Age."[19] Jupiter here lends his voice to the disillusionment expressed in the ending of Dryden's closely contemporaneous poem *Eleonora,* where the celebrated figure can only hope to escape "this bad Age." "So bad, that thou thy self had'st no defence,/From Vice, but barely by departing hence."[20] Such a figure of virtue, whose piety the poem extols, may be compared to Ovid's *Astraea fugax*. In Dryden's version of 1693: "Faith flies, and Piety in Exile mourns;/And Justice, here opprest, to Heav'n returns."[21] It is against this background of "Piety in Exile" that Dryden came by way of his political poetry to the translation of Vergil.

The Public Poems

As his plays amply illustrate, Dryden's frequent invocation of words derived from *pietas* is a distinctive fact of his literary vocabulary. More important than the mere frequency of *piety, impiety, pity, pious, impious* is the poet's evident awareness of their semantic history. Ideally Dryden would accommodate the political life of his time to a vocabulary that acknowledges the Vergilian authority of the word, but practically and reluctantly he recognizes the historical changes manifest in the divergence of English from Latin usage. The limitations of the English derivatives as positive terms of political discourse had been a subject of comment in the previous century, but they are contextualized for Dryden by the events of the 1640s and 1650s. After the separation of *piety* from *pity,* the former derivative assumes a predominately religious meaning at the very moment when religion had become a principal cause of resistance to the monarchy. Witness, for typical example from the period, the Puritan claim to possess *vera pietas,* as voiced by William Prynne. Writing in protest against government censorship in his *Newes from Ipswich,* Prynne proclaims: "this is the deploreable News of our present age, that our Presses formerly open only to Truth and Piety, are closed up against both of late, and patent for the most part to nought but error, superstition, and profanenesse."[22] That this Puritan brand of piety or "zeal" is for Dryden but a perversion of the ancient idea is perhaps most clearly expressed in his collaborative play *The Duke of Guise,* first performed in 1682:

> Saintship and zeal are still our best disguise:
> We mix unknown with the hot thoughtless crowd,
> And quoting Scriptures, (which too well we know,)
> With impious glosses ban the holy text,
> And make it speak rebellion, schism, and murder;
> So turn the arms of heaven against itself.[23]

The association of religious hypocrisy with revolutionary Puritanism sets off the classical ideals of duty and loyalty elaborated in Dryden's poetry by reference to the basic familial metaphor. Although Dryden will appeal to this metaphoric definition of pietas right to the end of his life, his poetry is evidence for the contemporary eclipse of pietas as a political term. Displaced by alternatives that express a contractual and commercial order, pietas remains for Dryden an ideal of an older society retained in his poetry to indict the "Impious Age" ushered in by the Revolution of 1688.

In the third edition of Elisha Coles's *Latin-English Dictionary,* published in 1692 (just five years before Dryden's *Aeneis*), *pietas* is defined by the English *piety,* which is in turn explained by a series of synonyms in an order that appears to descend from Christian to classical: "Holiness, natural Affection, Compassion, Tenderness, Duty to God and Man." This semantic range is fully exploited in Dryden's laudatory verse spanning half a century. Adapting his emphasis to suit his subject, Dryden celebrates the piety of such diverse figures as Lord Hastings, Cromwell, Charles II, Catherine of Braganza, James II, both of James's wives, Anne Killigrew, Eleonora, the Duke and Duchess of Ormond, Mary Frampton, and George Holman. Tracing this virtue chronologically through Dryden's occasional poetry illuminates his changing perception of late seventeenth-century England: his idea of pietas belongs to a changing vision of the present in relation to the past. The pious figures of the poems written in honor of the Restoration are seen as representative of England and its future under Charles II, both David and Aeneas in *Astraea Redux.* Thus, in the dedication to *Annus Mirabilis* Dryden confidently assumes that "Heaven never made so much Piety and Vertue to leave it miserable." One implication of the word here is suggested in the passage from the poem itself referring to the presentation of the *Loyal London* to the king: "This martial Present, piously design'd, / The Loyal City give their best-lov'd King."[24] But such confidence is conspicuously absent from the poems written after 1688. The pious figures of the later poems are seen as exceptions to the general rule of "impious Arms" and "impious Lucre."[25] At the nexus between the pietas of 1660 and the impietas of 1688 are the public poems written during the decade prior to the Revolution, from *Absalom and Achitophel,* which begins famously with the phrase "In pious times," to *The Hind and the Panther,* which concludes with the Hind's admonitory fable of the Buzzard and "the feather'd *Nimrods* of his Race."

The first note of *Absalom and Achitophel* is pietas, which serves to introduce the major issues of a poem that is expressly interested in historical semantics. In his concluding speech David himself recognizes language as a political issue.[26] Referring to the word *patriot* and anticipating the tone of Johnson's definition in the next century, Dryden's David here illustrates the poem's concern with the confusion of names:

> Gull'd with a Patriots name, whose Modern sense
> Is one that would by Law supplant his Prince:
> The Peoples Brave, the Politicians Tool;
> Never was Patriot yet, but was a Fool.
>
> (965–68)

This passage reveals the poem's sensitivity to semantic evolution, Dryden's understanding of words perverted to serve partisan causes: "My Rebel ever proves my Peoples Saint" (974). In the "Modern sense," moreover, the patriotic saint is victimized by a knave who also assumes "a Patriott's All-attoning Name" (179). This distinction between an ancient and a "Modern sense" bears directly on the question of *piety*, a word carefully abused by Achitophel, who plies the people with rhetorical arts of the sort that can take advantage of a word like *patriot:* "Mistaken Men, and Patriots in their Hearts; / Not Wicked, but Seduc'd by Impious Arts" (497–98). This emphasis affirms the running parallel between the Exclusion Crisis and the midcentury rebellion, the time when (according to *Astraea Redux*) "Religions name against it self was made" and the revolutionary Puritans—compared to the Titans—were ruined by their own "impious wit."[27]

In contrast to once and future impietas is the ideal expressed in the first line of the poem. The possibilities that this phrase initiates depend on meanings of "pious" vested in its literary history. The narrative from 2 Samuel announced by the title immediately provides a context for recalling David as the type of the ideal ruler and exemplar of royal pietas; at the same time it will be remembered that David's pietas had long been understood as an expression of his failures rather than of his successes. With regard to David, then, the opening phrase has a double edge. Opposite him is Absalom, commonly aligned with Cain to represent impietas, as in the poems of Prudentius, who nonetheless insists on the responsibility of David in accordance with the principle that we beget our own sins. In the Middle Ages this responsibility had been cast in political terms, as the rebellion of Absalom against David is taken to illustrate the aphorism of Coelestinus that pietas may beget impietas. Whether Dryden's David begot Absalom with "some diviner Lust" (19) or not, his procreative activities are emphasized in the poem's opening in a manner derivative from the Renaissance interest in David as lover.

> In pious times, e'r Priest-craft did begin,
> Before *Polygamy* was made a sin;
> When man, on many, multiply'd his kind,
> E'r one to one was, cursedly, confind:
> When Nature prompted, and no law deny'd
> Promiscuous use of Concubine and Bride;
> Then, *Israel's* Monarch, after Heaven's own heart,
> His vigorous warmth did, variously, impart
> To Wives and Slaves: And, wide as his Command,
> Scatter'd his Maker's Image through the Land.
>   (1–10)[28]

As these couplets establish a biblical context for understanding pietas, they simultaneously project upon this context a classical argument: the appeal to nature against custom and law that informs attempts to redefine pietas in defense of illicit desire. As made, for example, by Ovid's Myrrha in defense of incest, this argument is called in doubt by her own admission of traditional meanings of the word that would prohibit her desire. Taken over by Boccaccio's Fiammetta in defense of adultery, the argument is given a more sympathetic voice and supporting context, but even Fiammetta admits a counterimplication of marital fidelity. Although it is in comment on royal philandering that the argument is invoked here, it should be kept in mind that the immediate antecedent of this passage is Nourmahal's "Promiscuous love is Nature's general law" speech in *Aureng-Zebe,* where it is answered by the title character: "And man grows wild in Nature's common field."[29] Similarly in *Absalom and Achitophel,* the initial appeal to nature is answered later in the warning against rebellion: "Government it self at length must fall/To Nature's state; where all have Right to all" (793–94). By transferring this pattern of argument and its vocabulary organized around redefinitions of pietas to *Absalom and Achitophel,* Dryden expounds "Promiscuous use of Concubine and Bride" in terms regarded as specious even in his own earlier play.

But this implication is enriched by still others that turn its force against David's enemies. As a temporal expression, "pious times" has a traditional meaning illuminated by Roman poetry, in which the Latin adjective commonly refers to the golden age. Understood in this way, the opening lines establish the "times" as without need of "law" and without any idea of "sin." That Dryden should present this pre-historical golden age in terms of sexual freedom is both highly original and deftly appropriate, as pietas is connected, not with incest or adultery, but with Old Testament polygamy. By setting the polygamy of this golden age against the idea of priestcraft, Dryden distinguishes the classical valence of "pious" from its modern association with religion as an argument for rebellion. Just as Horace had taken civil war and Propertius luxury to mark the idea of *pietas victa,* so Dryden takes the establishment of organized religion to fix the advent of the iron age. The pejorative "Priest-craft" is subsequently developed in the poem along the lines suggested by the phrase "Priests of all Religions are the same" (99), and what they have in common is a tendency to confuse religion with rebellion. As the opening of *Absalom and Achitophel* recasts the words of Nourmahal, so it also updates and revalorizes the advice of Placidius in *Tyrannick Love:* "T'infected zeal you must no mercy show:/For, from Religion, all Rebellions grow."[30] Similarly in *Absalom and Achitophel* the repeated "zeal" expresses the perversion of classical *pietas,* which long had political loyalty as a dominant meaning. In the opening of the poem, then, Dryden evokes multiple contexts for the definition of "pious" in the first line. In fact, the only meaning clearly disclaimed is the one that is today the most obvious: piety is opposed to religion as loyalty is opposed to rebellion as the golden age is opposed to the iron.

From the beginning, then, the poem depends on the distinction between ancient and modern definitions of this word, the former sustaining the monarchy, the latter in collaboration with priestcraft attempting to subvert it. At the close of the classical period, it will be recalled, Cassiodorus had expressed the normative relationship of power and piety by taking *pietas* as the guardian of *imperium.* Translated into English by Gower, the axiom had been so modified by semantic change in the centuries following that for Dryden the ancient piety that would guard royal power is countered by a piety that would overthrow it.[31] The importance of this semantic history is again acknowledged by David himself; just as he recognizes the distortion of patriotism in the poem's final speech, so also does he subject to irony the twisted piety of those who would subvert the throne: "My Pious Subjects for my Safety pray, / Which to Secure they take my Power away" (983–84). The adjective repeated from the opening line here resonates between its modern religious and its older political significance, between its increasingly dominant English meaning and its Latin origin, as Dryden at once condemns the false piety of the "good old cause" and recalls the classical ideal of filial piety that sustains the patriarchal conception of monarchy. In effect, this single word here identifies both victim and norm of the satire, the ancient meaning endorsing what the modern would destroy.

Just as Dryden aims at removing religion as justification for rebellion by setting piety against priestcraft in the opening line, so in his portraits of the king's "Pious Subjects" he denies the Puritan claims on the word. A century and a half earlier, the Tudor translator of Erasmus's *Enchiridion* had offered twin definitions of the English word in his marginal glosses: in the first, "Pietie" signifies honor, reverence, and obedience due to God; in the second it is the reverent love and honor of inferiors toward their superiors. In the rich Shimei, Dryden portrays the intervening revolutionary attempt to set these definitions at odds. Rewarded (Dryden writes) for "pious Hate / Against his Master" (593–94), Shimei becomes a walking oxymoron by Christian as well as classical standards. In contrast to the loyalty and affection of London revealed in *Annus Mirabilis,* Shimei embodies the hatred and disloyalty of London in the time of the Popish Plot. The relationship of "pious" to "Master" in this passage is enhanced by contrast to the ideal figure of Barzillai, who suffered "his Masters Fate" (822) during the interregnum: "For him he Suffer'd, and with him Return'd" (824). The master in both passages is clearly the king, the "Monarch of *Jerusalem*" (602), but the word "Master" is ultimately invested with divine authority that affirms the analogy between God and king. In the introduction to David's final speech: "The God-like *David* spoke: with awfull fear / His Train their Maker in their Master hear" (938–39). This passage retrospectively completes the destruction of the revolutionary argument that piety toward God can be distinguished from piety to the king, that "pious Hate"—especially toward one's "Master"—can be anything but a contradiction in terms. That furor should be the consequence of such piety as Shimei's reveals the sense of paradox that governs Dryden's use of the word in this poem.

In the mouth of Achitophel the word is more than just paradoxical. Adapting to his own purposes the identification of *piety* with nature asserted in the opening lines, Achitophel attempts to circumvent the claims of custom and law. Invoking a deliberately classical definition of the word, he invites Absalom to "Commit a pleasing Rape upon the Crown" (474): "Urge now your Piety, your Filial Name" (419). Along with justice a traditional attribute of monarchy, piety here qualifies Absalom for rule; as an expression of obligation to David as father and as king, piety requires him to respect David's crown. The double meaning of the word as the virtue of both subject and king pinpoints Absalom's dilemma: he cannot have the crown without forfeiting his qualification for it. To accept Achitophel's argument is to assent to a complete inversion of meaning: the word that historically has protected monarchy is here adduced to promote usurpation. Achitophel's flagrant abuse of the word here defined as a filial virtue has the corollary effect of recalling the filial status of Absalom as illegitimate son. Without a legal claim, Absalom is encouraged by Achitophel to appeal to a definition of *piety* understood as a bond of nature. While highlighting the specious language of the tempter, this passage also suggests the limitations of pietas as an effective moral guardian of monarchy.

Although Absalom eventually accedes to Achitophel's argument, he is nonetheless allowed royal virtues that correspond very closely to those of his father, specifically: "Not stain'd with Cruelty, nor puft with Pride" (480). His character as Dryden develops it is remarkable precisely because it does not follow the type of impietas. On the contrary, Dryden's Absalom falls well outside the familiar character of tyrant ("Cruelty") or usurper ("Pride"), the traditional categories of political impietas. Nor does the portrait in any way recall the figure identified with Cain on the example of patristic literature. Rather, Dryden chooses to model Absalom on David.[32] As Barzillai and his son are bound together by "Honour" (818, 844), Achitophel and his son by images of "Anarchy" (172), the bond that connects David and Absalom goes by the name of "Mildness" (381), a critical term in the poem with a history of close connections with pietas. "*Absalom's* Mild nature" (478) is inherited from his father, who shares it in turn (*Astraea Redux* indicates) with his father: "By that same mildness which your Fathers Crown/Before did ravish, shall secure your own" (258–59). Although the King James Bible renders Matthew 11.29 with the word "meek," "mild" is a common synonym in accounts of this passage where the Vulgate reads "mitis." In Milton's sonnet on his blindness, for example: "who best/Bear his milde yoak, they serve him best, his State/Is Kingly."[33] Yet it should be noted that this same yoke, which

Ambrose had long since described as *pietatis iugum,* is described not only as "mild" but also as "just" in book 10 of *Paradise Lost* (10.1045–46). These complementary English words evoke the twin attributes of God commonly accorded by analogy to Christian kings, and designated in the Latin mirrors for magistrates as *iustitia* and *pietas.* A few lines later in book 10, Adam does use the English derivative of the Latin word in advising prayer: "How much more, if we pray him, will his ear/Be op'n, and his heart to pitie incline" (10.1060–61).

Although the Miltonic background of *Absalom and Achitophel* has been well appreciated,[34] the point here is not influence or literary indebtedness, but rather an inherited cluster of associations that bear upon the praise that Absalom accords his father.

> Mild, Easy, Humble, Studious of our Good;
> Enclin'd to Mercy, and averse from Blood.
> If Mildness Ill with Stubborn *Israel* Suite,
> His Crime is God's beloved Attribute.
> (325–28)

Here mildness is at once identified with "Mercy" ("God's beloved Attribute") and designated a "Crime," an apparent contradiction well explained by the above citation from *Astraea Redux,* which is here revised: the mildness that Dryden had earlier assumed would secure the throne is now perceived to threaten it. The problem is specified with reference to David's affection for his son: "Poor pitied Youth, by my Paternal care,/Rais'd up to all the Height his Frame coud bear" (961–62). In effect, Dryden's poem details a situation very similar to that which writers of the ninth century had discovered in the attitude of Louis the Pious toward his son, leading Hincmar of Rheims to insist—drawing upon 2 Samuel to illustrate—that royal *pietas* in the form of paternal indulgence may foster filial *impietas* in the form of rebellion. The eventual consequence of this thought was to deprive *pietas* of its traditional place in the discourse of rule in favor of such alternative terms as (especially) *clementia,* a distinction most emphatically conveyed into English by Elyot's *Governour.* It is precisely to *clemency* along with *mercy,* terms also preferred by Spenser, that Dryden turns in framing David's concluding speech.

> Thus long have I, by native mercy sway'd,
> My wrongs dissembl'd, my revenge delay'd:

> So willing to forgive th' Offending Age,
> So much the Father did the King asswage.
> But now so far my Clemency they slight,
> Th' Offenders question my Forgiving Right.
>
> (939–44)

By attaching the terms that express the king's characteristic mildness to the exercise of the royal pardon, the argument begins to right the balance between mercy and justice, later implied in the rhetorical question: "Must I at length the Sword of Justice draw?" (1002). But perhaps the most telling phrase in these lines is "th' Offending Age." The traditional virtues of kingship, here organized around the word "Father," are (Dryden suggests) lost upon the age: the "pious times" of the first line are never to be recovered. The "Series of new time" (1027) prophesied in the poem's last lines rests not on shared participation in the familial metaphor, not on nature, but rather on law sustained by the threat of force. As the "Lawfull Pow'r" of line 1024 is answered by the poem's concluding phrase "Lawfull Lord" of 1031, pietas that metaphorically defines the bond between subject and ruler is silently abandoned.

If Dryden recognizes in *Absalom and Achitophel* the gap separating contemporary realities from the traditional ideal of pietas, this does not prevent him from using the word in the negative to characterize "th' Offending Age." In this respect Dryden effectively repeats the history of usage already reflected in Spenser and Milton: as the political importance of pietas had contracted since the late Middle Ages, its negative had continued to thrive as an expression of political disorder, sedition, rebellion, with the added connotations of pride and madness. This cluster of connotations informs the contingent prophecy that concludes *The Medall*. Should "impious Arms prevail" (290):

> The Cut-throat Sword and clamorous Gown shall jar,
> In shareing their ill-gotten Spoiles of War:
> Chiefs shall be grudg'd the part which they pretend;
> Lords envy Lords, and Friends with every Friend
> About their impious Merit shall contend.
>
> (306–10)

This vision is the culmination of a poetic argument that compares the abuses of priestcraft—here the "clamorous Gown"—to the sectarian contentions of sixteenth-century France, as Dryden points to the parallel of "plotting Jesuite" and "*French* Puritan" (201–2). The impietas revealed in *The Medall* may thus be illuminated by Dryden's 1684 translation of Maimbourg's history of the Catholic League (of which book 4 includes allusion to the story of David and Absalom). Dryden's version belongs to the same context of political furor (with additional possibilities provided by the Rye House Plot of 1683) as *Absalom and Achitophel* and *The Medall,* and serves to underline the problem of pietas in contemporary political discourse. Indeed, the epigraph on the title page of Dryden's translation reads, suggestively: "Neque enim libertas gratior ulla est/ Quam sub Rege Pio . . . ,"[3] a quotation from Claudian that also graced closely contemporaneous editions of Robert Filmer's *Patriarcha.*[35]

In Dryden's postscript to the translation itself, one such *rex pius* is identified as England's Charles I, "incomparably more pious" than the French king, Henry III, though both kings owe the catastrophes of their respective reigns to "too much mildness" (405). Taking advantage of this mildness, the rebels in both cases claim the name of *piety* in attacking the crown: " 'tis an action of Piety in them to destroy their Enemies, having first pronounc'd them Enemies of God" (405). The irony here specifies a more general phrase from the translation, a reference to the characteristic way in which the Guisards "disguis'd Rebellion under a specious name" (234). The "specious name" in this translation is commonly *piety,* though *religion* and *zeal* function in essentially equivalent ways, as the translation addresses problems very similar to those considered in *Absalom and Achitophel.*[36] In fact, Dryden takes the opportunity of dedicating the translation to Charles II in the form of an answer to the question raised toward the conclusion of the earlier poem—"Must I at length the Sword of Justice draw?"

> But when that pity has been always found to draw into example of greater Mischiefs; when they continually behold both Your Majesty and themselves expos'd to Dangers, the Church, the Government, the Succession still threatned, Ingratitude so far from being Converted by gentle means, that it is turn'd at last into the nature of the damn'd, desirous of Revenge, and harden'd in Impenitence; 'Tis time at length, for self preservation to cry out for Justice, and to lay by Mildness when it ceases to be a Vertue. (4)

[3] Never is liberty more welcome than under a pious king.

Dryden's subsequent qualification of this vindictive argument involves defining "That sort of pity which is proper for them . . ." (7), a line that suggests the political history of *pity* in English as it may be traced over several centuries from (for example) Gower to Hoccleve to Elyot to Dryden, and with Mandeville's remarks on the horizon: "Pity, tho' it is the most gentle and the least mischievous of all our Passions, is yet as much a Frailty of our Nature, as Anger, Pride, or Fear. . . . [A]s it is an Impulse of Nature, that consults neither the publick Interest nor our own Reason, it may produce Evil as well as Good."[37] That this derivative of *pietas* is an impulse of "Nature" that must be balanced by justice and controlled by law is the strongly marked direction of English political usage down to the time of Dryden and beyond.

The danger of pity to a ruler is established by connection to "mildness" as the essential characteristic of the king to whom the translation is dedicated; likewise, the danger of piety to a ruler is established by connection to "pretences of Religion" that shield "Conspiracy." Whereas Maimbourg's history takes Livy as its classical model, Dryden's translation is replete with phrases that suggest his own favorite classical historian, Tacitus. As in the *Annals*, pietas is repeatedly connected to words such as *appearance* and *pretence,* and to other expressions of seeming and hypocrisy: "But it will not be difficult to discover in the process of this History, that the Authours of that Conspiracy made use of those pretences of Religion, to abuse the credulity, and even the Piety of the People; and to make them impious, without their perceiving it, by animating and arming them against their kings" (27). The play of "Piety" and "impious" effectively articulates the basic contradiction inherent in popular abuse of the word: to be disloyal to a legitimate ruler is (in Dryden's view) to be "impious" in a religious sense as well. This abuse of the word is associated with "credulity" and here identified with the popular folly exploited by such as the Duke of Lorraine (and in England Shaftesbury, to whom the French Duke is compared). In effect, the word that in the Latin of the epigraph defines an appropriate governmental norm, in the derivative modern languages has become a vehicle for deliberate subversion on the part of the rebel leaders, and unwitting cooperation on the part of their followers. Throughout, then, what the rebels undertake in the name of religion Dryden will label "impious," concluding the last sentence of his postscript with a statement of purpose to this effect: "This particular work was written by express order of the *French* King, and is now translated by our Kings Command: I hope the effect of it in this Nation will be, to make the well-meaning men of the other Party sensible of their past errors, the worst of them asham'd, and prevent Posterity from the like unlawful and impious designs" (415). Sustaining "impious" by conjunction with "unlawful," Dryden stresses the aptness of the parallel between England in the seventeenth century and France in the sixteenth. Remarking upon the dynastic connection between Charles II and his grandfather Henry IV, moreover, Dryden acknowledges the developed preference for "Clemency" and "Mercy" as the appropriate terms of qualification on the idea of justice.

> To come yet nearer, *Henry* the Fourth, Your Royal Grandfather, whose Victories, and the Subversion of the *League,* are the main Argument of this History, was a Prince most Clement in his Nature, he forgave his Rebels, and receiv'd them all into Mercy, and some of them into Favour, but it was not till he had fully vanquish'd them: they were sensible of their Impiety, they submitted, and his Clemency was not extorted from him, it was his Free-gift, and it was seasonably given. (5)

The phrase "sensible of their Impiety" is corrective to the notion of a people "impious, without their perceiving it." Part of what is at issue here, as in *Absalom and Achitophel,* is clarification of the reference for the derivatives of *pietas* and *impietas,* the survival of the latter and the continuing displacement of the former in English by *mercy* and *clemency.*

Such clarification is necessary because ancient meaning has been obscured by seditious preaching: "profaneing their Sacred Function of Preaching the Gospel, by their Seditious Tongues, and dealing out a thousand impostures from the Chair of Truth, [they] declaim'd venemously against the Lord's Annointed, all whose actions they bespatter'd, even those which were adorn'd with the greatest Piety" (113). Those ridiculing the hypocrisy of the king are now themselves guilty of "impostures," which has the effect of redeeming, however anachronistically, the "Piety" of the king. The precise wording—"adorn'd with the greatest Piety"— dates from the medieval governance tracts, in which Constantine is repeatedly described as "optimus imperator pietate decoratus."[38] The significance of this for Dryden, who later compares James II to Constantine in *Britannia Rediviva,*[39] may be observed in *The Hind and the Panther.* In the portrayal of James, Dryden appeals almost nostalgically to the older and increasingly irrelevant political vocabulary. Here pietas as a term claimed by radical Protestantism is even restored to a Catholic tradition that Dryden's Hind situates within a history that begins with Genesis.

> Thus kneaded up with milk, the new made man
> His kingdom o'er his kindred world began:
> Till knowledge misapply'd, misunderstood,
> And pride of Empire sour'd his balmy bloud.
> Then, first rebelling, his own stamp he coins;
> The murth'rer *Cain* was latent in his loins,
> And bloud began its first and loudest cry
> For diff'ring worship of the Deity.
> Thus persecution rose, and farther space
> Produc'd the mighty hunter of his race.
> Not so the blessed *Pan* his flock encreas'd,
> Content to fold 'em from the famish'd beast:
> Mild were his laws; the Sheep and harmless Hind
> Were never of the persecuting kind.
> Such pity now the pious Pastor shows,
> Such mercy from the *British Lyon* flows,
> That both provide protection for their foes.
>
> (1.274–90)

In this compressed history of religion from creation to the reign of James II, Dryden sets traditional exemplars of impietas, Cain and Nimrod ("the mighty hunter of his race") against Christ as *auctor pietatis,* whose "Mild . . . laws" are shown to be exercised by the contemporary Pope Innocent XI as well as by King James. The parallel structure—"Such pity . . . / Such mercy"—underlines the shared responsibility of church and state; the convergence of "pity" and "pious" in the description of the pope functions by extension to describe the English king, who is later characterized by "mildness" (3.1104) and who offers his care to the Catholic clergy: "And from His Pious Hands receiv'd their Bread" (3.996). In contrast, the Buzzard who emerges as false savior at the conclusion of part 3, is identified with Nimrod (1274) and described as both "Usurper" (1279) and "Tyrant" (1288). The Buzzard has been taken to represent both Bishop Burnet and William of Orange, thereby in one figure of impietas providing the antithesis to the pietas of Innocent and James. Consistent not only with the political allegory but also with the poem's beast fable, the triumphant Buzzard belongs to the hawk family, which is (according to the sacred zoographer Wolfgang Franzius) the type of all impious creatures ("omnium impiorum").[40]

Foreseeing the reign of the impious, Dryden performed his last service for James II by translating Bouhours's life of Francis Xavier. In this work Catholic patterns of piety are discovered that reveal in the spiritual life of a saint the providential order so difficult to find in the secular realm of English politics. Although the work reveals in the portrait of the Portuguese governor, Antonio Galvan, an exemplary ruler of "Piety and Valour,"[41] the real hero of this work represents a quite different version of pietas with religious devotion as its essential meaning. The hagiographic details describing this second Paul (442) emphasize a piety surpassing that of all secular rulers. The very quality that has become so doubtful in Dryden's rulers is here triumphant: "his countenance full of mildness, gave them to believe" (148). In the basic design of the life, as in individual passages, *impiety*—even amplified by connection with madness—is overcome by *mildness* in a manner that implies a providential order willing universal and permanent conversion. Throughout the translation, *devotion* is the word most closely aligned with *piety,* but the latter term suggests greater permanence: "This so sudden a change of manners, was none of those transient fits of Devotion, which pass away, almost as soon as they are kindled; Piety was establish'd in all places; and they who formerly came to confession once a year . . . now perform'd it regularly once a month" (67). Yet it is asserted in the life that the "seeds of Piety" (256) are within, even before conversion, and the most likely converts are women. Consider Xavier's conversion of the queen of Ternate: "He was not satisfy'd with barely making her a Christian. He saw in her a great stock of Piety, an upright Heart, a tenderness of Mind, inclinations truly great and noble; which he cultivated with admirable care, and set her forward by degrees, in the most sublime and solid ways of a spiritual life" (142). Although this passage retains the connection between piety and nobility, this is now redefined to refer not to social eminence but to the "spiritual life." And in the process, manners change: "she grew humble and modest, from disdainful, and haughty as she was, mild to others, and severe to her self" (142). Nor is it any accident that the exemplar of piety is female: "the weaker Sex, had greater advantages than ours, by reason of that modesty and piety, which is almost inherent in their nature" (309). The usage of Dryden's Bouhours, then, depends upon tendencies latent in the history of the word and increasingly to be emphasized in the century to come. Here piety is religious, feminine, and personally revealed in a manner that is modest and mild, as the word so important in Dryden's political poetry here retreats from the public to the private domain; or in larger perspective, it may be said that the heroic definition of *pietas* derivative from Vergil is submerged by the alternative of the church fathers. It is, then, not only against the background of an "Impious Age" that Dryden came to his translation of the *Aeneid,* but also at a time when the epithet *pious* had ceased to suggest anything heroic.

The Aeneis

In his postcript to the *Aeneis* Dryden sharply distinguishes his situation from that of Vergil: "What *Virgil* wrote in the vigour of his Age, in Plenty and at Ease, I have undertaken to Translate in my Declining Years: strugling with Wants, oppress'd with Sickness, curb'd in my Genius, lyable to be misconstrued in all I write."[42] As Vergil wrote his epic after revolution had brought Octavian to power, so Dryden translates it after revolution had brought William of Orange to power. But whereas Vergil secures entry to the court circle around Maecenas, Dryden is now evicted from his offices and content "if the Government will let me pass unquestion'd" (808). Vergil finds in the *pietas* of Aeneas the ideal expressing the new age ushered in by his patron Augustus; in sharp contrast, Dryden had already portrayed William of Orange under the figure of the Buzzard, the *omnium impiorum* type, in the beast fable of *The Hind and the Panther* and had characterized his own times in the conclusion to *Amphitryon* as "an Impious Age."

The impietas of the age in which Dryden translated the *Aeneid* is reflected in his versions of Juvenal published earlier in the same decade, where the "ill-gotten Spoiles" of the "impious," condemned in *The Medall,* are taken to measure the conflict between the old order and the new, in seventeenth-century England as in second-century Rome. Compare the Delphin Juvenal 6.551–52 with Dryden's expansive translation:

> Pectora pullorum rimatur, et exta catelli,
> Interdum et pueri. Faciet quod deferat ipse.[4]

---

[4] He probes the breast of a chicken, or the entrails of a dog, sometimes even of a boy; some things he will do with the intention of informing against them himself.

> In Dogs, a Victim more obscene, he rakes;
> And Murder'd Infants, for Inspection, takes:
> For Gain, his Impious Practice he pursues;
> For Gain will his Accomplices Accuse.[43]

The anaphoric "For Gain" is reminiscent of Dryden's description of Shimei, who "never broke the Sabbath, but for Gain" (588), although the increased intensity of the later satire is quite evident. Nor can this be explained entirely by reference to Juvenal, whose poem invokes *impietas* neither here nor in satire 1.45–47, rendered by Dryden: "What Indignation boils within my Veins, / When perjur'd Guardians, proud with Impious Gains, / Choak up the Streets, too narrow for their Trains!" (1.67–69). One measure of impietas in the decade that produces the *Aeneis,* then, is greed, and Dryden's Juvenalian indignation is captured in the phrase "Impious Gains." The implication of the adjective here is something more than the illegality expressed by the earlier "perjur'd." If such "Gains" are a reason to be "proud," then the very basis of public esteem has been commercialized in the manner expressed by the translation of Juvenal 3.140–41: "The Question is not put how far extends / His Piety, but what he yearly spends" (3.235–36). Again adding "Piety" to the original, Dryden sets ancient ideal against contemporary reality. In the present iron age, bereft of idealism, its relationships defined in metaphors of commerce, piety is a rare anachronism; in contrast, and going beyond the authority of Juvenal, Dryden identifies the ideal of piety with a past and unrecoverable golden age when social and political relationships could be defined in familial metaphors.

Judging from Dryden's translations of Juvenal, then, Vergil's Aeneas might be less at home in late seventeenth-century England than his Polymestor, who

> Broke ev'ry Bond of Nature, and of Truth;
> And murder'd, for his Wealth, the Royal Youth.
> O sacred Hunger of pernicious Gold,
> What bands of Faith can impious Lucre hold?[44]

In this account of Polydorus's murder, Dryden's words reveal a vision very much like that expressed by Dorax in *Don Sebastian* ("Why then no Bond is left on human kind . . .") combined with that of Mercury in *Amphitryon:* "Our Iron Age is grown an Age of Gold: / 'Tis who bids most; for all Men wou'd be sold" (4.1.556–57). Like the "impious Gains" of Dryden's Juvenal, then, the "impious Lucre" of his Vergil is understood to violate the "Bond" or "bands" holding society together. Lucre is "impious" because it here becomes something more worthy ("sacred") than religion, family, and state from which the ancient ideal derives its meaning.

Dryden's translation develops Vergil's religious emphasis by investing ritualistic passages of the poem with an understanding of *pietas* touched by Christianity at the point where ritual converges with ethics. In the Polydorus episode, for example, the English poet follows Vergil closely in rendering the first words from the bleeding branch. In Vergil: "jam parce sepulto, / Parce pias scelerare manus" (3.41–42). In Dryden: "O spare the Corps of thy unhappy Friend! / Spare to pollute thy pious Hands with Blood" (3.59–60). The repeated imperative indicates the double obligation of piety to bury the dead and not to stain the hands with "Blood," the latter word occurring three times over the next seven lines, as against the single instance of "cruor" in the Latin. The command thus has at once a ritual and a moral dimension, requires one kind of action while warning against another. The ritual aspect of this command is repeated in the prophecy of Helenus. Against the curse of the Harpies, "Dare you with Heav'n an impious War maintain . . . ?" (3.325), Helenus expands upon Anchises' prayer for relief: "And from th' impending Curse, a Pious People free" (3.347). He thus predicates the triumph of Trojan piety on performance of religious rites.

> Ev'n when thy Fleet is landed on the Shore,
> And Priests with holy Vows the Gods adore;
> Then with a Purple Veil involve your Eyes,
> Lest hostile Faces blast the Sacrifice.
> These Rites and Customs to the Rest commend;
> That to your Pious Race they may descend.
> (3.517–22)

Here understood as a cultural expression that unifies and preserves against adversity, religious ritual connects the future to the past. Throughout the poem the specific ritual answerable to Helenus's prophecy is burial of the dead, the "Fun'ral Rites" (3.88) performed for Polydorus repeated at intervals for others right through book 11 as a measure of the hero's piety.

But the warning of Polydorus attaches piety not only to ritual, but also to the moral injunction: "Spare to pollute thy pious Hands with Blood." More obviously than in the original, this negative command connects the words of Polydorus to Aeneas's own words at the end of the previous book, when he asks Anchises to carry the sacred relics from Troy.

> Our Country Gods, the Relicks, and the Bands,
> Hold you, my Father, in your guiltless Hands:
> In me 'tis impious holy things to bear,
> Red as I am with Slaughter, new from War:
> 'Till in some living Stream I cleanse the Guilt
> Of dire Debate, and Blood in Battel spilt.
>   (2.974–79)

Here capturing Vergil's noun "nefas" (2.719) in the adjective "impious," Dryden places the blood of war against the virtue that characterizes Aeneas. Dryden's word "Guilt"—for which there is no real equivalent in the Latin—narrows the gap between classical poem and Christian translation, as the confidence expressed by Aeneas at the efficacy of hand-washing is inevitably qualified in Dryden by contexts unknown to Vergil.

If latter-day associations serve to undermine the pious heroic represented by Aeneas, they tend to stress the opposing forces of the impious heroic. Thus Vergil's Polymestor is described in the English as a "faithless Tyrant" (3.75), Dryden's choice of words associating the Thracian king ("Threïcio regi," 3.51) with a developed type of impiety famously represented by Vergil's own Mezentius:

> 'Till curs'd *Mezentius*, in a fatal Hour,
> Assum'd the Crown, with Arbitrary Pow'r.
> What Words can paint those execrable Times;
> The Subjects Suff'rings, and the Tyrant's Crimes?
> That Blood, those Murthers, O ye Gods replace
> On his own Head, and on his impious Race!
>   (8.630–35)

Dryden condemns the tyrant in language that parallels the account of Polymestor, and goes on to describe him by comparison to Cacus as a "raging Monster" (8.642). This type, of which Western literature had provided numerous examples since Vergil, is accurately described not only in Dryden's preface ("A Man may be very Valiant, and yet Impious and Vicious"), but also in the conclusion to *Amphitryon,* where the figure of Hercules is opposed to "Tyrants . . . Monsters, and Monstermen." Dryden's emphatic pursuit of the analogy between the *labores* of Hercules and Aeneas in his translation elaborates upon the question raised at the end of his earlier play: what is the meaning of heroism in an age of impiety? or, more generally, what happens to piety in time?

Roman literature after Vergil had provided alternative answers to this question: one line confirming the triumph of *pietas* and the advent of an imperial golden age, the other arguing imperial triumph over *pietas* in an age of iron. The perspective of Dryden's *Aeneis* on these alternatives may be suggested by juxtaposition of a passage from book 6, which resonates with echoes of Dryden's Restoration panegyrics, and another from book 11, which suggests the impious age envisioned in the translations of Juvenal's satires. First, consider in translation the words of Anchises that thirty-seven years before Dryden had adapted to celebrate the Restoration of Charles II: "*Augustus,* promis'd oft, and long foretold,/Sent to the Realm that *Saturn* rul'd of old;/Born to restore a better Age of Gold" (6.1079–81). The resonant word "restore" here echoes line 7 of the first book, where religion promises a redemptive vision of history dependent on the pious heroism of Aeneas. "His banish'd Gods restor'd to Rites Divine,/And setl'd sure Succession in his Line" (1.7–8). The meaning of this couplet is revealed in Jupiter's promise to Venus later in book 1: "Then dire Debate, and impious War shall cease,/And the stern Age be softned into Peace:/Then banish'd Faith shall once again return" (1.396–98). The language of this prophecy evokes the Restoration, and can be compared to the language of *Astraea Redux* and, second, to that of Edmund Waller's poem on the same occasion:

> At home the hateful names of Parties cease
> And factious Souls are weary'd into peace.
>
> Faith, law, and piety, (that banished train!)
> Justice and truth, with you return again.[45]

The Restoration thus provides a touchstone for situating Vergilian *pietas* in time, as Dryden recreates the redemptive pattern of Roman history in the idiom of the panegyrics addressed to Charles II.

The alternative vision of Roman history is reflected in the words of Diomede to the Latian ambassadors in book 11: "*Ausonian* Race, of old / Renown'd for Peace, and for an Age of Gold, / What Madness has your alter'd Minds possess'd, / To change for War hereditary Rest?" (11.386–89). In contrast to the peaceful golden age, the furor of war is here characterized in a vocabulary that recalls the "Madness" of *Absalom and Achitophel* and the "impious Arms" of *The Medall*. Whereas books 1–6 of the *Aeneis* recapture the optimism of the poems Dryden had written in the 1660s, books 7–12 reflect an impious age in the making from the Exclusion Crisis to the Revolution and after. As Vergil had "maturely weigh'd the Condition of the Times in which he liv'd," so has Dryden weighed the "Condition" of his own times, and translated the poem accordingly.[46] The problem of Roman history in Latin poetry after Vergil thus returns to the *Aeneid* via English history in Dryden's translation.

At issue, then, is not just the time separating Vergil from Dryden, but the difference between the redemptive history of books 1–6 and the historical regression of 7–12. This difference is particularly well illustrated by the contrasting prospects of piety and governance evident in the first simile of book 1 and its revision in book 7. Dryden's version of the original simile is reminiscent of several passages from *The Medall*, and recalls in a general way David's speech at the conclusion of *Absalom and Achitophel*.

> As when in Tumults rise th' ignoble Crowd,
> Mad are their Motions, and their Tongues are loud;
> And Stones and Brands in ratling Vollies fly,
> And all the Rustick Arms that Fury can supply:
> If then some grave and Pious Man appear,
> They hush their Noise, and lend a list'ning Ear;
> He sooths with sober Words their angry Mood,
> And quenches their innate Desire of Blood:
> So when the Father of the Flood appears,
> And o're the Seas his Sov'raign Trident rears,
> Their Fury falls: He skims the liquid Plains,
> High on his Chariot, and with loosen'd Reins,
> Majestick moves along, and awful Peace maintains.
>   (1.213–25)[47]

In this version of the triumph of pietas over furor, the "Pious Man"—exactly Dryden's later description of Aeneas at 4.858—silences the "ignoble Crowd" and by analogy to Neptune secures "Peace." The pattern of this simile is thus very close to the larger pattern of *Astraea Redux,* in which Charles II is compared to Aeneas at sea early in the poem and to the triumphant Augustus at the end.

But this assertion of "Peace" (Dryden's rendering of Vergil's "aequora") is later revoked to illuminate the abdication of the Latian King Latinus in book 7. In his preface, Dryden contrasts Latinus to Mezentius, who "Govern'd Arbitrarily . . . And came to the deserv'd End of all Tyrants."[48]

> Our Author shews us another sort of Kingship in the Person of *Latinus.* He was descended from *Saturn,* and as I remember, in the Third Degree. He is describ'd a just and a gracious Prince; solicitous for the Welfare of his People; always Consulting with his Senate to promote the common Good. We find him at the head of them, when he enters into the Council-Hall: Speaking first, but still demanding their Advice, and steering by it as far as the Iniquity of the Times wou'd suffer him. And this is the proper Character of a King by Inheritance, who is born a Father of his Country. (284)

If Dryden appears to protest too much on behalf of Latinus, the implied comparison with James II is the likely reason.[49] In any case, Dryden goes out of his way to honor the piety of Latinus, to condemn the madness of those opposed to him, and to view the moment of his abdication as a reversal not only of the poem's first simile but of the entire first six books.

> With Fates averse, the Rout in Arms resort,
> To Force their Monarch, and insult the Court.
> But like a Rock unmov'd, a Rock that braves
> The rageing Tempest and the rising Waves,
> Prop'd on himself he stands: His solid sides
> Wash off the Sea-weeds, and the sounding Tides:
> So stood the Pious Prince unmov'd: and long
> Sustain'd the madness of the noisie Throng.
> But when he found that *Juno's* Pow'r prevail'd,
> And all the Methods of cool Counsel fail'd,
> He calls the Gods to witness their offence,

Disclaims the War, asserts his Innocence.
Hurry'd by Fate, he cries, and born before
A furious Wind, we leave the faithful Shore:
O more than Madmen! you your selves shall bear
The guilt of Blood and Sacrilegious War:
Thou, *Turnus,* shalt attone it by thy Fate,
And pray to Heav'n for Peace, but pray too late.
For me, my stormy Voyage at an end,
I to the Port of Death securely tend.
The Fun'ral Pomp which to your Kings you pay,
Is all I want, and all you take away.
He said no more, but in his Walls confin'd,
Shut out the Woes which he too well divin'd:
Nor with the rising Storm wou'd vainly strive,
But left the Helm, and let the Vessel drive.
                                                    (7.807–32)

It should be noted, first, that Vergil does not describe the Latian king as *pius.*[50] Dryden, on the other hand, not only gives to Latinus the epithet of Aeneas, but also capitalizes on the essential dualism of the couplet form to associate the contrast between royal piety and popular fury with the dominant polarities of the later books, specifying the contrast between the "Pious" and the "furious" in revealing terms: "Prince"–"Counsel"– "Innocence"–"Peace" versus *"Turnus"*–"Madmen"–"Guilt"–"War."

The classificatory pattern of these lines highlights the dynamic narrative they contain: a narrative that reverses the significance of the "Pious Man" simile of book 1 by providing an alternative version of *Aeneis* 1– 6. Dryden emphasizes the identification of Latinus with Aeneas in the phrase "Pious Prince" by then echoing the opening lines of the poem, as "Hurry'd by Fate" recalls "forc'd by Fate" in line 1 of the translation, confirmed by the echo of "Shoar" from line 3. It is at this point that the image of the rock begins to yield to the more obviously allegorical image of the ship—ship of state but also, as Dryden's translation of "O miseri" (7.596) to read "O more than Madmen" suggests, ship of fools as well. Dryden then encloses one nautical image within another to give his compressed revision of *Aeneis* 1 ("Tempest") to *Aeneis* 6 ("Port of Death") an ominously new conclusion: the abdication of the "Pious Prince" and the certain shipwreck of his subjects. Vergil had concluded, briefly: "Nec plura locutus, / Sepsit se tectis, rerumque reliquit habenas"

(7.599–600).[5] By adding to this the idea of Latinus as both visionary ("Woes which he too well divin'd") and realist ("Nor with the rising Storm wou'd vainly strive"), Dryden deflects blame from the Latian king, who represents an idealism once but no longer possible. Isolated and overwhelmed by the furious, Latinus must accept defeat in order to sustain his commitment to the ideal of pietas. His obstinate refusal to open the gates of Janus places him in opposition to a future represented by "the wicked Ministry of Arms" (7.856) that he is powerless to prevent. Dryden thus brings into sharp focus the conflict between virtue and destiny facing Aeneas, himself earlier described as the "Pious Prince" (4.404, 823) as he responds to the divine command to leave Carthage.

At the moment of decision in book 4 it is the feeling of pity that has to be overcome:

> But good *Aeneas,* tho' he much desir'd
> To give that Pity, which her Grief requir'd,
> Tho' much he mourn'd, and labour'd with his Love,
> Resolv'd at length, obeys the Will of *Jove.*
>
> (4.568–71)

Translating Vergil's "pius" as "good," Dryden transfers the English derivative to the subordinate construction where it expresses the alternative to "the Will of *Jove.*" The parallelism between "Pity" and "Love," moreover, not only evokes the traditional vocabulary of the European love lyric, but reverses the conventional pattern, as the male here controls both: for Dryden's Aeneas "Pity" and "Love" are finally subordinate to the divine will, the syntax reflecting the order of the hero's experience. Also to be noticed here, given Dryden's emphasis on the Aeneas–Hercules analogy, is the word "labour'd," which effectively puts "Love" in its place as a form of adversity that must be withstood. Adding this word without any real hint from Vergil suggests that for Dryden the challenge of Dido has less to do with the positive attractions of "Love" than it does with default of labor, also emphasized with reference to women in the narrative of the Trojan matrons in book 5.[51] Both books amplify the Penates' warning from book 3: that the weary mind may yield to the desire for release from labor. Twice including a negation of the word where there is no equivalent expression in the Latin, Dryden first offers and then rejects love

[5] Saying no more he shut himself in the palace, and let drop the reins of rule.

as a substitute for labor. In the first instance Dido is showing Aeneas her city, "Which Love, without his Labour, makes his own" (4.104). The implication of this entirely original line is that Aeneas may gain through love the city he has not so far been able to gain by his labor. But the translator denies this possibility with reference to Dido's Carthage in the second instance, where the significance of default is disclosed in an image not so vivid as Vergil's but still effective: "the rising Tow'rs are at a stand: / No Labours exercise the youthful Band" (4.123–24). Unfinished and undefended, the city cannot be gained with love nor without labor; nor does Dryden dignify the hero's later attempts at Tyrian city-building with the name of labor. Rather, the very absence of this word in a context that should recall the prophecy "with hard Labour, *Alba-Longa* build" (1.368) tends to justify Mercury's more than Vergilian severity: "Degenerate Man, / Thou Woman's Property . . ." (4.389–90).[52] What book 4 contributes to the design of the first six books is, then, an escape from the very idea of labor and from the comparison with Hercules.

Overcoming default in books 4 and 5, Dryden's Aeneas achieves the union of labor and piety in book 6. The correspondence of Aeneas to Hercules, intermittently acknowledged over the first five books of the translation, is vigorously reasserted and its meaning now clarified in the voyage to the underworld. Vergil specifically compares the two heroes: "Nec vero Alcides tantum telluris obivit" (6.801).[6] In Dryden this becomes: "Nor *Hercules* more Lands or Labours knew" (6.1093). The alliterative association of "Lands" with "Labours," of triumph with cost, not only evokes the epic question, but also refines the comparison between the two heroes. Whereas Hercules (according to Charon) had gained admission to the underworld by force, Aeneas relies on the talismanic power of the golden bough, obtained according to the instructions of the Sibyl.

> Then rend it off, as holy Rites command:
> The willing Metal will obey thy hand,
> Following with ease, if, favour'd by thy Fate,
> Thou art foredoom'd to view the *Stygian* State:
> If not, no labour can the Tree constrain:
> And strength of stubborn Arms, and Steel are vain.
>   (6.219–24)

[6] Nor, in truth, did Alcides range o'er such space of earth.

Rejecting the more obvious "no force" to translate Vergil's "non viribus ullis" (6.147), Dryden here repeats "labour" in a context that insists on the congruence of "labour" with "Fate," human endeavor with divine sanction. The outward manifestation of this congruence is the correct performance of "holy Rites," specifically extended in the Sibyl's explanation to include a funeral for Misenus. It is by paying the "Pious Dues" (6.229) of his lost comrade that Aeneas and his labor are finally—after all the false starts and misdirections of the preceding books—united. "Arm'd like the rest the *Trojan* Prince appears: / And, by his pious Labour, urges theirs" (6.269–70). Thus translating "opera" (6.183) as "Labour" and adding both "Prince" and "pious," Dryden here defines the responsibility of the heroic role in accordance with the historical pattern of *pietas victrix*. In the phrase "pious Labour," ritual and act, character and destiny, are in perfect balance. Aeneas's trial in the last six books will be to repatriate his piety in Latium, to carry this ethical burden through the "Toils of War," thus fulfilling the prophecy of Jupiter: "Then dire Debate, and impious War shall cease, / And the stern Age be softned into Peace" (1.396–97).

In Dryden's translation, however, it does not work out this way because "impious War" is never rendered compatible with the character of the "Pious Prince." This incompatibility, long a perception of commentary on Vergil's poem, is deeply felt in Dryden's version. The prophetic phrase "dire Debate" is recast in book 7 by the Fury Alecto, who "watch'd an Hour to work her impious Will" (7.714): "Behold, 'tis done, / The Blood already drawn, the War begun; / The Discord is compleat, nor can they cease / The dire Debate, nor you command the Peace" (7.755–58). This revision of the original prophecy bears heavily on Aeneas, who himself acknowledges "the Guilt / Of dire Debate, and Blood in Battel spilt" in book 2, and indicates his desire in book 7 to gain his kingdom without war. Consider Dryden's rendering of the initial mission to the Latians: "The Pious Chief, who sought by peaceful Ways, / To found his Empire, and his Town to raise" (7.203–4). Emphasizing the means fully as much as the end, Dryden identifies piety with peace: in the Latin there is no reference to the hero's *pietas,* nor is there any equivalent for the general phrase "who sought by peaceful Ways." Vergil does not allow this particular mission of peace either to reach beyond its immediate context or to define the character of the "Pious Chief." In Dryden it does both.

The problem, then, is the recurrent one of Renaissance epic: reconciling Vergilian *pietas* and *arma.* It is directly addressed in the encounter with Lausus in book 10. Presenting Vergil's "iuvenis" (10.793, 796) as "The pious Youth" (10.1131), Dryden so complicates the moral issues of the war as to render the prediction that "War shall end in lasting Peace" (8.57) entirely irrelevant; Aeneas himself now becomes the embodiment of "Fury" (10.1154) in opposition to Latian piety. Aeneas even acknowledges the piety of Lausus in an attempt to rationalize his own fury, succeeding only in emphasizing the reversal of roles that has taken place. Lausus becomes the mirror of what Aeneas once was.

> But when, with Blood, and Paleness all o'respread,
> The pious Prince beheld young *Lausus* dead;
> He griev'd, he wept, the sight an Image brought
> Of his own filial Love; a sadly pleasing Thought.
> (10.1164–67)

Its referent made momentarily ambiguous by Dryden's syntax, the adjective "pious" itself acquires a measure of ambiguity as well: if this formulaic expression here marks Aeneas's recovery from momentary fury, it also functions as a tragically ironic comment on the whole episode. The fate of Lausus may now be added to the fate of Latinus in Dryden's continuing exploration of the virtue to which Aeneas still clings at the beginning of the next book.

Three times in the burial scene that introduces book 11, Dryden describes Aeneas as "pious" without authority from Vergil. By carefully attending the ritual of mass funeral, the hero recovers his status as "the pious Man" (11.57) and stands ready to fulfill the terms of the truce. But again peace fails, in the Trojan camp as well as in the Latian, and Dryden's account of this failure in book 12 is revealing:

> Peace leaves the violated Fields; and Hate
> Both Armies urges to their mutual Fate.
> With impious Haste their Altars are o'return'd,
> The Sacrifice half broil'd, and half unburn'd.
>
> . . . .
>
> Brands from the Fire, are missive Weapons made . . .
> (12.423–26, 429)

The first four lines of this citation represent a bit more than one line of Vergil: "Sic omnes amor unus habet decernere ferro./Diripuere aras"

(12.282–83).[7] By specifying Vergil's "omnes" as "Both armies" and then adding "mutual Fate," Dryden makes moral discrimination between these two armies as hard to sustain as that between Christians and Saracens in the last canto of *Gerusalemme Liberata*. The "impious" transformation of altar fires into weapons in the lines that follow again tests the validity of the "Pious Man" simile from book 1: the figure of the bareheaded, unarmed Aeneas rushing through "Warm Blood, and mingled Brains" (12.466) in an effort to halt the conflict expresses as well as any passage in the translation the ultimate incapacity of piety to contain fury: "what new Desire of Blood/Inflames your alter'd Minds? *O Trojans* cease/From impious Arms, nor violate the Peace" (12.472–74). Expanding Vergil's "O cohibete iras" (12.314)[8], Dryden describes a world like that viewed by the allegorized Pietas of Statius, a world in which even friends are hostile to the piety Aeneas would represent. The phrase that describes them—"alter'd Minds"—exactly repeats the phrase earlier used by Diomede to place desire for war in historical perspective. The historical pattern illustrated by the last six books is that of *pietas victa,* most dramatically illustrated by Aeneas himself.

The war thus resumed is not only between two armies, or two ways of life, but also between the hero and his world, and in the process it is the hero, not the world, that changes. The decisive moment of change is marked with exceeding care.

> The Prince, whose Piety had long repell'd
> His inborn ardour, now invades the Field:
> Invokes the Pow'rs of violated Peace,
> Their Rites, and injur'd Altars to redress:
> Then, to his Rage abandoning the Rein,
> With Blood and slaughter'd Bodies fills the Plain.
> (12.719–94)

There is nothing in Vergil's original to suggest the explicitness of Dryden's distinction between "Piety" and "ardour"; what Aeneas himself earlier calls "impious Arms" (12.474) can no longer be held in check by his pious character. Here the thematic paradox latent in the opening

---

[7] Thus all are ruled by one passion, to let the sword decide. Lo! they have stripped the altars.

[8] O curb your rage!

phrase of the poem becomes finally untenable: the man has to change, must become in arms another man. The piety achieved in the first six books collapses under the stress of war in the last six; these lines mark the end of all "peaceful Ways." From this moment, the piety of Dryden's Aeneas is mentioned but once, in a context that recalls Servius's description of Aeneas as "innocens" and explicitly invites comparison with Latinus. As the Latian towers burn, "the Heroe stands, / And stretching out to Heav'n his Pious Hands; / Attests the Gods, asserts his Innocence" (12.849–51). It will be remembered that in book 7 the "Pious Prince" Latinus "calls the Gods to witness their offence, / Disclaims the War, asserts his Innocence" (7.817–18). The irony of this echo perfectly defines the dilemma of Dryden's idealists. Latinus can justly claim "Innocence," but the cost is high—the loss of his kingdom. Aeneas, whose "Pious Hands" are already stained with blood and will be stained with more, wins a kingdom, but the cost is again high—the loss of his claim to "innocence" and to piety as well. Aeneas wins in Dryden's translation by becoming so like Turnus as to be indistinguishable from him: "zeal of Slaughter fires their Souls alike" (12.771). Vergil's narrative represents for Dryden the fate of piety in the world: the triumph of Aeneas over Turnus in the outer war of action is thus the defeat of Aeneas in the inner war of moral struggle. Indeed, he is no longer the "pious Aeneas" but rather the "stern *Aeneas*" (12.1284); Dryden's adjective that earlier describes the age, now describes Aeneas as well. The triumph of Aeneas is not the triumph of piety. In the words of Dryden's epistle to his cousin, included in *Fables Ancient and Modern:* "Ev'n Victors are by Victories undone."[53]

The Fables

The anti-war dimension of Dryden's translation is a telling commentary on the age of William III. Yet it may be emphasized that in the dedication of the *Fables* to the Duke of Ormond, Dryden recounts in some detail his patron's involvement in King William's war. Praising Ormond's conduct in the aftermath of the battle of Landon, Dryden writes: "All Men, even those of a different Interest, and contrary Principles, must praise this Action, as the most eminent for Piety, not only in this degenerate Age, but almost in any of the former; when Men were made *de meliore luto.*"[54] Ormond's "Piety" is defined in context as "Heroick Charity,"[55] a phrase that brings together classical and Christian dimensions of its inherited meaning. The heroic idea is appropriately underlined by supporting quotation from the *Aeneid,* but in citing Dido's words from book 1 Dryden lends them a Christian significance: "The Heathen Poet, in commending the Charity of *Dido* to the *Trojans,* spoke like a Christian: *Non ignara mali miseris, succurrere disco*" (1443).[9] The idea thus voiced in the *Aeneid* through Dido is attached to the idealized Ormond in praise of his "Acts of Compassion, and of Charity" (1441). The second quotation is from *Aeneid* 6 and is obviously chosen to celebrate the heroic stature of Ormond while at the same time to confirm Juvenal's "*de meliore luto*": "Teucri pulcherrima proles, / Magnanimi Heroes nati melioribus annis" (1443).[10] The effect of the Latin quotations, then, is to define "Piety" in terms at once ancient and modern, and thus to poise Christian hero against the "degenerate" age that provides the background for the *Fables* as it had for the *Aeneis.*

Exactly when men were made of better clay, however, is not specified in the dedication except to call in doubt the age of Vergil as such a time.[56] At least Dryden now admits that "the *Felix, Pius,* and *Augustus* of the *Roman* Emperors . . . were Epithets of Flattery, deserv'd by few of them" (1440). In contrast he acknowledges the inherent goodness that may be transmitted from generation to generation in a single family, here the Ormonds, and hence the last lines of "To Her Grace the Dutchess of Ormond" that introduces the first of the fables: "All other Parts of Pious Duty done, / You owe Your *Ormond* nothing but a Son."[57] In the preface to the *Fables,* Dryden adapts the same metaphor to refer to the family of Western writers: "for we [poets] have our Lineal Descents and Clans, as well as other Families."[58] The act of translation thus becomes a familial duty by which Dryden asserts his kinship to authors in other European languages.[59] The metaphor assumes the integrity of Western literature that is expressed in the design of the *Fables:* Homer finds a place between Ovid and Chaucer in a collection that includes poems of Dryden's own and closes with a tale from Boccaccio. In asserting his own participation in the European tradition, Dryden compares Homer and Vergil, and declares: "the *Grecian* is more according to my Genius, than the *Latin* Poet" (1448). A sign of changing taste, Dryden's observation recognizes

[9] Not ignorant of ill do I learn to befriend the unhappy.
[10] Teucer's family most fair, high-souled heroes born in happier years

what is already quite evident: that the rediscovery of Greek literature, as well as the emergence of the European vernaculars as literary languages, has displaced Vergil from the dominant position that he had so long occupied.[60] The very diversity of the *Fables* admits alternatives to the pious heroic of Vergil, while Dryden's promise of a complete *Iliad* anticipates the accomplished version of Alexander Pope.[61] Even in Pope's proposed Vergilian epic of *Brutus*, the hero was to be drawn not according to pietas, but (as Maynard Mack has emphasized) as an example of the essential eighteenth-century virtue of benevolence.[62] Although translated in part by Wordsworth and in full by William Morris, the *Aeneid* has ceased to provide later writers what it provided Dryden: not just a model for his own literary ambition, nor just a pattern of analogy for describing England after the civil war, but also a vocabulary in which to express his ideas of history and governance.[63] What the *Fables* reveals is that the Vergilian vocabulary cannot be restricted to its Vergilian meaning.

Whereas the *Aeneis* is concerned with piety in time, *Fables Ancient and Modern* is organized to defeat historical inference, specifically so where governance is concerned.[64] Creon is as much a part of the poem's landscape as Numa, and Dryden's presentation of the two rulers reflects not historical development but rather the mingling, almost Augustinian in its implications, of pietas and impietas in the world. Although translated from Chaucer, the character of Dryden's Creon reflects the type of the impious ruler modelled on Statius, Chaucer's source, and catalogued with others of the same type in Ariosto.

> But *Creon*, old and impious, who commands
> The *Theban* City, and usurps the Lands,
> Denies the Rites of Fun'ral Fires to those
> Whose breathless Bodies yet he calls his Foes.
> Unburn'd, unbury'd, on a Heap they lie;
> Such is their Fate, and such his Tyranny.[65]

Dryden's translation accommodates this portrait to type by summing up Chaucer's "ire," "iniquitee," "tyrannye," and "vileynye" in the added "impious." In contrast to the tyrant, the traditional exemplar of the pious ruler is Numa.

> A king is sought to guide the growing State,
> One able to support the Publick Weight,

> And fill the Throne where *Romulus* had sat.
> Renown, which oft bespeaks the Publick Voice,
> Had recommended *Numa* to their choice:
> A peaceful, pious Prince . . .[66]

Although individual narratives have direction, some toward piety, others away from it, the collection itself moves to validate the rule of neither Creon nor Numa, an example of the "irreconciliation" that characterizes the *Fables* in Cedric D. Reverand's compelling interpretation of the work.[67] Government in the world reflects the larger cosmos of the *Fables*, which provides ultimately contradictory answers about the nature of piety, or more often impiety. "Heav'n . . . cannot impious Acts decree"; "Heav'n sometime may bless / An impious Act with undeserv'd Success"; "We to the Gods our impious Acts ascribe."[68] As a poem, the *Fables* declines to affirm the triumph of one principle over the other in history, but rather refers the problem to the unchanging character of "Mankind."

And indeed the conflict between pietas and impietas may be viewed in the microcosm as well as the macrocosm of the *Fables*. Witness, in particular, the struggles of Dryden's female characters drawn from Boccaccio and Ovid. In "Sigismonda and Guiscardo" and "Cinyras and Myrrha" the patriarchal order defined in Vergil by the relationship of father to son is challenged by the complexities of the father-daughter relationship. Dryden's translation of the story from *Metamorphoses* 10 well illustrates the ways in which Western literature has taken Ovidian pietas to rival and complicate the Vergilian. Rendering both the comedy and the melodrama of the Latin in contemporary terms of nature and law, will and reason, sin and guilt, Dryden nonetheless translates Ovid's *pietas* as *piety*, even adding the English word to the original to underline the dilemma that confronts the heroine. In her initial soliloquy Myrrha directly addresses the question of piety by arguing first one view then its opposite. At first she sets "sacred Laws" in opposition to "Nature" and, as in the opening lines of *Absalom and Achitophel*, the implications of this are strongly urged by the word "Sin":

> But is it Sin? Or makes my Mind alone
> Th' imagin'd Sin? For Nature makes it none.
> What Tyrant then these envious Laws began,
> Made not for any other Beast, but Man!
> The Father-Bull his Daughter may bestride,

> The Horse may make his Mother-Mare a Bride;
> What Piety forbids the lusty Ram
> Or more salacious Goat, to rut their Dam?
> The Hen is free to wed the Chick she bore,
> And make a Husband, whom she hatch'd before.[69]

Here "Piety" is interrogatively aligned with "sacred Laws" (36) and, subsequently, with the meddling of "busie Senates" (54) of the sort that create Sigismonda's "State-Laws."[70] The question thus raised by the English version of Ovid's barnyard analogy is extended to other "Nations" (58) where no such laws apply. The crucial step in the argument is then taken by transferring "Piety" from the realm of law to that of nature: "Where happy Daughters with their Sires are join'd, / And Piety is doubly paid in Kind" (60–61). The counterargument to this conclusion is largely a matter of self-accusation, as Myrrha repeatedly describes herself as "impious"—Dryden adding the word to Ovid twice in the succeeding twenty lines. In this argument, "Nature" itself is allowed to have "Sanctions" (97) against incest, so that the prior appeals, including that to other nations, cannot bring desire into harmony with piety. In this argument, then, piety belongs to nature, and the terms of the debate shift from nature-law to reason-will, reason confessing incest as "impious" but without the power to control the will. "So various, so discordant is the Mind, / That in our Will, a diff'rent Will we find. / Ill she presag'd, and yet pursu'd her Lust; / For guilty Pleasures give a double Gust" (260–63). In effect, Myrrha is pious and impious at once, as the struggle within her is an instance of the larger struggle between these two principles in the universe of *Fables Ancient and Modern*.

Her situation parallels that of Althaea, the "pious, impious Wretch" of "Meleager and Atalanta."[71] Whereas "Cinyras and Myrrha" finally locates the conflict between pietas and impietas in the will of Myrrha, here the conflict takes place in the conscience. "The Sister and the Mother long contest / Two doubtful Titles in one tender Breast" (268–69). Competing obligations of kinship effectively pull the idea of pietas apart in this case of a mother and a son who has killed her brothers. The account of her inner state is expressed by reference to the roles imposed on her as both mother and sister.

> And now her Eyes and Cheeks with Fury glow,
> Now pale her Cheeks, her Eyes with Pity flow:

. . . .
And as a Ship, which Winds and Waves assail,
Now with the Current drives, now with the Gale,
Both opposite, and neither long prevail:
She feels a double Force, by Turns obeys
Th' imperious Tempest, and th' impetuous Seas:
So fares *Althaea's* Mind; she first relents
With Pity, of that Pity then repents:
Sister and Mother long the Scales divide,
But the Beam nodded on the Sisters side.
                                    (270–71, 276–84)

The conflict of furor and pietas is here rendered as "Fury" and "Pity," but this Vergilian opposition breaks down under the Ovidian circumstances: Althaea cannot be pious without being impious no matter what she does. Her decision to kill her own son ("Perish this impious, this detested Son," 319) is an act that at once preserves and violates a patriarchal order that rests on pietas. Not only does this narrative situation generate sympathy for the Ovidian heroine, but it also calls in doubt an idea of pietas that compels her to choose wrongly, and like Sigismonda and Myrrha to die. In contrast to the critical moment in the fourth book of Dryden's *Aeneis,* where the piety of the hero overcomes his pity, there is no way that Althaea can escape her dilemma by setting one derivative of pietas against another. The history of Ovidian pietas as rival to the Vergilian is thus captured in Dryden's translation, in terms that effectively comment on his own version of the *Aeneid.*

As the *Fables* reconsiders pietas from the feminine perspective that had so notably failed to emerge from his version of *Aeneid* 4, so Dryden's last work also reconsiders the implications of *Aeneid* 12 by recasting the matter of Troy in terms that undermine the classical heroic. The meaning of the Trojan War is summed up in a phrase spoken by Nestor, with whom Dryden identifies himself in the dedication (1439). Nestor's description of the war as the "impious Thirst of Blood" is consistent with Dryden's frequent presentation of heroism in the *Fables* as barbarism.[72] The description of Aeneas at the conclusion of book 12—"Then rowz'd anew to Wrath, he loudly cries, / (Flames, while he spoke, came flashing from his Eyes:)" (12.1368–69)—has several echoes in passages of the *Fables* that show furor as fundamentally inhuman. The description of the Caledonian Boar in "Meleager and Atalanta" is the best example:

"His Eye-balls glare with Fire suffus'd with Blood" (22), and again: "his red Eye-balls roll with living Fire" (122). Terms similar to those that describe Aeneas serve in the *Fables* to describe the literally brutal; or half-brutal, as in the gory descriptions of the Centaurs: "For One, most Brutal, of the Brutal Brood, / Or whether Wine or Beauty fir'd his Blood, / Or both at once; beheld with lustful Eyes / The Bride . . ."[73] The inward-turning generalization of Homer's Calchas seems especially relevant to the end of the *Aeneis:* "Revenge, like Embers, rak'd within their Breast, / Bursts forth in Flames; whose unresisted Pow'r / Will seize th' unwary Wretch and soon devour."[74] The generalization is denied by Agamemnon, who becomes in the process simply another of the furious. "His Breast with Fury fill'd, his Eyes with Fire; / Which rowling round, he shot in Sparkles on the Sire" (153–54). In the *Fables,* then, furor is shown to be more compatible with the classical heroic, especially as the heroic is traced to Homer, than pietas.

The counterimpulse of the *Fables* toward religious ritual moderates this conclusion, but only by calling in doubt the confidence with which Christian writers had claimed an idea of pietas superior to the pagan. Also expressed in the imagery of fire, specifically the flame of funeral and altar, *piety* is invoked in reference to diverse religious rituals (including even Pythagorean vegetarianism) over the course of the entire poem. Yet where the context is Christian, the pietas of ritual and prayer is no more immune to hypocrisy and scandal than the heroic is to barbarism. The Good Parson and the Fair Maiden Lady—"So Pious, as she had no time to spare / For human Thoughts, but was confin'd to Pray'r"—share the world of the *Fables* with Chaucer's clerical fox—"This pious Cheat that never suck'd the Blood, / Nor chaw'd the Flesh of Lambs but when he cou'd."[75] In "The Cock and the Fox" Dryden captures Chaucer's "False dissymulour" as "O Hypocrite" and then completes the comparison: "O Traytor, worse than *Sinon* was to *Troy*" (500). In Chaucer the Vergilian allusion is of a piece with the comedy of the mock-heroic; in Dryden the "pious" added to describe the fox drives comedy toward satire. By an irony of literary history that says a good deal about the fate of pietas, the epithet of Aeneas is here metaphorically attached to the Greek whose falsehood brings the fall of Troy.

Dryden's phrase "pious Cheat" well indicates the shift from classical to Christian usage, and within Christian usage from a positive to a negative connotation. Whereas Dryden had described "False *Reynard*" (53) as progenitor of an "impious race" (56) in part I of *The Hind and the Panther,* in "The Cock and the Fox" even the positive term serves to convey a negative meaning. The *Fables* thus juxtaposes not only different claims on pietas, but exposes as well the false pretensions to its sanction. On the other side of the analogy between the cock and Sinon, the question of *vera pietas* had already been raised in Dryden's portrayal of the Greek liar in book 2 of the *Aeneis.* Sinon's appeal is to "Pity": "O if Pity mortal Minds can move!" (2.193). Once the appeal succeeds, Vergil's "His lacrymis vitam damus, et miserescimus ultro" (2.145)[11] becomes Dryden's "False Tears true Pity move" (2.197). As one English derivative of *pietas* lends itself in Dryden's English to irony, so the other yields vulnerability. Here underlined by the traditional play of "False" and "true" to establish the connotation of the word, pietas in the form of "Pity" returns to Vergil as a temptation, as a source of weakness rather than strength. Taken together, the *Aeneis* and the *Fables* instance nearly the whole range of meanings that attend pietas in Western literature. Taken as a commentary on the *Aeneis,* the *Fables* emphasizes the pressures that have historically weighed against the Vergilian definition and rendered the task of translation so difficult.

[11] To these tears we grant life and pity him besides.

Conclusion

In the century inaugurated by Dryden's *Fables, piety* is gradually displaced by moral terms that express public engagement and social responsibility, dimensions of meaning once but no longer conveyed by pietas. Reduced to the rank of subordinate partner in the recurrent phrase "virtue and piety," this once comprehensive ideal comes to signify revelation in an age of reason, religion in an age of philosophy. Even within the agreed boundaries of superstition and enthusiasm, the "happy medium of true Christian piety"[1] must fend against the charge of hypocrisy announced in Dryden's phrase "pious Cheat." With all these limitations, *piety* is a liability for reasons traceable to the basic conflict in its history between its classical and Christian, ancient and derived meanings: although its classical associations connect it to an ethic that is public, rational, noble, even heroic, the adoption of the word by Christianity eventually lends it quite different associations with what is private, emotional, humble, meek, feminine, with what David Hume calls "monkish virtues."[2] It is this latter cluster of connotations that ultimately prevails in English literature of the eighteenth century.

Although *piety* does not surrender its originally noble status without a struggle, its decline in authority after Dryden is unmistakable.[3] That it does not sink even more rapidly is due to its donning of a religious mantle that is natural rather than supernatural. The phrase "natural piety" has a considerable vogue that begins well before Locke and endures even after and in spite of Hume. Distinguishing atheism from superstition, Francis Bacon had written: "Atheism leaves a man to sense, to philosophy, to natural piety, to laws, to reputation: all which may be guides to an outward moral virtue, though religion were not; but superstition dismounts all these, and erecteth an absolute monarchy in the minds of men."⁴ Two centuries later, William Wordsworth concludes his brief lyric "My Heart Leaps up" with three lines that later become the epigraph for the immortality ode: "The Child is father of the Man; / And I could wish my days to be / Bound each to each by natural piety."⁵ As Bacon anticipates the constraints on the word elaborated during the eighteenth century, Wordsworth attempts to break through them by using a conventional phrase in an unusual way, but in each case the word *piety* depends for its value on its connection with *nature*. Compared to *nature,* which is highly consistent as a term of honor but notoriously various in meaning, *piety* has by this time acquired a stable meaning— "Discharge of duty to God" (according to Johnson's dictionary)—at the same time that its connotation has become highly variable. The passages from Bacon and Wordsworth are both annotated by William Blake, who takes the opportunity to ridicule the stock phrases "virtue and piety" and "natural piety."⁶ Blake's objection to both phrases is symptomatic of his rejection of the moral tradition that emerges between the time of Bacon's *Essays* and Wordsworth's poems, but he makes no attempt to rehabilitate in contrast some new version of "true piety." Rather, he simply lets the exhausted term go.

Its eighteenth-century decline may nonetheless be viewed as a measure of its prior importance in articulating the values of successive moments in Western culture. As the ideal from which Rome is said to have been born, pietas is centrally at issue in the struggle between divergent visions of Roman history. Claimed by the Caesars and their supporters against the dissent of Cicero, pietas is shaped to a political ideology of order and loyalty that traces its authority to Vergil. An essential term of imperial propaganda, pietas becomes the virtue of both rulers and subjects, and thereby the ideal that defends the political status quo. Identified with each new emperor and with each newly proclaimed golden age, it is defined by contrast to the impietas of rebellion, insistently condemned in the imagery of furor. As Vergilian epic is thus adapted to the goals of panegyric, pietas becomes a ceremonial rather than an active virtue, a term of ritual rather than of heroism. The repeated image of pietas in the literature of the later empire is the figure of the emperor himself in his triumphal chariot, cheered by hosts of loyal subjects. To dissent from the ideology represented by this image was to risk the fate of Lucan, whose spirit of opposition nonetheless survives in the historical works of Tacitus, where the ritual display of pietas is shown to be a mere cover for the abuse of power, a shield for crimes symptomatic of Roman decline.

This dissent from the imperial *pia spectacula* is reasserted in the Augustinian account of the two cities, where pietas articulates a theology of history and governance that later informs the Christian interpretation of Vergil for the Middle Ages. During this period, contention over the meaning and scope of pietas is a reflection of the larger political struggle between secular and ecclesiastical authorities. As defined by strong bishops and popes in the tradition of Ambrose, royal pietas entails obligation to the church and pastoral responsibility toward the governed. The intermittently perceived failure of this sacerdotal conception of monarchy encourages an imperial conception of the papacy: in the extreme case, Gregory VII recasts the two cities of Augustine to claim pietas as the exclusive virtue of the church. In the long run, this claim is simply conceded by the state, which from the thirteenth century onward bases its moral authority on the political vocabulary of the Latin Aristotle, on *iustitia, prudentia,* and their derivatives in the modern languages. Even as the traditional complement of justice, pietas attracts the negative connotation of political weakness and is thus superseded in vernacular discourse on government by derivatives and translations of Senecan *clementia.* By the end of the Middle Ages pietas has become a problematic, if not yet a consistently suspect virtue, in the character of the ruler.

It is especially problematic for the "good governour" of Renaissance epic, where pietas also defines the character of the "vertuous man." Here the moral legacy of Aeneas is specifically tested against latter-day incarnations of Dido and Turnus. Adaptations of *Aeneid* 4 variously acknowledge the heroine's claim on the love of Aeneas, even as revisions of *Aeneid* 12 admit the defeated hero's claim on his mercy. The asserted rights of both Dido and Turnus depend on evolved meanings of pietas that exist in tension with its classical origins, as the characteristic quality of Vergil's hero is suspended between competing definitions and discrepant connotations. Since the Renaissance hero cannot at once adhere to all its different meanings, the moment of hesitation ("cunctantem," 4.390, 12.940) that precedes the desertion of Dido in *Aeneid* 4 and the killing of Turnus in *Aeneid* 12 must be protracted or even repeated with an alternative resolution. To admit post-Vergilian understanding of pietas necessitates, above all, coming to terms with the meaning of compassion ascendant in Italian *pietà* and conveyed by the English *pity.* Yet this meaning is itself unstable, its connotation negatively touched by the erotic in the encounters with Dido, the vain in those with Turnus. In book 2 of *The Faerie Queene,* then, *pity* is an emotion to be repressed in the temperate mind. Here pietas in the form of *pity* has finally become a temptation rather than a virtue, a term parallel rather than antithetical to *furor.*

Whereas pietas is thus highly unstable in Renaissance epic, its antonym is a remarkably consistent term that evokes the Titan figure of both tyranny and rebellion. The culmination of this figure in Milton's Satan later influences Dryden's characterization of Achitophel, who himself advances *piety* as an argument for usurpation. Only one entirely ignorant of the history of pietas could fall for this abuse of meaning, as the specious semantics of Achitophel's rhetoric discloses Dryden's own recognition of the gulf that separates ancient meaning from modern usage. This, then, is the linguistic situation that the poet must confront directly in translating the *Aeneid.* Dryden's translation tests the capacity of his own age to accommodate Latin *pietas* in the form of English *piety.* The first six books of his version project the possibility of such accommodation by evoking the Vergilian prophecies of Restoration panegyric, but in the last six the "Impious Age" condemned in Dryden's satires finally prevails over the piety of the hero. The shape of the *Aeneis* thus reflects the shape of Dryden's career, which concludes not with an original epic on the Vergilian model, but three years after the translation with a collection effectively recapitulating the meanings that rival the Vergilian definition of pietas in European literature.

The historical trajectory of these meanings leads away from epic toward satire, from the public and aristocratic realm of classical heroism to the private domain of middle- and finally lower-class religion. After Dryden the very notion of a pious hero typically signifies either irony or oxymoron.[7] Yet a knowledge of the semantic history traced in this book may still prove useful in reading literature after Dryden, for pietas does not escape its past even as it descends the scale of society and the hierarchy of literary genres. This is true even in such a satiric novel as *The Expedition of Humphry Clinker,* whose titular hero is an illegitimate Methodist servant, "so stout, and so pyehouse, that he fears neither man nor devils."[8] In Clinker, Smollett remarkably creates a protagonist who is at once heroic and pious. His courage is both demonstrated and praised, most notably in his rescue of Matt Bramble (later discovered to be his father) in a scene at least remotely suggestive of Aeneas and Anchises in *Aeneid* 2. Admirable as he is, however, Clinker is not socially redeemed in the manner of Tom Jones but remains lower-class, married in the end to the maid whose deformation of "pious" has a double effect in the novel. On the one hand, it serves to detach the Methodist hero from the negative connotations that have rendered doubtful the honor conveyed by the word, as correctly spelled but ironically used to describe less praiseworthy characters; on the other hand, the repeated "pyehouse" affirms this positive connotation only by depressing the social level at which it operates. What was once a term of power, of contention between pagan and Christian, republican and imperialist, emperor and pope, hero and king, Puritan and Royalist, is now a marginal term left to society's marginal groups.

Notes

Introduction

1. For an overview of Vergil's epic and its importance in Western culture, see the entry "Virgil" by Paul J. Alpers in *Atlantic Brief Lives: A Biographical Companion to the Arts,* ed. Louis Kronenberger (Boston, 1971). I am indebted to this essay (844) for the phrasing of my first sentence. R. D. Williams and T. S. Pattie provide a useful introduction to the history of response to the *Aeneid* in *Virgil: His Poetry Through the Ages* (London, 1982). For introduction to modern scholarship, see the essays gathered in *Vergil at 2000: Commemorative Essays on the Poet and his Influence,* ed. John D. Bernard (New York, 1986). As a starting point for further reading, see the bibliographical essay in this collection by William R. Nethercut, "American Scholarship on Vergil in the Twentieth Century," 303–30, and the references indicated in note 16 below. The standard guide to Vergil studies is *The Classical World Bibliography of Vergil,* Garland Reference Library of the Humanities, vol. 96 (New York and London, 1978).

2. John Dryden, "Dedication of the Aeneis," *The Works of John Dryden,* eds. Edward N. Hooker, H. T. Swedenberg, et al. (Berkeley and Los Angeles, 1956–) v, 286. Unless otherwise indicated, all citations from Dryden will be repeated from this edition and referenced as *Works.*

3. Ibid., 288. This passage is quoted and helpfully discussed by Paul J. Korshin, *Typologies in England: 1650–1820* (Princeton, 1982), 151. That Dryden's translation of Segrais's phrase "tous les devoirs de l'homme" should suggest the title of Richard Allestree's popular moral treatise affirms the conclusion that more is less. What Dryden says the Romans could express in a word, *The Whole Duty of Man* takes seventeen chapters to explain.

4. Vergil, *Aeneid,* 6.687–88, ed. and trans. H. Rushton Fairclough, rev. ed., 2 vols., LCL (Cambridge, Mass., and London, 1986), i, 552–54. Unless otherwise indicated, all quotations from the *Aeneid* will be cited from this edition and referenced parenthetically in the text by book and line numbers.

5. Dante, *Inferno,* 2.4–5. *The Divine Comedy,* translated, with a commentary by Charles S. Singleton, 6 vols. (Princeton, 1970), i, 12. All subsequent quotations from the *Commedia* will be cited from this edition and referenced in the text by canto and line numbers.

6. Robert Ball, "Theological Semantics: Virgil's *Pietas* and Dante's *Pietà*," *Stanford Italian Review* 2 (Spring 1982): 61. See also John Freccero, "Dante's Prologue Scene," *Dante Studies* 84 (1966): 1–25; Robert Hollander, "Dante's Use of *Aeneid* I in *Inferno* I and II," *Comparative Literature* 20, no. 2 (Spring 1968): 142–56; Giorgio Padoan, *Il pio Enea l'empio Ulisse* (Ravenna, 1977), especially 192–97; and Albert R. Ascoli, *Ariosto's Bitter Harmony: Crisis and Evasion in the Italian Renaissance* (Princeton, 1987), 144ff., especially 152.

7. Erasmus, *Enchiridion militis christiani,* canon tertius. *Desiderius Erasmus Roterdamus: Ausgewählte Werke,* ed. Hajo Holborn and Annemarie Holborn (Munich, 1964), 61. The translation is adapted from Charles Fantazzi's new English version of the *Enchiridion.* In his introduction to this translation, John W. O'Malley observes: "When we deal with Erasmian *pietas* . . . we must deal with it as a seamless robe that envelops all he wrote. . . . In his *Enchiridion* Erasmus used the words *pius* or *pietas* over a hundred times, a good indication of the centrality of the idea in his thinking." *Collected Works of Erasmus,* ed. John W. O'Malley (Toronto, 1988), LXVI, xi. It may be added that Erasmus repeats the precise phrase "pietatis via" in other works. See, for example, *De libero arbitrio,* 1a8, *Ausgewählte Schriften,* ed. Werner Welzig, 8 vols. (Darmstadt, 1969), IV, 10.

8. Erasmus, *Enchiridion militis christiani,* 60.

9. Jonathan Swift, *Gulliver's Travels,* 4.12. *The Prose Works of Jonathan Swift,* ed. Herbert Davis, 14 vols. (Oxford, 1941), XI, 278.

10. Georg W. F. Hegel, *Grundlinien der Philosophie des Rechts,* 166. *Georg Wilhelm Friedrich Hegel: Sämtliche Werke,* ed. Georg Lasson, 21 vols. (Leipzig, 1930), VI, 145. The translations from Hegel are by T. M. Knox. On Hegel and pietas, see Roger Scruton, *From Descartes to Wittgenstein: A Short History of Modern Philosophy,* U.S. edition (New York, 1982), 208.

11. Hegel, *Grundlinien der Philosophie des Rechts,* in *Sämtliche Werke,* VI, 145.

12. Ibid., 142.

13. Paul Tillich, *Systematic Theology,* 3E2e, 3 vols. in one (Chicago, 1967), II, 86. Elsewhere Tillich qualifies this judgment by distinguishing generally between American and European usage. "What is Pietism? The term is much less respectable in America than in Europe. There the words 'pious' and 'pietist' can be used of people, but hardly in America, because here they carry the connotations of hypocrisy and moralism. Pietism does not necessarily have these connotations." Tillich, *A History of Christian Thought,* ed. Carl Braaten (New York, 1968), 284. Taking this passage as a starting point, Dale Brown has shown how the negative connotations that attend the word have influenced modern perception of the pietist movement. "Nevertheless," he writes, "piety and Pietism are not to be completely equated. Pietism represents one of the historic forms of piety which are part of our heritage. *Pietismus* . . . was an uncomplimentary nickname bequeathed to posterity by Pietism's detractors." Brown, *Understanding Pietism* (Grand Rapids, Mich., 1978), 12. On the origins of pietism and the significance of the name, see also F. Ernest Stoeffler, *The Rise of Evangelical Pietism* (Leiden, 1965), chap. 1.

14. Owen Barfield has correlated the degeneration of "the word pious . . . towards an imputation of feeble-mindedness" with the emergence at the end of the seventeenth century of the "unpleasant derivative, *pietism,* which in turn produced its adjective *pietistic.*" Barfield, *History in English Words,* new edition (London, 1954), 191. It

may be noted, however, that ironical use of the word, especially in the phrase "pious fraud," has been current in English since the end of the sixteenth century. Indeed, in the speech of Shakespeare's Polonius, ironical usage is already accommodated to platitude: "Tis too much prov'd—that with devotion's visage / And pious action we do sugar o'er / The devil himself," Shakespeare, *Hamlet,* 3.1.47–49, *Riverside Shakespeare,* ed. G. Blakemore Evans (Boston, 1974). The decline of positive meaning in English is matched in the other modern languages, although it is not hard to find instances of usage that resist this tendency. A particularly striking counterindication is provided by Guido Piovene's end-of-the-war novel *Pietà contro pietà.* Against the dominant trajectory of the word in the modern period toward the periphery of the European vocabulary, pietas is here unmistakably central: "una parola che spiega tutto e rende tutto inevitabile" (a word that explains everything and makes everything inevitable). Piovene, *Pietà contro pietà,* in *Opere narrative,* ed. Clelia Martignoni, 2 vols. (Milan, 1976), I, 791.

15. The contemporary French poet Edmond Jabès has written: "You must not think the word is without memory. Where we have erased everything, it is present to remind us of our past." Jabès, "Answer to a Letter," trans. Rosemarie Waldrop. *Twentieth-Century French Poetry,* ed. Paul Auster (New York, 1982), 413. Compare the observation of Thomas M. Greene: "Just as an amnesiac recovers his identity with his memory, so it is with words; we learn them as they acquire a past for us." Greene, *The Light in Troy: Imitation and Discovery in Renaissance Poetry* (New Haven, 1982), 16.

16. On the significance of *pietas* in the *Aeneid* there is naturally a considerable body of modern as well as ancient commentary. See first W. R. Johnson, "Aeneas and the Ironies of *Pietas,*" *Classical Journal* 60 (1965): 360–64; G. Karl Galinsky, *Aeneas, Sicily, and Rome* (Princeton, 1969), 53–61; M. Owen Lee, *Fathers and Sons in Virgil's Aeneid: Tum Genitor Natum* (Albany, N.Y., 1979), 17–23, 142–43, 180–81; and M. C. J. Putnam, "*Pius* Aeneas and the Metamorphosis of Lausus," *Arethusa* 14 (1981): 139–56. For other studies addressing the problem over the last half-century, see Erich Burck, "Drei Grundwerte der römischen Lebensordnung," *Gymnasium* 58 (1951): 161–83, especially 174–80; Brooks Otis, *Virgil: A Study in Civilized Poetry* (Oxford, 1964), 307–8, 341–42; Kenneth Quinn, *Virgil's Aeneid: A Critical Description* (Ann Arbor, Mich., 1968), 111–12, 391; Mario A. Di Cesare, *The Altar and the City: A Reading of Vergil's Aeneid* (New York, 1974), 192–97; Gordon Williams, *Technique and Ideas in the Aeneid* (New Haven, 1983), 117, 212–13. Francis Cairns, *Virgil's Augustan Epic* (Cambridge, 1989), 29–32, 52–53, 71–77.

17. See page 12.

18. See Adam Parry, "The Two Voices of Vergil's *Aeneid,*" *Arion* 2 (1963): 66–80.

Chapter 1

1. As Roger Fowler has expressed the idea: "the majority of meanings in languages . . . are crystallized in response to the social, economic, technological, and theoretical needs of the cultures concerned." Fowler, *Literature as Social Dis-*

course: The Practice of Linguistic Criticism (London, 1981), 21. This approach to meaning is predicated on the research of M. A. K. Halliday, *Language as a Social Semiotic: The Social Interpretation of Language and Meaning* (Baltimore, 1978). Considered as dialogue, moreover, the history of meaning illustrated in this chapter corresponds closely to the description of semantic change offered by Mikhail Bakhtin. "The life of the word is in its transferral from one mouth to another, one context to another, one social collective to another, and one generation to another. In the process the word does not forget where it has been and can never wholly free itself from the dominion of the contexts of which it has been a part." Mikhail Bakhtin, *Problems of Dostoevsky's Poetics,* trans. R. W. Rotsel (Ann Arbor, Mich., 1973), 167. This passage is quoted and persuasively discussed by Greene, *The Light in Troy,* 143.

2. Lucretius, *De rerum natura,* 5.1198–1203, ed. and trans. W. H. D. Rouse, rev. M. F. Smith, LCL (Cambridge, Mass., and London, 1975), 424. To help establish the "meaning of *pietas* in the first century B.C.," M. Owen Lee quotes and discusses this passage in juxtaposition with Catullus 76. Lee, *Fathers and Sons in Virgil's Aeneid,* 19–21. The lines from Lucretius are also cited and discussed under the rubric of "Epicureanism" by Frederick J. Copleston, book I of *A History of Philosophy,* reprinted, 3 vols. in one (New York, 1985), I, 406. See also William H. FitzGerald, "Pietas Epicurea," *Classical Journal* 46 (1950–51): 195–99.

3. Seneca, *Thyestes,* 549, *Seneca: Tragedies,* ed. and trans. Frank Justus Miller, 2 vols., LCL (Cambridge, Mass., and London, 1987), II, 138. This sentence is spoken by the chorus.

4. Cicero, *De inventione,* 2.53.161, ed. and trans. H. M. Hubbell, LCL (Cambridge, Mass., and London, 1988), 328. For an excellent account of Cicero's use of the word, see Hendrik Wagenvoort, *Pietas: Selected Studies in Roman Religion* (Leiden, 1980), 5–16. Wagenvoort argues from ample evidence that the content of the word for Cicero changes in response to events of the 40s: "As we see clearly from these quotations, which are so essential to my argument, up to the year 46 Cicero uses *pietas* at one moment in connection with blood relations and at another with the fatherland, and, frequently, with both. But after that year this suddenly changes. . . . [I]nstead of being applied to one's country, parents and relatives, it is applied, in the first place, to the gods" (9).

5. Cicero, *De republica,* 6.16.1, ed. and trans. Clinton Walker Keyes, LCL (Cambridge, Mass., and London, 1988), 268. Cicero's Dream of Scipio derives from Plato's Vision of Er, his Romans cultivating *iustitia* and *pietas* from the "δίκαιοι καὶ ὅσιοι" rewarded in the *Republic,* 10.13.615C, trans. Paul Shorey, 2 vols., LCL (Cambridge, Mass., and London, 1970), II, 496. The Latin word, more comprehensive than the specifically religious Greek word ὁσιότης, is broad enough to be common in translating other Greek words as well, most importantly εὐσέβεια. See the passage from Augustine cited here, page 12.

6. Lactantius, *De divinis institutionibus adversus gentes,* 5.10, *Lactantii opera omnia,* PL (Paris, 1844), VI, 581A. The translations from Lactantius are by Sister Mary Francis McDonald, who observes: "It is difficult to find a good English word for *pietas.* Piety, especially in its usual meaning, is not adequate." This is a virtual refrain of translators working from Latin to the modern languages. See Lactantius,

The Divine Institutes, trans. Sister Mary Francis McDonald, *The Fathers of the Church,* ed. Roy Joseph Deferrari (Washington, D.C., 1964), XLIX, 352.

7. 5.10, p. 581B. In weighing Lactantius's deprecating attitude toward Vergil's hero, it should be kept in mind that skepticism about the *pietas* of Aeneas was not limited to Christian writers. This has been emphasized by Galinsky, *Aeneas, Sicily, and Rome,* chap. 1. See p. 4 and the authorities cited in note 3, especially V. Ussani, "Enea traditore," *Studi Italiani di Filologia Classica,* n.s. 22 (1947): 108–23.

8. 5.23, p. 626B. The importance of *pietas* in the thought of Lactantius has been emphasized by Charles N. Cochrane, *Christianity and Classical Culture: A Study of Thought and Action from Augustus to Augustine* (London, 1944), 193–94.

9. "Pietas fundamentum est omnium virtutum" (filial affection is the basis of all virtues). Cicero, *Pro Cnaeo Plancio,* 12.29, ed. and trans. N. H. Watts, LCL (Cambridge, Mass., and London, 1961), 442.

10. Lactantius, *De divinis institutionibus,* 2.16, p. 336A for the Greek, 5.15, p. 597B for the Latin translation.

11. Augustine, *De civitate Dei contra paganos,* 10.1., ed. and trans. George E. McCracken et al., LCL (Cambridge, Mass., and London, 1957), 7 vols., III, 252–54.

12. 4.23.2, II, 82.

13. Bernard of Clairvaux, *De consideratione,* 1.7, *Sancti Bernardi opera,* ed. J. Leclercq and H. M. Rochais, 8 vols. (Rome, 1963), III, 403. The translation is by John D. Anderson and Elizabeth T. Kennan.

14. *Epistola seu tractatus ad fratres de Monte Dei,* 1.4, *S. Bernardi opera omnia,* PL (Paris, 1879), CLXXXIV, 313C. On the image of the yoke, see page 34.

15. *Biblia vulgata,* ed. Alberto Colunga and Laurentio Turrado, 7th edition (Madrid, 1985). All references to books of the Latin Bible are repeated from this edition and referenced in the text by chapter and verse. For a more detailed account of this passage in scriptural exegesis, see chapter 2.

16. Thomas Aquinas, *Summa theologiae,* 2a2ae.101,3.2, ed. and trans. Thomas Gilby et al., 60 vols. (London and New York, 1963–), XLI, 12.

17. 2a2ae.102,3.3, XLI, 28.

18. Dante, *Convivio,* 2.11, *Le opere di Dante,* ed. E. Moore, rev. P. Toynbee, 5th edition (Oxford, 1963), 262. For comment on this and other passages relevant to the problem of pietas in Dante, see Antonio Lanci, "Pietà," in the *Enciclopedia dantesca* (Rome, 1970). The translation is by William W. Jackson. To see how much confusion can be generated by this word, compare the nineteenth-century translation of Elizabeth Price Sayer: "Wherefore Virgil, speaking of Aeneas, in his greater praise calls him compassionate, pitiful; and that is not pity such as the common people understand it, which is to lament over the misfortunes of others; nay, this is an especial effect which is called Mercy, Pity, Compassion; and it is a passion. But compassion is not a passion; rather a noble disposition of the mind, prepared to receive Love, Mercy, and other charitable passions."

19. Brunetto Latini, *Li livres dou tresor,* 2.2.82, ed. P. Chabaille (Paris, 1863), 423, and also 497.

20. Erasmus, *Enchiridion Militis Christiani: An English Version,* ed. Anne M. O'Donnell, Early English Text Society, no. 282 (Oxford, 1981), xliv. O'Donnell's introduction to this anonymous translation includes an excellent discussion of *pietas*

in Erasmus and the variable ways in which it is translated into sixteenth-century English. On the diverse spellings, see also chapter 5, especially page 120. For typical examples, note the case of Malory's Sir Brewnys, who is both "Saunze Pité" and "Saunze Pieté" without any apparent shift in meaning, and the case of Francis Thynne's Aeneas in the *Emblemes and Epigrames* published in 1600. The first emblem in this collection is titled "Pietie and Impietie" and contrasts Aeneas to Nero. In the following verses Aeneas is "full of pittie" for rescuing father and son from Troy, a deed eight lines later said to be a "lovinge deede of famous pietie." See Thomas Malory, *Le Morte d'Arthur*, 10.53 and 10.65, *The Works of Thomas Malory*, ed. Eugene Vinaver, 3 vols. (Oxford, 1967), II, 687, 721; Francis Thynne, *Emblemes and Epigrames*, ed. F. J. Furnivall, for the Early English Text Society (London, 1876), 5–6.

21. Erasmus, *Enchiridion militis christiani*, 53; *An English Version*, 80. On this passage see Richard L. DeMolen, "The Interior Erasmus," *Leaders of the Reformation*, ed. Richard L. DeMolen (London, 1984), 20.

22. *An English Version*, 98.

23. Ibid., 103.

24. John Locke, *Of Civil Government*, 2.6.74, *Two Treatises of Government*, ed. Peter Laslett (Cambridge, 1960), 334.

25. Joseph Butler, Sermon 12, *Fifteen Sermons Preached at the Rolls Chapel*, ed. W. R. Matthews (London, 1953), 201.

26. David Hartley, *Observations on Man, His Frame, His Duty, and His Expectations*, 1.4.2.95, reprinted (Gainesville, Fla., 1966), 452–53.

27. Henry Fielding, *The History of Tom Jones, A Foundling*, 3.2, ed. Fredson Bowers with introduction and commentary by Martin C. Battestin (Wesleyan, Conn., 1975), 118. See James E. Evans, "Blifil as Tartuffe: The Dialogic Comedy of *Tom Jones*," *Comparative Literature Studies* 27, no. 2 (1990): 101–12, especially 105.

28. Charles Dickens, *The Life and Adventures of Nicholas Nickleby*, 4 (Oxford, 1950), 33.

29. Ibid., 33–34.

30. Although Wordsworth's rhetorical question—"Is ancient Piety for ever flown?"—refers specifically to the decline of Christian devotion, the addition of the adjective is a telling comment on the connotations of "Piety." Sonnet XXII, *The Poetical Works of William Wordsworth*, ed. E. de Selincourt and Helen Darbishire, 5 vols., 2d edition (Oxford, 1954), III, 13. See page 256.

31. John Ruskin, *Val d'Arno*, 9.222, *The Works of John Ruskin*, ed. E. T. Cook and Alexander Wedderburn (London, 1906), XXIII, 129–30.

32. 9.222, p. 130.

33. 9.223, p. 130.

34. Ruskin, *Fors Clavigera*, 5.49.6, *Works*, XXVIII, 239.

35. George Santayana, *The Life of Reason; or The Phases of Human Progress*, 3.10, rev. ed. (New York, 1954), 260. Subsequent quotations from Santayana in this paragraph may be found in this edition on 258, 262, and 263.

36. Kenneth Burke, *Permanence and Change: An Anatomy of Purpose*, 2.1, 3d edition (Berkeley and Los Angeles, 1984), 71.

37. Ibid., 74.

38. Ibid., 75.

39. Raymond Williams, *Keywords: A Vocabulary of Culture and Society,* rev. ed. (New York, 1976); and see also Peggy Rosenthal, *Words and Values: Some Leading Words and Where They Lead Us* (Oxford, 1984). Both works are indebted to William Empson, *The Structure of Complex Words* (London, 1951). With specific reference to American values, see Daniel T. Rodgers, *Contested Truths: Keywords in American Politics Since Independence* (New York, 1987), especially 3–16.

40. See Rodgers, "Keywords: A Reply," *Journal of the History of Ideas* 49 (October–December 1988): 669–76, especially the eloquent statement on 671, where it is argued that keywords "are words which matter enough for persons to fight . . . for the power to redefine, redeploy, and gain possession of them." Rodgers goes on to describe the class of words to which, I believe, pietas belongs: "Words . . . of this sort acquire their power because compacted in their histories are profound ambiguities, possibilities, and antagonisms." To situate these remarks in the context of other approaches to intellectual history, see Donald R. Kelley, "What is Happening to the History of Ideas?" *Journal of the History of Ideas* 51 (January–March 1990): 3–25, especially 15.

Chapter 2

1. Ovid, *Fasti,* 2.543, ed. and trans. Sir James George Frazer, LCL (Cambridge, Mass., and London, 1951), 96.

2. Chromatius Aquilensis, Sermo 11, 1.9, ed. R. Etaix and J. Lemarié, CC, IX A, 48.

3. George Herbert, *A Priest to the Temple or, The Country Parson,* 11.30–32, *The Works of George Herbert,* ed. F. E. Hutchinson (Oxford, 1941), 243.

4. Julius Caesar Scaliger, *Poetices libri septem,* 3.12, facsimile of 1561 Lyons edition (Stuttgart, 1964), 92.

5. Servius Grammaticus, *In Vergilii carmina commentarii,* ed. George Thilo and Hermann Hagen, 3 vols. (Leipzig, 1881–1902), I, 127. This passage is cited by Ball, "Theological Semantics," 65. Ball here follows Alois Walde in suggesting that *"pius* may be an etymological double of *purus."* Walde, *Lateinisches etymologisches Wörterbuch,* ed. J. B. Hofmann, 3d edition (Heidelberg, 1954). For a detailed etymological discussion, see Huguette Fugier, *Recherches sur l'expression du sacré dans la langue latine* (Paris, 1963), chaps. 8 and 9, especially 371–75. It may be noted that Servius later reinforces this cluster of associations by glossing "casti" (3.409) as "pii" (I, 415). Although the reference in this passage of the poem is not to Aeneas himself but to his descendants ("hac casti maneant in religione nepotes"), the effect of the gloss is to confirm the fundamental connection between *pietas* and the sacred rites, especially the purification rituals, of Roman religion. For the cultural milieu to which Servius's commentary belongs, see Robert Kaster, *Guardians of Language: The Grammarian and Society in Late Antiquity* (Berkeley and Los Angeles, 1988), 169–97. For discussion of Servius in relation to medieval traditions of commentary, see J. W. Jones, Jr., "The Allegorical Traditions of the *Aeneid,*" *Vergil at 2000,* 107–32, especially the note on *pietas,* 130 n. 5.

6. Servius, I, 15; and I, 167, commenting on *Aeneid* 1.545.

7. Servius, II, 649, and see Ball, 68.

8. Tiberius Claudius Donatus, *Interpretationes vergilianae*, ed. H. Georgii, 2 vols., reprinted (Stuttgart, 1969), I, 2–3. On this passage, see Galinsky, *Aeneas, Sicily, and Rome*, 51.

9. Specifically: "virtus in exercitatione bellandi" (valor in the practice of war). Donatus, I, 109.

10. *Aeneid* 8.84–85; Donatus, II, 126.

11. Donatus, II, 126.

12. Donatus, II, 388. The contrast affirmed here between Aeneas (*cultor deorum*) and Mezentius (*contemptor deorum*) will later become a standard illustration of the difference between *pietas* and *impietas*. See Macrobius, *Saturnalia*, 3.5.9–10, *I Saturnali*, ed. Nino Marinone (Turin, 1967), 386.

13. Donatus, II, 389.

14. Donatus, II, 641.

15. Fulgentius, *Expositio virgilianae continentiae secundum philosophos moralis*, 160, *Opera*, ed. R. Helm, reprinted (Stuttgart, 1970), 101. On Fulgentius and allegorical interpretation of the *Aeneid*, see Domenico Comparetti, *Vergil in the Middle Ages*, trans. E. F. M. Benecke (London, 1895); R. R. Bolgar, *The Classical Heritage and its Beneficiaries* (Cambridge, 1963), especially 218–19; and the chapter on Vergil in Don Cameron Allen, *Mysteriously Meant: The Rediscovery of Pagan Symbolism and Allegorical Interpretation in the Renaissance* (Baltimore, 1970), 135–62.

16. Bernardus Silvestris, *Commentum super sex libros Eneidos Virgilii*, ed. Julian Ward Jones and Elizabeth Frances Jones (Lincoln, Neb., 1977), 2–3. In a later passage allegorizing the seven bulls of *Aeneid* 6.38, Bernardus situates *pietas* alongside six closely related terms: "innocentia, amicicia, concordia" come first, then "pietas" followed by "religio, affectus, humanitas." The distinctions that Bernardus then makes among these terms convey the appearance of semantic refinement, but in his actual usage they tend to overlap. See Bernardus, 39–40. On his interpretation, see Giorgio Padoan, "Tradizione e fortuna del commento all'*Eneide* di Bernardo Silvestre," *Italia Medioevale e Umanistica* 3 (1960): 227–40; Winthrop Wetherbee, *Platonism and Poetry in the Twelfth Century: The Literary Influence of the School of Chartres* (Princeton, 1972), 105–11; J. W. Jones, Jr., "The Allegorical Traditions of the *Aeneid*," especially 117–27. On the cultural context, with specific reference to manuscript evidence, see Birger Munk Olsen, "Virgile et la renaissance du XIIe siècle," *Lectures médiévales de Virgile* (Rome, 1985), 31–48.

17. John of Salisbury, *Polycraticus*, 8.24, *Opera omnia*, ed. J. A. Giles, 5 vols., reprinted (Leipzig, 1969), IV, 371.

18. 8.24, IV, 371–72.

19. 8.24, IV, 372.

20. 8.24, IV, 373.

21. Although Aeneas as founder of Rome is repeatedly taken by John of Salisbury to illustrate the virtues indispensable to rule, it may be observed that in the larger context of the *Polycraticus* the role of Aeneas and the ideal of *pietas* do not always perfectly coincide. See, for example, book 2, chap. 15, where Aeneas is less the

author of *pietas* than the author of the Roman state, bearing responsibility for its putative evils as well as for its benefits. John of Salisbury, *Opera omnia*, III, 85–86.

22. Cristoforo Landino, *Disputationes camaldulenses*, 4, ed. Peter Lohe (Florence, 1980), 191. All subsequent references are to this edition. A selection from the disputations may also be found, with facing Italian translation, in *Prosatori latini del Quattrocento*, ed. Eugenio Garin (Milan, 1952), 716–91; a facsimile text with an English translation is provided by Thomas Stahel, "Cristoforo Landino's Allegorization of the *Aeneid*: Books III and IV of the *Camaldolese Disputations*," dissertation, Johns Hopkins University, 1968. All translations from Landino are Stahel's. On Landino's interpretation, see in addition to Stahel's introduction: Allen, *Mysteriously Meant*, 142–54; Michael Murrin, *The Allegorical Epic: Essays in its Rise and Decline* (Chicago, 1980), 27–50; Annabel Patterson, *Pastoral and Ideology: Virgil to Valéry* (Berkeley and Los Angeles, 1987), 62–81; and Craig Kallendorf, *In Praise of Aeneas* (Hanover, 1989), 129–65.

23. Landino, 3, p. 176.

24. 4, p. 251.

25. 3, pp. 172ff. and 4, pp. 197ff.

26. See especially 3, pp. 173–74. This argument may also be found in the selection made by Garin, *Prosatori latini del Quattrocento*, 750.

27. Stahel, "Cristoforo Landino's Allegorization of the *Aeneid*," 21.

28. See Chapter 1, notes 8 and 10.

29. Augustine, *Enchiridion*, 1.2, ed. and trans. J. Rivière, *Oeuvres de Saint Augustin*, Bibliothèque Augustinienne, 37 vols. (Paris, 1947), IX, 102.

30. Landino, 3, p. 175.

31. 3, p. 175. The pastoral epistles were still assumed to be the work of Paul. Whether or not Landino believed it, the legend that Paul wept over Vergil's tomb at Naples was still alive in the fifteenth century and is preserved in medieval verse. See Sir Paul Harvey, "Virgil" in the *Oxford Companion to Classical Literature* (Oxford, 1980).

32. This emphasis is evident from the beginning, as this passage is from the gloss on *Aeneid* 1.148–53. Compare Landino's remarks on the opening of book 7: "Ponunt platonici duas alas: per quas animi humani ad caelum evolent: iustitiam et religionem: et per iustitiam: cuius pars est pietas: intelligunt morales virtutes: per religionem et intellectivas" (The Platonists posit two wings on which human souls may rise to heaven: justice and religion. By justice, to which piety belongs, they understand moral virtues, by religion, the intellectual ones as well). In his account of the final battle, then, Landino emphasizes the *pietas* that binds Aeneas to Pallas, and denies that killing Turnus is motivated by *crudelitas*. Glossing "furiis accensus et ira / terribilis" (12.946–47) as "Implacabili indignatione," Landino instead lays the charge of cruelty at the feet of Turnus himself. Vergil, *Vergilii Maronis poetarum principis opera* (Florence, 1487).

33. Vergil, *Opera*, Garland facsimile of 1544 Venice edition, 2 vols. (New York, 1976), I, 152. All citations from Datho may be found on 152. Cicero continues: "quibus sublatis perturbatio vitae sequitur et magna confusio, atque haud scio an pietate adversus deos sublata fides etiam et societas generis humani et una excellentissima virtus iustitia tollatur" (And when these are gone, life soon becomes a

welter of disorder and confusion; and in all probability the disappearance of piety towards the gods will entail the disappearance of loyalty and social union among men as well, and of justice itself, the queen of all the virtues). See Cicero, *De natura deorum*, 1.2, ed. and trans. H. Rackham, LCL (Cambridge, Mass., and London, 1979), 6. Note that Datho's quotation differs slightly from modern texts of Cicero.

34. See Cicero, *De natura deorum*, 1.42, LCL, 112.

35. Scaliger, *Poetices libri septem*, 3.12, p. 92. All citations from Scaliger may be found in this chapter, 90–95.

36. Jacobus Pontanus, *Symbolarum libri XVII Virgilii*, Garland facsimile of 1599 Augsburg edition, 3 vols. (New York, 1976), ii, 633. On the importance of this work, see Allen, *Mysteriously Meant*, 184.

37. Pontanus, iii, 2097.

38. Pontanus, ii, 2064.

39. The full expression is "caritas erga parentes." Vergil, *P. Vergilii Maronis opera*, ed. Carolus Ruaeus (London, 1687), 486, glossing *Aeneid* 9.294.

40. Martin Luther, *Operationes in Psalmos*, 1.1, *Martin Luthers Werke*, 58 vols. (Weimar, 1883–1938), v, 29.

41. Ambrose, *De officiis ministrorum*, 1.27, PL (Paris, 1880), xvi, 65C–66A. The translation is by H. de Romestin. On this subject, see Cochrane, *Christianity and Classical Culture*, 347–50, 374–76; and M. L. W. Laistner, *Thought and Letters in Western Europe A.D. 500 to 900* (New York, 1931), 117–58. Specifically on Roman *pietas* in the first centuries A.D., see H. D. Weiss, "Piety in Latin Writers in Early Christian Times," dissertation, Duke University, 1964, especially 19–47.

42. Ambrose, *Expositio Evangelii secundum Lucam*, 7.199, ed. M. Adriaen, CC (Turnhout, Belgium, 1957), xiv, 283. See F. Homes Dudden, *The Life and Times of St. Ambrose*, 2 vols. (Oxford, 1935), ii, 692–94.

43. Ambrose, *Expositio Evangelii secundum Lucam*, 10.58, p. 362.

44. See especially 7.135–36, pp. 260–61, and 8.73, pp. 325–26. It may be noted that the boy Jesus is himself taken to illustrate filial *pietas* earlier in Ambrose's commentary on Luke 2.51, 2.65–66, pp. 58–59.

45. 7.146, p. 265.

46. "Magnum pietatis officium, sed religionis uberius" (Great is the duty of piety, but more fruitful is that of religion). Ambrose, *De viduis*, 1.6, PL, xvi, 249B.

47. Ambrose, Epistolarum Classis ii, 66.7, PL, xvi, 1279C.

48. See Jerome, *In Matheum*, 1.1795–97, ed. M. Adriaen, CC (Turnhout, 1969), lxxvii, 74. On Jerome's manner of interpreting Scripture, see Louis N. Hartmann, "St. Jerome as an Exegete," *A Monument to St. Jerome*, ed. Francis X. Murphy (New York, 1952), 35–81.

49. Jerome, *Select Letters*, 14.2, trans. F. A. Wright, LCL (Cambridge, Mass., and London, 1980), 30–32.

50. 117.4, p. 380.

51. See, for example, this same letter, 117.2, p. 374.

52. Jerome, *In Malachiam*, 3.13–15, ed. M. Adriaen, CC (Turnhout, 1969), lxxvi A, 937–38.

53. See the relevant entries in F. P. Dutripon, *Bibliorum sacrorum concordantiae*, reprinted (Hildesheim and New York, 1976). On the linguistic importance of Je-

rome's translation, see G. Q. A. Meershoek, *Le latin biblique d'après Saint Jérôme: Aspects linguistiques de la rencontre entre la Bible et le monde classique* (Utrecht, 1966), 1–30.

54. Jerome, *In Zachariam*, 1.5.5–8, CC, LXXVI A, 789.

55. 1.5.9–11, p. 791.

56. Jerome, *In Matheum*, 1.1795–97, CC, LXXVII, 86.

57. Augustine, *De sermone domini in monte*, 1.4.11, ed. A. Mutzenbecher, CC (Turnhout, 1967), XXXV, 10. The content of this correlation is fairly complicated. Among the seven spiritual gifts of Isaiah 11.1–3, *pietas* is listed sixth, right after *scientia*, with which it is syntactically paired. Whereas Jerome views the order of the list as essentially irrelevant, Augustine takes the numerical order seriously and in his explication of the Sermon on the Mount attempts to correlate the Old Testament gifts with the New Testament beatitudes. No little ingenuity is required to manage this, but Augustine finally develops the correspondence by using a mirror figure, so that the sixth gift is equated with the second beatitude, *pius* with *mitis*. In turn *mitis* becomes for Augustine a bridge from *pius* to *misericors* ("mitis autem et misericors unum videntur"), rather inconsistently with the emphasis of his remarks on the two words in the *City of God*. It may be added that at least one commentary on the Sermon on the Mount contemporary with Augustine's makes this connection directly, identifying *pietas* not with the second but with the fifth beatitude. Chromatius Aquilensis, Sermo 41, CC, IX A, 177. It is, moreover, this correlation that Gregory repeats in his massive commentary on Job (where the seven gifts are identified with Job's seven sons). Gregory, *Moralia in Job*, 1.32.44, ed. M. Adriaen, CC (Turnhout, 1979), CXLIII, 49.

58. Gregory, *Moralia*, 11.11.17, CXLIII A, 595. Set against divine *pietas*, human *crudelitas* is equated by Gregory with *impietas*, and the ultimate example is the crucifixion: "Quis umquam impius esse putandus est, si ille populus, qui ipsam pietatem persecutus est, impius non est?" (Who is ever to be considered impious, if not that people who persecuted piety itself?) In this formulation, Christ becomes *pietas* itself. Gregory, *Moralia*, 9.29.45, CXLIII, 487–88, and see also 6.18.32, CXLIII, 307. Consider further how *pietas* is invoked by Gregory to explain events on the road to Damascus: "ei superna pietas caelos aperit seseque illi Iesus de sublimibus ostendit" (for him celestial piety opens the heavens and Jesus shows himself to him from on high), Gregory, *Moralia*, 19.6.11, CXLIII A, 963. On the assumptions that guide Gregory's interpretation, see G. R. Evans, *The Thought of Gregory the Great* (Cambridge, 1986), especially 87–95.

59. That is, grammatically "ὅς" cannot refer to "μυστήριον," but "quod" does refer to "sacramentum."

60. Ambrosiaster, *In epistolam B. Paulus ad Timotheum primam*, 3.16, ed. J. P. Migne, PL (Paris, 1879), XVII, 498B.

61. Hrabanus Maurus, *Enarrationum in epistolas beati Pauli*, 23.3, ed. J. P. Migne, PL (Paris, 1878), CXII, 608C.

62. Herveus Burgidolensis, *Commentaria in epistolas divi Pauli*, 3, ed. J. P. Migne, PL (Paris, 1854), CLXXXI, 1425C.

63. See Ambrosiaster, *Ad Timotheum primam*, 4, PL, XVII, 500C; Hrabanus Maurus, 23.4, PL, CXII, 613A; Peter Lombard, *In epistolam I ad Timotheum*, 4, ed.

J. P. Migne, PL (Paris, 1880), CXCII, 348D. In his lengthy homily on 1 Timothy, well known in the West in Latin translation, John Chrysostom carefully remarks on the phrase "πάσῃ εὐσεβείᾳ" ("omni pietate") in 2.2, calling particular attention to the adjective, which he assumes would not be there if the noun had one clear meaning. John Chrysostom, *In epistolam primam ad Timotheum commentarius*, 7.1, ed. J. P. Migne, PG (Paris, 1862), LXII, 535.

64. Aquinas, *Summa theologiae*, 1a2ae.68,7, XXIV, 32. On Aquinas and scholastic exegesis, see especially, M.-D. Chenu, *Toward Understanding Saint Thomas*, trans. A.-M. Landry and D. Hughes (Chicago, 1964), 233–63.

65. Nicolaus of Lyra, *Postilla super totam Bibliam*, facsimile reprint of 1492 Strasbourg edition, 4 vols. (Frankfurt, 1971), IV, n.p., glossing 1 Timothy 4.8. See Jerry H. Bentley, *Humanists and Holy Writ: New Testament Scholarship in the Renaissance* (Princeton, 1983), 21–31.

66. Aquinas, 2a2ae.157.4, XLIV, 46–48.

67. Lorenzo Valla, *In Bartolemaeum Facium Ligurem, invectivarum seu recriminationum*, 2, *Opera omnia*, facsimile reprint of 1540 Basel edition, 2 vols. (Turin, 1962), I, 584. Charles Trinkaus has emphasized that for Valla "the evidence for the nature of thought is to be found in the language or the words in which it is expressed." Trinkaus, *In Our Image and Likeness: Humanity and Divinity in Italian Humanist Thought*, 2 vols. (Chicago, 1970), II, 572. For a helpful discussion with additional references, see Bentley, *Humanists and Holy Writ*, 32–69. On Valla and Fazio, see Salvatore Camporeale, *Lorenzo Valla: Umanesimo e teologia* (Florence, 1972), especially 308–15.

68. Marsiglio Ficino, *In epistolas D. Pauli*, 8, *Opera omnia*, facsimile of 1576 Basel edition, 2 vols., 2 parts each, repaginated (Turin, 1959), I, i, 469 (439). On the commentary on Romans, see Bentley, *Humanists and Holy Writ*, 9. On Ficino's Platonism, see P. O. Kristeller, *Renaissance Thought and its Sources*, ed. Michael Mooney (New York, 1979), especially 188–91; "Lay Religious Traditions and Florentine Platonism," *Studies in Renaissance Thought and Letters* (Rome, 1956), 99–122; *The Philosophy of Marsilio Ficino* (New York, 1943), especially 309–23.

69. 6, p. 465 (435).

70. Ficino, *In Platonem*, in *Opera omnia*, II, i, 517 (1517). See in contrast to Plato, the "impii duo" of Epicurus and Lucretius, *Theologica platonica*, ed. and trans. Raymond Marcel, 2 vols. (Paris, 1964), II, 76–79. On the piety of Ficino's Plato, see Trinkaus, *In Our Image and Likeness*, II, 461–504, especially 464–66; and Marcel, *Marsile Ficin* (Paris, 1958), 647–78, especially 654–55.

71. Ficino, *Theologica platonica*, II, 281.

72. Jacques Lefèvre d'Etaples, *Commentarii initiatorii in quatuor Evangelia*, in *The Prefatory Epistles of Jacques Lefèvre d'Etaples*, ed. Eugene F. Rice (New York and London, 1972), 436. Lefèvre had earlier been influenced by Ficino, but by the time of the commentary he has turned away from the ancient philosophers. See Philip Edgcumbe Hughes, *Lefèvre: Pioneer of Ecclesiastical Renewal in France* (Grand Rapids, Mich., 1984), 54. Specifically on Lefèvre and the problem of interpreting Scripture, see Guy Bedouelle, *Lefèvre d'Etaples et l'intelligence des Ecritures* (Geneva, 1976), chap. 5. The epigraph for this book comes from another telling

passage in Lefèvre's commentary on the Gospels: "Sola veritas quae est verbum Dei salvat" (The only truth which saves is the word of God).

73. Lefèvre d'Etaples, *Commentariorum libri quatuordecim,* in *Prefatory Epistles* 296–97.

74. Ibid., 298.

75. Erasmus, *Novum Testamentum . . . adnotationes,* in *Opera omnia,* reprint of 1703–6 edition by Jean LeClerc, 10 vols. (London, 1962), VI, 936.

76. Martin Luther, *Annotationes in priorem epistolam ad Timotheum,* 4, *Werke,* XXVI, 67. The translation is by Richard J. Dinda.

77. Ibid., 78.

78. Erasmus, *Ratio seu methodus compendio perveniendi ad veram theologiam,* in *Ausgewählte Werke,* 303. See Albert Rabil, *Erasmus and the New Testament: The Mind of a Christian Humanist* (San Antonio, Tex., 1972), 99–113; Marjorie O'Rourke Boyle, *Erasmus on Language and Method in Theology* (Toronto, 1977), 33–57; Bentley, *Humanists and Holy Writ,* 112–93.

79. Erasmus, *Ratio seu methodus,* 304–5.

80. Philipp Melancthon, for example, dedicated his *Loci communes* to Tilemann Plettener, "pio et erudito viro," and in the work itself Melancthon finds several opportunities to reflect on the "stulti et impii" of the world. See *Loci communes seu hypotyposes theologicae,* ed. Hans Engelland, *Melancthons Werke,* ed. Robert Supperich, 7 vols. (Hamburg, 1951–75), II, i, 3, 16. Similar passages occur in the work of Erasmus's friends John Colet and Juan-Luis Vives. Vives adopts the phrase "stultus aut impius" in his epistle to Henry VIII and Colet joins the noun forms by "et" in his commentary on *Romans,* in both cases as if the ideas conveyed by the two words were naturally related. See Juan-Luis Vives, "Epistola Henrico VIII. Regi Angliae," *Opera omnia,* reprint of the eighteenth-century Valencia edition, 8 vols. (London, 1964), V, 179; John Colet, *Enarratio in epistolam B. Pauli ad Romanos,* 10, *Dean Colet's Lectures on Romans,* ed. J. H. Lupton (London, 1873), 172.

81. Erasmus, *Encomium moriae,* 65, *Ausgewählte Schriften,* II, 196.

82. Erasmus, *Ratio seu methodus,* 249.

83. Ibid., 250.

84. Ibid., 253.

85. See, for example, *Enchiridion militis christianae,* 16. In the prefatory epistle, Erasmus summarizes the purposes of his manual: "Et tamen eius laboris me non omnino paenitet, si tam multos exstimulat ad verae pietatis studium" (Nevertheless, I do not altogether regret this labor, if it encourages many people in their devotion to true piety), 3.

86. Ibid., 85.

87. Ibid., 89.

88. Luther, *Annotationes in priorem epistolam ad Timotheum,* 3, p. 64.

89. Luther, *Operationes in Psalmos,* in *Werke,* V, 28. The translation is by Edward Sittler.

90. For both passages, see Luther, *Epistolas ad Romanos,* 11.4, *Werke,* LVI, 430. The translation is by Jacob A. D. Preus. For comment on this work, see David C. Steinmetz, *Luther in Context* (Bloomington, Indiana, 1986), 12–31.

91. Erasmus, *De libero arbitrio,* 1b3, *Ausgewählte Schriften,* IV, 26. This passage is quoted and discussed by John William Aldridge, *The Hermeneutic of Erasmus,* Basel Studies of Theology, 2 (Richmond, Va., 1966), 95.

92. Luther, *De servo arbitrio,* in *Werke,* XVIII, 606. The translation is by Ernst F. Winter. See Heinrich Bornkamm, *Luther in Mid-Career, 1521–1530,* trans. E. Theodore Bachmann (Philadelphia, 1983), 337–53, 417–58.

93. See especially 641.

94. For example, 609.

95. Ibid., 614.

96. Ibid., 758, and see earlier 650ff.

97. Ibid., 759.

98. Ibid., 761.

99. Ibid., 632, 743.

100. Luther, *Annotationes in epistolam Pauli ad Titum,* in *Werke,* XXV, 11. The translation is by J. Pelikan.

101. The importance of *pietas* in Calvin's vocabulary has been rightly emphasized by John T. McNeill in his introduction to the English translation by Ford Lewis Battles, *Calvin: Institutes of the Christian Religion,* 2 vols. (Philadelphia, 1960), lii. McNeill observes: "To the modern mind the word 'piety' has lost its historic implications and status. It has become suspect, as bearing suggestions of ineffectual religious sentimentality or canting pretence. For Calvin and his contemporaries, as for ancient pagan and Christian writers, *pietas* was an honest word, free from any unsavory connotation. It was praiseworthy dutifulness or faithful devotion to one's family, country, or God. Calvin insistently affirms that piety is a prerequisite for any sound knowledge of God." It may be added that Calvin's Christian sense of the word is informed by his classical studies. His commentary on Seneca's *De clementia,* for prime example, provides a considerable account of the word based on a range of classical sources. See *Calvin's Commentary on Seneca's De Clementia,* ed. and trans. Ford Lewis Battles and Andre Hugo (Leiden, 1969), 92–93, 226–28.

102. Calvin, *Christianae religionis institutio* (London, 1576), 1.2.1, p. 3. In the *Institutes* Calvin assumes that God's original plan, according to which the universe would be a school of *pietas,* was wrecked by the rebellion of Adam, and *vera pietas* then disappeared from the earth, to be reawakened in those who acknowledge God as father.

103. "[Pietas] ex qua demum religio nascitur" (Piety, from which religion takes its source), 1.4.4, p. 7.

104. 4.10.12, p. 577.

105. 4.20.32, p. 742. This is the second to last sentence of the *Institutes;* the very last sentence is a quotation from Paul warning against *impietas.*

106. Vives, *De officio mariti,* 1.1, *Opera omnia,* IV, 330.

107. Andrea Alciati, *Emblemata cum commentariis,* Garland reprint of 1621 Padua edition (New York, 1976), 828–31. All citations concerning Emblem 195 are from this text. See Elbert N. S. Thompson, *Literary Bypaths of the Renaissance* (New Haven, 1924), 29–67, and the specific reference to Alciati's "Pietas filiorum in parentis," 29–30; Robert J. Clements, *Picta Poesis: Literary and Humanistic Theory in Renaissance Emblem Books* (Rome, 1960), especially 68; Huston Diehl, *An Index*

of Icons in English Emblem Books 1500–1700 (Norman, Okla., 1986), 3–6. For more extensive bibliography on the emblem tradition, see Peter M. Daly, *The English Emblem Tradition* (Toronto, 1988), and William S. Heckscher, *The Princeton Alciati Companion* (New York, 1989). On emblems and typology, see especially Korshin, *Typologies in England,* where the typological relationship between Aeneas and Christ is emphasized, 5, 135, 140. On the sixteenth-century context, see Ruth Mortimer, "Vergil in the Light of the Sixteenth Century," *Vergil at 2000,* 159–84.

108. See Valerius Maximus, *Factorum et dictorum memorabilium libri novem,* book 5. This is one of two significant collections of *exempla pietatis* in antiquity. The other is Pliny's *Naturalis historia,* 7.36.121–22. As Galinsky has emphasized, Aeneas is not mentioned in either one. Galinsky, *Aeneas, Sicily, and Rome,* 54.

109. See Tacitus, *Historiae,* 3.25, ed. and trans. Clifford H. Moore, 4 vols. (with *Annales*), LCL (Cambridge, Mass., and London, 1963), I, 372.

110. Seneca, *De beneficiis,* 3.37.2, *Moral Essays,* ed. and trans. John W. Basore, LCL, 3 vols. (Cambridge, Mass., and London, 1975), III, 200.

111. It may be observed here that the connection between "Pietas filiorum in parentes" (Emblem 195) and "Gratiam referendam" (Emblem 30) is acknowledged at some distance in Santayana's chapter on "Piety" in *The Life of Reason:* "This consciousness that the human spirit is derived and responsible, that all its functions are heritages and trusts, involves a sentiment of gratitude and duty which we may call piety." Santayana, *The Life of Reason,* 3.10 (New York, 1954), 258. Unless otherwise indicated, all citations concerning Emblem 30 are from the Padua Alciati of 1621, 172–75.

112. Padua Alciati of 1621, 827.

113. Valeriano Bolzani, *Hieroglyphica,* 20, Garland facsimile of 1602 Lyons edition (New York, 1976), 200–201. All citations from the *Hieroglyphica* are from this edition. On the emblem of the pelican, see Peter M. Daly, *Literature in the Light of the Emblem* (Toronto, 1979), 98.

114. Filippo Picinelli, *Mundus symbolicus,* trans. August Erath, Garland facsimile of the 1694 edition, 2 vols. (New York and London, 1976), I, 318. All citations from the *Mundus symbolicus* are from this edition.

115. The commentary refers specifically to kings of Spain and Portugal who adopt the pelican as a royal symbol.

Chapter 3

1. Ovid, *Metamorphoses,* 1.149, ed. and trans. Frank Justus Miller, rev. G. P. Goold, 2 vols., LCL (Cambridge, Mass., and London, 1984), I, 12. Compare the ironic version of this idea as expressed by Phaedra in *Heroides* 4: "ista vetus pietas, aevo moritura futuro, / rustica Saturno regna tenente fuit" (such old-fashioned regard for virtue was rustic even in Saturn's reign, and doomed to die in the age to come). Ovid, *Heroides,* 4.131–32, *Heroides and Amores,* ed. and trans. Grant Showerman, rev. G. P. Goold, LCL (Cambridge, Mass., and London, 1977), 54. For an excellent discussion of *pietas* in the *Heroides,* see Howard Jacobson, *Ovid's*

"*Heroides*" (Princeton, 1974), 129–33 on Hypermestra and 154 on Phaedra. See also G. Karl Galinsky, *Ovid's Metamorphoses: An Introduction to the Basic Aspects* (Oxford, 1975), 220–28, 232, 246; and Edgar M. Glenn, *The Metamorphoses: Ovid's Roman Games* (Lanham, Md., 1986), 101–14. For further example, see the parallel to Ovid's "victa iacet pietas" in Propertius, *Elegies*, 3.13, line 48: "aurum omnes victa iam pietate colunt" (piety is vanquished and all men worship gold). Propertius, *Elegies*, ed. and trans. H. E. Butler, LCL (Cambridge, Mass., and London, 1976), 224.

2. See J. H. W. G. Liebeschuetz, *Continuity and Change in Roman Religion* (Oxford, 1979), 1; and specifically on *pietas* in the writing of Roman history, Gerhard Stübler, *Die Religiosität des Livius* (Amsterdam, 1964), especially the accounts of Numa, 34–43 and Scipio, 123–52.

3. Probably written near the time of Actium, the Horatian epode takes civil war as the defining characteristic of an impious age ("impia . . . aetas"). The conclusion of the poem thus represents an alternative to contemporary Rome in the pastoral vision of a *locus pietatis* isolated from the moral regression of history by special dispensation of Jove: "Iuppiter illa piae secrevit litora genti, / ut inquinavit aere tempus aureum" (Jupiter set apart these shores for a righteous folk, ever since with bronze he dimmed the lustre of the golden age, 63–64). Horace, Epode 16, *Odes and Epodes*, ed. and trans. C. E. Bennett, LCL (Cambridge, Mass., and London, 1989), 412. On the politics of pastoral poetry, see Patterson, *Pastoral and Ideology*, especially 1–17.

4. Horace writes: "cui per ardentem sine fraude Troiam / castus Aeneas patriae superstes / liberum munivit iter, daturus / plura relictis" (they for whom righteous Aeneas, survivor of his country, unscathed 'mid blazing Troy, prepared a way to liberty, destined to bestow more than had been left behind). *Carmen saeculare*, 41–44, *Odes and Epodes*, LCL, 352.

5. Propertius, *Elegies*, 4.1.39–50. The first six lines of this passage represent Vergil's epic, concluding with the scene later taken to define the hero's *pietas*, expressed by Propertius: "cum pater in nati trepidus cervice pependit, / et verita est umeros urere flamma pios" (when the father hung trembling on his son's neck, and the flame feared to burn those pious shoulders). The lines that follow explain Roman history in light of the epic, including an elliptical and problematic reference to Romulus and Remus, whose death is apparently offered as atonement ("pianda") for the violation of the city's first boundary. This poem has much in common with Tibullus's elegy, 2.5, considered below.

6. In Ovid's description of the temple of Mars the Avenger in book 5, Aeneas and Romulus are presented as co-founders of Rome. This leads in turn to reconciliation of *pietas* and *arma* in the figure of Augustus. Extraordinary even in this celebratory context, Ovid's phrase "pia . . . arma"—taken to honor the victory of Octavian—is here specifically applied to civil war. The collaboration of Aeneas and Romulus, of *pietas* and *arma* thus signifies the collapse of idealized past and idealized future into the idealized present of panegyric. Ovid, *Fasti*, 5.567–70, LCL, 302.

7. Tibullus, *Elegies*, 2.5, line 119, ed. and trans. J. W. Mackail, Rev. G. P. Goold, *Catullus, Tibullus, Pervigilium Veneris*, LCL (Cambridge, Mass., and London, 1988), 278. All subsequent citations from this poem will be repeated from this edition and referenced in the text by line numbers.

8. Benedetto Riposati, *Introduzione allo studio di Tibullo* (Como, 1945), 158. See also Evan T. Sage, "The Non-Virgilian Aeneas," *Classical Journal,* 15 (1919–20): 350–57.

9. Tibullus writes: "haec dedit Aeneae sortes, postquam ille parentem/dicitur et raptos sustinuisse Lares/nec fore credebat Romam, cum maestus ab alto/Ilion ardentes respiceretque deos" (Twas she that gave responses to Aeneas after the hour when, as story tells, he bore away in his arms his sire and household gods, never dreaming that a Rome would be, when from the deep he turned his eyes in sorrow on Ilion and its gods ablaze, 19–22). Tibullus's "dicitur" may reflect the "aiunt" of *Aeneid* 4.598 ("en dextra fidesque,/quem secum patrios aiunt portare Penatis,/quem subiisse umeris confectum aetate parentem!").

10. Bright observes: "The slaying of Remus by the favored Romulus opened the panel on pre-Aenean Rome, and now the first words of the Sibyl point (as ancient authors rarely did) to the fact that [Aeneas and Cupid] are brothers. Since we have also just seen how Latium favored lovers, the vigorous exploits of Aeneas cannot help but be recognized as a threat to his brother. In fact the fratricide of Romulus emerges almost as a consequence of the eviction of Amor by Aeneas as he comes to Italy." David F. Bright, *Haec mihi fingebam: Tibullus in his World* (Leiden, 1978), 84.

11. For the editorial problem, see *Albii Tibulli aliorumque carminum libri tres,* ed. F. W. Lenz and G. Karl Galinsky (Leiden, 1971), 106.

12. Velleius Paterculus, *Historia,* 2.86, ed. and trans. Frederick W. Shipley, LCL (Cambridge, Mass., and London, 1955), 230. Subsequent citations are repeated from this edition and referenced parenthetically by book and section numbers.

13. Calpurnius Siculus, *Eclogues,* 1.42, ed. Charles H. Keene (Hildesheim, 1969). All quotations are repeated from this edition and referenced parenthetically by poem and line numbers. On the disputed historical context of the *Eclogues,* see most recently R. Mayer, "Calpurnius Siculus: Technique and Date," *Journal of Roman Studies* 70 (1980): 166–74; T. P. Wiseman, "Calpurnius Siculus and the Claudian Civil War," *Journal of Roman Studies* 72 (1982): 57–67; Edward Champlin, "History and the Date of Calpurnius Siculus," *Philologus* 130 (1986): 104–12; David Armstrong, "Stylistics and the Date of Calpurnius Siculus," *Philologus* 130 (1986): 113–36. Whether the poems were written in the reign of Nero or later is less important for my purposes than the attitude they take toward the imperial office. On this point see Paul J. Alpers, *The Singer of the Eclogues* (Berkeley and Los Angeles, 1979), 165 n. 13.

14. Silius Italicus, *Punica,* 3.614–15, ed. and trans. J. D. Duff, 2 vols., LCL (Cambridge, Mass., and London, 1949–50), I, 158. Subsequent references are cited from this edition in the text by book and line numbers.

15. Pliny, *Panegyricus,* 2, *Letters and Panegyricus,* ed. and trans. Betty Radice, 2 vols., LCL (Cambridge, Mass., and London, 1969), II, 326.

16. See James D. Garrison, *Dryden and the Tradition of Panegyric* (Berkeley and Los Angeles, 1975), 46–52.

17. Mamertinus, *Panegyricus genethliacus Maximiano Augusto dictus,* 11. *Panégyriques latins,* ed. and trans. Edouard Galletier, 3 vols. (Paris, 1949), I, 60–61.

18. Claudian, *Panegyricus de tertio consulatu Honorii Augusti,* 126–30, ed. and trans. Maurice Platnauer, 2 vols., LCL (Cambridge, Mass., and London, 1963), I,

278–80. On fourth-century panegyric, see Alan Cameron, *Claudian: Poetry and Propaganda at the Court of Honorius* (Oxford, 1970), especially 22–23, 30–45, 253–55.

19. Claudian, *In Rufinum*, 1.51–53, I, 30. Compare Vergil, *Eclogues* 4, Calpurnius's imitation in *Eclogues* 1, and Horace, *Carmen saeculare*, 57–60, and see also Claudian's *Panegyricus de quarto consulatu Honorii Augusti*, 111–21, I, 294.

20. Nazarius, *Panegyricus Constantino Augusto dictus*, 6, *Panégyriques*, II, 171.

21. Later in the oration the *fortitudo-pietas* pair is modified to *fortitudo-clementia*, thus affirming *pietas* and *clementia* as synonyms, II, 183.

22. Claudian, *Panegyricus dictus Manlio Theodoro Consuli*, 166–68, I, 350.

23. To desecrate a statue of Constantine, for example, is to demonstrate a form of "caeca dementia" that provokes Nazarius to exclaim: "O manus impiae! o truces oculi!" (O impious hands! o fierce eyes!) Nazarius, *Panegyricus*, 12, *Panégyriques*, II, 176.

24. Pacatus, *Panegyricus Theodosio Augusto dictus*, 34, *Panégyriques*, III, 101.

25. For example: "en ades, Omnipotens, concordibus influe terris: / iam mundus te, Christe, capit, quem congrege nexu / pax et Roma tenent" (Come then, Almighty; here is a world in harmony; do Thou enter it. An earth receives Thee now, O Christ, which peace and Rome hold in a bond of union). Prudentius, *Contra orationem Symmachi*, 2.634–36, *Prudentius*, trans. H. J. Thomson, 2 vols., LCL (Cambridge, Mass., and London, 1979), II, 56. On *pietas* in Prudentius, see Anne-Marie Palmer, *Prudentius on the Martyrs* (Oxford, 1989), especially 147: "The word 'inpias' used of the martyrs' activities in war implicitly expresses a condemnation of warlike activities which are traditionally included in any definition of *pietas*, and obliquely sets forth a redefinition of the latter in a Christian context."

26. Prudentius, *Hamartigenia*, 564–68, I, 242–44.

27. Ibid., 575, I, 244.

28. Ibid., 580, I, 244.

29. Prudentius, *Apotheosis*, 446–48, I, 154.

30. Prudentius, *Contra orationem Symmachi*, 2.677–83, II, 60. All subsequent quotations from the oration will be cited in the text by book and line numbers.

31. Claudian, *Panegyricus de sexto consulatu Honorii Augusti*, 116–18, II, 82.

32. Lucan, *De bello civili*, 1.22–66, trans. J. D. Duff, LCL (Cambridge, Mass., and London, 1951), 4–6. Subsequent passages will be referenced in the text by book and line numbers from this edition. On the invocation to Nero, see G. K. Gresseth, "The Quarrel between Lucan and Nero," *Classical Philology* 52 (1957): 24–27; P. Grimal, "L'Eloge de Neron au début de la *Pharsale*, est-il ironique?" *Revue des Etudes Latins* 38 (1960): 296–305. On Lucan, see Frederick M. Ahl, *Lucan: An Introduction* (Ithaca, N.Y., 1976). I am generally indebted to Ahl's book, especially to his discussion of *pietas* on 275–78, but also to his observations on the poem's principal characters—Pompey, Caesar, and Cato. See also Joseph Hellegouarc'h, *Le vocabulaire latin des relations et des partis politiques sous la République* (Paris, 1963), especially 276–79.

33. See Ahl, *Lucan*, 274–79.

34. Statius writes: "sic et tu—rabidi nefas tyranni!—/iussus praecipitem subire Lethen,/dum pugnas canis arduaque voce/das solacia grandibus sepulcris,/—o dirum scelus! o scelus!—tacebis" (Even so on thee—ah! the impious frenzied tyrant!—bidden while singing of battles and with lofty utterance solacing the mighty dead to plunge in Lethe's rushing stream—O crime, o most foul crime!—on thee too shall silence fall). Statius, *Sylvae* 2.7.100–104, ed. and trans. (with the *Thebaid*) J. H. Mozley, 2 vols. (Cambridge, Mass., and London, 1967), I, 134.

35. Statius, *Sylvae*, 2.7.52. All quotations from the *Thebaid* are also repeated from the LCL edition and referenced parenthetically by book and line numbers.

36. "εἴπερ γὰρ ἀδικεῖν χρή, τυραννίδος πέρι/κάλλιστον ἀδικεῖν, τἆλλα δ᾽ εὐσεβεῖν χρεών." Euripides, *Phoenissae*, 524–25, ed. and trans. A. S. Way, LCL (Cambridge, Mass., and London, 1978), 386.

37. Cicero, *De officiis*, 3.21, ed. and trans. Walter Miller, LCL (Cambridge, Mass., and London, 1990), 356.

38. See also Seneca's adaptation of Euripides, *Phoenissae*, 662–64, and David Vessey, *Statius and the Thebaid* (Cambridge, 1973), 76–77.

39. See J. H. Burgess, "*Pietas* in Virgil and Statius," *Proceedings of the Virgil Society* 11 (1971–72): 48–60; and Gordon Williams, "Statius and Vergil: Defensive Imitation," *Vergil at 2000*, 207–24.

40. Ronald Syme, *Tacitus*, 2 vols. (Oxford, 1958), I, 414.

41. Vessey, *Statius and the Thebaid*, 316.

42. Tacitus, *Agricola*, 3.21, *Agricola and Germania*, ed. and trans. Maurice Hutton, LCL, revised edition (Cambridge, Mass., and London, 1980), 30. All subsequent quotations will be referenced in the text from this edition by paragraph and line numbers.

43. Syme, *Tacitus*, I, 206.

44. Tacitus, *Historiae*, 2.69, *Histories and Annals*, ed. and trans. C. H. Moore and J. Jackson, 4 vols., LCL (Cambridge, Mass., and London, 1963), I, 270. Subsequent quotations from both works will be referenced in the text from this edition by book and section numbers.

45. Lactantius, *De divinis institutionibus*, 1.15, PL, VI, 196.

46. On the golden and Iron Ages in Lactantius, see 368 in Arthur L. Fisher, "Lactantius' Ideas Relating Christian Truth and Christian Society," *Journal of the History of Ideas* 43 (July–September, 1982): 355–77. Lactantius's concluding celebration of Constantine (claimed by many to be an interpolation) idealizes the Christian emperor as one who rules in accordance with *vera pietas*, thus providing a model for Augustine's portrayal of Theodosius in the *City of God*. Exploiting the conventions of panegyric for the purposes of apology, Lactantius makes "Vera maiestas" dependent on "vera pietas," which in the manner of third- and fourth-century panegyric specifically includes "paterna clementia" (7.26). Yet in the end, this vision of restoration pales by comparison with the reconciliation to come, as Lactantius admonishes his reader in a final prayer: "Nemo divitiis, nemo fascibus, nemo etiam regia potestate confidat: immortalem ista non faciunt" (Let no one trust in riches, in public office, even in royal power; those things do not make a man immortal, 7.27). With this scriptural warning against placing faith in princes,

Lactantius leaves it for Augustine to work out the distinction here implied between the city of man and the city of God.

47. See Peter Brown, *Augustine of Hippo: A Biography* (London, 1967), 306.

Chapter 4

1. Augustus, *Res gestae divi Augusti,* 34, ed. and trans. (with the *History* of Paterculus) Frederick W. Shipley, LCL (Cambridge, Mass., and London, 1955), 400.

2. M. P. Charlesworth, "The Virtues of a Roman Emperor: Propaganda and the Creation of Belief," *Proceedings of the British Academy,* vol. 23 (London, 1937), 105–33. The passage quoted appears on 113–14. See also Galinsky, *Aeneas, Sicily, and Rome,* 51–54.

3. Cassiodorus, *Variarum liber duodecim,* 12.13, ed. A. J. Fridh, CC (Turnhout, 1973), xcvi, 478. A. J. Carlyle remarks that, according to Cassiodorus, the king feels bound by his own *pietas* when he is not bound by anything else. See A. J. Carlyle and Sir Robert W. Carlyle, *A History of Medieval Political Theory in the West,* 6 vols. (New York, 1936), i, 171.

4. Isidore, *Etymologiarum libri XX,* 9.3.5, ed. W. Lindsay (Oxford, 1966), i, n.p. See chapter 1 for classical versions of this conjunction in Cicero's Dream of Scipio (page 10) and chapter 3 for Ovid's historical myth (page 61), and compare the conception of the divine nature held by Gregory the Great: "Deus autem noster iustus et pius est" (Indeed our God is just and pious). Gregory, *Registrum epistolarum libri xiv,* 11.31, ed. D. Norberg, CC (Turnhout, 1982), cxl A, 920.

5. Its importance is indicated, for example, in a letter on the subject of *pietas regia* written by a bishop of the Western church to Pippin the Short, who is addressed as "piissime rex." See *Epistolae merovingici et karolini aevi,* 1.7.15, ed. W. Gundlach, MGH Epp. (Berlin, 1892), iii, 457–60.

6. The phrase is common in late imperial panegyric, in the dedicatory passages of the Augustan History, and in correspondence between church and state.

7. *Epistolae merovingici et karolini aevi,* MGH Epp., iv, 504.

8. Alcuin, *Epistolae,* 50, ed. J. P. Migne, PL (Paris, 1863), c, 215, and compare the passage from Dante's *Convivio,* cited earlier, page 14. For Alcuin and his Carolingian successors, I am indebted to Walter Ullmann, *The Carolingian Renaissance and the Idea of Kingship* (London, 1969). For the entire medieval period the indispensable volumes of the Carlyles (see above, note 3) have been a constant resource.

9. Alcuin, *Epistolae,* 38, PL, c, 197C. The expression "inaestimabilis pietas" had figured in Salvian, *De gubernatione Dei,* MGH Auctores Antiqui, Ii ii ii, 45.

10. Alcuin, *Epistolae* 120, PL, c, 354C.

11. *Epistolae 50,* PL, c, 214–15.

12. Gregory, *Regulae pastoralis liber,* 2.6, ed. J. P. Migne, PL (Paris, 1896), lxxvii, 38A.

13. 1.10 and 3.28, pp. 23B and 105D.

14. Smaragdus of St. Mihiel, *Via regia,* 30, ed. J. P. Migne, PL (Paris, 1865), cii, 968B.

15. Ermoldus Nigellus, *In honorem Hludowici Christianissimi Caesaris Augusti*, 3.619 and 4.761, ed. G. H. Pertz, MGH Scriptores (Hanover, 1829), II, 501 and 515.

16. Theganus, *Vita Hludowici Imperatoris, 55*, MGH Scriptores, II, 602.

17. 49, p. 601.

18. 44, p. 600.

19. *Vita Hludowici Imperatoris, 55*, MGH Scriptores, II, 641, and see also 42, p. 631. This anonymous life has been translated by Allen Cabaniss, *Son of Charlemagne: A Contemporary Life of Louis the Pious* (Syracuse, N.Y., 1961). In his introduction, Cabaniss remarks that the cognomen "the Pious" has been "devastating" (11) to the historical reputation of Louis. In his account of this reign, Will Durant places "the Pious" in quotation marks and adds in a note: "A time-ingrown mistranslation of *pius*, which means reverent, faithful, kind, gentle, and much besides." Durant, *The Age of Faith*, volume 4 in *The Story of Civilization* (New York, 1950), 472.

20. *Vita Hludowici Imperatoris, 56*, p. 642.

21. 62, p. 646.

22. Nithard, *Nithardi historiarum libri IV*, 1.7, MGH Scriptores, II, 654.

23. The phrase is interchangeable with "solita clementia," *Annalium Bertinianorum liber*, 834, MGH Scriptores, I, 428.

24. 832, p. 425.

25. 839, p. 432.

26. Sedulius Scotus, *Liber de rectoribus christianis*, 13, ed. J. P. Migne, PL (Paris, 1864), CIII, 314C–D. Compare Jonas, who (for the benefit of Louis's son Pippin) had written: "pietas, iustitia et misericordia stabiliant regnum" (piety, justice, and mercy stabilize a kingdom). Jonas of Orleans, *Opusculum de institutione regia*, 6, ed. J. P. Migne, PL, CVI (Paris, 1864), 295D, and see also 287B.

27. 13, p. 315B. Although Sedulius goes on to acknowledge that David did not always spare his enemies, he clearly distinguishes him from Saul, described as a figure of furor who puts tyranny ahead of piety ("pietatem tyrannidi postponens," 315A).

28. Hincmar of Rheims, *Opuscula varia*, 11 ("Ad regem: De coercendo et exstirpando raptu viduarum, puellarum ac sanctimonialium"), 4, ed. J. P. Migne, PL (Paris, 1879), CXXV, 1020B–C.

29. Hincmar writes: "Regiae virtutes praecipue duae sunt, iustitia videlicet et pietas. Verumtamen in regibus plus laudatur pietas: nam iustitia per se sine pietate severa est" (There are two main royal virtues, namely justice and piety. Nevertheless, piety is more praised in kings, for justice by itself without piety is cruel). Hincmar, *Opuscula* 10 ("Ad episcopos regni"), 17, PL, CXXV, 1016–17.

30. Hincmar, *Opuscula* 1 ("De regis persona et regio ministerio"), 31, PL, CXXV, 855B.

31. Ibid., 855C–D, 856A–B.

32. Peter Damian, *Opusculum 57* ("De principis officio in coercitione improborum"), 1, ed. J. P. Migne, PL (Paris, 1867), CXLV, 820C–D.

33. Hincmar, *Opuscula varia*, 1.31, PL, CXXV, 855B. See Gregory, *Regulae pastoralis liber*, 2.6, PL, LXXVII, 37C–D, and 1 Samuel 2.

34. Peter Damian, *Opusculum 57.3*, PL, CXLV, 821D.

35. Ibid., 822D.

36. Damian later added an "alia dissertatio" that is well summarized in one

phrase: "Noli esse nimium pius" (Refuse to be too pious). Damian, *Opusculum* 57, Alia Dissertatio 1, PL, CXLV, 826A.

37. Damian, *Opusculum* 57.4 and 57.5, PL, CXLV, 823D, 825B.

38. Damian writes: "noxiae pietatis imaginem a te procul exclude, et erga populum, qui tibi commissus est, satage semper iustitiam custodire" (keep the idea of noxious piety far from you; and toward the people, who are entrusted to you, always do enough to guard justice). *Opusculum* 57.5, PL, CXLV, 825B.

39. See note 11 above. In his famous book on this subject, Ernst Kantorowicz briefly mentions *pietas*. Kantorowicz, *The King's Two Bodies: A Study in Medieval Political Theology* (Princeton, 1957), 108 and note 61; see also 240–43. Taken as guardian of *iustitia, pietas* is part of the iconography of kingship, as Kantorowicz points to the evidence of a church window displaying these complementary qualities of rule (114). Evidence that this conjunction endures well into the Renaissance is presented by Victor E. Graham and W. McAllister Johnson in their excellent discussion of the *impresa* of the French king Charles IX. See Graham and Johnson, *Estienne Jodelle: Le recueil des inscriptions* (Toronto, 1972), 26–28.

40. John of Salisbury, *Polycraticus*, 5.10, *Opera omnia*, III, 306. See Lucan, *De bello civili*, 8.493–94.

41. John of Salisbury, *Polycraticus*, 4.8, *Opera omnia*, III, 246.

42. A still thoughtful discussion is provided by Johannes Althusius, *Politica*, 19.25, facsimile reprint of the 1614 edition (1961), 338. In the introduction to his translation of Althusius, Frederick S. Carney observes that political life for Althusius is "characterized by piety and justice. . . . He repeatedly asserts that piety is required by the first table of the Decalogue and justice by the second." *The Politics of Johannes Althusius,* translated with an introduction by Frederick S. Carney (Boston, 1964), xix.

43. Vincent de Beauvais, *Speculum quadruplex,* facsimile reprint of 1624 edition, 4 vols. (Graz, Austria, 1964–65), IV, 69.

44. Ibid., IV, 1255.

45. Salvian, *De gubernatione Dei,* 1.5, MGH Auctores Antiqui Ii ii, II, 8. Translations from Salvian are by Jeremiah F. O'Sullivan.

46. Vincent de Beauvais, *Speculum,* IV, 674. The phrases describing Constantine in the encyclopedia derive from Latin translations of Eusebius. In eulogizing Constantine, the Greek bishop emphasizes the Christian emperor's place in history by adapting the historical pattern of Roman panegyric to redemptive theology; the pagan past is superseded in the reign of Constantine by a pious present that will extend into the future. Eusebius, *De laudibus Constantini,* 10, ed. J. P. Migne, PG (Paris, 1857), XX, 1373. In his later account of Constantine's rise to power in the *Ecclesiastical History,* Eusebius develops this vision of history to reflect the contrast between emperor and tyrant, between the piety of the victorious Constantine and the impiety of his vanquished enemies. Still more influential in the later legend of the first Christian emperor is the bishop's panegyrical biography, which identifies εὐσέβεια as the imperial virtue above all others and Constantine as its supreme representative. Eusebius, *De vita Constantini,* 5.75, PG, XX, 1229.

47. Cassiodorus, *Historia ecclesiastica tripartita,* 1.1, *Corpus Scriptorum Ecclesiasticorum Latinorum* (Vienna, 1952), LXXI, 5, 8. The translation renders the Greek εὐσέβεια, which has a long life as the essential virtue of the monarch in the political

writing of the Eastern Empire. For comment and references, see Cyril Mango, *Byzantium: The Empire of New Rome* (New York, 1980), 219. For later reflection of the translated phrase in the Latin West, see Sedulius Scotus, *Liber de rectoribus christianis*, 18, PL, CIII, 327A.

48. It should be pointed out that Theodosius was not the first emperor to be thus accused, nor Ambrose the first to define the governmental obligations of *pietas* by direct criticism of a reigning emperor. Earlier in the fourth century Hilary of Poitiers had issued a warning against the contagion of Arianism to Constantine's imperial son Constantius. Addressing him as "piissime imperator," Hilary appeals directly to the ruler's *pietas* on behalf of the orthodox party, warning that Arianism will be taken as a sure sign of *impietas*. When the letter proved useless and Constantius affirmed his favor to the Arians, Hilary responded by denying to Constantius the preeminent imperial virtue. Now addressing him not as "piissime" but as "omnium crudelium crudelissime," Hilary conjures with the names of Nero, Decius, and Maximinus in defining the *impietas* of the imperial Antichrist. The price for this assertion of ecclesiastical prerogative was four years of exile. See Hilary, "Ad Constantium Augustum" and "Contra Constantium Imperatorem," ed. J. P. Migne, PL (Paris, 1879), X, 563D and 585A.

49. Ambrose, *Epistolarum classis I, 51, Opera*, PL, XVI, 1210C. See also the account of David's "agon pietatis" in Ambrose, *De apologia prophetae David ad Theodosium Augustum*, where David's sins are emphasized in order to highlight his repentance. Here Ambrose situates David between two figures of *impietas*, his son Absalom and Cain. Ambrose, *De apologia prophetae David ad Theodosium Augustum*, 6, ed., Pierre Hadot, trans. Marius Cordier (Paris, 1977), 78. On the importance of the letter to Theodosius ("a milestone on the road to Canossa"), see W. H. C. Frend, *The Rise of Christianity* (Philadelphia, 1984), 625.

50. 51, p. 1212D.

51. 61, p. 1238C.

52. See, for example, the correspondence of Pope Leo I, who forthrightly proclaims imperial responsibility to the grandson and namesake of Theodosius: "Siquidem praeter imperiales et publicas curas, piissimam sollicitudinem Christianae religionis habetis, ne scilicet in populo Dei aut schismata, aut haereses, aut ulla scandala convalescant" (Indeed, beyond your imperial and public responsibilities, the most pious care of the Christian religion is yours, to prevent schisms, heresies, and any scandals from gaining strength among the people of God). Although the phrases are deferential, Leo is obviously determined to align the imperial authority behind the orthodoxy of Nicaea (and, in later correspondence, of Chalcedon). By doing so he will be combating what he views as the "furor et impietas caeca" of theological dissent. See Leo I, *Epistolae*, 24, ed. J. P. Migne, PL (Paris, 1881), LIV, 735B, and 156, p. 1129B–C.

53. See Gelasius, *Epistolae et decreta*, Epistola 8, ed. J. P. Migne, PL (Paris, 1862), LIX, 42.

54. Gregory I, *Registrum epistolarum libri XIV*, 1, 24, CC, CXL, 30. This was a favorite comparison with Gregory, whose *Moralia* shows the Samaritan healing the injured man with the wine of *iustitia* and the oil of *pietas*. See chapter 2, note 58. On the importance of this distinction in Gregory's theology, see Carole Straw, *Gregory the Great: Perfection in Imperfection* (Berkeley and Los Angeles, 1988), 173–78.

55. See Gregory I, *Registrum epistolarum libri XIV*, 5.42, p. 327.

56. 5.37, p. 308.

57. Gregory II, Epistola 12, *Epistolae et canones*, ed. J. P. Migne, PL (Paris, 1863), LXXXIX, 518B.

58. Nicholas I, *Epistolae et decreta*, 86, ed. J. P. Migne, PL (Paris, 1880), CXIX, 932C. On this letter, see Ullmann, *The Carolingian Renaissance and the Idea of Kingship*, 72.

59. Nicholas I, *Epistolae et decreta*, 931C.

60. Ibid., 944A.

61. Ibid., 934–35.

62. *Le liber pontificalis*, ed. L'Abbé L. Duchesne, 3 vols. (Paris, 1955), II, 7.

63. Leo III, *Epistolae . . . ad Imperatorem Carolum missae*, 4, ed. J. P. Migne, PL (Paris, 1862), XCVIII, 529A–B.

64. 5, p. 532A. See also 4, p. 528B.

65. Already in the ninth century, for example, Hincmar of Rheims develops the Gelasian theory of the two powers to expound clerical authority and remind the king of his duty, *cura subiectorum*. Hincmar, *Opuscula* 9 ("Ad proceres regni, pro institutione Carolomanni Regis"), 5, PL, CXXV, 995C–D. Contemporaneously, the letters of Gelasius to Anastasius and Leo to Theodosius II cited above were published in the artful collection of genuine, altered, and forged documents now known as the False Decretals or Pseudo-Isidore, thus lending their views of *pietas regia* the aura of legal authority. The letters are preceded in the False Decretals by a gathering of canons from various church councils, most significantly where relations with the secular power are concerned, the Councils of Toledo. As now revived to address the concerns of the ninth century, the canonical point is that the church holds the power to punish not only rebellious people but also rebellious kings. Royal obligations are thus clearly spelled out and the penalty for neglect is specified as excommunication.

66. Gregory VII, *Monumenta gregoriana*, 2.49, ed. Philipp Jaffé, reprinted (Darmstadt, 1964), 164.

67. 4.2, p. 243. On the context, see Walter Ullmann, *The Growth of Papal Government in the Middle Ages*, 2d edition (London, 1962), 262–309; Uta-Renate Blumenthal, *The Investiture Controversy: Church and Monarchy from the Ninth to the Twelfth Century* (Philadelphia, 1988), especially 106–34. For remarks on this specific passage, see Carlyle and Carlyle, *A History of Medieval Political Theory in the West*, IV, 187–91. The passage is quoted at the foot of 189.

68. Manegold, *Ad Gebehardum liber*, 30, ed. K. Francke, MGH Libelli de Lite (Hanover, 1891), I, 365.

69. Henry IV, *Epistolae*, 436, ed. D. von Gladiss, MGH Diplomatum Regum et Imperatorum Germaniae (Weimar, 1952), VI, ii, 584.

70. Innocent III, *Opera omnia*, ed. J. P. Migne, PL, CCXIV–CCXVII. See, for example, *Prima collectio decretalium*, Titulus II ("Quod sacerdotium maius sit regno"), CCXVI, 1179–86, especially 1184A.

71. Innocent III, *Regestorum sive epistolarum liber XII*, 10.69, PL, CCXV, 1167B–C.

72. Innocent III, *Registrum de negotio romani imperii*, PL, CCXVI, 1163B.

73. As Paul Johnson has observed: "The Christian society of the ninth century, say, had been an entity. There was then no such thing as a 'clerical world' and a

'secular world.' The Gregorian reforms had brought the idea of the secular state into existence by stripping the ruler of his sacerdotal functions." Paul Johnson, *A History of Christianity* (New York, 1976), 215.

74. Innocent III, *Registrum,* PL, ccxvi, 1162D.

75. Julius Capitolinus, *Antoninus Pius,* 13, *Scriptores historiae augustae,* ed. and trans. David Magie, LCL (Cambridge, Mass., and London, 1954), 3 vols., i, 130. Although nothing is known about Capitolinus or any of the other putative authors of this history, its value as a source of information about the lives of the various emperors is generally acknowledged.

76. Orosius, *Historiarum adversum paganos libri VII,* 7.14, ed. C. Zangemeister (Hildesheim, 1967), 469.

77. Vincent de Beauvais, *Speculum,* iv, 400. See John of Salisbury, *Polycraticus,* 8.19, *Opera omnia,* iv, 330.

78. In the Carolingian period this is already evident in the political writing of Sedulius Scotus, who characteristically identifies his ideal of the king with Antoninus Pius. See note 26 above. Arguing that heavenly reward is especially appropriate for those kings who secure the peace of the church ("ac de pace et securitate pia solertia pertractat ecclesiastica"), Sedulius explains that this obligation proceeds from the authority that kings have been granted by God to regulate ecclesiastical affairs: it is by the rule of the *pius rector* that *serenitas pacis* is guaranteed to the church. Sedulius thus anticipates the arguments of the pro-imperial writers of the investiture controversy. Sedulius Scotus, *Liber de rectoribus christianis,* 19, PL, ciii, 328D.

79. See Carlyle and Carlyle, *A History of Medieval Political Theory in the West,* iv, 242–49.

80. *Liber de unitate ecclesiae conservanda,* 1.6, ed. W. Schwenkenbecher, MGH Libelli de lite, ii, 192.

81. 1.7, p. 193.

82. 1.8, p. 219.

83. Dante, *De monarchia,* 1.11, *Le Opere di Dante Alighieri,* 346. In the words of an eminent historian: "The problem of the fourteenth century was how to restore tranquillity to the distracted and demoralised fragments of what had lately been Christendom." F. J. C. Hearnshaw, *The Social and Political Ideas of Some Great Medieval Thinkers,* reprinted (New York, 1950), 195.

84. William of Ockham, *Octo quaestiones de potestate papae,* 5, *Opera politica,* ed. J. G. Sikes, 3 vols. (Manchester, 1940), i, 109; John Wycliffe, *Tractatus de potestate papae,* 12, ed. Johann Loserth for the Wyclif Society, reprinted (New York, 1966), 379.

85. Dante, *De monarchia,* 2.5, *Opere,* 354.

86. See, for example, Jean of Paris on the donation of Constantine, *De potestate regia et papali,* 21, *Jean de Paris et l'écclésiologie du XIIIe siècle,* ed. Dom Jean Leclercq (Paris, 1942), 245, and compare the comments of Wycliffe, *Tractatus de potestate papae,* 10, p. 227.

87. Dante, *De monarchia,* 3.3, *Opere,* 365.

88. Marsilius of Padua, *Defensor pacis,* 2.23.7, ed. C. W. Previté-Orton (Cambridge, 1928), 364. The translation is by Alan Gewirth.

89. 2.25.17, 2.26.14, 2.26.9, pp. 394, 414, 405.

90. 2.26.13, p. 413.

91. 2.22.20, p. 358.

92. Aristotle, *Ethics*, 5, quoted from Thomas Aquinas, *Ethicorum Aristotelis ad Nicomachum expositio*, ed. Raymundi M. Spiazzi (Rome, 1949), 246.

93. Aquinas, *De regimine principum*, ed. Joseph Mathis, 2d edition revised (Rome, 1948), especially book 1.

94. Jean of Paris, *De potestate regia et papali*, 17, p. 225.

95. Ibid. The translation is by Arthur P. Monahan.

96. 18, p. 229.

97. Pierre Dubois, *De recuperatione terre sancte*, 3, ed. Angelo Diotti (Florence, 1977), 119–20.

98. 64, p. 183.

99. Marsilius, *Defensor pacis*, 1.14, p. 61.

100. Dubois, *De recuperatione terre sancte*, 64, p. 183.

101. Ockham, *Opus nonaginta dierum*, 24, *Opera politica*, II, 479. The proviso of Arthur McGrade should be kept in mind here: "Ockham's involvement in political issues was complex, for he acted and wrote at many levels of concreteness and abstraction, passion and reflection, individuality and group loyalty." McGrade, *The Political Thought of William of Ockham: Personal and Institutional Principles* (Cambridge, 1974), 43.

102. Ockham, *Tractatus contra Benedictum*, 16, *Opera politica*, III, 211.

103. Ockham, *An princeps pro suo succursu*, 8, *Opera politica*, revised edition (Manchester, 1974), I, 256–57.

104. Ockham, *Dialogus de imperio et pontificia potestate*, 3.1.2.3, *Opera plurima*, facsimile reprint of the 1494–96 Lyons edition (London, 1962), I, 232.

105. 3.2.1.20, p. 200.

106. It may be observed, for example, how traditional is the vocabulary of Dante's portrait of Albert I in *Purgatorio* 6.106–17. Dante's characterization is achieved by negating in terms the same in Italian as in Latin the image of the *pius princeps*. This image depends on the association of *cura* and *pietà* to describe the obligations of prince to people, as the poet adapts the traditional vocabulary to his own critique of the secular ruler. In neglecting the obligations expressed by these terms, the German "uom sanza cura" attracts to himself the adjective "crudel," the antithesis of *pietà* and a code word for tyranny. Seen against the background of the Latin mirrors for magistrates, this portrait of Albert is that of a man failing the essential requirements of his office.

107. Dante, *De monarchia*, 1.11, *Opera*, 346.

108. John Wycliffe, *Tractatus de officio regis*, 7, ed. Alfred W. Pollard and Charles Sayle for the Wyclif Society (London, 1887), 195.

109. The long connection between the Latin words should be evident from various passages cited in each of the three sections above.

110. Marcus Aurelius quoted in Vulcacius Gallicanus, *Avidius Cassius*, 11, *Scriptores historiae augustae*, LCL, I, 254–56. See note 75 above.

111. In his praise of Julian, Ammianus calls him "clemens ut Antoninus." Ammianus Marcellinus, *Rerum gestarum libri qui supersunt*, 16.1.4, ed. and trans. John C. Rolfe, LCL, 3 vols. (Cambridge, Mass., and London, 1986), I, 202. The idea

is frequently repeated, perhaps most succinctly by the fourth-century historian Eutropius: "Pius propter clementiam dictus est" (He is called Pius on account of his clemency). Eutropius, *Eutropii breviarum historiae romanae*, 8.8, ed. C. G. Baumgarten-Crusius, rev. H. R. Dietsch (Leipzig, 1883), 57.

112. The lives dedicated to Constantine in the *Augustan History* refer to him almost interchangeably as *tua pietas* and *tua clementia*, and on occasion he is addressed as "Clementiae ac Pietati tuae." See Aelius Lampridius, *Severus Alexander*, 65, *Scriptores historiae augustae*, LCL, II, 308. Later, what is said of God in 2 Chronicles 30.9 ("pius enim et clemens est Dominus Deus vester") is readily applied to a long list of rulers. In Cardinal Humbert's *Adversus simoniacos* of 1057, for example, quotation of the biblical passage leads to affirmation of the Augustinian contrast between David and Jeroboam. See Humbert, *Adversus simoniacos libri tres*, 3.16, ed. J. P. Migne, PL (Paris, 1882), CXLIII, 1165C.

113. Claudian, *De quarto consulatu Honorii Augusti*, 276–77, LCL, I, 306.

114. Seneca, *De clementia*, 1.2.3, *Moral Essays*, ed. and trans. John W. Basore, LCL, 3 vols. (Cambridge, Mass., and London, 1975), I, 364. On the importance of this work in the English Renaissance, with specific reference to Elyot, see Howard Erskine-Hill, *The Augustan Idea in English Literature* (London, 1983), 56.

115. John Gower, *Miroir de l'homme*, 23053–54, *The Complete Works of John Gower*, ed. G. C. Macaulay, 4 vols. (Oxford, 1899), I, 254.

116. The fourteenth-century French translation of Aegidius Romanus's Latin *De regimine principum*, for example, takes *débonnaireté* to render *pietas* as a monarchical ideal. See Aegidius Romanus, *Li livres du gouvernement des rois* 21.28, ed. Samuel Paul Molenaer, reprinted (New York, 1966), 83–95. Also, *débonnaireté* commonly appears in passages on governance whose Latin precedents read *pietas*, as for example Robert de Blois's *L'enseignement des princes*, 1159–62, in John Howard Fox, *Robert de Blois, son oeuvre didactique et narrative* (Paris, 1950), 126. See note 126 below.

117. Gower, *Confessio Amantis*, 7.10, III, *Complete Works*, 233. Subsequent quotations from the poem are cited from this chapter and parenthetically referenced by page from this edition. On Gower's debt to Cassiodorus, see Maria Wickert, *Studies in John Gower*, trans. Robert J. Meindl (Washington, D.C., 1981), 139, 159–60; and John H. Fisher, *John Gower: Moral Philosopher and Friend of Chaucer* (New York, 1964), especially 203, 360.

118. Thomas Hoccleve, *The Regiment of Princes*, 473, *Hoccleve's Works*, ed. Frederick J. Furnivall, The Early English Text Society, extra series, vol. 72 (London, 1897), 119. Subsequent quotations are parenthetically indicated by stanza number from this edition.

119. Sir Thomas Elyot, *The Book Named the Governor*, 2.7, ed. S. E. Lehmberg (New York, 1962), 115. All subsequent quotations are parenthetically referenced from this edition by page number.

120. Machiavelli, *Il principe*, 17, *Niccolò Machiavelli: Tutte le opere*, ed. M. Martelli, 2 vols. (Florence, 1971), 281. All subsequent citations are referenced parenthetically by chapter number. All translations from Machiavelli are by Luigi Ricci and Christian E. Detmold.

121. Praising Ferdinand for his great undertakings, Machiavelli writes in chap.

21: "per potere intraprendere maggiori imprese, servendosi sempre della religione, si volse a una pietosa crudeltà, cacciando e spogliando, el suo regno, de' Marrani: né può essere questo esemplo più miserabile né più raro" (And in order to accumulate resources for yet greater enterprises, he next turned to a policy of pious cruelty, always under the pretext of religion, and expelled the Moriscos and rid his kingdom of them: which was a most extraordinary and most pitiable example, 21). It should be pointed out that in this context, with specific reference to the history of Spain, the adjective "pietosa" here also expresses the public justification for the king's cruelty, namely religion, as Machiavelli exploits the polysemy of the Italian derivative.

122. Machiavelli, *Discorsi sopra la prima deca di Tito Livio*, 3.19, *Tutte le opere*, 225. All subsequent citations from the *Discorsi* are repeated from this edition and referenced parenthetically by book and chapter. On *pietà* in the *Discorsi*, see Harvey C. Mansfield, Jr., *Machiavelli's New Modes and Orders* (Ithaca, N.Y., 1979), 133.

123. Livy, *Ab urbe condita*, 5.25.2–3, ed. and trans, Evan T. Sage and Alfred Schlesinger, LCL (Cambridge, Mass., and London, 1988), 13 vols., III, 84–86.

124. The political significance of *reverenza* is accurately defined by Machiavelli's near contemporary Francesco Guicciardini: "nessuna cosa offende più lo animo di uno superiore, che el parergli che non gli sia avuto el rispetto o reverenza che guidica convenirsegli" (For nothing offends a superior more than to think he is not receiving the respect and reverence he believes his due). Guicciardini, *Ricordi* B 148, ed. Sergio Marconi (Milan, 1983), 146. Compare also Dante, *Purgatorio* 1.31–33: "vidi presso di me un veglio solo,/degno di tanta reverenza in vista/che più non dee a padre alcun figliuolo" (I saw close to me an old man alone, worthy in his looks of so great reverence that no son owes more to his father).

125. Innocent Gentillet, *Discours contre Machiavel*, "Epistre," ed. A. D'Andrea and P. O. Stewart (Florence, 1974), 4. All subsequent citations are repeated from this edition and parenthetically referenced by page number. On Machiavelli in France, see Donald R. Kelley, "Murd'rous Machiavel in France: A Post Mortem," *Political Science Quarterly* 85 (December 1970): 545–59; and Edmond M. Beame, "The Use and Abuse of Machiavelli: The Sixteenth Century French Adaptation," *Journal of the History of Ideas* 43 (January–March 1982): 33–54. On Gentillet, in comparison to his more famous contemporaries, see Erskine-Hill, *The Augustan Idea in English Literature*, 58–67.

126. The phrase "clemence et debonnaireté" is especially common in the political works of Christine de Pisan. See, for example, *Le livre de la paix*, 3.1, ed. Charity Cannon Willard (The Hague, 1958), 116. In *Le livre du corps de policie*, ed. Robert H. Lucas (Geneva, 1967), this combination of ideas is accorded a brief chapter to itself, and *débonnaireté* is a leading virtue of Charles V in her panegyrical biography. See Christine de Pisan, *Le livre des fais et bonnes meurs du sage Roy Charles V*, 2 vols., ed. S. Solante (Paris, 1936–40), I, 69.

127. In one passage Gentillet comes close to defining the French *piété* in the manner of Latin *pietas*: "pieté que nous devons tous avoir envers nostre patrie, nos parens et amis" (piety which we all owe toward our country, our parents, and friends, 230). In actual usage, however, the word functions as a synonym for *religion*.

128. In the words of the French humanist Guillaume Budé: "les vertuz royales

doibent etres presque semblables aux vertuz heroiques" (the royal virtues ought to be almost the same as the heroic virtues). Budé, *De l'institutione du prince* (Paris, 1547), 196.

Chapter 5

1. The categories are those of Hallett Smith, *Elizabethan Poetry* (Cambridge, Mass., 1952). See also Paul J. Alpers, "Mode in Narrative Poetry," *To Tell a Story: Narrative Theory and Practice* (Los Angeles, 1973), 23–56.

2. See two essays by Julia Kristeva, "The Father, Love, and Banishment" and "Motherhood According to Giovanni Bellini," both collected in *Desire in Language* (New York, 1980), 148–58 and 237–70. Kristeva's assertion that "*To love* is to survive paternal meaning" (150) seems very much to the point of this chapter. See also, with specific reference to Aeneas and Dido in Renaissance drama, Barbara Bono, *Literary Transvaluation: From Vergilian Epic to Shakespearean Tragicomedy* (Berkeley and Los Angeles, 1984), 92–97, 107–16, 129–37.

3. See Ascoli, *Ariosto's Bitter Harmony*, 289; John M. Fyler, *Chaucer and Ovid* (New Haven, 1979), 33–39; Kallendorf, *In Praise of Aeneas*, 58–76.

4. See Boccaccio, *Genealogiae deorum gentilium liber XIV*, 14.13, *Boccaccio in Defence of Poetry*, ed. Jeremiah Reedy (Toronto, 1978), 59; *De mulieribus claris*, 42, *Tutte le opere di Giovanni Boccaccio*, 12 vols., ed. Vittore Branca (Milan, 1964–83), x, 168. On Penelope as feminine model of *pietas*, see Propertius, *Elegies*, 3.13, where "pia Penelope" joins "fida Evadne" to express marital fidelity in contrast to the satirized "avidis . . . puellis" of contemporary Rome.

5. Boccaccio, *Elegia di Madonna Fiammetta*, in *Opere di Giovanni Boccaccio*, ed. Cesare Segre, 5th edition (Milan, 1975), 1068. All subsequent citations will be repeated from this edition and referenced parenthetically by page numbers. The translations are adapted from Edward Hutton's revision of the Renaissance translation by Bartholomew Yong. For discussion with emphases different from mine, see Robert Hollander, *Boccaccio's Two Venuses* (New York, 1977), 40–49; Thomas G. Bergin, *Boccaccio* (New York, 1981), 168–80, and Janet Levarie Smarr, *Boccaccio and Fiammetta: The Narrator as Lover* (Urbana, 1986), 129–48.

6. See Ovid, *Metamorphoses* 10.331–33, LCL, II, 86–88. For the importance of *pietas* in the narrative, see the commentary in *Ovid's Metamorphoses Books 6–10*, ed. with introduction and commentary by William S. Anderson (Norman, Okla., 1972), 511–12. For comparison, see *Heroides* 4.129–34, where Phaedra addresses to Hippolytus the contemptuous phrase "ista vetus pietas" as a way of dismissing any claim on this virtue as impossibly out of date.

7. On the Senecan background, see Mario Serafini, "Le tragedie di Seneca nella Fiammetta di Giovanni Boccaccio," *Giornale Storico della Letteratura Italiana* 126 (1949): 95–105.

8. The adjective used to describe Myrrha (1067) has Ovidian authority, but comes more immediately from Dante, who refers in his seventh epistle to "Myrrha scelesta et impia" (Myrrha wicked and impious) and makes her an exemplum of

deceit in *Inferno* 30: "Quell'è l'anima antica/di Mirra scellerata, che divenne/al padre, fuor del dritto amore, amica" (That is the ancient spirit of infamous Myrrha, who became loving of her father beyond rightful love). Dante: *Epistolae, 7.7, Tutte le opere di Dante Alighieri*, 411; *Inferno*, 30.37–39.

9. This in turn creates a problem for Boccaccio's readers and interpreters. Janet Smarr comments: "Yet intent on creating and nourishing her own hell, [Fiammetta] wants to arouse the pity of others not in order to console herself but in order to increase her grief, to justify her own self-pity." Smarr, *Boccaccio and Fiammetta*, 132.

10. Notice that when Fiammetta recasts Dido's curse as part of her meditation on suicide, she denies the comparisons that Dido affirms. Her Aeneas is not an oak, not a stone; he was not nursed by a tigress, does not have a heart of steel (1049). This is all the more striking, as it contrasts with other Renaissance adaptations of Dido's curse, including an instance in Sannazaro's *Arcadia* where Dido's words are echoed by the lovesick male Carino in his contemplation of suicide. Sannazaro, *Arcadia*, Prosa 8, *Opere di Iacopo Sannazaro*, ed. Enrico Carrara (Turin, 1963), 125. And see note 25 below.

11. Ovid, *Metamorphoses* 10.345, 366, LCL, II, 88, 90.

12. The vision is adapted from Seneca, *Hippolytus*, 483–564, *Tragedies*, I, 356–60.

13. In Seneca, Hippolytus names "femina" as "dux malorum" (559). On this passage, see Smarr, *Boccaccio and Fiammetta*, 138, and observe that the original version of the passage from Seneca is effectively restored in the antifeminist complaints of Renaissance pastoral.

14. This phrase from the Yong–Hutton version well indicates the difficulties posed to the English translator by *pietà*. Boccaccio, *Amorous Fiammetta*, trans. Bartholomew Yong, revised Edward Hutton (London, 1952), 353.

15. The assumption of some special, usually religious, affinity between pietas and rural life is explicit in Mantuan's sixth eclogue, which contrasts city and country in a passage that begins: "nostra etiam pietas pietate potentior urbis" (our piety is still more powerful than the piety of the city). The idea is often repeated. Pope observes that "an Air of piety to the Gods should shine thro' the [pastoral] Poem." William Cowper affirms this view when he announces the intention of his own "descriptions . . . from Nature": "To discountenance the modern enthusiasm after a London Life, and to recommend rural ease and leisure as friendly to the cause of piety and virtue." Although echoes of this view are still heard, more common is H. L. Mencken's satiric type of "the pious husbandman," who survives (for example) in John Updike's description of Christmas dinner in the country: "served up in an atmosphere heavy with barnyard innuendo as well as lugubrious piety." See Baptista Mantuanus, *Eclogues*, 6.193, *The Eclogues of Baptista Mantuanus*, ed. Wilfred P. Mustard (Baltimore, 1911), 94; Alexander Pope, "A Discourse on Pastoral Poetry," *Pastoral Poetry and An Essay on Criticism*, ed. E. Audra and Aubrey Williams, vol. 1 of *The Poems of Alexander Pope*, ed. John Butt (New Haven, 1961), 26; William Cowper, *The Letters and Prose Writings of William Cowper*, ed. James King and Charles Ryskamp, 2 vols. (Oxford, 1979–81), II, 285; H. L. Mencken, "The Husbandman," *The American Scene: A Reader*, ed. Huntington Cairns (New York, 1965), 47; John Updike, *Roger's Version* (New York, 1986), 92.

16. Petrarch, *Bucolicum Carmen*, 5, ed. and trans. Thomas G. Bergin (New

Haven, 1974). For comparison, see Ronsard's observation that "Les Rois et les Pasteurs ont mesme estat de vivre" (Kings and shepherds have the same manner of life). Ronsard, Dedication to *Les eclogues et mascarades* in *Oeuvres complètes,* ed. Gustave Cohen, Bibliothèque de la Pléiade, 2 vols. (Paris, 1950), I, 915. It may be added that Ronsard introduces his *Bergerie* with verses emphasizing the analogy between shepherd and king: "David, d'un simple pastre et de bas sang issu/Par les Prophetes oingt, au thrône fut receu" (David, from a simple shepherd and humble birth, was by the prophets consecrated and came to the throne). On the political uses of Renaissance pastoral, see chapter 1 in Margaret M. McGowan, *Ideal Forms in the Age of Ronsard* (Berkeley and Los Angeles, 1985), especially 35–39; and chapter 2 in Patterson, *Pastoral and Ideology,* especially 85–92, 131–32.

17. Mantuan, *Eclogues,* 4.150–51, 181, 207–10, *The Eclogues of Baptista Mantuanus,* 81–83.

18. It may be noted that Augustine acknowledges but then quickly excuses David's passion in his tract on Christian doctrine, and in book 17 of the *City of God* he explains that whatever sins David was guilty of, his *pietas* overcame them ("delicta eius tanta pietate superata sunt"). See Augustine: *De doctrina christiana,* 3.21, ed. Joseph Martin, CC (Turnhout, 1962), XXXII, 96; *De civitate Dei,* 17.20, LCL, V, 338. The association of David with pietas is unusually durable, lasting into the twentieth century. Joseph Heller's biblical king even makes a point of disavowing it: "I've led a full, long life, haven't I? You can look it up. Samuel I and II. Kings. Chronicles also, but that's a prissy whitewash in which the juiciest parts of my life are discarded as unimportant or unworthy. Therefore, I hate Chronicles. In Chronicles I am a pious bore, as dull as dishwater and as preachy and insipid as that self-righteous Joan of Arc, and God knows I was never anything like that." Here the typical modern associations—"preachy," "prissy," "dull," "self-righteous"—are set against the "juiciest parts" of the David legend that make him an appropriate focus for the conflict of love and pietas in the literature of the sixteenth century. See Heller, *God Knows* (New York, 1984), 13.

19. Remy Belleau, "Les Amours de David et de Bersabee," *La bergerie,* in *Oeuvres complètes de Remy Belleau,* ed. A. Gouverneur, 3 vols. (Paris, 1867), II, 344–45. Subsequent references will be repeated from this edition and, because the lines are not numbered, referenced by page.

20. As lust is an important but a temporary distraction for Augustine's David, so embarrassed medieval commentators follow the bishop's lead, usually passing quickly from passion to penitence, from Bathsheba to Nathan, even from 2 Samuel to Psalm 50. In his exposition of this psalm, for example, Cassiodorus so readily loses sight of the specific sin involved that he can gloss "humiliatum" in verse 19 by taking pride rather than lust as the fault. Cassiodorus, *Expositio Psalmorum* 50.19, ed. M. Adriaen, CC (Turnhout, 1958), XCVII, 467.

21. She appears just prior to Dido in canto 5 of the *Inferno,* is also one of the figures mentioned by Fiammetta, and her crime of incest is described with horror in Boccaccio's *De mulieribus claris.*

22. See, for example, Augustine, *De civitate Dei,* 16.30, LCL, V, 144, where Sodom is called *civitas impia,* an expression elsewhere (e.g., 17.16) used to designate Babylon.

23. Smith, *Elizabethan Poetry*, 8.

24. *La bergerie* includes a version of the Ixion myth, where "amour ambitieux" specifically takes the form of "impiété." See "L'amour ambitieux d'Ixion," *La bergerie*, in *Oeuvres complètes*, II, 207.

25. See diversely Dante, *Rime*, 80, ed. and trans. Patrick S. Diehl (Princeton, 1979), 182–87; Ronsard, *Amours de Marie*, 14, *Oeuvres complètes*, I, 125 (in his commentary on this poem, Belleau makes a note of the source: "Ce que Virgile en son quatriesme livre des Aeneides a imité, feignant ainse parler Didon courroucée, contre Aenee, lequel secrettement la voiloit abandonner"); DuBellay, *Olive*, 91, *Oeuvres poétiques*, ed. Henri Chamard (Paris, 1982), I, 105 (which may be compared to the poet's translation of Vergil in *Le quatriesme livre de l'Enéide de Vergile*, 651–54, *Oeuvres poétiques* [Paris, 1931] VI, 282); Samuel Daniel, *To Delia*, 18, *Poems and a Defence of Ryme*, ed. Arthur Colby Sprague (Cambridge, Mass., 1930), 19; Spenser, *Amoretti 56*, *Spenser's Minor Poems*, ed. E. de Selincourt, 3 vols. (Oxford, 1910), I, 399; Sidney, *Astrophil and Stella*, 44, *The Poems of Sir Philip Sidney*, ed. William A. Ringler, Jr. (Oxford, 1962), 186–87. All subsequent citations are repeated from these editions and referenced by poem and line numbers.

26. Ronsard, *Amours de Marie*, II ("Chanson"), *Les oeuvres de Pierre Ronsard*, ed. Isidore Silver, 8 vols. (Chicago, 1966), II, 29.

27. Spenser, *Amoretti*, 10.5.

28. Cino da Pistoia, "Mille volte richiamo 'l di mercede," 30, *Le rime di Cino da Pistoia*, ed. Guido Zaccagnini (Geneva, 1925), 227. On the key terms as they derive from Provençal, see Glynnis M. Cropp, *Le vocabulaire courtois des troubadours de l'époque classique* (Geneva, 1975), 174–77.

29. Gianni Alfani, "Donne, la donna mia ha d'un disdegno," 8–10, *Poeti del Duecento*, ed. Gianfranco Contini, 2 vols. (Milan, 1960), II, 608.

30. "In te misericordia, in te pietate,/in te magnificenza, in te s'aduna/quantunque in creatura è di bontate" (In thee is mercy, in thee pity, in thee munificence, in thee is found whatever of goodness is in any creature). Dante, *Paradiso*, 33.19–21. The range of the word in Italian is greater than in French or English, and yet it should be kept in mind that the distinction between *piété/pitié* and *piety/pity* was still incomplete in the sixteenth century. In the English sonnet cycles *pity* can translate both *pietà* and *piété*, and thus receives a dimension of its meaning from its continental sources. Thus the phrase "gracefull Pitty" in *Astrophil and Stella* 100 has religious as well as carnal significance, and even Shakespeare's phrase "Pitiful thrivers" has been understood in relation to the more explicitly religious vocabulary of sonnet 125. In his gloss on this phrase, Stephen Booth remarks: "although *Pitiful* meaning 'pious' was rare . . . , 'pity' and 'piety' were interchangeable throughout the sixteenth century." *Shakespeare's Sonnets*, edited with analytic commentary by Stephen Booth (New Haven, 1977), 427.

31. Petrarch, *Rime sparse*, 285, *Petrarch's Lyric Poems: The Rime sparse and Other Lyrics*, ed. and trans. Robert M. Durling (Cambridge, Mass., 1976), 465. All citations from Petrarch are repeated from this edition and cited by poem and line numbers. On "doppia pietate," compare Raleigh's English poem to the queen, where the phrase "double pity" is explained by the repeated rhyme of "passion" and "compassion." Raleigh, "Sir Walter Ralegh to the Queen," especially lines 8, 10, 36,

and 38. *The Poems of Sir Walter Ralegh,* ed. Agnes M. C. Latham (London, 1951), 18–19.

32. Nicholas Mann, for example, speaks of the *Rime* as being "without ultimate resolution." Mann, *Petrarch* (Oxford, 1984), 66. But see Thomas P. Roche, Jr., *Petrarch and the English Sonnet Sequences* (New York, 1989), 1–69. There is a vast literature on Petrarch's followers; where Maurice Scève is concerned, Joann DellaNeva observes: "Scève participates in a kind of scriptural exegesis of the sacred Petrarchan text and reveals new meanings behind its verses." DellaNeva, *Song and Counter-Song: Scève's Délie and Petrarch's Rime* (Lexington, Ky., 1983), 105.

33. Maurice Scève, "Non de Venus les ardentz estincelles," *The Délie of Maurice Scève,* ed. I. D. McFarlane (Cambridge, 1966), 119. The parenthetical description is from 217.2. All references will be repeated from this edition and referenced parenthetically by poem and line numbers. For comparison, see "une mère si douce" of Ronsard, *Amours de Marie,* 14.14, and note 25 above.

34. Dorothy Gabe Coleman, *Maurice Scève: Poet of Love* (Cambridge, 1975), 108.

35. On the general problem of how conventions derived from other poetic modes operate in Renaissance heroic, see Paul J. Alpers, *The Poetry of the Faerie Queene* (Princeton, 1967), 370–405.

36. Ariosto, *Orlando furioso,* 7.53–54, ed. Cesare Segre (Milan, 1976). All citations are repeated from this edition and referenced parenthetically by canto, stanza, and line numbers. All translations are by Guido Waldman.

37. This aspect of the situation is firmly grasped by Sir John Harington, whose English version renders this passage by turning the key words into rhyme: "compassion . . . passion." Harington, *Ludovico Ariosto's Orlando Furioso,* 7.12.3.5, ed. Robert McNulty (Oxford, 1972). And see this chapter, note 31. Subsequent citations from Harington's translation are repeated from this edition and referenced by canto, stanza, and line numbers.

38. Harington, *Ludovico Ariosto's Orlando Furioso,* 89. In his fine book on Ariosto, Albert Russell Ascoli considers Alcina and Logistilla as paradigmatic figures of the poem's allegory, and then goes on to argue that criticism of Ariosto tends to organize itself in accordance with this opposition. Ascoli, *Ariosto's Bitter Harmony,* 122–35. Ascoli's argument depends on, and diverges from A. Bartlett Giamatti's chapter on this episode. Giamatti, *The Earthly Paradise and the Renaissance Epic* (Princeton, 1966), 137–64.

39. The extent to which Ruggiero lives up to this definition is well remarked by one of Ariosto's earliest commentators, who takes Ruggiero as the poem's lone illustration of "inconstanza." Oratio Toscanella, *I luochi communi di tutta l'opera di Lodovico Ariosto* (Venice, 1574), unpaginated but alphabetized by topic. Compare the mention of Ruggiero's cruelty in Simon Fornari, *La spositione sopra l'Orlando furioso* (Florence, 1549), 64.

40. Tasso, *Discorsi del poema eroico,* 2, *Scritti sull'arte poetica,* ed. Ettore Mazzali, 2 vols., reprinted (Turin, 1977), I, 199.

41. 2, I, 201.

42. 3, II, 238.

43. Tasso, *Gerusalemme liberata,* 4.36.7–8, *Opere di Torquato Tasso,* ed. Bor-

tolo Tommaso Sozzi, 2 vols., 3d edition (Turin, 1974), i, 178. Subsequent citations will be from this edition and will be referenced parenthetically by canto, stanza, and line numbers. All translations are by Ralph Nash.

Chapter 6

1. Drances' description of Turnus as "rabidus" typifies the strategy. See Maphaeus Vegius, *Aeneidos XIII*, 339–43, *Maphaeus Vegius and His Thirteenth Book of the Aeneid*, ed. Anna Cox Brinton (Stanford, Calif., 1930), 72. Subsequent references are indicated parenthetically by line numbers. On the thirteenth book Kallendorf observes that "Vegio's decision to complete the *Aeneid* probably suggests that [he] felt some dissatisfaction with the moral world of the poem as he found it." Kallendorf's chapter on Vegio shows how the supplement addresses the problem of the poem's "moral ambivalence." Kallendorf, *In Praise of Aeneas*, 100–128. On the ending of the *Aeneid* itself, see especially W. R. Johnson, *Darkness Visible* (Berkeley and Los Angeles, 1976), 114–34.

2. Lodovico Dolce, *L'Achille e l'Enea* (Venice, 1571), 530. Subsequent references will be indicated parenthetically by page numbers.

3. Gavin Douglas, *Virgil's Aeneid*, 12.14.113, ed. David F. C. Coldwell for the Scottish Text Society, 4 vols. (Edinburgh and London, 1957–64), iv, 137. Subsequent citations will be referenced parenthetically by book, stanza, and line numbers.

4. Douglas, "The Comment" (on "Rewthful Ene Am I"), *The Poetical Works of Gavin Douglas*, ed. John Small, 4 vols. (Edinburgh and London, 1874), ii, 294–95.

5. Maphaeus Vegius, *Aeneidos XIII*, 99; Thomas Twyne, *The Thirteenth Booke of Aeneidos supplied by Maphaeus Vegius Laudensis*, in *Maphaeus Vegius and His Thirteenth Book of the Aeneid*, 59; Douglas, *Virgil's Aeneid*, 13.2.99–100.

6. Marco Girolamo Vida, *Christiados libri sex*, 6.27–30, *The Christiad*, ed. and trans. Gertrude C. Drake and Clarence A. Forbes (Carbondale, Ill., 1978), 242. All subsequent references will be cited parenthetically by book and line numbers.

7. As reported by William of Tyre, *Historia rerum in partibus transmarinis gestarum*, 1.15, *Recueil des historiens des croisades* (Paris, 1844), i, 40. Subsequent references to this text will be indicated parenthetically by page numbers from this edition. All translations are by E. A. Babcock and A. C. Krey.

8. Turpin (or Pseudo-Turpin), *Historia Karoli Magni et Rotholandi*, 24, 33, ed. C. Meredith-Jones, Slatkine Reprints (Geneva, 1972), 202, 236.

9. This is argued in detail by Peter V. Marinelli, *Ariosto and Boiardo: The Origins of Orlando Furioso* (Columbia, Mo., 1987), 125–47.

10. The Vergilian matrix of the conclusion is perceived by Ariosto's first commentators to involve more than the struggle between Aeneas and Turnus. Oratio Toscanella, for example, compares Rodomonte to Mezentius as well as Turnus, recognizing that the Turnus problem is also the Mezentius problem. Toscanella, *Bellezze del Furioso*, 329, and see the catalogue of "tiranni atrocissimi et . . . mostri" in canto 17, where Rodomonte and Mezentius both appear.

11. A. Bartlett Giamatti, "Sfrenatura: Restraint and Release in the *Orlando Furioso*," *Ariosto 1974 in America*, ed. Aldo Scaglione (Ravenna, 1976), 31–39.

12. On this point see S. K. Heninger, Jr., "The Orgoglio Episode in *The Faerie Queene*," *English Literary History*, 26 (1959): 171–87.

13. Natalis Comes, *Mythologiae*, 6.21, Garland reprint of the 1616 Padua edition (New York, 1979), 342–44.

14. Augustine, *De civitate Dei*, 16.4, LCL, v, 26.

15. Philippe Desportes, "La mort de Rodomont," *Oeuvres de Philippe Desportes*, ed. Alfred Michiels (Paris, 1858), 339–40. Subsequent citations are repeated from this edition and referenced parenthetically by page numbers.

16. He also fights, for example, under the Gallicized Greek name of Phovère in the second book of Ronsard's unfinished *Franciade*. For all its Homeric allusions, the epic battle between Phovère and Francus is another version of the encounter between the heirs of Turnus/Mezentius and those of Aeneas.

17. On the opening phrase, note the translation of John Hoole: "Arms, and the chief I sing . . ." Hoole, *Jerusalem Delivered* in *The Works of the English Poets*, ed. Alexander Chalmers, 21 vols. (London, 1810), xxi, 405. On the significance of the Italian "capitano," see Machiavelli, *Discorsi* 1.49, *Tutte le opere*, 132.

18. Perhaps the closest parallel is in the second book of the *Franciade*, where the two opponents Francus and Phovère merge into "une horreur, une rage." After his victory, Francus kneels on the stomach of Phovère and repeatedly strikes his defeated adversary: "Trois, quatre fois de toute sa puissance" (Three, four times with all his force). Ronsard, *Oeuvres complètes*, i, 706–7.

19. Tasso, *Gerusalemme conquistata*, 23.100, ed. Luigi Bonfigli, 2 vols. (Bari, 1934), ii, 326. Subsequent citations will be repeated from this edition and referenced parenthetically by canto and line numbers.

20. Compare *Gerusalemme liberata*, 19.116–17, with *Gerusalemme conquistata*, 23.116–29. In the revision the lament of Argantes's wife is in 23.126, 5–6.

21. Tasso thus invites indictment even on the classical authority of *Aeneid* 2.717–20: "tu, genitor, cape sacra manu patriosque Penatis;/me, bello e tanto digressum et caede recenti,/attrectare nefas, donec me flumine vivo/abluero" (Father, do thou take in thy hand the sacred things and our country's household gods; for me, fresh from such a conflict and recent carnage, it were sin to handle them, until I have washed me in a running stream). Lauren Scancarelli Seem has called attention to the relevance of Antonio Possevino's *Dialogo dell'honore* for understanding Tasso's conclusion. Seem, "The Limits of Chivalry: Tasso and the End of the *Aeneid*," *Comparative Literature* 42, no. 2 (Spring 1990): 116–25.

22. Edward Fairfax, *Godfrey of Bulloigne*, 9.32.3, ed. Kathleen M. Lea and T. M. Gang (Oxford, 1981), 302.

23. The importance of *pity* in book 2 has been carefully noted by A. C. Hamilton in his edition of *The Faerie Queene* (London, 1977); the parallel phrasing of Elyot and Spenser has been remarked by James Nohrnberg. *The Analogy of The Faerie Queene* (Princeton, 1976), 383–84.

24. Spenser, *The Faerie Queene*, 1.3.7.4–5, *The Poetical Works of Edmund Spenser*, ed. J. C. Smith, 3 vols., reprinted (Oxford, 1964), ii, 32. All subsequent citations from the poem will be repeated from this edition and referenced parenthetically by book, canto, stanza, and line numbers.

25. Nohrnberg, *The Analogy of The Faerie Queene*, 385.

26. The Aristotelian distinction between disposition and passion seems to lie in

the background of this episode. See Dante's account with specific reference to pietas in chapter 1, page 14.

27. Spenser's allegorical figuration of Furor derives from *Aeneid* 1.294–96, where Vergil envisions a time when the gates of Janus will be closed and Furor bound: "Furor impius intus / saeva sedens super arma et centum vinctus aënis / post tergum nodis fremet horridus ore cruento" (within, impious Rage, sitting on savage arms, his hands fast bound behind with a hundred brazen knots, shall roar in the ghastliness of blood-stained lips). Compare *The Faerie Queene:* "And both his hands fast bound behind his backe, / And both his feet in fetters to an yron racke. // With hundred yron chaines he did him bind, / And hundred knots that did him sore constraine: / Yet his great yron teeth he still did grind, / And grimly gnash, threatning revenge in vaine" (2.4.14.8–9, 2.4.15.1–4).

28. Both readings can be found in the secondary literature: see *The Faerie Queene*, ed. A. C. Hamilton, 211; and Nohrnberg, *The Analogy of The Faerie Queene*, 382–83.

29. Chaucer, *The Knight's Tale*, 1761, *The Works of Geoffrey Chaucer*, ed. F. N. Robinson, 2d edition (Boston, 1961), 34.

30. On this passage, see Alpers, *The Poetry of the Faerie Queene*, 316–18.

31. Milton, *Paradise Lost*, 1.41–44, *The Poetical Works of John Milton*, ed. Helen Darbishire, 2 vols. (Oxford, 1952), I, 6. All subsequent citations from the poem will be repeated from this edition and referenced parenthetically by book and line numbers.

32. Stella Purce Revard, *The War in Heaven: Paradise Lost and the Tradition of Satan's Rebellion* (Ithaca, N.Y., 1980), 253.

33. John M. Steadman has argued that the relevant classical parallel is the single-handed pursuit of Hector by Achilles in *Iliad* 22. Steadman, *Epic and Tragic Structure in Paradise Lost* (Chicago, 1976), 110–12.

34. Revard, *The War in Heaven*, 304.

Chapter 7

1. Dryden, "Dedication" to the *Aeneis,* in *Works,* v, 330–31. On the contemporary context of these remarks and of Dryden's translation, see James Anderson Winn, *John Dryden and His World* (New Haven, 1987), 475–92. This splendid biography may be profitably consulted on all the works of Dryden considered below.

2. Dryden, "Preface" to *Fables Ancient and Modern,* in *The Poems of John Dryden,* ed. James Kinsley, 4 vols. (Oxford, 1958), IV, 1455.

3. Judith Sloman shows how fruitfully the *Aeneis* and the *Fables* can be discussed in relation to one another. See Sloman, *Dryden: The Poetics of Translation* (Toronto, 1985), chap. 6.

4. Dryden, "Of Heroique Plays: An Essay," prefatory to *The Conquest of Granada,* in *Works,* xi, 10. On the epic analogy, see Arthur C. Kirsch, *Dryden's Heroic Drama* (Princeton, 1965), 8–15; and Derek Hughes, *Dryden's Heroic Plays* (London, 1981), 15–21.

5. Reuben Brower, "Dryden's Epic Manner and Virgil," *PMLA* 55 (1940): 119–38.

6. See chapter 4, p. 102.

7. Dryden, "Preface" to *Tyrannick Love*, in *Works*, x, 110. All citations are referenced parenthetically from this edition. For discussion, see Kirsch, *Dryden's Heroic Drama*, 97–106; Eugene M. Waith, *The Herculean Hero in Marlowe, Chapman, Shakespeare, and Dryden* (New York, 1962), 147–49; Anne T. Barbeau, *The Intellectual Design of John Dryden's Heroic Plays* (New Haven, 1970), 94–105; Hughes, *Dryden's Heroic Plays*, 59–78. On the political topicality of the play, see Winn, *John Dryden and His World*, 200–207. On the larger context of dramatic history and performance, see Robert D. Hume, *The Development of English Drama in the Late Seventeenth Century* (Oxford, 1976), especially 192–99.

8. See the commentary of Maximillian E. Novak, *Works*, x, 391.

9. On the importance of pity in Restoration heroic plays, see Eric Rothstein, *Restoration Tragedy: Form and the Process of Change* (Madison, Wisc., 1967), 77–79.

10. Dryden, "Preface" to *Tyrannick Love*, in *Works*, x, 109.

11. See the commentary, *Works*, x, 412.

12. Dryden, *Aureng-Zebe*, 1.1.175, *The Works of John Dryden*, 18 vols, cd. Walter Scott, rev. George Saintsbury (Edinburgh, 1883), v, 209. The reader may more conveniently consult the edition of Frederick M. Link in The Regents Restoration Drama Series (Lincoln, Neb., 1971). On this play, see Kirsch, *Dryden's Heroic Drama*, 118–28; Barbeau, *The Intellectual Design of Dryden's Heroic Plays*, 126–41; George McFadden, *Dryden the Public Writer, 1660–1685* (Princeton, 1978), 183–202; and Hughes, *Dryden's Heroic Plays*, 118–49.

13. Brower, "Dryden's Epic Manner and Virgil," 127.

14. Saintsbury's note on the source is more accessible in *John Dryden: Three Plays*, Mermaid Dramabook, 5th printing (New York, 1967), 322.

15. Ovid, *Heroides* 4.133–34, and see chapter 4, note 1.

16. Dryden, "Preface" to *Don Sebastian*, in *Works*, xv, 68, and see Earl Miner's commentary on 388–89. Subsequent quotations from the preface are parenthetically referenced by page numbers. Winn judges this to be Dryden's "most complex, most mature tragedy," and finds a rich vein of reference to the recent revolution. Winn, *John Dryden and His World*, 438–42. See Derek Hughes, "Dryden's *Don Sebastian* and the Literature of Heroism," *Yearbook of English Studies* 12 (1982): 72–90; and on the political parallels, David Bywaters, "Dryden and the Revolution of 1688: Political Parallel in *Don Sebastian*," *Journal of English and Germanic Philology* 85 (1986): 346–65.

17. See the commentary, *Works*, xv, 417.

18. Dryden, *Don Sebastian*, 1.1.103, *Works*, xv, 83. All citations are repeated from this edition and referenced by act, scene, and line numbers.

19. Dryden, *Amphitryon*, 5.1.417–18, *Works*, xv, 316. All citations are repeated from this edition and referenced by act, scene, and line numbers.

20. Dryden, *Eleonora*, 368–70, *Works*, iii, 246.

21. Dryden, "The First Book of Ovid's Metamorphoses," 190–91, *Works*, iv, 381. Judith Sloman has aptly titled her chapter on *Examen Poeticum*, in which this

translation appeared, "Dryden against His Age." Sloman, *Dryden: The Poetics of Translation*, 108–24.

22. Quoted in William Haller, *The Rise of Puritanism* (New York, 1957), 224. Prynne may be a political radical, but his rhetoric—what we write is truth and piety, what our opponents write is error and profanity—is highly traditional. The attempt to identify one's own ideology with *vera pietas* has, as should be evident from earlier chapters of this book, a long history. Yet if Prynne is traditional, he is also modern in an important respect: he goes on in this same passage to use the word ironically. After calling his royalist opposition "impious," Prynne refers contemptuously to "his Majesties pious Declarations." That "impious" and "pious" have effectively the same referent is a sure sign that honorific usage is being displaced by the ironic.

23. Dryden (and Nathaniel Lee), *The Duke of Guise*, 4.2.13–14, *The Works of John Dryden*, ed. Scott, rev. Saintsbury, vii, 78. These words are spoken by the evil spirit Melanax, "a zealous, godly, canting devil," vii, 79.

24. Dryden, "Dedication" to *Annus Mirabilis*, in *Works*, i, 49; *Annus Mirabilis*, stanza 154 (lines 613–14), *Works*, i, 83.

25. See pages 228, 235–36. On the modes of Restoration poetry, see Rachel Trickett, *The Honest Muse* (Oxford, 1967), 16–26, 31–35; Earl Miner, *The Restoration Mode from Milton to Dryden* (Princeton, 1974), 288–364; Eric Rothstein, *Restoration and Eighteenth-Century Poetry* (Boston, 1981), 2–38; Margaret Ann Doody, *The Daring Muse* (Cambridge, 1985), 57–83, 97–98.

26. Dryden, *Absalom and Achitophel*, 939–1025, *Works*, ii, 33–35. This volume also contains *The Medall*. Citations from both poems are repeated from this edition and referenced in the text by line numbers. On the final speech, see Bernard Schilling, *Dryden and the Conservative Myth* (New Haven, 1961), 266–90; and Dustin Griffin, "Dryden's Charles: The Ending of *Absalom and Achitophel*," *Philological Quarterly* 57 (1978): 359–82. More generally, see chapter 4 ("Doubletalk in *Absalom and Achitophel*") in Ruth Salvaggio, *Dryden's Dualities* (Victoria, 1983), 60–78; and Steven N. Zwicker, *Politics and Language in Dryden's Poetry: The Arts of Disguise* (Princeton, 1984), 85–103.

27. Dryden, *Astraea Redux*, 191, 200, *Works*, i, 27. All subsequent references to this poem will be repeated from this edition and cited in the text by line numbers. It may be pointed out that identification of the Titans with impiety has a pedigree that may be traced at least as far back as the patristic period, when Irenaeus uses the comparison to condemn heretics. Irenaeus, *Libros quinque adversus haereses*, 2.46.1, ed. W. Wigan Harvey, 2 vols. (Ridgewood, N.J., 1965), i, 362. The further connotations of sedition as a form of insanity have, in turn, classical roots. A repeated pattern of action in Quintus Curtius Rufus's first-century life of Alexander, for example, is conspiracy against royal authority, and the vocabulary of conspiracy—*seditio, coniuratio, insidiae*—effectively defines *impietas*. Quintus Curtius Rufus, *History of Alexander*, 6.9, ed. and trans. John C. Rolfe, LCL (Cambridge, Mass., and London, 1946), 2 vols., ii, 78.

28. Although the opening lines have been very often discussed, the significance of "pious" has not usually been stressed beyond mention of its ironic juxtaposition with "Priest-craft." See, however, Anne D. Ferry, *Milton and the Miltonic Dryden* (Cambridge, Mass., 1968), 116–17.

29. Dryden, *Aureng-Zebe*, 4.1, *The Works of John Dryden*, ed. Scott, rev. Saintsbury, v, 261. See page 213 above.

30. Dryden, *Tyrannick Love*, 2.1.141–42, *Works*, x, 131.

31. On this point it is instructive to consider the sixteenth-century example of Jean Bodin, who has no trouble identifying rebellion with *impiété* and *parricide*. Jean Bodin, *Les six livres de la République*, facsimile reprint of the 1576 Lyons edition, 6 vols. (Paris, 1986), I, 74. On Bodin and Dryden, see Alan Roper, *Dryden's Poetic Kingdoms* (London, 1965), 66–74.

32. Directly on this topic, see Jerome Donnelly, "Fathers and Sons: The Normative Basis of Dryden's *Absalom and Achitophel*," *Papers on Language and Literature*, 17 (1981): 363–80; Larry Carver, "*Absalom and Achitophel* and the Father Hero," *The English Hero, 1660–1800*, ed. Robert Folkenflik (Newark, Del., 1982), 35–45; Howard D. Weinbrot, " 'Nature's Holy Bands' in *Absalom and Achitophel*: Fathers and Sons, Satire and Change," *Modern Philology* 85, no. 4 (May 1988): 373–92, reprinted in *Eighteenth-Century Satire: Essays on Text and Context from Dryden to Peter Pindar* (Cambridge, 1988), 80–99.

33. Milton, *Sonnets*, 19.10–12, *The Poetical Works of John Milton*, II, 155.

34. In general, examples of pietas in Milton and Dryden reveal that their common literary culture transcends their political differences. See Ferry, *Milton and the Miltonic Dryden*, especially 94–121.

35. Dryden, *The History of the League*, in *Works*, XVIII, 476. All citations are repeated from this edition and referenced by page numbers. For the passage from Claudian, see *De consulato Stilichonis*, 3.114–15, LCL, II, 50.

36. See Zwicker, *Politics and Language in Dryden's Poetry*, 222 n. 20.

37. Bernard Mandeville, "An Enquiry into the Origin of Moral Virtue," *The Fable of the Bees: Or, Private Vices, Publick Benefits*, ed. F. B. Kaye, 2 vols., reprinted (Oxford, 1957), I, 56.

38. For example: Cassiodorus, *Historia ecclesiastica tripartita*, 3.3, *Corpus Scriptorum Ecclesiasticorum Latinorum*, LXXI, 141; Sedulius Scotus, *Liber de rectoribus christianis*, 18, PL, CIII, 327A.

39. Dryden, *Britannia Rediviva*, 81, *Works*, III, 212. *The Hind and the Panther* is also included in this volume, which is the source of all citations from both poems, hereafter referenced parenthetically by line numbers. On the latter poem in relation to the development of Dryden's religious views, see Phillip Harth, *Contexts of Dryden's Thought* (Chicago, 1969), 245–91.

40. See the commentary on the poem by Earl Miner, *Works*, III, 456.

41. Dryden, *The Life of St. Francis Xavier*, in *Works*, XIX, 113, 144. All subsequent citations are from this text and are referenced parenthetically by page numbers.

42. Dryden, "Postscript to the Reader," appended to the *Aeneis*, in *Works*, VI, 807. Subsequent quotations are indicated parenthetically by page number.

43. Dryden, *Juvenal: Satyr VI*, 711–14, *Works*, IV, 191. Juvenal's Latin is quoted from the Delphin edition of Juvenal and Persius, ed. Ludovicus Prateus (Paris, 1684). Subsequent references to Dryden's Juvenal will be referenced parenthetically by satire and line numbers. David Hopkins has shown how helpful it is to consider Dryden's Juvenal and his Vergil together. Hopkins, *John Dryden* (Cambridge, 1986), 134–67.

44. Dryden, *Aeneis*, 3.78–81, *Works*, V, 419. All subsequent references will be to

this edition and will be cited parenthetically by book and line numbers. Dryden's translation is also conveniently available in one volume with helpful notes by Howard Clarke, ed., *Vergil's Aeneid and Fourth ("Messianic") Eclogue in the Dryden Translation* (University Park, Pa., 1989). The current surge of interest in Dryden's Vergil is also indicated by the recent publication of Taylor Corse's study of the poem, *Dryden's "Aeneid": The English Virgil* (Newark, Del., 1991), which has reached me just as this book goes to press. The text from which Dryden worked, almost exclusively, was the second edition of Charles de la Rue's Delphin Vergil. *P. Virgilii Maronis, opera, interpretatione et notis,* ed. Carolus Ruaeus (Paris, 1682). First published in Paris seven years earlier, this was a very popular edition complete, as the title indicates, with marginal *interpretatio* and ample footnotes, which sometimes influence Dryden's translation. Quotations from Vergil in this chapter are from the Delphin edition. See J. McG. Bottkol, "Dryden's Latin Scholarship," *Modern Philology* 40 (February 1943): 241–54, and Arvid Losnes, "Dryden's *Aeneis* and the Delphin *Virgil*," *The Hidden Sense and Other Essays* (Oslo, 1963), 113–57. I am generally indebted to William Frost's commentary in volume VI of Dryden's *Works*, to his earlier book *Dryden and the Art of Translation* (New Haven, 1955), and to the essays gathered in *John Dryden: Dramatist, Satirist, Translator* (New York, 1988). For one translator's view of another, see Robert Fitzgerald, "Dryden's *Aeneid*," *Arion* 2 (1963): 17–31. To see just how forceful Dryden's rendering of this passage is, and how much is contributed by the word "impious," compare Wordsworth: "Breaking through sacred laws without remorse, / Slew Polydore, and seized the gold by force, / What mischief to poor mortals has not thirst / Of gold created! appetite accurs'd!" And William Morris: "He brake all right, slew Polydore, and all the gold he got / Perforce: O: thou gold-hunger cursed, and whither driv'st thou not / The hearts of men?" Wordsworth, Translations of Virgil's *Aeneid*, 3, 77–80, *The Poetical Works of William Wordsworth*, IV, 338; Morris, *The Aeneids of Virgil*, 3, 55–57, *The Collected Works of William Morris*, 24 vols. (New York, 1910–15), XI, 47–48.

45. Dryden, *Astraea Redux*, 312–13; Edmund Waller, "To the King. Upon his Majesty's Happy Return," 109–10, *The Poems of Edmund Waller*, ed. George Thorn-Drury, reprinted (New York, 1968), 167.

46. Dryden, "Dedication" to the *Aeneis*, in *Works*, V, 281.

47. On this passage, see the discussion by L. D. Proudfoot, *Dryden's "Aeneid" and Its Seventeenth-Century Predecessors* (Manchester, 1960), 197–99.

48. Dryden, Dedication to the *Aeneis*, in *Works*, V, 284.

49. See Zwicker, *Politics and Language in Dryden's Poetry*, chap. 6, especially 184–85, separately reprinted in *Vergil at 2000*, 281–302, especially 285–86. On the larger context—biographical, cultural, and political—of the translation, see Thomas H. Fujimura, "Dryden's Virgil: Translation as Autobiography," *Studies in Philology* 80 (1983): 67–83; Michael West, "Dryden and the Disintegration of Renaissance Heroic Ideals," *Costerus* 7 (1973): 193–222, and "Dryden's Ambivalence as a Translator of Heroic Themes," *Huntington Library Quarterly*, 36 (1973): 347–66; William Myers, *Dryden* (London, 1973), 162–69, especially 167.

50. This has been emphasized by T. W. Harrison, "Dryden's *Aeneid*," *Dryden's Mind and Art*, ed. Bruce King (Edinburgh, 1969), 143–67.

51. Repeated emphasis on the word *labour* and its synonym *toil* is a pronounced

feature of *Aeneis* 1–6. The first instance of *labores* in the original comes at 1.10, but Dryden introduces the word already in line 4. "Long Labours, both by Sea and Land he bore." The Ruaeus *interpretatio* is also emphatic on this point. See Ruaeus, 176.

52. Compare Vergil, 4.265–66. Perhaps influenced by the *interpretatio* (300), Dryden is noticeably harder on Aeneas in this passage than Vergil is. On Dryden's version of *Aeneid* 4, see especially Hopkins, *John Dryden*, 163–67.

53. Dryden, "To my Honour'd Kinsman," 164, *Fables Ancient and Modern*, in *The Poems of John Dryden*, IV, 1534. All subsequent citations from the *Fables* are repeated from this edition and referenced by title and line numbers.

54. Dryden, "Dedication" to *Fables Ancient and Modern*, in *The Poems of John Dryden*, IV, 1443. All subsequent citations from the dedication are given parenthetically by page numbers to this edition.

55. Ibid. It may be recalled that Ruaeus had invoked *caritas* to explain *pietas*. See page 32 above.

56. On this topic see Howard D. Weinbrot, *Augustus Caesar in "Augustan" England: The Decline of a Classical Norm* (Princeton, 1978), especially 122.

57. Dryden, "To Her Grace the Dutchess of Ormond," 165–66, *Poems*, IV, 1467.

58. Dryden, Preface to *Fables Ancient and Modern*, IV, 1445.

59. See Reuben Brower, *Alexander Pope: The Poetry of Allusion* (Oxford, 1959), 1–14.

60. Charles Cotton's burlesque of the *Aeneid*, published over three decades before Dryden's translation, is a prior indication of the displacement of Vergil from the position of eminence he had so long held. See Cotton, *Scarronides; Or, Virgil Travestie* (Durham, 1807). On the decline in esteem for the poem during the eighteenth century, see T. W. Harrison, "English Vergil: The *Aeneid* in the XVIII Century," *Philologica Pragensia* 10 (1967): 1–11.

61. On contemporary attitudes toward Homer, see Howard D. Weinbrot, "*The Rape of the Lock* and the Contexts of Warfare," *The Enduring Legacy: Alexander Pope Tercentenary Essays*, ed. Pat Rogers and G. S. Rousseau (Cambridge, 1988), 21–48, reprinted in *Eighteenth-Century Satire*, especially 101–9.

62. Maynard Mack, *Alexander Pope: A Life* (New York, 1985), 773.

63. See Erskine-Hill, *The Augustan Idea in English Literature*, chap. 8, especially 231–33.

64. See Earl Miner, *Dryden's Poetry* (Bloomington, 1967), chap. 8; Judith Sloman, "An Interpretation of Dryden's *Fables*," *Eighteenth-Century Studies*, 4 (1971): 199–211; Myers, *Dryden*, 170–91, and the book-length study of the *Fables* by Cedric D. Reverand, *Dryden's Final Poetic Mode: The Fables* (Philadelphia, 1988).

65. Dryden, "Palamon and Arcite," 1.81–86.

66. Dryden, "Of the Pythagorean Philosophy," 1–6.

67. Reverand, *Dryden's Final Poetic Mode*, 218.

68. Dryden, "Theodore and Honoria," 226, "Cymon and Iphigenia," 469–70, "Of the Pythagorean Philosophy," 187.

69. Dryden, "Cinyras and Myrrha," 39–48. See David Hopkins, "Nature's Laws and Man's: The Story of Cinyras and Myrrha in Ovid and Dryden," *Modern Language Review* 80 (1985): 786–801.

70. "State-Laws may alter: Nature's are the same;/Those are usurp'd on helpless

Woman-kind,/Made without our Consent, and wanting Pow'r to bind." Dryden, "Sigismonda and Guiscardo," 418–20.

71. Dryden, "Meleager and Atalanta," 287.

72. Dryden, "The Speeches of Ajax and Ulysses," 328. See the chapter in Reverand devoted to "The Anti-Heroic *Fables," Dryden's Final Poetic Mode,* 11–45, especially 31–35.

73. Dryden, "The Twelfth Book of Ovid His Metamorphoses," 308–9.

74. Dryden, "The First Book of Homer's Ilias," 119–21.

75. Dryden, "The Monument of a Fair Maiden Lady," 28–29; "The Cock and the Fox," 484–85.

Conclusion

1. George Whitefield, Sermon 10, *Sermons on Important Subjects* (London, 1832), 131. As Whitefield uses the word in his journals, it identifies those who share or are coming to share the Methodist theology, usually common, uneducated folk. The inclination of *piety* toward Methodism is a pronounced feature of its eighteenth-century history. See especially the satires of enthusiasm by Swift, Shaftesbury, Fielding, and Graves.

2. Hume, *An Inquiry Concerning the Principles of Morals,* 9.1, ed. Charles W. Hendel (Indianapolis, 1957), 91; and see *A Treatise of Human Nature,* 3.3.2, ed. with introduction by Ernest C. Mossner, reprinted (London, 1985), 649–52.

3. This is not, of course, a sudden or uniform process. Ironic usage is already well in evidence among Dryden's contemporaries. Rochester, for example, portrays a hypothetical honest man "Whose pious life's a proof he does believe/Mysterious truths, which no man can conceive." Rochester, "A Satyr against Reason and Mankind," lines 214–15, *The Complete Poems of John Wilmot, Earl of Rochester,* ed. David M. Vieth (New Haven, 1968). On the other hand, evidence for the persistence of a more traditional understanding may be found under "Piety" in Nathan Bailey's *Dictionarium Britannicum* (London, 1730). Samuel Johnson's secondary definition of *piety* should also be noted: "Duty to parents or those in superior relation." Of those eighteenth-century writers who still consistently use the word with an honorific meaning, Johnson is the most important. As Dryden had dramatized "patterns of piety" in his heroic plays, so Johnson adopts the same phrase with minimal irony to indicate the last ambition of Nekayah in the closing paragraphs of *Rasselas,* in *Samuel Johnson,* ed. Donald Greene (Oxford, 1984), 418. Similarly, Johnson summarizes the design of *The Rambler* in the very last paper as the inculcation of "wisdom" and "piety." Johnson, *Rambler,* 208, ed. Walter Jackson Bate and Albrecht B. Strauss, The Yale Edition of the Works of Samuel Johnson (New Haven, 1969), v, 319. On the other side is Hume, whose irony undermines the "piety" of Demea in the *Dialogues Concerning Natural Religion,* 2, ed. Richard H. Popkin (Indianapolis, 1980), 13. Demea's later exit from the discussion effectively marks the impossibility, in Hume's view, of providing revelation with a basis in philosophy and may be taken symbolically to represent the retreat of *piety* to the periphery of the English moral

vocabulary. Although the word may still be seriously invoked in the eighteenth century, it may not always be seriously understood. This situation is well represented by William Hogarth's picture "Before," which shows in an open drawer the reading material of a young lady about to be seduced. One book in evidence is Lewis Bayley's seventeenth-century religious classic *The Practice of Piety*, but right next to it is a volume of Rochester's poems. This engraving graces the cover of the edition by Sean Shesgreen, *Engravings by Hogarth* (New York, 1973), and is discussed in relation to Hogarth's other conversation pictures by Ronald Paulson, *Hogarth: His Life, Art, and Times* (New Haven, 1974), 101–2.

4. Bacon, *Essays*, 17 ("Of Superstition"), *Essays, Advancement of Learning, New Atlantis*, ed. R. F. Jones (New York, 1937), 50.

5. Wordsworth, "My Heart Leaps Up," 7–9, *Poetical Works*, I, 226.

6. Blake, Marginalia, in *Poetry and Prose*, ed. D. V. Erdman (New York, 1965), 619, 626, 665.

7. William Paley's apologetic *View of the Evidences of Christianity* illustrates this particularly well. Admitting that "no two things can be more different than the Heroic and the Christian character," Paley identifies Christian piety with what is "poor-spirited, tame and abject." His best effort to redeem the pious character from these associations is to give the exemplary piety of Christ an eighteenth-century veneer: "Our Saviour uttered no impassioned devotion. There was no heat in his piety, or in the language in which he expressed it; no vehement or rapturous ejaculations, no violent urgency in his prayers. The Lord's Prayer is a model of calm devotion. His words in the garden are unaffected expressions of a deep indeed, but sober piety." William Paley, *A View of the Evidences of Christianity*, 2.2, 10th edition revised (Cambridge, 1901), 223, 239. As Paley would restrict the word to what is "sober," so James Beattie would limit it to what is "rational," both adjectives attempting to guard true piety from the sort whom Hume designates "gloomy, hair-brained enthusiast[s]." James Beattie, *Elements of Moral Science*, reprinted (Delmar, N.Y., 1976), I, 305; Hume, *An Inquiry Concerning the Principles of Morals*, 9.1, pp. 91–92.

8. Tobias Smollett, *The Expedition of Humphrey Clinker*, ed. James L. Thorson (New York, 1983), 242.

Selected Bibliography

Primary Sources

Aegidius Romanus (Egidio Colonna). *Li Livres du Gouvernement des Rois: A XIIIth Century French Version of Egidio Colonna's Treatise De Regimine Principum.* Ed. Samuel Paul Molenaer. New York: Columbia University Press, 1899; reprinted, Studies in Romance Philology and Literature, Columbia University, vol. 1. New York: AMS Press, 1966.

Alciati, Andrea. *Emblemata cum commentariis.* Padua: P. P. Tozzium, 1621; facsimile reprint, New York: Garland, 1976.

———. *Emblematum liber.* Augsburg: H. Steyner, 1531; facsimile reprint Hildesheim: Georg Olms, 1977.

Alcuin. *Epistolae.* Patrologiae Cursus Completus: Series Latina, vol. 100. Ed. J. P. Migne. Paris, 1863.

Alighieri, Dante. *The Banquet of Dante Alighieri.* Trans. Elizabeth Price Sayer. London: Routledge, 1887.

———. *Dante's Convivio.* Trans. William W. Jackson. Oxford: Clarendon Press, 1909.

———. *The Divine Comedy.* 6 vols. Ed. and trans. with commentary by Charles Singleton. Princeton: Princeton University Press, 1970.

———. *Le opere di Dante Alighieri.* Ed. E. Moore, rev. P. Toynbee, 5th edition. Oxford: Oxford University Press, 1963.

———. *Rime.* Ed. and trans. Patrick S. Diehl. Princeton: Princeton University Press, 1979.

Allestree, Richard. *The Whole Duty of Man.* London: T. Garthwait, 1659.

Althusius, Johannes. *Politica.* Herborn, 1614; facsimile reprint, 1961.

———. *The Politics of Johannes Althusius.* Trans. Frederick S. Carney. Boston: Beacon Press, 1964.

Ambrose. *De apologia prophetae David ad Theodosium Augustum.* Ed. Pierre Hadot, with French translation by Marius Cordier. Paris: Editions du Cerf, 1977.

———. *Expositio Evangelii secundum Lucam.* Corpus Christianorum, Series Latina, vol. 14. Ed. M. Adriaen. Turnhout, Belgium: Brepols, 1957.

————. *On the Duties of the Clergy.* In *Some of the Principal Works of St. Ambrose.* Trans. H. de Romestin. The Nicene and Post-Nicene Fathers, second series, vol. 10. Ed. Philip Schaff and Henry Wace. New York: Christian Literature, 1896.

————. *Opera.* Patrologiae Cursus Completus: Series Latina, vol. 16. Ed. J. P. Migne. Paris, 1880.

"Ambrosiaster." *In epistolam B. Paulus ad Timotheum primam.* Patrologiae Cursus Completus: Series Latina, vol. 17. Ed. J. P. Migne. Paris, 1879.

Ammianus Marcellinus. *Rerum gestarum libri qui supersunt,* vol. 1. Ed. and trans. John C. Rolfe. Loeb Classical Library. Cambridge, Mass., and London: Harvard University Press and William Heinemann, 1935; reprinted 1986.

Annalium Bertinianorum liber. Monumenta Germaniae Historica: Scriptores, vol. 2. Ed. G. H. Pertz. Hannover, 1829.

Aquinas, Thomas. *De regimine principum.* Ed. Joseph Mathis, 2d edition revised. Rome: Marietti, 1948.

————. *Ethicorum Aristotelis ad Nicomachum expositio.* Ed. Raymundi M. Spiazzi. Rome: Marietti, 1949.

————. *Summa theologiae,* vol. 41. Ed. and trans. Thomas Gilby et al. London and New York: Blackfriars with McGraw-Hill and Eyre and Spottiswoode, 1963.

Ariosto, Ludovico. *Orlando furioso.* Ed. Cesare Segre. Venice: Mondadori, 1976.

————. *Orlando Furioso.* Trans. Guido Waldman. London: Oxford University Press, 1974.

Augustine. *City of God.* 7 vols. Ed. and trans. G. E. McCracken et al. Loeb Classical Library. Cambridge, Mass., and London: Harvard University Press and William Heinemann, 1957.

————. *De doctrina christiana.* Corpus Christianorum: Series Latina, vol. 32. Ed. Joseph Martin. Turnhout, Belgium: Brepols, 1962.

————. *De sermone domini in monte.* Corpus Christianorum: Series Latina, vol. 35. Ed. A. Mutzenbecher. Turnhout, Belgium: Brepols, 1967.

————. *Enchiridion.* In *Oeuvres de Saint Augustin,* vol. 9. Ed. with French translation by J. Rivière. Bibliothèque Augustinienne. Paris: Desclée de Brouwer, 1947.

Bacon, Sir Francis. *Essays.* In *Essays, Advancement of Learning, New Atlantis.* Ed. R. F. Jones. New York: Odyssey, 1937.

Bailey, Nathan. *Dictionarium Britannicum.* London: T. Cox, 1730.

Beattie, James. *Elements of Moral Science.* Edinburgh: T. Cadell, 1790; facsimile reprint Delmar, N.Y.: Scholars Facsimiles and Reprints, 1976.

Belleau, Remy. *La bergerie.* In *Oeuvres complètes de Remy Belleau,* vol. 2. Ed. A. Gouverneur. Paris: Franck, 1867.

Bernard of Clairvaux. *De consideratione.* In *Sancti Bernardi opera,* vol. 3. Ed. J. Leclercq and H. M. Rochais. Rome: Editiones Cistercienses, 1963.

————. *Epistola seu tractatus ad fratres de Monte Dei.* In *Bernardi opera omnia.* Patrologiae Cursus Completus: Series Latina, vol. 184. Ed. J. P. Migne. Paris, 1879.

————. *Five Books on Consideration.* Trans. John D. Anderson and Elizabeth T. Kennan. *The Works of Bernard of Clairvaux,* vol. 13. Kalamazoo, Mich.: Cistercian Publications, 1976.

Blake, William. *Poetry and Prose.* Ed. D. V. Erdman. Garden City, N.Y.: Doubleday, 1965.

Blois, Robert de *L'enseignement des princes.* In *Robert de Blois: Son oeuvre didactique et narrative.* Ed. John Howard Fox. Paris: Nizet, 1950.

Boccaccio, Giovanni. *Amorous Fiammetta.* Trans. Bartholomew Yong, rev. Edward Hutton. London: Navarre Society, 1952.

———. *De mulieribus claris,* ed. V. Zaccaria. *Tutte le opere di Giovanni Boccaccio,* vol. 10. Ed. Vittore Branca. Milan: Mondadori, 1964.

———. *Genealogiae deorum gentilium liber XIV.* In *Boccaccio in Defense of Poetry.* Ed. Jeremiah Reedy. Toronto: Pontifical Institute of Medieval Studies, 1978.

———. *Opere de Giovanni Boccaccio.* Ed. Cesare Segre. 5th edition. Milan: Mursia, 1975.

Bodin, Jean. *Les six livres de la république.* Lyons: Gabriel Cartier, 1576. Reprint in six vols., ed. C. Frémont, M.-D. Couzinet, H. Rochais. Paris: Fayard, 1986.

Budé, Guillaume. *De l'institutione du prince.* Lyons: G. Gazeau, 1547.

Burke, Kenneth. *Permanence and Change: An Anatomy of Purpose,* 3d edition. Berkeley and Los Angeles: University of California Press, 1984; first published 1935.

Butler, Joseph. *Fifteen Sermons Preached at the Rolls Chapel.* Ed. W. R. Matthews. London: G. Bell, 1953.

Calpurnius Siculus. *Eclogues.* In *The Eclogues of Calpurnius and Nemesianus.* Ed. Charles H. Keene. Hildesheim: Georg Olms, 1969.

Calvin, John. *Calvin: Institutes of the Christian Religion.* Ed. John T. McNeill, trans. Ford Lewis Battles. Philadelphia: Westminster Press, 1960.

———. *Calvin's Commentary on Seneca's De Clementia.* Ed. and trans. Ford Lewis Battles and André Hugo. Leiden: E. J. Brill, 1969.

———. *Christianae religionis institutio.* London, 1576.

Cassiodorus. *Historia ecclesiastica tripartita.* Ed. W. Jacob and R. Hanslik. Corpus Scriptorum Ecclesiasticorum Latinorum, vol. 71. Vienna: Hoelder-Pichler-Tempsky, 1952.

———. *Variarum liber duodecim.* Corpus Christianorum: Series Latina, vol. 96. Ed. A. J. Fridh. Turnhout, Belgium: Brepols, 1973.

Chaucer, Geoffrey. *The Canterbury Tales.* In *The Works of Geoffrey Chaucer.* Ed. F. N. Robinson, 2d edition. Boston: Houghton Mifflin, 1961.

Christine de Pisan. *Le livre de la paix.* Ed. Charity Cannon Willard. The Hague: Mouton, 1958.

———. *Le livre des fais et bonnes meurs du sage Roy Charles V.* Ed. S. Solente. Paris: Champion, 1940.

———. *Le livre du corps de policie.* Ed. Robert H. Lucas. Geneva: Droz, 1967.

Chromatius Aquilensis. *Opera.* Corpus Christianorum: Series Latina, vol. 9A. Ed. R. Etaix and J. Lemarié. Turnhout, Belgium: Brepols, 1974.

Cicero. *De inventione.* Ed. and trans. H. M. Hubbel. Loeb Classical Library. Cambridge, Mass., and London: Harvard University Press and William Heinemann, 1949; reprinted 1968.

———. *De natura deorum.* Ed. and trans. H. Rackham. Loeb Classical Library.

Cambridge, Mass., and London: Harvard University Press and William Heinemann, 1933; reprinted 1979.

————. *De officiis*. Ed. and trans. Walter Miller. Loeb Classical Library. Cambridge, Mass., and London: Harvard University Press and William Heinemann, 1913; reprinted 1990.

————. *De republica*. Ed. and trans. Clinton W. Keyes. Loeb Classical Library. Cambridge, Mass., and London: Harvard University Press and William Heinemann, 1928; reprinted 1988.

————. *Pro Cnaeo Plancio*. Ed. and trans. N. H. Watts. Loeb Classical Library. Cambridge, Mass., and London: Harvard University Press and William Heinemann, 1923; reprinted 1961.

Cino da Pistoia. *Le rime di Cino da Pistoia*. Ed. Guido Zaccagnini. Geneva: Olschki, 1925.

Claudian. *The Poems of Claudian*. Ed. and trans. Maurice Platnauer. Loeb Classical Library. Cambridge, Mass., and London: Harvard University Press and William Heinemann, 1922; reprinted 1963.

Coles, Elisha. *A Dictionary, English-Latin, and Latin-English*. London: Thomas Guy, 1692.

Colet, John. *Enarratio in epistolam B. Pauli ad Romanos*. In *Dean Colet's Lectures on Romans*. Ed. J. H. Lupton. London: Gregg, 1873.

Colunga, Alberto, and Turrado, Laurentio, eds. *Biblia vulgata*. 7th edition. Madrid: Biblioteca de Autores Cristianos, 1985.

Contini, Gianfranco, ed. *Poeti del Duecento: Poesie popolare e guillaresca*. In *La letteratura italiana: Storia e testi*, vol. 2. Milan and Naples: Ricciardi, 1960.

Cotton, Charles. *Scarronides; Or, Virgil Travestie: A Mock Poem of the First and Fourth Books of Virgil's Aeneid, In English Burlesque*. Durham: G. Walker, 1807.

Cowper, William. *The Letters and Prose Writings of William Cowper*, vol. 2. Ed. James King and Charles Ryskamp. Oxford: Clarendon Press, 1979.

Curtius, Quintus. *History of Alexander*. 2 vols. Ed. and trans. J. C. Rolfe. Loeb Classical Library. Cambridge, Mass., and London: Harvard University Press and William Heinemann, 1946.

Daniel, Samuel. *To Delia*. In *Poems and a Defence of Ryme*. Ed. Arthur Colby Sprague. Cambridge, Mass.: Harvard University Press, 1930.

Desportes, Philippe. *Oeuvres de Philippe Desportes*. Ed. Alfred Michiels. Paris: A. Delahays, 1858.

Dickens, Charles. *The Life and Adventures of Nicholas Nickleby*. Intro. Dame Sybil Thorndike. London: Oxford University Press, 1950.

Dolce, Lodovico. *L'Achille e l'Enea*. Venice: Gabriel Giolito, 1571.

Donatus, Tiberius Claudius. *Interpretationes vergilianae*. 2 vols. Ed. H. Georgii. Stuttgart: Teubner, 1905–6; reprinted 1969.

Douglas, Gavin. *The Poetical Works of Gavin Douglas*, vol. 2. Ed. John Small. Edinburgh: W. Paterson, 1874.

————. *Vergil's Aeneid*. 4 vols. Ed. David F. C. Coldwell. Scottish Text Society. Edinburgh: W. Blackwood, 1957–64.

Dryden, John. *Aureng-Zebe*. Ed. Frederick M. Link. Regents Restoration Drama Series. Lincoln: University of Nebraska Press, 1971.

———. *John Dryden: Three Plays*. Ed. George Saintsbury. Mermaid Dramabook, 5th printing. New York: Hill and Wang, 1967.

———. *The Poems of John Dryden*. 4 vols. Ed. James Kinsley. Oxford: Clarendon Press, 1958.

———. *Vergil's Aeneid and Fourth ("Messianic") Eclogue in the Dryden Translation*. Ed. Howard Clarke. University Park: The Pennsylvania State University Press, 1989.

———. *The Works of John Dryden*, vols. 5, 7. Ed. Walter Scott, rev. George Saintsbury. Edinburgh: W. Paterson, 1883.

———. *The Works of John Dryden*. Eds. Edward N. Hooker and H. T. Swedenberg, Jr., et al. Berkeley and Los Angeles: University of California Press, 1956–.

DuBellay, Joachim. *Oeuvres poétiques*, vols. 1–2. Ed. Henri Chamard, rev. Yvonne Bellenger. Paris: Nizet, 1982.

———. *Oeuvres poétiques*, vol. 6. Ed. Henri Chamard. Paris: Droz, 1931.

Dubois, Pierre. *De recuperatione terre sancte*. Ed. Angelo Diotti. Florence: Olschki, 1977.

Dummler, E., gen. ed. *Epistolae merovingici et karolini aevi*. Monumenta Germaniae Historica: Epistolae, vols. 4–5. Berlin, 1892.

Duchesne, L., ed. *Le liber pontificalis*, vol. 2. Paris: Boccard, 1955.

Elyot, Sir Thomas. *The Book Named the Governor*. Ed. S. E. Lehmberg. New York: Dutton, 1962.

Erasmus, Desiderius. *Desiderius Erasmus Roterdamus: Ausgewählte Werke*. Ed. Hajo Holborn and Annemarie Holborn. Munich: C. H. Beck, 1964.

———. *Enchiridion militis christiani*. Trans. Charles Fantazzi. *The Collected Works of Erasmus*. Ed. John W. O'Malley. Toronto: University of Toronto Press, 1988.

———. *Enchiridion Militis Christiani: An English Version*. Ed. Anne M. O'Donnell. Early English Text Society, no. 282. Oxford: Oxford University Press, 1981.

———. *Erasmus: Ausgewählte Schriften*, vols. 2 and 4. Ed. with German translation by Werner Welzig. Darmstadt: Wissenschaftliche Buchgesellschaft, 1969.

———. *Novum Testamentum . . . Adnotationes*. In *Opera Omnia*, vol. 6. Ed. Jean LeClerc. Lyons: P. Vander, 1703–6; reprinted 1962.

Erasmus, Desiderius, and Luther, Martin. *Discourse on Free Will*. Ed. and trans. Ernst F. Winter. New York: Ungar, 1962; 13th printing, 1982.

Ermoldus Nigellus. *In honorem Hludowici Christianissimi Caesaris Augusti libri IV*. Monumenta Germaniae Historica: Scriptores, vol. 2. Ed. G. H. Pertz. Hannover, 1829.

Euripides. *Phoenissae*. In *Tragedies*, vol. 3. Ed. and trans. A. S. Way. Loeb Classical Library. Cambridge, Mass., and London: Harvard University Press and William Heinemann, 1912; reprinted 1978.

Eusebius. *Opera*. Patrologiae Cursus Completus: Series Graeca, vol. 20. Ed. J. P. Migne. Paris, 1857.

Eutropius. *Eutropii breviarum historiae romanae*. Ed. C. G. Baumgarten-Crusius, rev. H. R. Dietsch. Leipzig: Teubner, 1883.

Fairfax, Sir Edward. *Godfrey of Bulloigne: A Critical Edition of Edward Fairfax's Gerusalemme Liberata*. Ed. Kathleen M. Lea and T. M. Gang. Oxford: Clarendon Press, 1981.

Ficino, Marsiglio. *Opera omnia*. Basle, 1576; facsimile reprint with introduction by P. O. Kristeller, 2 vols. Turin: Bottega d'Erasmo, 1959.

———. *Theologica platonica*. Ed. and trans. Raymond Marcel. 2 vols. Paris: Société d'Edition Les Belles Lettres, 1964.

Fielding, Henry. *The History of Tom Jones, A Foundling*. Ed. Fredson Bowers with introduction by Martin C. Battestin. Wesleyan, Conn.: Wesleyan University Press, 1975.

Fornari, Simon. *La spositione di Simon Fornari . . . sopra l'Orlando furioso di Ludovico Ariosto*. Florence: Lorenzo Torrentino, 1549.

Fulgentius. *Expositio virgilianae continentiae secundum philosophos moralis*. In *Opera*. Ed. R. Helm. Stuttgart: Teubner, 1898; reprinted 1970.

Galletier, Edouard, ed. with French translation. *Panégyriques latins*. Paris: Société d'Edition Les Belles Lettres, 1949.

Garin, Eugenio, ed. with Italian translation. *Prosatori latini del Quattrocento*. Milan: Ricciardi, 1952.

Gelasius. *Epistolae et decreta*. Patrologiae Cursus Completus: Series Latina, vol. 59. Ed. J. P. Migne. Paris, 1862.

Gentillet, Innocent. *Discours contre Machiavel*. Ed. A. D'Andrea and P. O. Stewart. Florence: Casalini Libri, 1974.

Gower, John. *The Complete Works of John Gower*. 4 vols. Ed. G. C. Macaulay. Oxford: Clarendon Press, 1899.

Gregory I. *Moralia in Job*. Corpus Christianorum: Series Latina, vol. 143. Ed. M. Adriaen. Turnhout, Belgium: Brepols, 1979.

———. *Registrum epistolarum libri XVI*. Corpus Christianorum: Series Latina, vol. 140A. Ed. D. Norberg. Turnhout, Belgium: Brepols, 1982.

———. *Regulae pastoralis liber*. Patrologiae Cursus Completus: Series Latina, vol. 77. Ed. J. P. Migne. Paris, 1896.

Gregory II. *Epistolae et canones*. Patrologiae Cursus Completus: Series Latina, vol. 89. Ed. J. P. Migne. Paris, 1863.

Gregory VII. *Monumenta gregoriana*. Ed. Philipp Jaffé. Bibliotheca Rerum Germanicarum, vol. 2. Berlin, 1845; reprinted 1964.

Guicciardini, Francesco. *Ricordi*. Ed. Sergio Marconi. Milan: Feltrinelli, 1983.

Harington, Sir John. *Ludovico Ariosto's Orlando Furioso*. Ed. Robert McNulty. Oxford: Clarendon Press, 1972.

Hartley, David. *Observations on Man, His Frame, His Duty, and His Expectations*. London: J. Leake and W. Frederick, 1749; facsimile reprint, Gainesville, Fla.: Scholars Facsimiles and Reprints, 1966.

Hegel, Georg W. F. *Grundlinien der Philosophie des Rechts*. In *Georg Wilhelm Friedrich Hegel: Sämtliche Werke*, vol. 6. Ed. Georg Lasson. Leipzig: F. Meiner, 1930.

———. *Hegel's Philosophy of Right*. Trans. T. M. Knox. London: Oxford University Press, 1952; reprinted 1977.

Heller, Joseph. *God Knows*. New York: Knopf, 1984.

Henry IV. *Epistolae*. Monumenta Germaniae Historica: Diplomatum Regum et Imperatorum Germaniae, vol. 6. Ed. D. von Gladiss. Weimar, 1952.

Herbert, George. *A Priest to the Temple or, The Country Parson*. In *The Works of George Herbert*. Ed. F. E. Hutchinson. Oxford: Oxford University Press, 1941.

Herveus Burgidolensis. *Commentaria in epistolas divi Pauli*. Patrologiae Cursus Completus: Series Latina, vol. 181. Ed. J. P. Migne. Paris, 1854.

Hilary of Poitiers. *Opera*. Patrologiae Cursus Completus: Series Latina, vol. 10. Ed. J. P. Migne. Paris, 1845.

Hincmar of Rheims. *Opuscula varia*. Patrologiae Cursus Completus: Series Latina, vol. 125. Ed. J. P. Migne. Paris, 1879.

Hoccleve, Thomas. *The Regement of Princes*. In *Hoccleve's Works*. Ed. Frederick J. Furnivall. Early English Text Society, extra series, vol. 72. London: Kegan Paul, Trench, Trübner, 1897.

Hoole, John. *Jerusalem Delivered*. In *The Works of the English Poets*, vol. 21. Ed. Alexander Chalmers. London: J. Johnson, et al., 1810.

Horace. *Odes and Epodes*. Ed. and trans. C. E. Bennett. Loeb Classical Library. Cambridge, Mass., and London: Harvard University Press and William Heinemann, 1914; reprinted 1989.

Hrabanus Maurus. *Enarrationum in epistolas beati Pauli*. Patrologiae Cursus Completus: Series Latina, vol. 112. Ed. J. P. Migne. Paris, 1878.

Humbert. *Adversos simoniacos libri tres*. Patrologiae Cursus Completus: Series Latina, vol. 143. Ed. J. P. Migne. Paris, 1882.

Hume, David. *Dialogues Concerning Natural Religion*. Ed. Richard H. Popkin. Indianapolis: Hackett, 1980.

———. *An Inquiry Concerning the Principles of Morals*. Ed. Charles W. Hendel. Indianapolis: Bobbs-Merrill, 1957.

———. *A Treatise of Human Nature*. Ed. Ernest C. Mossner. London: Penguin Books, 1969; reprinted 1985.

Innocent III. *Opera omnia*. Patrologiae Cursus Completus: Series Latina, vol. 216. Ed. J. P. Migne. Paris, 1891.

———. *Regestorum sive epistolarum liber XII*. Patrologiae Cursus Completus: Series Latina, vol. 215. Ed. J. P. Migne. Paris, 1891.

Irenaeus. *Libros quinque adversus haereses*, vol. 1. Ed. W. Wigan Harvey. Cambridge: Cambridge University Press, 1857; reprinted Ridgewood, N.J.: Gregg, 1965.

Isidore of Seville. *Etymologiarum sive originum libri XX*. 2 vols. Ed. W. Lindsay. Oxford: Clarendon Press, 1966.

Jean of Paris. *De potestate regia et papali*. In *Jean de Paris et l'ecclésiologie du XIIIe siècle*. Ed. Dom Jean Leclercq. Paris: J. Vrin, 1942.

———. *On Royal and Papal Power*. Trans. Arthur P. Monahan. New York: Columbia University Press, 1974.

Jerome. *Opera exegetica*. Corpus Christianorum: Series Latina, vols. 76–77. Ed. M. Adriaen. Turnhout, Belgium: Brepols, 1969.

———. *Select Letters*. Ed. and trans. F. A. Wright. Loeb Classical Library. Cambridge, Mass., and London: Harvard University Press and William Heinemann, 1933; reprinted 1980.

John Chrysostom. *In epistolam primam ad Timotheum commentarius.* Patrologiae Cursus Completus: Series Graeca, vol. 62. Ed. J. P. Migne. Paris, 1862.

John of Salisbury. *Polycraticus.* In *Opera omnia.* Ed. J. A. Giles. Oxford: J. H. Parker, 1848; reprinted Leipzig: Zentralantiquariat, 1969.

Johnson, Samuel. *A Dictionary of the English Language.* London: W. Strahan, 1755.

———. *The Rambler.* Ed. Walter Jackson Bate and Albrecht B. Strauss. Yale Edition of the Works of Samuel Johnson, vol. 5. New Haven: Yale University Press, 1969.

———. *Rasselas.* In *Samuel Johnson.* Ed. Donald Greene. Oxford: Oxford University Press, 1984.

Jonas of Orleans. *Opusculum de institutione regia.* Patrologiae Cursus Completus: Series Latina, vol. 106. Ed. J. P. Migne. Paris, 1864.

Juvenal. *Satirae.* In *Juvenal and Persius.* Ed. L. Prateus. Paris: Delphin Edition, 1684.

Lactantius. *De divinis institutionibus adversus gentes.* In *Lactantii opera omnia.* Patrologiae Cursus Completus: Series Latina, vol. 6. Ed. J. P. Migne. Paris, 1844.

———. *The Divine Institutes.* Trans. Sister Mary Francis McDonald. *The Fathers of the Church,* vol. 49. Ed. Roy Joseph Deferrari. Washington, D.C.: Catholic University of America Press, 1964.

Landino, Cristoforo. *Disputationes camaldulenses.* Ed. P. Lohe. Florence: Sansoni, 1980.

Latini, Brunetto. *Li livres dou tresor.* Ed. P. Chabaille. Paris: Impériale, 1863.

Lefèvre d'Etaples, Jacques. *The Prefatory Epistles of Jacques Lefèvre d'Etaples.* Ed. Eugene F. Rice, Jr. New York: Columbia University Press, 1972.

Leo I. *Epistolae.* Patrologiae Cursus Completus: Series Latina, vol. 54. Ed. J. P. Migne. Paris, 1881.

Leo III. *Epistolae . . . ad Imperatorem Carolum missae.* Patrologiae Cursus Completus: Series Latina, vol. 98. Ed. J. P. Migne. Paris, 1862.

Liber de unitate ecclesiae conservanda. Monumenta Germaniae Historica: Libelli de Lite Imperatorum et Pontificum, vol. 2. Ed. W. Schwenkenbecher. Hannover, 1892.

Livy. *Ab urbe condita,* vol. 3. Ed. and trans. Evan T. Sage and Alfred C. Schlesinger. Loeb Classical Library. Cambridge, Mass., and London: Harvard University Press and William Heinemann, 1988.

Locke, John. *Of Civil Government.* In *Two Treatises of Government.* Ed. Peter Laslett. Cambridge: Cambridge University Press, 1960.

Lopez, Diego. *Declaración magistral sobre las emblematas de Andrés Alciata.* Valencia: Geronimo Vilagrasa, 1655; facsimile reprint Menston, England: Scolar Press, 1973.

Lucan. *De bello civili.* Ed. and trans. J. D. Duff. Loeb Classical Library. Cambridge, Mass., and London: Harvard University Press and William Heinemann, 1928; reprinted 1951.

Lucretius. *De rerum natura.* Ed. and trans. W. H. D. Rouse, rev. M. F. Smith. Loeb Classical Library. Cambridge, Mass., and London: Harvard University Press and William Heinemann, 1975.

Luther, Martin. *Luther's Work,* vols. 10, 14, 25, 28, 29, 33. Gen. eds. Jaroslav

Pelikan and Helmut T. Lehmann. St. Louis and Philadelphia: Concordia Press and Fortress Press, 1958–86.

———. *Martin Luthers Werke,* vols. 4, 5, 18, 25, 26, 56. Weimar: Hermann Böhlau, 1883–1938.

Machiavelli, Niccolò. *Niccolò Machiavelli: Tutte le opere.* Ed. M. Martelli. Florence: Sansoni, 1971.

———. *The Prince and the Discourses.* Trans. Luigi Ricci and Christian E. Detmold. New York: Random House, 1950.

Macrobius. *Saturnalia.* In *I Saturnali.* Ed. with Italian translation by Nino Marinone. Turin: UTET, 1967.

Magie, D., ed. and trans. *Scriptores historiae augustae.* 3 vols. Loeb Classical Library. Cambridge, Mass., and London: Harvard University Press and William Heinemann, 1932; reprinted 1954.

Malory, Sir Thomas. *Le Morte d'Arthur.* In *The Works of Thomas Malory.* 3 vols. Ed. Eugene Vinaver. Oxford: Oxford University Press, 1954.

Mandeville, Bernard. *The Fable of the Bees: Or, Private Vices, Publick Benefits,* vol. 1. Ed. F. B. Kaye. Oxford: Clarendon Press, 1924, reprinted 1957.

Manegold of Lautenbach. *Ad Gebehardum liber.* Monumenta Germaniae Historica: Libelli de Lite Imperatorum et Pontificum, vol. 1. Ed. K. Francke. Hannover, 1891.

Mantuan, Baptista. *The Eclogues of Baptista Mantuanus.* Ed. Wilfred P. Mustard. Baltimore: Johns Hopkins University Press, 1911.

Marsilius of Padua. *The Defender of Peace.* Trans. Alan Gewirth. New York: Columbia University Press, 1956; reprinted New York: Harper and Row, 1967.

———. *Defensor pacis.* Ed. C. W. Previté-Orton. Cambridge: Cambridge University Press, 1928.

Melancthon, Philipp. *Loci communes seu hypotyposes theologicae.* Ed. Hans Engelland. In *Melancthons Werke,* vol. 2. Ed. Robert Supperich. Hamburg: C. Bertelsmann, 1952.

Mencken, H. L. *The American Scene: A Reader.* Ed. Huntington Cairns. New York: Knopf, 1965.

Milton, John. *The Poetical Works of John Milton.* 2 vols. Ed. Helen Darbishire. Oxford: Clarendon Press, 1952.

Morris, William. *The Aeneids of Virgil.* In *The Collected Works of William Morris,* vol. 11. New York: Longmans, Green, 1911.

Natalis Comes (Conti). *Mythologiae.* Padua: M. Antonio Tritonio, 1616; facsimile reprint, New York: Garland, 1979.

Nicholas I. *Epistolae et decreta.* Patrologiae Cursus Completus: Series Latina, vol. 119. Ed. J. P. Migne. Paris, 1880.

Nicolaus of Lyra. *Postilla super totam bibliam.* Strasbourg, 1492; facsimile reprint, 4 vols. Frankfurt: Minerva, 1971.

Nithard. *Nithardi historiarum libri IV.* Monumenta Germaniae Historica: Scriptores, vol. 2. Ed. G. H. Pertz. Hannover, 1829.

Orosius. *Historiarum adversum paganos libri VII.* Ed. Karl Zangemeister. Leipzig: Teubner, 1889, reprinted Hildesheim: G. Olms, 1967.

Ovid. *Fasti.* Ed. and trans. Sir James G. Frazer. Loeb Classical Library. Cambridge,

Mass., and London: Harvard University Press and William Heinemann, 1931; reprinted 1951.

———. *Heroides*. In *Heroides and Amores*. Ed. and trans. Grant Showerman, rev. G. P. Goold. Loeb Classical Library. Cambridge, Mass., and London: Harvard University Press and William Heinemann, 1977.

———. *Metamorphoses*. 2 vols. Ed. and trans. F. J. Miller, rev. G. P. Goold. Loeb Classical Library. Cambridge, Mass., and London: Harvard University Press and William Heinemann, 1984.

———. *Ovid's Metamorphoses Books 6–10*. Ed. William S. Anderson. Norman: University of Oklahoma Press, 1972.

Paley, William. *A View of the Evidences of Christianity*. 10th edition, revised. Cambridge: J. Hall, 1901.

Peter Damian. *Opuscula*. Patrologiae Cursus Completus: Series Latina, vol. 145. Ed. J. P. Migne. Paris, 1867.

Peter Lombard. *In epistolam I ad Timotheum*. Patrologiae Cursus Completus: Series Latina, vol. 192. Ed. J. P. Migne. Paris, 1880.

Petrarch, Francesco. *Bucolicum carmen*. Ed. and trans. Thomas G. Bergin. New Haven: Yale University Press, 1974.

———. *Petrarch's Lyric Poems: The Rime sparse and Other Lyrics*. Ed. and trans. Robert M. Durling. Cambridge, Mass.: Harvard University Press, 1976.

Picinelli, Filippo. *Mundus symbolicus*. Ed. and trans. August Erath. Cologne: H. Demen, 1694; facsimile reprint, 2 vols., New York: Garland, 1976.

Piovene, Guido. *Pietà contro pietà*. In *Opere narrative*, vol. 1. Ed. Clelia Martignoni. Milan: Mondadori, 1976.

Plato. *Republic*. 2 vols. Ed. and trans. Paul Shorey. Loeb Classical Library. Cambridge, Mass., and London: Harvard University Press and William Heinemann, 1930; reprinted 1970.

Pliny the Elder. *Natural History,* vol. 2. Ed. and trans. H. Rackham. Loeb Classical Library. Cambridge, Mass., and London: Harvard University Press and William Heinemann, 1938; reprinted 1979.

Pliny the Younger. *Panegyricus*. In *Letters and Panegyricus*, vol. 2. Ed. and trans. Betty Radice. Loeb Classical Library. Cambridge, Mass., and London: Harvard University Press and William Heinemann, 1969.

Pontanus, Jacobus (J. J. Spanmueller). *Symbolarum libri XVII Virgilii*. Augsburg: Praetorii, 1599; facsimile reprint, New York: Garland, 1976.

Pope, Alexander. *Pastoral Poetry and an Essay on Criticism*. Ed. E. Audra and Aubrey Williams. In *The Poems of Alexander Pope*, vol. 1. Ed. John Butt. New Haven and London: Yale University Press and Methuen, 1961.

Propertius. *Elegies*. Ed. and trans. H. E. Butler. Loeb Classical Library. Cambridge, Mass., and London: Harvard University Press and William Heinemann, 1912; reprinted 1976.

Prudentius. *Opera*. 2 vols. Ed. and trans. H. J. Thomson. Loeb Classical Library. Cambridge, Mass., and London: Harvard University Press and William Heinemann, 1949; reprinted 1979.

Raleigh, Sir Walter. *The Poems of Sir Walter Ralegh*. Ed. Agnes M. C. Latham. London: Routledge and Kegan Paul, 1951.

Ronsard, Pierre de. *Oeuvres complètes*. 2 vols. Ed. Gustave Cohen. Bibliothèque de la Pléiade. Paris: Gallimard, 1950.

———. *Les oeuvres de Pierre de Ronsard*, vol. 2. Ed. Isidore Silver. Chicago: University of Chicago Press, 1966.

Ruskin, John. *The Works of John Ruskin*, vols. 23 and 28. Ed. E. T. Cook and Alexander Wedderburn. London: G. Allen and Longmans, Green, 1906.

Salvian. *De gubernatione Dei*. Monumenta Germaniae Historica: Auctores Antiqui, vol. 1. Ed. C. Halm. Berlin, 1877.

———. *The Governance of God*. In *The Writings of Salvian, the Presbyter*. Trans. Jeremiah F. O'Sullivan. Fathers of the Church. Ed. Ludwig Schopp. New York: Cima, 1947.

Sannazaro, Jacopo. *Arcadia*. In *Opere di Iacopo Sannazaro*. Ed. Enrico Carrara. Turin: UTET, 1963.

Santayana, George. *The Life of Reason; or The Phases of Human Progress*. Revised edition. New York: Scribner's, 1954.

Scaliger, Julius Caesar. *Poetices Libri Septem*. Intro. August Buck. Stuttgart: F. Fromman, 1964.

Scève, Maurice. *The Délie of Maurice Scève*. Ed I.D. McFarlane. Cambridge: Cambridge University Press, 1966.

Sedulius Scotus. *Liber de rectoribus christianis*. Patrologiae Cursus Completus: Series Latina, vol. 103. Ed. J. P. Migne. Paris, 1864.

———. *"On Christian Rulers" and the "Poems."* Trans. Edward Gerard Doyle. Binghamton: State University of New York Press, 1983.

Segrais, Jean Regnault de. *Traduction de l'Eneide de Virgile*. Paris, 1668.

Seneca. *Moral Essays*. 3 vols. Ed. and trans. J. W. Basore. Loeb Classical Library. Cambridge, Mass., and London: Harvard University Press and William Heinemann, 1928; reprinted 1975.

———. *Tragedies*, vol. 1. Ed. and trans. F. J. Miller. Loeb Classical Library. Cambridge, Mass., and London: Harvard University Press and William Heinemann, 1917; revised and reprinted 1987.

Servius. *Vergilii carmina commentarii*. 3 vols. Eds. George Thilo and Hermann Hagen. Leipzig: B. G. Teubner, 1881–1902; reprinted Special Publication of the American Philological Association, 1, 2. Lancaster, Pennsylvania, 1946.

Shakespeare, William. *Hamlet*. In *The Riverside Shakespeare*. Ed. G. Blakemore Evans. Boston: Houghton Mifflin, 1974.

Sidney, Sir Philip. *Astrophil and Stella*. In *The Poems of Sir Philip Sidney*. Ed. William A. Ringler, Jr. Oxford: Clarendon Press, 1962.

Silius Italicus. *Punica*. 2 vols. Ed. and trans. J. D. Duff. Loeb Classical Library. Cambridge, Mass., and London: Harvard University Press and William Heinemann, 1934; reprinted 1949–50.

Silvestris, Bernardus. *Commentary on the First Six Books of the "Aeneid" of Virgil Commonly Attributed to Bernardus Silvestris*. Eds. J. W. Jones and E. F. Jones. Lincoln: University of Nebraska Press, 1977.

Smaragdus of St. Mihiel. *Via regia*. Patrologiae Cursus Completus: Series Latina, vol. 102. Ed. J. P. Migne. Paris, 1865.

Smollett, Tobias. *The Expedition of Humphry Clinker.* Ed. James L. Thorson. New York: Norton, 1983.

Spenser, Edmund. *Amoretti.* In *Spenser's Minor Poems,* vol. 1. Ed. E. de Selincourt. Oxford: Clarendon Press, 1910.

———. *The Faerie Queene.* In *The Poetical Works of Edmund Spenser,* vols. 2–3. Ed. J. C. Smith. Oxford: Oxford University Press, 1909; reprinted 1964.

———. *The Faerie Queene.* Ed. A. C. Hamilton. London: Longman, 1977.

Statius. *Sylvae and Thebaid.* 2 vols. Ed. and trans. J. H. Mozley. Loeb Classical Library. Cambridge, Mass., and London: Harvard University Press and William Heinemann, 1928; reprinted 1967.

Swift, Jonathan. *Gulliver's Travels.* In *The Prose Works of Jonathan Swift,* vol. 11. Ed. Herbert Davis. Oxford: B. Blackwell, 1941.

Tacitus. *Agricola.* In *Agricola and Germania.* Ed. and trans. Maurice Hutton. Loeb Classical Library. Cambridge, Mass., and London: Harvard University Press and William Heinemann, revised edition 1970; reprinted 1980.

———. *Histories and Annals,* 4 vols. Ed. and trans. C. H. Moore and J. Jackson. Loeb Classical Library. Cambridge, Mass., and London: Harvard University Press and William Heinemann, 1937; reprinted 1963.

Tasso, Torquato. *Discorsi del poema eroico.* In *Scritti sull'arte poetica,* vol. 1. Ed. Ettore Mazzali. Milan and Naples: Ricciardi, 1959; reprinted Turin: G. Einaudi, 1977.

———. *Gerusalemme conquistata.* 2 vols. Ed. Luigi Bonfigli. Bari: G. Laterza, 1934.

———. *Gerusalemme liberata.* In *Opere di Torquato Tasso.* 2 vols. Ed. Bortolo Tommaso Sozzi, 3d edition. Turin: UTET, 1974.

———. *Jerusalem Delivered: An English Prose Version.* Ed. and trans. Ralph Nash. Detroit: Wayne State University Press, 1987.

Theganus. *Vita Hludowici Imperatoris.* Monumenta Germaniae Historica: Scriptores, vol. 2. Ed. G. H. Pertz. Hannover, 1829.

Thynne, Francis. *Emblemes and Epigrames.* Ed. F. J. Furnivall. Early English Text Society, original series no. 64. London: N. Trübner, 1876.

Tibullus. *Albii Tibulli aliorumque carminum libri tres.* 3d edition. Ed. F. W. Lenz and G. Karl Galinsky. Leiden: E. J. Brill, 1971; first published 1959.

———. *Elegies.* In *Catullus, Tibullus, Pervigilium Veneris.* Ed. and trans. J. W. Mackail, rev. G. P. Goold. Cambridge, Mass., and London: Harvard University Press and William Heinemann, 1988.

Tillich, Paul. *A History of Christian Thought, from its Judaic and Hellenistic Origins to Existentialism.* Ed. Carl Braaten. New York: Harper and Row, 1968; reprinted New York: Simon and Schuster, 1972.

———. *Systematic Theology,* 3 vols. in one. Chicago: University of Chicago Press, 1967; first published 1951.

Toscanella, Oratio. *Bellezze del Furioso.* Venice: Giovanni Bariletto, 1574.

———. *I luochi communi di tutta l'opera di Lodovico Ariosto.* Venice: Pietro dei Franceschi, 1574.

Turpin (Pseudo-Turpin). *Historia Karoli Magni et Rotholandi.* Ed. C. Meredith-Jones. Paris, 1936; reprinted Geneva: Slatkine Reprints, 1972.

Updike, John. *Roger's Version.* New York: Alfred A. Knopf, 1986.

Valeriano, Giovanni Piero Bolzani. *Hieroglyphica*. Lyons: P. Frelon, 1602; facsimile reprint, New York and London: Garland, 1976.

Valerius Maximus. *Factorum et dictorum memorabilium libri novem*. Ed. C. Kempfius. Hildesheim: Georg Olms, 1976.

Valla, Lorenzo. *In Bartolemaeum Facium Ligurem, invectivarum seu recriminationum*. In *Opera omnia*, vol. 1. Basel: Henricum Petrum, 1540; facsimile reprint, Turin: Bottega d'Erasmo, 1962.

Vegius, Maphaeus (Maffeo Vegio). *Aeneidos XIII*. In *Maphaeus Vegius and His Thirteenth Book of the Aeneid*. Ed. Anna Cox Brinton. Stanford: Stanford University Press, 1930.

Velleius Paterculus. *Historia;* and Augustus, *Res gestae divi Augusti*. Ed. and trans. Frederick W. Shipley. Loeb Classical Library. Cambridge, Mass., and London: Harvard University Press and William Heinemann, 1924; reprinted 1955.

Vergil. *Opera*. Venice: Giunta, 1544; facsimile reprint, 2 vols., New York: Garland, 1976.

———. *P. Vergilii Maronis opera*. Ed. Carolus Ruaeus (Charles de la Rue). London: T. Dring, G. Wells, A. Swalle, 1687; first published Paris: Delphin Edition, 1675.

———. *Vergilii Maronis poetarum princeps, opera*. Florence: Bernardus Nerlius, 1487.

———. *Virgil: Eclogues, Georgics, Aeneid*. 2 vols. Ed. and trans. H. R. Fairclough, revised edition. Loeb Classical Library. Cambridge, Mass., and London: Harvard University Press and William Heinemann, 1935; reprinted 1986.

Vida, Marco Girolamo. *The Christiad*. Ed. and trans. Gertrude C. Drake and Clarence Forbes. Carbondale: Southern Illinois University Press, 1978.

Vincent de Beauvais, comp. *Speculum quadruplex, sive speculum maius*. Douai: B. Belieri, 1624; facsimile reprint, 4 vols. Graz, Austria: Akademische Druck, 1964–65.

Vita Hludowici Imperatoris. Monumenta Germaniae Historica: Scriptores, vol. 2. Ed. G. H. Pertz. Hannover. 1829.

Vives, Juan-Luis. *Opera omnia*, vols. 4, 5. Valencia: Benedicti Montfort, 1782–90; reprinted London: Gregg, 1964.

Waller, Edmund. *The Poems of Edmund Waller,* vol. 1. Ed. George Thorn-Drury. London: Routledge and Dutton, 1893; reprinted New York: Greenwood Press, 1968.

Whitefield, George. *Sermons on Important Subjects*. London: H. Fisher, 1832.

William of Ockham. *Dialogus de imperio et pontificia potestate*. In *Opera plurima*, vol. 1. Lyon, 1494–96; facsimile reprint, London: Gregg, 1962.

———. *Opera politica*, 3 vols. Ed. J. G. Sikes. Manchester: University of Manchester Press, 1940; vol. 1 revised 1974.

William of Tyre. *Historia rerum in partibus transmarinis gestarum*. In *Recueil des historiens des croisades,* vol. 1. Paris: L. Techener, 1844.

———. *A History of Deeds Done Beyond the Sea*. 2 vols. Trans. Emily Atwater Babcock and A. C. Krey. New York: Columbia University Press, 1943.

Wilmot, John (Earl of Rochester). *The Complete Poems of John Wilmot, Earl of Rochester*. Ed. David M. Vieth. New Haven: Yale University Press, 1968.

Wither, George. *A Collection of Emblemes, Ancient and Modern.* London: Henry Taunton, 1635; facsimile reprint Columbia: University of South Carolina Press, 1975.

Wordsworth, William. *The Poetical Works of William Wordsworth,* vols. 1, 3, 4. Ed. E. de Selincourt and Helen Darbishire. 2d edition. Oxford: Clarendon Press, 1954; first published 1940.

Wycliffe, John. *Tractatus de officio regis.* Ed. Alfred W. Pollard and Charles Sayle. Wyclif Society. London: Trübner, 1887.

———. *Tractatus de potestate papae.* Ed. Johann Loserth. Wyclif Society. Trübner, 1907; reprinted New York: Johnson Reprint, 1966.

Secondary Sources

Ahl, Frederick M. *Lucan: An Introduction.* Ithaca: Cornell University Press, 1976.

Aldridge, John William. *The Hermeneutic of Erasmus.* Basel Studies in Theology, 2. Richmond, Va.: John Knox Press, 1966.

Allen, Don Cameron. *Mysteriously Meant: The Rediscovery of Pagan Symbolism and Allegorical Interpretation in the Renaissance.* Baltimore: Johns Hopkins University Press, 1970.

Alpers, Paul J. "Mode in Narrative Poetry." *To Tell a Story: Narrative Theory and Practice.* Papers Read at a Clark Library Seminar, 4 February 1972. Los Angeles: William Andrews Clark Memorial Library, 1973.

———. *The Poetry of The Faerie Queene.* Princeton: Princeton University Press, 1967.

———. *The Singer of the Eclogues: A Study of Virgilian Pastoral with a New Translation of the Eclogues.* Berkeley and Los Angeles: University of California Press, 1979.

———. "Virgil." *Atlantic Brief Lives: A Biographical Companion to the Arts.* Ed. Louis Kronenberger. Boston: Little, Brown, 1971.

Armstrong, David. "Stylistics and the Date of Calpurnius Siculus." *Philologus* 130 (1986): 113–36.

Ascoli, Albert Russell. *Ariosto's Bitter Harmony: Crisis and Evasion in the Italian Renaissance.* Princeton: Princeton University Press, 1987.

Bakhtin, Mikhail. *Problems of Dostoevsky's Poetics.* Trans. R. W. Rotsel. Ann Arbor: University of Michigan Press, 1973; first published in Russian, 1929.

Ball, Robert. "Theological Semantics: Virgil's *Pietas* and Dante's *Pietà.*" *Stanford Italian Review* 2 (Spring 1982): 59–79.

Barbeau, Anne T. *The Intellectual Design of John Dryden's Heroic Plays.* New Haven: Yale University Press, 1970.

Barfield, Owen. *History in English Words.* New Edition. London: Faber, 1954; first published 1926.

Beame, Edmond M. "The Use and Abuse of Machiavelli: The Sixteenth-Century

French Adaptation." *Journal of the History of Ideas* 43 (January–March 1982): 33–54.

Bedouelle, Guy. *Lefèvre d'Etaples et l'intelligence des Ecritures.* Geneva: Droz, 1976.

Bentley, Jerry H. *Humanists and Holy Writ: New Testament Scholarship in the Renaissance.* Princeton: Princeton University Press, 1983.

Bergin, Thomas G. *Boccaccio.* New York: Viking, 1981.

Blumenthal, Uta-Renate. *The Investiture Controversy: Church and Monarchy from the Ninth to the Twelfth Century.* Philadelphia: University of Pennsylvania Press, 1988.

Bolgar, R. R. *The Classical Heritage and its Beneficiaries.* Cambridge: Cambridge University Press, 1963; first published 1954.

Bono, Barbara. *Literary Transvaluation: From Vergilian Epic to Shakespearean Tragicomedy.* Berkeley and Los Angeles: University of California Press, 1984.

Booth, Stephen. *Shakespeare's Sonnets.* New Haven: Yale University Press, 1977.

Bornkamm, Heinrich. *Luther in Mid-Career, 1521–1530.* Trans. E. Theodore Bachmann. Philadelphia: Fortress Press, 1983; first published in German, 1979.

Bottkol, J. McG. "Dryden's Latin Scholarship." *Modern Philology* 40 (1943): 241–55.

Boyle, Marjorie O'Rourke. *Erasmus on Language and Method in Theology.* Toronto: University of Toronto Press, 1977.

Bright, David F. *Haec mihi fingebam: Tibullus in his World.* Leiden: E. J. Brill, 1978.

Brower, Reuben. *Alexander Pope: The Poetry of Allusion.* Oxford: Clarendon Press, 1959.

———. "Dryden's Epic Manner and Virgil." *PMLA* 55 (1940): 119–38.

Brown, Dale. *Understanding Pietism.* Grand Rapids, Mich.: W. B. Eerdmans, 1978.

Brown, Peter. *Augustine of Hippo: A Biography.* London: Faber, 1967.

Burck, Erich. "Drei Grundwerte der römischen Lebensordnung." *Gymnasium* 58 (1951): 161–83.

Burgess, J. F. "*Pietas* in Virgil and Statius." *Proceedings of the Virgil Society* 11 (1971–72): 48–61.

Bywaters, David. "Dryden and the Revolution of 1688: Political Parallel in *Don Sebastian.*" *Journal of English and Germanic Philology* 85 (1986): 346–65.

Cabaniss, Allen. *Son of Charlemagne: A Contemporary Life of Louis the Pious.* Syracuse: Syracuse University Press, 1961.

Cairns, Francis. *Virgil's Augustan Epic.* Cambridge: Cambridge University Press, 1989.

Cameron, Alan. *Claudian: Poetry and Propaganda at the Court of Honorius.* Oxford: Oxford University Press, 1970.

Camporeale, Salvatore. *Lorenzo Valla: Umanesimo e teologia.* Florence: Istituto Nazionale di Studi sul Rinascimento, 1972.

Carlyle, A. J., and Robert W. *A History of Medieval Political Theory in the West,* 4th impression, 6 vols. New York: Barnes and Noble, 1936; first published New York, Edinburgh, and London: G. P. Putnam and W. Blackwood, 1903.

Carver, Larry. "Absalom and Achitophel and the Father Hero." In *The English*

Hero, 1660–1800. Ed. Robert Folkenflik. Newark: University of Delaware Press, 1982.

Champlin, Edward. "History and the Date of Calpurnius Siculus." *Philologus* 130 (1986): 104–12.

Charlesworth, M. P. "The Virtues of a Roman Emperor: Propaganda and the Creation of Belief." *Proceedings of the British Academy* 23 (1937): 105–33.

Chenu, M.-D. *Toward Understanding Saint Thomas.* Trans. A.-M. Landry and D. Hughes. Chicago: H. Regnery, 1964; first published in French, 1950.

Clements, Robert J. *Picta Poesis: Literary and Humanistic Theory in Renaissance Emblem Books.* Rome: Edizioni di Storia e Letteratura, 1960.

Cochrane, Charles N. *Christianity and Classical Culture: A Study of Thought and Action from Augustus to Augustine,* revised and corrected. London: Oxford University Press, 1944; first published Oxford: Clarendon Press, 1940.

Coleman, Dorothy Gabe. *Maurice Scève: Poet of Love.* Cambridge: Cambridge University Press, 1975.

Comparetti, Domenico. *Vergil in the Middle Ages.* Trans. E. F. M. Benecke. London: Sonnenschein, 1895; first published in Italian, 1867.

Copleston, Frederick. *A History of Philosophy.* New York: Doubleday, 1985; first published 1946–53.

Corse, Taylor. *Dryden's "Aeneid": The English Virgil.* Newark: University of Delaware Press, 1991.

Cropp, Glynnis M. *Le vocabulaire courtois des troubadours de l'époque classique.* Geneva: Droz, 1975.

Daly, Peter M. *The English Emblem Tradition.* Toronto: University of Toronto Press, 1988.

———. *Literature in the Light of the Emblem: Structural Parallels between the Emblem and Literature in the Sixteenth and Seventeenth Centuries.* Toronto: University of Toronto Press, 1979.

DellaNeva, Joann. *Song and Counter-Song: Scève's Délie and Petrarch's Rime.* Lexington, Ky.: French Forum, 1983.

DeMolen, Richard L. "The Interior Erasmus." In *Leaders of the Reformation.* Ed. Richard L. DeMolen. London: Associated University Presses, 1984.

Di Cesare, Mario A. *The Altar and the City: A Reading of Vergil's Aeneid.* New York: Columbia University Press, 1974.

Diehl, Huston. *An Index of Icons in English Emblem Books 1500–1700.* Norman: University of Oklahoma Press, 1986.

Donnelly, Jerome. "Fathers and Sons: The Normative Basis of Dryden's *Absalom and Achitophel.*" *Papers on Language and Literature* 17 (1981): 363–79.

Doody, Margaret Anne. *The Daring Muse: Augustan Poetry Reconsidered.* Cambridge: Cambridge University Press, 1985.

Duckworth, G. E., and McKay, A. G., contributors. *The Classical World Bibliography of Vergil,* intro. W. Donlan. Garland Reference Library of the Humanities, vol. 96. New York: Garland, 1978.

Dudden, F. Homes. *The Life and Times of St. Ambrose.* 2 vols. Oxford: Oxford University Press, 1935.

Durant, Will. *The Age of Faith*. Vol. 4 in *The Story of Civilization*. New York: Simon and Schuster, 1950.

Dutripon, F. P. *Bibliorum sacrorum concordantiae*. Reprinted Hildesheim and New York: Georg Olms, 1976; first published Paris: Bloud et Barral, 1880.

Empson, William. *The Structure of Complex Words*. London: Chatto and Windus, 1951.

Erskine-Hill, Howard. *The Augustan Idea in English Literature*. London: E. Arnold, 1983.

Evans, G. R. *The Thought of Gregory the Great*. Cambridge: Cambridge University Press, 1986.

Evans, James E. "Blifil as Tartuffe: The Dialogic Comedy of *Tom Jones*." *Comparative Literature Studies*, 27, no. 2 (1990): 101–12.

Ferry, Anne D. *Milton and the Miltonic Dryden*. Cambridge, Mass.: Harvard University Press, 1968.

Fisher, Arthur L. "Lactantius' Ideas Relating Christian Truth and Christian Society." *Journal of the History of Ideas* 43 (July–September 1982): 355–77.

Fisher, John H. *John Gower: Moral Philosopher and Friend of Chaucer*. New York: New York University Press, 1964.

Fitzgerald, Robert. "Dryden's *Aeneid*." *Arion* 2 (1963): 17–31.

FitzGerald, William H. "Pietas Epicurea." *Classical Journal* 46 (1950–51): 195–99.

Fowler, Roger. *Literature as Social Discourse: The Practice of Linguistic Criticism*. London: Batsford, 1981.

Freccero, John. "Dante's Prologue Scene." *Dante Studies* 84 (1966): 1–25.

Frend, W. H. C. *The Rise of Christianity*. Philadelphia: Fortress Press, 1984.

Frost, William. *Dryden and the Art of Translation*. New Haven: Yale University Press, 1955.

———. *John Dryden: Dramatist, Satirist, Translator*. New York: AMS Press, 1988.

Fugier, Huguette. *Recherches sur l'expression du sacré dans la langue latine*. Paris: Société d'Editions Les Belles Lettres, 1963.

Fujimura, Thomas H. "Dryden's Virgil: Translation as Autobiography." *Studies in Philology* 80 (1983): 67–83.

Fyler, John M. *Chaucer and Ovid*. New Haven: Yale University Press, 1979.

Galinsky, G. Karl. *Aeneas, Sicily, and Rome*. Princeton: Princeton University Press, 1969.

———. *Ovid's Metamorphoses: An Introduction to the Basic Aspects*. Oxford: Basil Blackwell, 1975.

Garrison, James D. *Dryden and the Tradition of Panegyric*. Berkeley and Los Angeles: University of California Press, 1975.

Glenn, Edgar M. *The Metamorphoses: Ovid's Roman Games*. Lanham, Md., University Press of America, 1986.

Giamatti, A. Bartlett. *The Earthly Paradise and the Renaissance Epic*. Princeton: Princeton University Press, 1966.

———. "Sfrenatura: Restraint and Release in the *Orlando Furioso*." In *Ariosto 1974 in America*. Ed. Aldo Scaglione. Ravenna: Longo, 1976.

Graham, Victor E., and Johnson, W. McAllister. *Estienne Jodelle: Le Recueil des*

Inscriptions, 1558: A Literary and Iconographical Exegesis. Toronto: University of Toronto Press, 1972.

Greene, Thomas M. *The Light in Troy: Imitation and Discovery in Renaissance Poetry.* New Haven: Yale University Press, 1982.

Gresseth, G. K. "The Quarrel between Lucan and Nero." *Classical Philology* 52 (1957): 24–27.

Griffin, Dustin. "Dryden's Charles: The Ending of Absalom and Achitophel." *Philological Quarterly* 57 (1978): 359–82.

Grimal, P. "L'Eloge de Neron au début de la *Pharsale,* est-il ironique?" *Revue des Etudes Latins* 38 (1960): 296–305.

Haller, William. *The Rise of Puritanism.* New York: Harper and Row, 1938; reprinted 1957.

Halliday, M. A. K. *Language as a Social Semiotic: The Social Interpretation of Language and Meaning.* Baltimore: University Park Press, 1978.

Harth, Phillip. *Contexts of Dryden's Thought.* Chicago: University of Chicago Press, 1968.

Harrison, T. W. "Dryden's *Aeneid.*" In *Dryden's Mind and Art.* Ed. Bruce King. Edinburgh: Oliver and Boyd, 1969.

———. "English Vergil: The *Aeneid* in the XVIII Century." *Philologica Pragensia* 10 (1967), 1–11.

Hartmann, Louis N. "St. Jerome as an Exegete." In *A Monument to St. Jerome.* Ed. Francis X. Murphy. New York: Sheed and Ward, 1952.

Harvey, Paul. "Virgil." In *The Oxford Companion to Classical Literature.* Oxford: Oxford University Press, 1980; first published 1937.

Hearnshaw, F. J. C. *The Social and Political Ideas of Some Great Medieval Thinkers.* New York: Barnes and Noble, 1950; first published London: G. G. Harrap, 1923.

Heckscher, William S. *The Princeton Alciati Companion.* New York: Garland, 1989.

Hellegouarc'h, Joseph. *Le vocabulaire latin des relations et des partis politiques sous la République.* Paris: Société d'Editions Les Belles Lettres, 1963.

Heninger, S. K., Jr. "The Orgoglio Episode in *The Faerie Queene.*" *English Literary History* 26 (1959): 171–87.

Hollander, Robert. *Boccaccio's Two Venuses.* New York: Columbia University Press, 1977.

———. "Dante's Use of *Aeneid* I in *Inferno* I and II." *Comparative Literature* 20, no. 2 (Spring 1968): 142–56.

Hopkins, David. *John Dryden.* Cambridge: Cambridge University Press, 1986.

———. "Nature's Laws and Man's: The Story of Cinyras and Myrrha in Ovid and Dryden." *Modern Language Review* 80 (1985): 786–801.

Hughes, Derek. "Dryden's *Don Sebastian* and the Literature of Heroism." *Yearbook of English Studies* 12 (1982): 72–90.

———. *Dryden's Heroic Plays.* London: Macmillan, 1981.

Hughes, Philip Edgcumbe. *Lefèvre: Pioneer of Ecclesiastical Renewal in France.* Grand Rapids, Mich.: W. B. Eerdmans, 1984.

Hume, Robert D. *The Development of English Drama in the Late Seventeenth Century.* Oxford: Clarendon Press, 1976.

Jabès, Edmond. "Answer to a Letter." Trans. Rosemarie Waldrop. In *Twentieth-Century French Poetry*. Ed. Paul Auster. New York: Random House, 1982; originally published in French, 1972.

Jacobson, Howard. *Ovid's "Heroides."* Princeton: Princeton University Press, 1974.

Johnson, Paul. *A History of Christianity*. New York: Atheneum, 1976.

Johnson, W. R. "Aeneas and the Ironies of *Pietas*." *Classical Journal* 60 (1965): 360–64.

———. *Darkness Visible: A Study of Vergil's Aeneid*. Berkeley and Los Angeles: University of California Press, 1976.

Jones, J. W., Jr. "The Allegorical Traditions of the *Aeneid*." In *Vergil at 2000: Commemorative Essays on the Poet and His Influence*. Ed. John D. Bernard. New York: AMS Press, 1986.

Kallendorf, Craig. *In Praise of Aeneas: Virgil and Epideictic Rhetoric in the Early Italian Renaissance*. Hanover, N.H.: University Press of New England, 1989.

Kantorowicz, Ernst. *The King's Two Bodies: A Study in Medieval Political Theology*. Princeton: Princeton University Press, 1957.

Kaster, Robert A. *Guardians of Language: The Grammarian and Society in Late Antiquity*. Berkeley and Los Angeles: University of California Press, 1988.

Kelley, Donald R. "Murd'rous Machiavel in France: A Post Mortem." *Political Science Quarterly* 85 (December 1970): 545–59.

———. "What is Happening to the History of Ideas?" *Journal of the History of Ideas* 51 (January–March 1990): 3–25.

Kirsch, Arthur C. *Dryden's Heroic Drama*. Princeton: Princeton University Press, 1965.

Korshin, Paul J. *Typologies in England: 1650–1820*. Princeton: Princeton University Press, 1982.

Kristeller, P. O. "Lay Religious Traditions and Florentine Platonism." In *Studies in Renaissance Thought and Letters*. Rome: Edizioni di Storia e Letteratura, 1956.

———. *The Philosophy of Marsilio Ficino*. Trans. Virginia Conant. New York: Columbia University Press, 1943.

———. *Renaissance Thought and its Sources*. Ed. Michael Mooney. New York: Columbia University Press, 1979.

Kristeva, Julia. *Desire in Language: A Semiotic Approach to Literature and Art*. Trans. Thomas Gora, Alice Jardine, Leon S. Roudiez. Ed. Leon S. Roudiez. New York: Columbia University Press, 1980; first published in French, 1969.

Laistner, M. L. W. *Thought and Letters in Western Europe A.D. 500 to 900*. New York: Dial Press, 1931.

Lanci, Antonio. "Pietà." *Enciclopedia dantesca*. Rome: Istituto della Enciclopedia Italiana, 1970.

Lee, M. Owen. *Fathers and Sons in Virgil's Aeneid: Tum Genitor Natum*. Albany: State University of New York Press, 1979.

Liebeschuetz, J. H. W. G. *Continuity and Change in Roman Religion*. Oxford: Oxford University Press, 1979.

Losnes, Arvid. "Dryden's *Aeneis* and the Delphin Vergil." *The Hidden Sense and Other Essays*. Ed. M. Sofie Rostvig et al. Oslo: Universitetsforlaget, 1963.

McFadden, George. *Dryden the Public Writer, 1660–1685.* Princeton: Princeton University Press, 1978.

McGrade, Arthur. *The Political Thought of William of Ockham: Personal and Institutional Principles.* Cambridge: Cambridge University Press, 1974.

Mack, Maynard. *Alexander Pope: A Life.* New York: Norton, 1985.

Mango, Cyril. *Byzantium: The Empire of New Rome.* New York: Scribner's, 1980.

Mann, Nicholas. *Petrarch.* Oxford: Oxford University Press, 1984.

Mansfield, Harvey C. *Machiavelli's New Modes and Orders.* Ithaca: Cornell University Press, 1979.

Marcel, Raymond. *Marsile Ficin.* Paris: Société d'Editions Les Belles Lettres, 1958.

Marinelli, Peter V. *Ariosto and Boiardo: The Origins of Orlando Furioso.* Columbia: University of Missouri Press, 1987.

McGowan, Margaret M. *Ideal Forms in the Age of Ronsard.* Berkeley and Los Angeles: University of California Press, 1985.

Meershoek, G. Q. A. *Le latin biblique d'après Saint Jérôme: Aspects linguistiques de la rencontre entre la Bible e le monde classique.* Utrecht: Dekker and Van de Vegt, 1966.

Miner, Earl. *Dryden's Poetry.* Bloomington: Indiana University Press, 1967.

———. *The Restoration Mode from Milton to Dryden.* Princeton: Princeton University Press, 1974.

Mortimer, Ruth. "Vergil in the Light of the Sixteenth Century: Selected Illustrations." In *Vergil at 2000: Commemorative Essays on the Poet and His Influence.* Ed. John D. Bernard. New York: AMS Press, 1986.

Murrin, Michael. *The Allegorical Epic: Essays in its Rise and Decline.* Chicago: University of Chicago Press, 1980.

Myers, William. *Dryden.* London: Hutchinson and Co., 1973.

Nethercut, William R. "American Scholarship on Vergil in the Twentieth Century." In *Vergil at 2000: Commemorative Essays on the Poet and His Influence.* Ed. John D. Bernard. New York: AMS Press, 1986.

Nohrnberg, James. *The Analogy of The Faerie Queene.* Princeton: Princeton University Press, 1979.

Olsen, Birger Munk. "Virgile et la renaissance du XIIe siècle." *Lectures Médiévales de Virgile.* Rome: Ecole Française de Rome, 1985.

Otis, Brooks. *Virgil: A Study in Civilized Poetry.* Oxford: Oxford University Press, 1964.

Padoan, Giorgio. *Il pio Enea l'empio Ulisse.* Ravenna: Longo, 1977.

———. "Tradizione e fortuna del commento all'*Eneide* di Bernardo Silvestre." *Italia Medioevale e Umanistica* 3 (1960): 227–40.

Palmer, Anne-Marie. *Prudentius on the Martyrs.* Oxford: Oxford University Press, 1989.

Parry, Adam. "The Two Voices of Vergil's *Aeneid*." *Arion* ii (1963): 66–80.

Patterson, Annabel. *Pastoral and Ideology: Virgil to Valéry.* Berkeley and Los Angeles: University of California Press, 1987.

Paulson, Ronald. *Hogarth: His Life, Art, and Times.* Abridged by Anne Wilde. New Haven: Yale University Press, 1974.

Proudfoot, L. D. *Dryden's "Aeneid" and its Seventeenth-Century Predecessors.* Manchester: Manchester University Press, 1960.

Putnam, M. C. J. "*Pius* Aeneas and the Metamorphosis of Lausus." *Arethusa* 14 (1981): 139–56.

Quinn, Kenneth. *Virgil's Aeneid: A Critical Description.* Ann Arbor: University of Michigan Press, 1968.

Rabil, Albert. *Erasmus and the New Testament: The Mind of a Christian Humanist.* San Antonio, Tex.: Trinity University Press, 1972.

Revard, Stella Purce. *The War in Heaven: Paradise Lost and the Tradition of Satan's Rebellion.* Ithaca: Cornell University Press, 1980.

Reverand, Cedric D. *Dryden's Final Poetic Mode: The Fables.* Philadelphia: University of Pennsylvania Press, 1988.

Riposati, Benedetto. *Introduzione allo studio di Tibullo.* Como: Marzorati, 1945.

Roche, Thomas P., Jr. *Petrarch and the English Sonnet Sequences.* New York: AMS Press, 1989.

Rodgers, Daniel T. *Contested Truths, Keywords in American Politics Since Independence.* New York: Basic Books, 1987.

———. "Keywords: A Reply." *Journal of the History of Ideas* 49 (October–December 1988): 669–76.

Roper, Alan. *Dryden's Poetic Kingdoms.* London: Routledge and Kegan Paul, 1965.

Rosenthal, Peggy. *Words and Values: Some Leading Words and Where They Lead Us.* Oxford: Oxford University Press, 1984.

Rothstein, Eric. *Restoration and Eighteenth-Century Poetry 1660–1780.* Boston: Routledge and Kegan Paul, 1981.

———. *Restoration Tragedy: Form and the Process of Change.* Madison: University of Wisconsin Press, 1967.

Sage, Evan T. "The Non-Virgilian Aeneas." *Classical Journal* 15 (1919–20): 350–57.

Salvaggio, Ruth. *Dryden's Dualities.* English Literary Studies. Victoria: University of Victoria Press, 1983.

Schilling, Bernard. *Dryden and the Conservative Myth: A Reading of Absalom and Achitophel.* New Haven: Yale University Press, 1961.

Scruton, Roger. *From Descartes to Wittgenstein: A Short History of Modern Philosophy.* U.S. Edition. New York: Harper and Row, 1982.

Seem, Lauren Scancarelli. "The Limits of Chivalry: Tasso and the End of the *Aeneid*." *Comparative Literature* 42, no. 2 (Spring 1990): 116–25.

Serafini, Mario. "Le tragedie di Seneca nella Fiammetta di Giovanni Boccaccio." *Giornale Storico della Letteratura Italiana* 126 (1949): 95–105.

Shesgreen, Sean. *Engravings by Hogarth.* New York: Dover, 1973.

Sloman, Judith. *Dryden: The Poetics of Translation.* Toronto: University of Toronto Press, 1985.

———. "An Interpretation of Dryden's *Fables.*" *Eighteenth-Century Studies* 4 (1971): 199–211.

Smarr, Janet Levarie. *Boccaccio and Fiammetta: The Narrator as Lover.* Urbana: University of Illinois Press, 1986.

Smith, Hallett. *Elizabethan Poetry: A Study in Conventions, Meaning, and Expression.* Cambridge, Mass.: Harvard University Press, 1952.

Stahel, Thomas H. "Cristoforo Landino's Allegorization of the *Aeneid:* Books III and IV of the *Camaldolese Disputations.*" Diss. Johns Hopkins University, 1968.

Steadman, John M. *Epic and Tragic Structure in Paradise Lost.* Chicago: University of Chicago Press, 1976.

Steinmetz, David C. *Luther in Context.* Bloomington: Indiana University Press, 1986.

Stoeffler, F. Ernest. *The Rise of Evangelical Pietism.* Leiden: E. J. Brill, 1965.

Straw, Carole. *Gregory the Great: Perfection in Imperfection.* Berkeley and Los Angeles: University of California Press, 1988.

Stübler, Gerhard. *Die Religiosität des Livius.* Amsterdam: Hakkert, 1964.

Syme, Ronald. *Tacitus.* 2 vols. Oxford: Clarendon Press, 1958.

Thompson, Elbert N. S. *Literary Bypaths of the Renaissance.* New Haven: Yale University Press, 1924.

Trickett, Rachel. *The Honest Muse: A Study in Augustan Verse.* Oxford: Clarendon Press, 1967.

Trinkaus, Charles. *In Our Image and Likeness: Humanity and Divinity in Italian Humanist Thought.* 2 vols. Chicago: University of Chicago Press, 1970.

Ullmann, Walter. *The Carolingian Renaissance and the Idea of Kingship.* London: Methuen, 1969.

———. *The Growth of Papal Government in the Middle Ages.* 2d edition. London: Methuen, 1962; first published 1955.

Ussani, V. "Enea traditore." *Studie Italiani di Filologia Classica,* n.s. 22 (1947): 108–23.

Vessey, David. *Statius and the Thebaid.* Cambridge: Cambridge University Press, 1973.

Wagenvoort, Hendrik. *Pietas: Selected Studies in Roman Religion.* Leiden: E. J. Brill, 1980.

Waith, Eugene M. *The Herculean Hero in Marlowe, Chapman, Shakespeare, and Dryden.* New York: Columbia University Press, 1962.

Walde, Alois. *Lateinisches etymologisches Wörterbuch.* Rev. J. B. Hofman. 3d ed. Heidelberg: C. Winter, 1954; first published 1906.

Weinbrot, Howard D. *Augustus Caesar in "Augustan" England: The Decline of a Classical Norm.* Princeton: Princeton University Press, 1978.

———. *Eighteenth-Century Satire: Essays on Text and Context from Dryden to Peter Pindar.* Cambridge: Cambridge University Press, 1988.

Weiss, Herold David. "Piety in Latin Writers in Early Christian Times." Diss. Duke University, 1964.

West, Michael. "Dryden and the Disintegration of Renaissance Heroic Ideals." *Costerus* 7 (1973): 193–202.

———. "Dryden's Ambivalence as a Translator of Heroic Themes." *Huntington Library Quarterly* 36 (1973): 347–66.

Wetherbee, Winthrop. *Platonism and Poetry in the Twelfth Century: The Literary*

Influence of the School of Chartres. Princeton: Princeton University Press, 1972.

Wickert, Maria. *Studies in John Gower*. Trans. Robert J. Meindl. Washington, D.C.: University Press of America, 1981; originally published in German, 1953.

Williams, Gordon. "Statius and Vergil: Defensive Imitation." In *Vergil at 2000: Commemorative Essays on the Poet and His Influence*. Ed. John D. Bernard. New York: AMS Press, 1986.

———. *Technique and Ideas in the Aeneid*. New Haven: Yale University Press, 1983.

Williams, Raymond. *Keywords: A Vocabulary of Culture and Society*. Revised edition. New York: Oxford University Press, 1976.

Williams, Robert D., and Pattie, T. S. *Virgil: His Poetry Through the Ages*. London: British Library, 1982.

Winn, James Anderson. *John Dryden and His World*. New Haven: Yale University Press, 1987.

Wiseman, T. P. "Calpurnius Siculus and the Claudian Civil War." *Journal of Roman Studies* 72 (1982): 57–67.

Zwicker, Steven N. *Politics and Language in Dryden's Poetry: The Arts of Disguise*. Princeton: Princeton University Press, 1984.

———. "Reading Vergil in the 1690's." In *Vergil at 2000: Commemorative Essays on the Poet and His Influence*. Ed. John D. Bernard. New York: AMS Press, 1986.

Index of Words and Phrases

ENGLISH

FRENCH

charité, 125
chaste, chasteté, 136, 143
clemence, 124–26, 288 n. 126
contempteur des dieux / de toute piété, 125,
    176
cruauté, cruel, 124, 135, 138–39, 178
débonnaire, débonnaireté, 118, 124–26,
    287 n. 116, 288 n. 126
despiteux, 144–45
fureur, 176
honneste pitié, 143
impiété, 126, 135
justice, 118, 124–25, 138
miséricorde, 125
piété, 15, 118, 125–26, 137, 265–66 n. 20,
    288 n. 127, 292 n. 30
pité, 118, 265–66 n. 20
piteux, 144–45
pitié, 14–15, 118, 139, 142–43, 177–78,
    292 n. 30
religion, 126
severement piteux, 144, 146

GERMAN

Pietät, 4
Pietismus, 262 n. 13

GREEK

eusebeia, 11–12, 40, 55, 109, 264 n. 5, 271–
    72 n. 63, 282 n. 47
hosios, hosiotēs, 51, 55, 264 n. 5
storgē, philostorgia, 55
theosebeia, 12, 28–29

ITALIAN

amor(e), 123, 130, 132–33, 140, 147–48,
    152, 154–55, 157, 159, 173
arme, 155, 179, 181–82, 185–86
arme pietose, 179, 182, 184–87
bella petra, 140, 147
bombarda, 174, 176
capitano, 179–80, 295 n. 17
castità, casto, 132, 155
cortesia, 159, 174
cristiano, 163, 169
crudel(e), crudeltà, crudeltade, 122, 147,
    154, 162–63, 172, 174

cura, 153, 173, 185, 286 n. 106
di pietà sublime esempio, 187
d'ogni Dio sprezzatore, 182, 211
empio, 146, 150, 153, 155–56, 170, 174–
    76, 178, 180, 182, 184–85, 202
empio re / tyranno, 174–75, 180
furor(e), 152, 172–73, 184
ira, 172, 184
misericordia, 14, 18
opera pia, 171
orgoglioso, 162
pietà, pietate, pietade, 2, 14, 18, 121–24,
    128, 130–33, 139–41, 146–56, 158–
    59, 162–63, 169–70, 172–73, 180,
    182, 183, 185, 187, 257, 263 n. 14
pietosa crudeltà, 122
pietoso, 14, 122, 131, 140, 145–46, 150–
    51, 181, 184–86
pietoso affetto, 153, 198
pio, 154, 162, 169, 181, 185
pio Goffredo, 152, 180, 185–86
pudicizia, pudico, 152, 158–59
religioso, 163
reverenza, 123–24, 126
sommo duce, 185–86
superbia, superbo, 122, 150, 153, 156, 162–
    63, 176, 183
titolo di pio, 153, 180
troppa pietà, 122
ubbidienza filiale, 130, 150
ufficio, 180
vana e folle pietà, 188

LATIN

affectus, 30, 34, 60, 86, 99
agon pietatis, 283 n. 49
amor, 7, 127, 129, 145, 148, 150, 213, 245
amor filiorum, 55
arma, 11, 22, 65, 71, 74, 80–87, 162, 167,
    179, 244
auctor pietatis, 21, 59, 120, 165, 232
caerimonia, 29, 42, 44–45, 109
caritas, 13, 32–34, 37, 39, 56, 60, 104, 112
civitas impiorum, 6, 87–88, 90–91, 136,
    200
civitas piorum, 6, 87–88, 90
clemens, clementia, 7, 30, 67–69, 73, 82,
    93–94, 96–98, 101, 103, 117–18, 121,
    125, 166, 169, 197, 227, 257, 286–
    87 nn. 111, 112
concordia, 11, 72, 109–10
consideratio, 13
contemptor deorum, 31, 267 n. 12

General Index

Authors are indexed only when discussed in the text or quoted in a note.